ARISTOPHANES

CLOUDS

ABRIDGED EDITION

EDITED WITH

INTRODUCTION AND COMMENTARY

BY

K. J. DOVER, F.B.A.

PROFESSOR OF GREEK IN THE

UNIVERSITY OF ST. ANDREWS

OXFORD UNIVERSITY PRESS

Oxford University Press, Walton Street, Oxford OX2 6DP

OXFORD LONDON GLASGOW
NEW YORK TORONTO MELBOURNE WELLINGTON
KUALA LUMPUR SINGAPORE HONG KONG TOKYO
DELHI BOMBAY CALCUTTA MADRAS KARACHI
NAIROBI DAR ES SALAAM CAPE TOWN

ISBN 0 19 912009 9

Reprinted 1976, 1980

Cover photograph:
Hellenistic statuette of Socrates.
British Museum.

Printed in Great Britain
at the University Press, Oxford
by Eric Buckley
Printer to the University

PREFACE

THE text of the play is reproduced from my larger edition, but the Introduction (Sections I and III–X) and the Commentary have been abridged and new Sections (II and XI–XII) have been added to the Introduction.

As in my abridged commentaries on Thucydides VI and VII, I have in many places substituted assertion for the detailed treatment of evidence. The reader's attention is drawn especially to four hypotheses which seem to me, but not to everyone, indicated by the data:

(i) Aristophanes' portrayal of Socrates as a man who, in his forties, expounded scientific theories is not adequately supported by evidence from other sources.

(ii) In the contest between the two Logoi ('Right' and 'Wrong') 'Right' is caricatured and is not to be treated as the mouthpiece of Aristophanes.

(iii) Aristophanes had at his disposal temporary 'sets' (cheaply made and easily moved), and stage-properties were commonly brought on or taken off during the action of the play.

(iv) Texts of the original version of *Clouds*, differing substantially from the revised version which we possess, survived at least until the first century A.D.

The purpose of the Commentary is not only to explain the Greek but also to relate what is said to its social and cultural context and to enable the reader to visualize the action in the theatre. He should try to see every movement in the mind's eye and hear every syllable in the mind's ear; in short, to study the play as if he were producing it and the actors might at any moment turn to him for instructions. Much humour which lies hidden under lines of print emerges when the resources of the voice and the limbs are brought to bear upon those lines.

K. J. DOVER

University of St. Andrews

July 1968

An asterisk indicates a note in the Corrigenda.

CONTENTS

ABBREVIATIONS

Manuscripts and Scholia. See pp. xxx and xxxix.

Dates. Unless otherwise stated, all three-figure dates are B.C. and four-figure dates A.D. Unless otherwise stated, the Roman numerals from I to IX refer to centuries B.C. and those from X upwards to centuries A.D.

Punctuation. In order to avoid confusion with the Greek mark of interrogation, I use a colon after a Greek word in circumstances in which I would have used a semicolon if the word had been English.

Aristophanes. Reference is made to editions of Aristophanes and to commentaries on his work by the editor's (or commentator's) name alone.

LSJ = LIDDELL, H. G., and SCOTT, R., *A Greek–English Lexicon*, ed. 9 (revised by Sir HENRY STUART JONES and R. McKENZIE), Oxford, 1940.

References to ancient authors and works are given either as in LSJ or more fully; but all except a handful of names are Hellenized, e.g. 'Kratinos' is preferred to 'Cratinus'.

INTRODUCTION

I. ARISTOPHANES

THE career of Aristophanes as a writer of comedies lasted forty years, from 427 to *c.* 386. At least forty plays were attributed to him in antiquity, eleven of which survived into the Middle Ages and thus to our own day; the earliest of these eleven is *Acharnians* (425) and the last *Wealth* (388). *Clouds* was produced in 423, and was placed by the judges third of the three plays competing at the City Dionysia that year. The original version has not survived; what we have is an incompletely revised version (see Section IX below).

Considering how much we know about Ar. as poet and dramatist, it is remarkable how little we know about him as a man. We do not know whether he was rich or poor, or in what section of Athenian society the poet moved.[1] If we reflect that he survived two oligarchic revolutions and two democratic restorations, we may conclude that his positive political involvement was not remarkable. For his generation, to be conventional or conservative was to accept the radical democracy which had been created and consolidated by the previous three generations. Radical democracy was 'the establishment', and revolution could come only from factions which took as their model a state of affairs which existed, or was imagined to have existed, further back than living memory could reach. Despite his venomous ridicule of individuals and his keen perception of human weaknesses, there is nothing in Ar. to suggest that he believed Athens would be a better and wiser community if political and juridical power were restricted by law to one class.

[1] There is ample scope for differences of opinion on the relevance of Plato's *Symposium*, where Ar. is portrayed as a guest at a party given by Agathon in 416.

Ar. does not directly reflect or express the culture and spirit of Periclean Athens, for he did not begin to write until after the death of Perikles. His Athens is the Athens which fell from wealth, power, and confidence to starvation and humiliation and regained, before his death, stability and prosperity. It is most important that modern students of Ar. should not credit him with foreknowledge of historical events with which we are familiar—a mistake commonly made in the interpretation of *Birds* (414) and *Frogs* (405). When Ar. wrote *Clouds*, the plague had come, but it had also gone; the Peloponnesian invasions of Attica were suspended while the Athenians held as hostages the Spartiate prisoners they had taken on Sphakteria; the Athenians had suffered reverses on land, and the steady diminution of their financial reserves warned them that they could not sustain naval operations on the same scale as in the first years of the war, but it was unthinkable that the Peloponnesians should successfully assault the Athens–Peiraieus perimeter or win a major naval battle or interfere significantly with the movement of an Athenian fleet.

Ar. is the only poet of the 'Old Comedy' whose work we can assess through the reading of complete plays; therefore we cannot help treating him as the representative of Old Comedy. He represents, however, the last stage of the genre. Comedies had been officially recognized as part of the City Dionysia for sixty years before he wrote his first play; his last two extant plays show striking departures in plot and structure from his earlier work.

II. OLD COMEDY

Production. The comic plot is more complicated than the tragic plot, and sometimes includes several changes of scene. Different parts of *Clouds* represent the interior and exterior of Strepsiades' house and of Socrates' school. It is hard to decide how far what is implied by the text was realistically portrayed in the theatre. A modern audience makes very exacting demands, but audiences at other times and places have been readier to use their imagination whenever the words of a play tell them what to imagine, and (as in charades) much can be conveyed by mime. We must remember that although Greek plays were performed in daylight the words often require us to imagine that it is dark.

Archaeological and literary evidence are alike inadequate for the fifth-century Athenian theatre. We know that the audience sat in concentric rows, each row being approximately semicircular. The area in which the performance took place was a flat, nearly circular 'orchestra', and beyond this was a building ('skene'). There was a broad way into the orchestra, next to the skene, on each side. The skene had stone foundations, but a wooden façade was built out from it, and there was a door in the centre of this. The area immediately in front of the façade was probably a little higher than the orchestra. There is some evidence that temporary representational 'sets', which would necessarily be placed in front of the façade, were already being used in tragedy by Ar.'s time, and there are no mechanical or economic reasons why Ar. should not have used them too. Thus, although the same door can represent different buildings in different parts of a play—just as the orchestra can change its role and represent different parts of the world, the heavens, or the underworld—it is not necessary to believe that the same door can represent different buildings simultaneously.

In tragedy the revelation of interior scenes was effected by pushing a low trolley out from the door, but the tragic characters thus revealed are often immobile through death, sickness, or insanity, and it does not follow that Athenian ingenuity could not rise to anything better for (e.g.) the revelation of the interior of the school in *Clouds*. Nor, again, should we assume that the audience objected to seeing stage-hands bringing on and removing properties in the course of the play, any more than a Greek would be distracted from talking to a householder by the comings and goings of his slaves. The demand that scene-shifters and stage-hands should be neither seen nor heard is modern.

The actors were supplemented by 'extras' (e.g. the Creditor's Witness in *Clouds*) who did not speak. All speaking parts were acted by men (though, so far as we know, extras could be slave-girls when appropriate). Apart from *Clouds*, which creates unique problems because we possess it only in an incompletely revised version (see pp. xxviii ff.), no extant play of Ar. requires more than four actors except *Ach.* 1–203, where the fifth actor plays a Persian and speaks two partially intelligible lines. An actor was accustomed to taking two or more parts, and the play was so constructed as to give him time for changes of costume. We can, if we wish, assign most of the work in each play to three actors, leaving only a little for the fourth, but the fact that we can do this does not prove that the Athenians did it.

The actors wore masks (probably grotesque, but direct evidence on fifth-century masks is scanty) and costume of a kind which provokes unsophisticated laughter, with artificial genitals of prodigious size and padding to exaggerate the paunch. We do not know how far these conventions went; in *Clouds* it would obviously be inappropriate for Pheidippides (before his transformation) to have a pot-belly or for Right to have a monstrous penis, but convention may have taken precedence over fidelity to character.

Nothing is known about style and elocution in Greek comic acting.

Dramatic technique. The chorus plays an essential part in Aristophanic comedy. Its entry, which comes 200 lines or more after the start of the play, is dramatically exciting and spectacular. The plot is so constructed that in the middle of the play the actors are all off-stage, and the chorus addresses the audience; this part of the play, the 'parabasis', has an elaborate structure in each of the plays down to *Birds* (414), but thereafter it is modified and in the fourth century eliminated. The chorus in the parabasis is half in and half out of its dramatic role; in *Clouds* we find that in 518–62 it is simply the poet's mouthpiece (ἐγώ there = Ar.), while in 563–626 it sings and speaks as if it were a body of clouds visiting Athens on the occasion of the City Dionysia. The parabasis concluded, it reverts to its role within the story of the play, but in 1115–30 it again becomes clouds addressing the judges at the festival.

It is in keeping with this practice that whereas the spectator of tragedy looks across a gulf of time at the grandeur and horror of heroic events, comedy is anchored to the moment of performance and repeatedly breaks dramatic illusion, as if to remind us that we are watching fellow citizens dressed up. Hence we find direct allusion to the theatre (e.g. 326) or the audience (e.g. 889 f.), and for the purpose of a joke a character may momentarily adopt a standpoint alien to himself but appropriate to the poet or the audience (e.g. 316).

Fantasy in the comic plot is unrestricted. Supernatural and magical elements are introduced at will and dropped equally at will. As the plot unfolds, we cannot ask 'But how . . .?' or 'But why . . .?', as we would ask in respect of the causes, motives, and consequences of a real situation. The dramatist supplies motives and explores consequences only so far as they form part of his comic purpose, and he selects only those elements of a causal sequence which he needs, ignoring practical impossibilities. Metaphors and abstract conceptions can be presented in concrete form, often personified; so in *Clouds* the fact that the sophists taught pupils how to present both sides of a case is dramatized by making Right and Wrong inmates of Socrates' school.

Comedy and society. By contrast with modern comedy, Aristophanic comedy is remarkably uninhibited. All aspects of sex and excretion are fully exploited in word and deed. Contemporaries, no matter how eminent, are slandered without restraint and ridiculed for their diseases, physical disabilities, ugliness, family misfortunes, poverty, bad manners, perversions, cowardice, conceit, incompetence, and dishonesty. Although a law of slander existed at Athens, it had a very limited application; comedy and political and forensic oratory were, for all practical purposes, what we should call 'privileged'. Gods (with a few important exceptions) are also subject to ridicule and are sometimes portrayed in discreditable and undignified predicaments. Although comedy, being performed at two festivals of Dionysos, the City Dionysia and the Lenaia, was to that extent 'religious', solemnity did not play a great part in Greek religious observance, and a festival in honour of a god (who was assumed to enjoy what men enjoy) was more like a gala than a church service. Whatever the reservations of intellectuals, the ordinary Greek felt himself in continuous, intimate contact with his gods, as with his parents, elders, military commanders and administrative officials, and the audience which was unwilling to forgo ridicule of gods in the festive atmosphere of comedy was prompt to execute men suspected of deliberately mutilating statues of Hermes.

The paradox of comedy is that it was written for a mass audience by sophisticated poets with high technical standards. It represents the poet's concept of the ordinary man hitting out at whatever is in some way or other above average in power and prestige: generals, politicians, gods, artists, and intellectuals. Noisy, philistine ridicule is directed against what is new in poetry and music and against ideas which upset comfortable assumptions. These are sitting targets in all ages; compare modern jokes against Picasso and Freud.

By convention the poet was a 'teacher' and adviser, but the originality of Ar.'s 'teaching' should not be exaggerated. It is certain that in *Peace* (421) Ar. was not forming public opinion but expressing what was already formed, and almost certain that in *Frogs* (405) he was doing likewise. Nor should the effect of his 'teaching' be exaggerated. *Acharnians* in 425 made the point that peace is more enjoyable than war and that continuation of the war at that time was unnecessary, but there is no sign that the play had any effect on the Athenians' bellicosity. *Knights*, a virulent attack on Kleon, won first prize at the Lenaia of 424, but the Athenians none the less elected Kleon general for 424/3. Plato may have been right in saying (*Ap.* 18 CD, 19 BC) that the man in the street derived his picture of Socrates from *Clouds*; but no harm befell Socrates until 399, when intense bitterness had been created by the political careers of two men who had been his associates, Alkibiades and Kritias (cf. Xen. *Mem.* i. 1. 12 ff.).

III. THE CHARACTER OF THE PLAY

Clouds strikes an unusual note. The 'hero', Strepsiades, is stupid and excitable, never truly resourceful, never in control of the situation, and at the end pitiable. He believes that he has solved his problem, the lawsuits with which his creditors threaten him, by having his son, Pheidippides, educated in rhetoric in the school of Socrates; but one of the lessons which Pheidippides learns is reckless contempt for his father. Strepsiades revenges himself on Socrates by brute force, burning down the school; but he will still have to live with his son and his creditors, who are now his implacable enemies because of the insolence and violence with which he has treated them. The Chorus, which in *Knights* and *Peace* is well disposed to the hero from first to last, and in *Acharnians*, *Wasps*, and *Birds* is converted from initial hostility in the course of the play, has a strange and equivocal role in *Clouds*; cf. p. xxviii.

On a closer examination the peculiarities of *Clouds* diminish. In *Knights* the Sausage-seller defeats Kleon not by championing virtue against vice but by outdoing Kleon in vulgar and impudent flattery of their master, the People. The patriotic optimism which pervades the closing scene is consonant with the tradition of the genre but has no rational justification in what has been enacted. In *Wasps* Philokleon, once converted from his immoderate zeal for jury service, is no less immoderate in his pursuit of pleasure. The dancing with which the play ends simply serves to stifle with noise and excitement any inclination on our part to construct a sequence of events beyond the point to which Ar. has led us.

We are bound to wonder how the original version of *Clouds* ended (cf. p. xxx): whether, in particular, it exploited satire and ambivalence in the direction indicated by *Knights*, and whether the design of *Wasps* was influenced in any way by the judges' adverse verdict on *Clouds*. *Knights* in 424 and *Wasps* in 422 suffice to show that during the period when the first version of *Clouds* was written the type of comedy which ends with unalloyed triumph and leaves no uncomfortable questions in the audience's mind was not the only type in which Ar. was interested.

IV. STREPSIADES AND HIS FAMILY

Strepsiades is *γέρων* (129, 746, 1304; cf. 263, 358, 513 ff.); Pheidippides is *νεανίας* (8), and addressed by Right and Wrong as *ὦ μειράκιον* (990, 1000, 1071). It would be wrong to suppose that these terms admit of precise numerical translation. Neither of the two men is old enough for the father to have handed over to the son the management of the family estate. Strepsiades is responsible for Pheidippides' debts (1267 ff.); presumably he could not stand up to the contemptuous and exacting demands made by his wife and son in alliance against him. Pheidippides will, of course, inherit the debts when the estate comes to him (39 f.). Pheidippides speaks (119 f.) as if already a member of 'the cavalry'. It is therefore unlikely that he can be under 18, but he need not be more than 20, and might be only 19. Strepsiades is to be imagined as past, or nearly past, the age-limit for military service; conceivably in his late fifties, but more probably in his sixties. But people notoriously age at different rates, and so long as we realize that Strepsiades' mental and physical condition is such that he is regarded as an old man by himself and by others, his sum of years is irrelevant.

Strepsiades lives 'far off in the country' (138). He is ignorant, stupid, and boorish, a son of the soil and smelling of the soil (43 ff.)—but one of its richer sons. He seems to have had no difficulty in borrowing, from people who knew him (cf. p. xviii), very large sums of money, such as are not readily lent to farm-labourers or poor peasants. A distinguished aristocratic family sought him out (41 f.) as a husband for one of its daughters, and since this (to us) surprising marriage is taken for granted, we may be justified in supposing that it did not surprise Ar.'s audience. Strepsiades, although he knows how to tighten his belt and has a farmer's mistrust of extravagance (421), is to be thought of as owning farm land which would nowadays sell for £60,000.

The tension between Strepsiades and Pheidippides is not first created by sophistic education; it has arisen because the young man has been encouraged by his mother and her family to associate with other young men of aristocratic pretensions and extravagant tastes. But Pheidippides, however defiant and sulky, observes in the last resort (865, 1112) the outward convention of filial obedience. This convention he discards when he has been through Socrates' school; and at the same time he emerges (1399 ff. ~ 102 ff., 119 f.) from the anti-intellectual pose and inarticulateness characteristic of young men who devote all their energies to currently fashionable competitive sports. He is now fluent, dexterous, ready with equal coolness to use violence or argument to make sure that he gets what he wants. His verbal facility, sang-froid, and intellectual enthusiasm distinguish him very sharply from the highly emotional 'protester' of the present day.

The conservatism of Strepsiades' tastes, the artistic innovations of late fifth-century Athens, and the contrast between old-fashioned obedience and modern rebelliousness, are all exaggerated by Ar. for the sake of comic effect; see further Section VII and pp. 182 f.

V. THE CREDITORS

Early in the play Strepsiades tells us of two debts: he owes twelve mnai to Pasias and three to Ameinias.

At 1214 one of his creditors appears to demand his money; he is a fellow demesman of Strepsiades (1219), not a professional money-lender or banker, for he speaks of the loan as a favour to a friend. The sum owed to him is 12 mnai (1224). Not surprisingly, therefore, he is called 'Pasias' in the *dramatis personae* of most manuscripts. Whether Ar. really means us to think of the man as Pasias is doubtful; if he does, he has altered one of the two possible clues by making the creditor speak not of the brand of horse called κοππατίας (as in 21 ff.) but of ψαρός, an adjective of colour.

The Second Creditor appears at 1259. The naming of this creditor as 'Amynias' (i.e. Ameinias) first appears in the Middle Ages; there is no sign of the identification in the scholia of ancient origin. If Ar. intended us to think of this man as Ameinias, he has hidden the clues altogether, for there is no mention either of the sum borrowed or of the use to which it was put.

Since neither of the two creditors is represented as a money-lender, I call them χρήστης α′ and χρήστης β′, dropping the non-Attic term δανειστής* by which they are designated in the medieval MSS.

VI. SOCRATES

Socrates was 70 at the time of his trial in 399 and therefore 45 when the original version of *Clouds* was composed. He was physically hard and in good training; in the previous autumn he had acquitted himself well as a hoplite in the gruelling retreat from Delion. Probably his hair was greying, but even if he was bald in later life there is no reason to suppose that he was already bald. His eyes were prominent, his nose upturned, and his lips thick—ugly features of the type customarily attributed by the Athenians to satyrs and silenoi.

There is no reference in the play to his face. The actor who took the part may have worn a portrait-mask (it is a fair inference from *Knights* 230–3 that such masks were used in Old Comedy), but it is possible that a mask embodying features like Socrates' would not have been easily distinguishable from a type of ugly mask commonly used for fictitious characters. Aelian, telling the famous story of how Socrates answered the question whispered among the foreigners in the theatre, 'Who is this man Socrates?', by standing up in silence, assumes in parenthesis that a portrait-mask was probably worn, but the story is a good one even without the assumption.

Socrates in the play is the head of a school; Chairephon, who seems in certain passages to be treated as his partner, is classed in 502 ff. among his students, and has no part in the teaching of Strepsiades or Pheidippides. The work of the school comprises research and teaching in astronomy, meteorology, natural history, geology, geometry, metre, and grammar. Socrates teaches for payment, and the school is residential. Above all, he teaches forensic oratory, by means of which a man in the wrong may convince a jury that he is in the right. This is cardinal to the plot of the play; it is, after all, why Strepsiades seeks him out in the first place, and it is what Pheidippides learns.

Socrates is represented as holding a varied collection of scientific doctrines; he rejects the gods of cult and myth, putting in their place sometimes the impersonal operation of physical laws, sometimes deities of his own. There is no consistency in the portrayal of his 'atheism'; since the Greeks tended to personify natural phenomena and abstractions, they also tended to assume that a man who rejected the traditional gods worshipped gods of his own devising and did not abjure worship as such.

All the characteristics attached to Socrates by Ar. are to be found in various intellectuals of his own and earlier generations. Attempts to explain astronomical and meteorological phenomena on more or less scientific principles had been made ever since the beginning of the sixth century, and continued to be made. Each of the scientific theories caricatured in the play can be identified and ascribed to one or another of writers and teachers whose works were in circulation at the time of the play, and it is known that metre and language had already come under systematic scrutiny. The teaching of oratorical technique was well established, and this naturally included teaching the student how to refute a strong case and win with a weak one. If the evidence of Plato is to be trusted, the eminent 'sophists' who taught this art and the philosophical and linguistic studies which were its ancillaries charged high fees.

So far it appears that Ar. has created a composite portrait. A distinct element in this portrait is that Socrates and his students are pale from their indoor life, unkempt and dirty, unshod, ill-clothed, and verminous. Since they do nothing which the man in the street (or the field) regards as real work, they are poor and rely for a living on stealing other people's clothes. Anyone who enrols in the school must be prepared to endure cold and hunger and to abstain from wine and athletic exercise. Similar language is used of Socrates in *Birds* 1554 ff. and *Frogs* 1491 ff. Here there is a combination of contradictory elements, for living indoors is not conducive to endurance out of doors, nor is poverty reconcilable with the exaction of exorbitant fees (cf. 876). Each element, however, can be treated separately as a consequence of alienation from ordinary life, and Ar. casts his net wide in representation of all the types thus 'alienated'. In 331 ff. seers, medical writers, and lyric poets are included, under the heading *σοφισταί*, as 'idle', and the parasitic philosopher typified by the comic Socrates has affinities with other parasitic figures in Old Comedy, notably the seer (*Peace* 1043 ff.), the oracle-monger (*Birds* 959 ff.) and the beggar-poet (*Birds* 904 ff.). The eminent sophists who earned high fees did not need to save money on haircuts, baths, and sandals, and they are not represented by Plato and Xenophon as ascetics. It was in the fourth century that nakedness and dirt became trade-marks of certain types of philosopher; but possibly people of this kind were already familiar in the latter part of the fifth century.

The asceticism of Socrates is one of the two features on which Ar.'s caricature agrees with Plato and Xenophon (cf. Pl. *Smp.* 220 B, Xen. *Mem.* i. 2. 1, 3. 5 ff.); the other is Socrates' bearing and expression, described in *Clouds* 362 in words which Pl. *Smp.* 221 B cites with approval. Agreement on other points of detail—notably in 'tutorial' methods and terminology—is much smaller than has sometimes been suggested, and the hard core of agreement is fortuitous and insignificant; see the notes on 137, 140, 145, 179, 479, 489, 703, 742 ff. On the issues which matter Plato and Xenophon are in conflict with Aristophanes. Their Socrates is not interested in science, linguistics, or metre; he believes in taking part in the religious observances of his city, and he has faith in the providential government of the world by the gods; above all, he is hostile to the theory and teaching of oratory (see especially Plato's *Gorgias*), and he is so far from exacting fees from 'pupils' that he likens such a procedure to prostitution (Xen. *Mem.* i. 6. 13). It is sometimes believed that the 'intellectual autobiography' of Socrates in Pl. *Phaedo* 96 A ff. is evidence that at one time in his life Socrates' interests were scientific, and that to this extent *Clouds* is a telling caricature. But although *Phaedo* is evidence that Socrates at one time felt intense curiosity about scientific causation, this is not the same thing as the dogmatic exposition of scientific doctrines which is so prominent in *Clouds*. Also, the more we rely on *Phaedo* to bring the Platonic and Aristophanic Socrates together, the less we can rely on the historical accuracy of *Ap.* 19 CD, where Plato's Socrates says, with specific reference to the portrayal of himself in *Clouds*, that no one has ever on any occasion heard him talking at all about the subjects there associated with him. In any case, *Phaedo* does not touch the issue of teaching oratory for money, which is central to the play.

Other items of evidence which can be traced back to the time of Socrates (they include a fragment of Lysias, information transmitted via Aristippos and Aristoxenos, and a significant silence in the material used by Aristotle for his *Sophistes* [a lost work about which we learn something from later writers]) support Plato and Xenophon against Aristophanes, but also provide an important clue to Ar.'s standpoint. Socrates enjoyed the friendship and hospitality of wealthy, eminent, and ambitious young men (cf. Pl. *Ap.* 23 c); among them was Alkibiades, who was already well known by 427 (Ar. fr. 198, from *Banqueters*) and whose subsequent career, as we see from Xen. *Mem.* i. 2. 12 ff., was debited to Socrates. Ar. treated Socrates essentially as a parasitic intellectual. To philosophers and historians of philosophy this seems a bad mistake and a cruel injustice; but Ar. was not a philosopher. We are all familiar with the fact that distinctions which seem fundamental to those whose interests lie in a particular field are scarcely perceived by those who stand outside. To the man who has no ear for music, Mozart and Rachmaninov sound the same, and to the man of conservative tastes in painting a Picasso and a Matisse look the same. Protestants often say that Catholics 'worship' the Virgin Mary; Catholics normally deny this; to the agnostic they seem to be splitting a hair so fine that it is hard to focus one's eyes on it at all. Which distinctions are to be judged important, and which trivial, depends on the standpoint of the judge; and to Ar. the differences between Socrates and other intellectuals of his day, so momentous to the Socratics, were insignificant beside the respects in which both Socrates and the other intellectuals differed from the comic poet and his audience.

VII. RIGHT AND WRONG

Names. The two contestants in 889–1114 are designated in the hypotheses, the dramatis personae, the scholia, and the sigla beside the text ὁ δίκαιος λόγος and ὁ ἄδικος λόγος. I prefer ὁ κρείττων λόγος and ὁ ἥττων λόγος, which is what they are called when they are first mentioned (112 ff.) and what they call themselves (893 ff., 990, 1038); cf. 882 ff., 1336 f., 1444 f., 1451 f.

The best translation of the names is 'Right' and 'Wrong', for this combines the appropriate moral, legal, and intellectual overtones; cf. our expressions 'in the right', 'in the wrong', 'he has no idea of right or wrong', and 'right's right'.

That the two λόγοι should be personified and brought before us as speaking characters is fully in accord with traditional Greek categories of thought and with the technique of comedy. λόγοι are included by Hesiod in the abstract brood of Eris, and the personification of the Laws in Plato's *Crito* has its roots in ordinary linguistic usage (ὁ νόμος κελεύει and ὁ νόμος ἀπαγορεύει). Dramatically, Strepsiades' words at 112 ff. prepare us for the eventual dispute between personified Right and Wrong.

Education. The contest is focused on education. If we had no other evidence but the play, we should probably believe that an old system of education was yielding to a new system in the 420s, but no one, so far as we know, ever suggested that sophistic education should or could be substituted for music, poetry, and physical training in boyhood. The sophists taught young men; it is implied by Plato that their teaching came after that of the γραμματιστής, κιθαριστής, and παιδοτρίβης, and this is consistent with the age of individuals mentioned in Plato and Xenophon as undergoing sophistic education. Provided that he was not prevented by poverty or parental opposition, anyone could continue into adult life advanced instruction in music and gymnastics or embark on a technical apprenticeship or on a course of a different (sometimes, perhaps, a more intellectual) kind. But sophists' fees were high, and it is unlikely that more than a minute proportion of Athenian youths received any education at all which compelled them to exercise the intellect.

If, therefore, Right were a real person (and capable, as he is not, of rational exposition), he would say:

1. Among the wealthiest and most influential families, there is a tendency to prefer sophistic education to advanced training in the traditional techniques of music and gymnastics.

2. This sets the tone which (*a*) is superficially imitated by society at large, and (*b*) has its effect also on boys still undergoing ordinary education, because they look up to distinguished young men as models of behaviour.

If he were more than ordinarily percipient, he might add:

3. The authority of the family and the state is undermined by rootless individuals who stimulate intellectual curiosity and independence of thought in the young and so minister to an appetite which family and state have been unable to satisfy.

The New Education, as represented by Wrong and criticized by Right, differs strikingly from what we have so far seen of Socrates' school. When Strepsiades is enrolled in the school he is warned that he must cheerfully endure cold and hunger and abstain from the pleasures of life (414 ff., cf. 440 ff.)—precisely the opposite of what Wrong encourages. Ar.'s Socrates is interested in scientific speculation and experiment and in linguistic analysis; in the contest of Right and Wrong these matters are not mentioned, and it is only in the light of the earlier part of the play that we can, if we wish, imagine them subsumed under the 'chatter' of the young men. The reason for these discrepancies is that the contest is accommodated by Ar. to the familiar theme of

'New vs. Old', in which the older generation represents itself as tough, upright, and virtuous and represents the younger generation as soft, dishonest, and dissolute. That is why there is so much in common between this debate on education and the debate in *Frogs* on poetry, which has undergone a similar accommodation to conventional themes. The Greeks of any given generation tended to believe that their ancestors were supermen, and in both *Clouds* and *Frogs* emphasis is strongly laid on ancestral virtues, not simply on contemporary change. Right claims that his system of education 'bred the men who fought at Marathon' (986)—men, that is, of whom very few indeed can still have been alive when Ar. wrote *Clouds*.

There is a good deal of nonsense in Right's argument. The implication that criticism of mythology is a new phenomenon overlooks the teaching of Xenophanes and Herakleitos in the time of the *Μαραθωνομάχαι*. As for the belief that young men have only just learned to open their mouths, Xenophon hits the target when, at the end of a story of how the young Alkibiades trapped Perikles in an argument, he makes Perikles say (*Mem.* i. 2. 46) 'We were clever at that kind of argument when we were young!' From our vantage-point twenty-four centuries later we can identify possible internal causes of the decline of Athenian power; but it is difficult, and perhaps impossible, to connect any of them in any way with the intellectual developments of which Right so strenuously disapproves.

Homosexuality. Apart from the inability to meet reasonable argument with anything better than an outburst of bad temper (906 f., 1052 f.), the most striking characteristic of Right is his obsession with boys' genitals (966, 973 ff., 1014).

Greek society, at least from the sixth century and probably from a somewhat earlier date, differed notably from ours in its attitude to homosexuality. The undifferentiated sex-play characteristic of puberty in most cultures was prolonged into adult life, perhaps in consequence of the segregation of girls in those families which could afford to entrust all errands to slaves. It was universally assumed that the co-existence of heterosexual and homosexual desire in the same person was natural and normal. In Aristophanic comedy heterosexuality is more prominent, but homosexual practices and attitudes are by no means excluded; Philokleon in *Wasps* 578 ranks 'looking at the genitals of the youths undergoing their δοκιμασία' as one of a juror's pleasures and privileges.

Just as in many modern cultures a boy who seduces girls is applauded, while the girls whom he seduces are condemned, so it was taken for granted by the Greeks that a young man who pursues a boy deserves sympathy and encouragement, while the boy is expected to resist his lover's advances. Plato puts an excellent exposition of this situation into the mouth of Pausanias in *Smp.* 182 A ff.

That Right should condemn a boy who ogles a lover (979 f.) is in accord with Greek convention. What goes beyond convention is his own obsession; see 966, 973 ff., 977 f.

There is, I believe, an adequate reason for Ar.'s depiction of Right in this way. Given the evidence of literature from 450 to 300 B.C., it would be hard to sustain the hypothesis that homosexual practices were more widespread and homosexual emotions more intense during the preceding hundred years, but at least there is no denying that their expression and depiction were much less inhibited. It is from the period 550–450 that we find on vase-paintings straightforward portrayal of a virtually unlimited range of sexual behaviour—in later vase-painting there is a sharper distinction between the serious and the grossly humorous—and in conjunction with the visual arts of the early fifth century we must remember the earthy directness with which Pindar and Aischylos portray homosexual activity and emotion. It must have seemed to Ar. (and tales told by his grandfather's generation will have strengthened the impression) that the *Μαραθωνομάχαι* combined frugality, endurance, and physical courage with a homosexual zest which in his own day could not find completely uninhibited expression except in a comic context.

Thus Right, who is ignominiously vanquished in the contest, is caricatured no less than triumphant Wrong; and, in an author with so sharp an eye and so deeply imbued with irreverence, it would be strange if it were otherwise.

VIII. THE CHORUS

There were three possibilities open to Ar. for the chorus of a play ridiculing intellectuals: students, abstractions (e.g. φροντίδες), and phenomena of the heavens. The third possibility had two outstanding advantages. First, the intellectual was by tradition preoccupied with astronomy and meteorology. Secondly, the words μετέωρος, ἀνεπτερῶσθαι, etc., are used metaphorically of insecurity, suspense, and excitement, and are associated with the unknown, the spiritual, all that is divorced from ordinary life (cf. the treatment of poets in 331 ff., *Peace* 827 ff., *Birds* 1373 ff., and our expressions 'his head is in the clouds' and 'his feet aren't on the ground'). Stars and winds were unsuitable for Ar.'s purpose, for the winds had long been regarded as fierce gods and the stars include in their number formidable powers bringing the seasons which govern the round of human life. Clouds were the perfect answer. The Greeks did not worship them as deities; they regarded them simply as part of the mechanism by which Zeus sent rain; but as natural phenomena outside human control, they could be personified and treated as divine agents or ministers of Zeus. Since they look like steam or smoke (καπνός: cf. 330) they suggest what is vain, empty, deceptive, and insubstantial; καπνός has this metaphorical sense in Eur. *Hipp.* 954. Since μετάρσιος (= μετέωρος) occurs as an epithet of κόμπος in Eur. *Andr.* 1220, the clouds, as 'smoke up in the air', not only are a characteristic object of intellectual speculation (cf. p. xx) but also represent in visible form two different metaphorical descriptions of such speculations.

Clouds have one other association which is most important for the comic representation of misguided intellectuals. Ixion, believing that he had seduced Hera, 'lay with a cloud' (Pindar, *Py.* 2. 36) created by Zeus to deceive him as a preliminary to eternal punishment for his evil intentions. In the version of the Helen myth adopted by Euripides (in *Helena*) from Stesichoros, the phantom Helen who went to Troy while the real Helen was transported to Egypt was a 'cloud' (Eur. *Hel.* 705 f., 750, 1219) created by divine malice.

The majestic opening song of the Chorus is formally much closer to tragedy and serious choral lyric than to comedy, and this befits their status as deities responding to Socrates' invocation. In the parabasis they conform to the traditions of comedy, speaking partly for the poet. After the parabasis, when in other comedies the Chorus tends to degenerate into the hero's claque, the Clouds' alienation from Strepsiades becomes apparent. They give the first hint of their change of role at 1113 f., and openly foretell disaster in 1303 ff. In the argument between Strepsiades and Pheidippides they revert to 'holding the ring' in the manner expected of a Chorus during a formal contest; but when Strepsiades is worsted they reveal themselves at the end (1454 ff.) as true deities, who have behaved towards Strepsiades as the gods in tragic legend behave, leading him on to disaster to punish him for the wrongdoing on which he set his heart. They have no mercy to spare for Socrates, who has treated them as goddesses, for they are representatives and agents of the true divine hierarchy, which he has slighted.

IX. THE TWO VERSIONS OF THE PLAY

The Chorus says in 520 ff.: 'I thought this the best of my comedies, but I retreated worsted by vulgar men.' Since a play cannot refer to its own failure in the past tense, this part of the parabasis must belong to a revised version. Confirmation that this is so is found in 545 ff.: 'Other poets . . . keep on pounding Hyperbolos. Eupolis began it with *Marikas* . . .' Hypothesis II, which precedes the play in the MSS. and is derived ultimately from the official records kept at Athens, says that *Clouds* was performed at the City Dionysia of 424/3. But Eupolis' *Marikas* was performed at the Lenaia of 422/1. Since Eupolis is described (553) as the first to write a comedy ridiculing Hyperbolos, 'and then Hermippos wrote one . . . and now all the rest of them bash away at Hyperbolos' (557 f.), and since we know that Hermippos did not compete at the City Dionysia of 422/1, Ar. cannot have written these lines before the spring of 420 at the earliest. Hyperbolos was ostracized in 416 (cf. 551 n.), and on the assumption that the comic poets spared their ammunition on him when he was gone, the limits for the composition of *Clouds* 518–62 are spring 420 and winter 417.

Later in the parabasis the Chorus refers (575 ff.) to the election of Kleon as general, and concludes (590 ff.): 'If you convict Kleon of embezzlement . . . everything will turn out all right.' Kleon was killed in the summer of 422 (Thuc. v. 10. 9); therefore *Clouds* 575–94 belong to the original play (Kleon was in fact a general in 424/3).

It follows that the play as we have it was partially, but not completely, revised. Hypothesis II says that a revised version was performed in 423/2; but this statement must be rejected, for (*a*) that is not early enough for the reference to the plays attacking Hyperbolos, and (*b*) we can see from the researches of Kallimachos and Eratosthenes on the subject, summarized by the Scholiast on 552, that the official records contained no entry relating to a second performance of *Clouds* and no room for such an entry. Moreover, the easiest explanation of the structural oddity at 706 (see ad loc.) is that Ar. cancelled what he had originally written there but did not fill the gap; and whereas 887 suggests that he envisaged the performance of the play by four actors, the absence of a choral song after 888 allows no actor any time for a change of costume.

It is interesting that Ar. allowed an incompletely revised version of a play, unperformable within the framework of Athenian theatrical convention, to go into circulation as a written text. This is an indication that he, at least (we cannot speak for other comic poets), was not exclusively concerned with theatrical effect but also took into account a reading public.

It appears from statements in Hypothesis I and in the scholia on 520 and 543 that the contest between Right and Wrong was quite different in the two versions and that the final scene, in which the school is burned, belongs entirely to the revised version. It is interesting to speculate how the original version ended. In view of the prominence given to Chairephon 'off-stage' in 104, 144 ff., 156 ff., and 1465, it is also legitimate to wonder whether he had a part in the original version or in an early (but superseded) stage of revision.

X. THE HISTORY OF THE TEXT

Scraps of five ancient copies survive, the oldest written in III A.D. and the others in V–VII A.D.

136 medieval MSS. contain the whole or the greater part of *Clouds*. Only two—R (Ravennas 429, written *c.* 1000) and V (Marcianus 474, probably XII but possibly XI)—are known to have been written before the sack of Constantinople by the Crusaders in 1204; the remainder belong to the end of XIII or later. V is more closely related to R in *Clouds* than in the other plays of Ar. Comparison of R with the ancient scraps suggests that it is not markedly inferior to the kind of text one might have expected to find in IV or V A.D.

R, V, and E (Estensis *α*. U.5.10) contain marginal scholia derived ultimately (as can be shown by comparing them with the partly legible scholia in one of the ancient fragments) from ancient commentaries. These commentaries were probably compiled in the period A.D. 250–350, and they drew on earlier work which in its turn drew on the Alexandrian scholars. The scholia include some metrical analyses of lyric passages, and these go back to Heliodoros (I A.D.). Since copyists often did not concern themselves with the relation between scholia and text, a reading incorporated in a scholion or implied by it may be older and better than the reading of the text itself.

Byzantine scholars edited the text of the play from XII onwards, and (especially *c.* 1300) introduced their own emendations. One of the tasks of a modern editor is, as it were, to by-pass the Byzantines by identifying their emendations and distinguishing them from readings which were transmitted from antiquity.

Many ancient and medieval authors quote from *Clouds*, and these 'testimonia' are sometimes a source of good readings when the MSS. of the play itself let us down. The most important source of testimonia is the great early medieval lexicon known as the Suda.

XI. LANGUAGE

1. Phonology and Morphology. Ar.'s language differs very little from that of Attic prose, except: (*a*) In certain passages of lyric, original ᾱ is retained (as in tragic lyric) and *ρσ* and *σσ* may be substituted for the normal Attic *ρρ* and *ττ*. (*b*) Proper names in -*κλῆς* have an alternative form in -*κλέης*. (*c*) The optative ending -*οιντο* has an alternative -*οίατο*. (*d*) MSS. present both *ἐς* and *εἰς*, but the metre (with one or two disputed exceptions) never requires *ἔ̆ς*. (*e*) Both *ξύν* and *σύν* occur, and metre seldom makes a decision between them possible.

2. Syntax. (*a*) Complex sentences containing more than one subordinate clause are not common. In narrative units tend to be strung together by means of the connectives *εἶτα*, *κᾆτα* (= *καὶ εἶτα*), *ἔπειτα*, and *κἄπειτα*, e.g. 46, 66, 151, 390; and these connectives sometimes appear between a participle and a main verb, e.g. 624 *λαχὼν . . . κἄπειτ' . . . ἀφῃρέθη*. (*b*) Ellipse of a verb is common, e.g. 3 *ἀπέραντον*, 'Endless!'; 5 *ἀλλ' οὐκ ἂν πρὸ τοῦ*, 'But they wouldn't have done so in the old days'; 227 *εἴπερ*, 'If that's what you're doing'.

3. Vocabulary. (*a*) *Reinforcement.* It follows from the nature of comic action that the ratio of questions and exclamations to statements is high, and they tend to be reinforced in ways familiar to us from colloquial usage in modern languages:

(i) Exclamations, e.g. *ἰού* and *οἴμοι*.

(ii) Vocatives, e.g. *ὦ μέλε* and *ὦ δαιμόνιε*.

(iii) Oaths and adjurations. *νὴ (τὸν) Δία* (or *ναὶ μὰ Δία*) and *μὰ (τὸν) Δία* are normal ways of saying 'Yes' and 'No'; (*ὦ*) *Ἡράκλεις* is a common exclamation of surprise; and questions and requests are accompanied by *πρὸς τῶν θεῶν*, *πρὸς τοῦ Διός*, etc.

(iv) An order can be reinforced by *ἀνύσας* (e.g. 181), lit. 'Having hastened', i.e. 'Buck up and . . .!'

(v) Questions are reinforced by *γάρ* (e.g. 200; it is seldom translatable); *ἀντιβολῶ* or *ἱκετεύω*, 'I beseech you!'; *ἴθι*, *φέρε*, or *φέρ' ἴδω*; *ἐτεόν* (e.g. 35, 'Really'); and *εἰπέ* (*μοι*).

(vi) Pronouns (and more rarely, other words) are reinforced by *μέν* (e.g. 29) or *μέντοι* (e.g. 126), which correspond to an increased volume of voice in English.

(vii) Demonstratives in -*ί*, e.g. *οὑτοσί* and *ὡδί*, are much commoner in Comedy than in any other genre.

(viii) The interrogatives *τιή* and *ὁτιή* = *τί* and *ὅτι*, and interrogatives may be accumulated, e.g. 784 *ὁτιὴ τί;* 'Whatever for?'

(ix) *πρῶτα (μέν)* and *πρῶτον (μέν)* are used, like 'To start with' and 'First of all' in English, when the speaker has no precise idea of what, if anything, would come second; e.g. 224.

(x) δῆτα is extremely common (e.g. 58) in replying to the previous speaker: 'Then . . .', 'Well, then, . . .', 'Why, . . .'.

(*b*) *Poetic words*. The vocabulary of Ar.'s lyrics is sometimes indistinguishable in character from that of serious poetry, e.g. 275 ff., 563 ff. When words of this character occur in dialogue, they normally indicate quotation or parody (e.g. 335 ff.) or achieve humorous effect by some kind of incongruity (e.g. 357 οὐρανομήκη). There are, however, occasions on which our classification of a word as 'poetic' may only reflect our comparative ignorance of the prose vocabulary of the fifth century B.C., e.g. 105 νήπιον, 'childish', 'silly'.

(*c*) *Derived and compound words*. The meaning of such words is normally discoverable by analysis, e.g. 15 ξυνωρικεύεται, 'Practises his skill as the driver of a racing pair', 101 μεριμνοφροντισταί, 'Intellectual excogitators'. Sometimes, however, these words would be mysterious if divorced from their contexts, e.g. 166 διεντερεύματος, 'Thorough gutting', which takes its point from 160 ff.

(*d*) *Slang and vulgarisms*. The large anatomical and physiological vocabulary of Comedy consists in part of words which never occur in serious literature at all (e.g. 9 πέρδεται, 734 πέος); the correct translation of these is the vulgarest words known to the translator. There are in addition very many slang words, i.e. words which in serious literature bear a different meaning (e.g. 1371 ἐκίνει, lit. 'moved', 'stirred', but in the context 'had sexual intercourse with'). Slang of other kinds is undoubtedly an ingredient in the vocabulary of Comedy, but its identification is often difficult because of our lack of direct access to the spoken language of Aristophanes' time.

XII. METRE

Symbols

(i) *In abstract description of a metre*
(e.g., 'The usual form of a glyconic is . . .')

–	position occupied by a long syllable
ᴗ	position occupied by a short syllable
×	('anceps') position which may be occupied by either
oo	position occupied by one or other of: – ᴗ, ᴗ –, and – –
⌢̣	last position in verse
|	('caesura') point at which word-end always occurs
⁝	point at which word-end usually occurs
:	point at which word-end occurs if it has not occurred at ⁝
	('bridge') two successive positions are occupied by syllables of the same word.

(ii) *In scanning a given sequence of words*
(e.g., 'The scansion of line 1312 is . . .')

–	long syllable
ᴗ	short syllable
×	syllable which may be scanned as either
‿	open syllable ending in long vowel or diphthong but scanned short because the next word begins with a vowel
⌢	syllable which would be short if the next syllable belonged to the same verse
|	('diaeresis') (1) in responding verses: word-end occurs at this point in both strophe and antistrophe; (2) in other verses: word-

end occurs at a point which is, or might be, of interest to students of metre

|| (1) within a verse: hiatus; (2) verse-end

When a verse is constructed of smaller units which are common and easily recognizable, a space equivalent to one long is left between units.

Definitions

acatalectic — When two kola or verses differ only in that one ends in – ⏑ – and the other in – ⏑ – ◠, or one in ⏑ – – and the other in ⏑ – ⏑ ◠, the longer form is called 'acatalectic' and the shorter 'catalectic'.

aeolic — A generic term for kola which contain at least one choriambic metron preceded and followed by other sequences.

anapaestic metron (*an*) — ⏔ – ⏔ –, – ⏑ ⏑ – –, or (if – ⏔ follows) ⏔ – – ⏑ ⏑

anapaestic tetrameter catalectic (verse) — ⏔ – ⏔ – ⋮ ⏔ – ⏔ – | ⏔ – ⏔ – ⏑ ⏑ – ◠
One may substitute – ⏑ ⏑ for ⏔ – (except in the fourth metron), but the sequence ⏑ ⏑ ⏑ ⏑ is avoided. Occasionally there is no caesura.

antistrophe — When the metrical pattern of a sequence of verses is repeated, the first occurrence is the 'strophe' and the second the 'antistrophe'.

aristophanean kolon — – ⏑ ⏑ – ⏑ – –

bacchiac metron (*ba*) — ⏑ – –

catalectic — *See* acatalectic.

choriambic metron (*ch*) — – ⏑ ⏑ –

clausula — The last verse or kolon of a sequence.

correption — The process which gives ⏑.

cretic metron (*cr*) — ⏕ ⏑ ⏕

dactyl	– ⏔
dactylic hemiepes (kolon)	– ⏑ ⏑ – ⏑ ⏑ –
dactylo-epitrites	*See* p. 114.
dochmiac metron	Most commonly × – – ⏑ – or – ⏑ ⏑ – ⏑ –; there are many variants.
eupolidean verse	o o – × – ⏑ ⏑ – ⁝ o o – × – ⏑ ⌒
foot	Half a metron, when the metron is divisible into halves.
glyconic kolon	o o – ⏑ ⏑ – ⏑ –
iambic metron (*ia*)	× – ⏑ –
iambic tetrameter catalectic (verse)	× – ⏑ – × – ⏑ – ⁝ × – ⏑ – ⏑ – ⌒ Resolution is not common in this verse.
iambic trimeter	{× ⏕ / ⏑ ⏑ –} {⏑ ⏕ / ⏑ ⏑ –} {× ⁝ ⏕ / ⏑ ⏑ –} {⏑ : ⏕ / ⏑ ⏑ –} {× ⏕ / ⏑ ⏑ –} ⏑ ⌒ Lack of caesura is commoner in Comedy than in Tragedy. When there are three syllables in a foot, certain distributions of the syllables between two different words tend to be avoided; the only common distributions are – | ⏖ and ⏑ | ⏖.
iambo-choriambic verse	A verse composed of *ia* and *ch* in equal quantities or with *ia* predominating.
ionic (*io*) metron	⏑ ⏑ – – In an ionic verse one or more *io* may have the form ⏑ ⏑ –
ithyphallic kolon (*ith*)	– ⏑ – ⏑ – –
kolon	A sequence larger than any of those normally called metra; it may constitute a verse by itself or be part of a verse.
lekythion (kolon: *lek*)	– ⏑ – × – ⏑ –

lyric dactyls — *See* p. 99.

metron — The smallest unit of a recognizable rhythm.

paroemiac (kolon) — { ⏔ – ⏔ – / – ⏑ ⏑ – – } ⏑ ⏑ – –

pause — Verse-end.

pherecratean kolon — o o – ⏑ ⏑ – –

pnigos — A sequence of anapaestic, cretic, iambic, or trochaic metra which comes at the end of a passage of verses of the same metre but is not divisible into verses of the same size.

reizianum (kolon) — o – ⏑ ⏑ – –

resolution — Substitution of ⏑ ⏑ for –.

responsion — The repetition of the same metrical sequence.

strophe — *See* antistrophe.

trochaic metron (*tr*) — ⏕ ⏑ ⏕ ×

trochaic tetrameter catalectic (verse) — – ⏑ – × – ⏑ – × ⋮ – ⏑ – × – ⏑ 𝄐
Resolution is not common in this verse.

verse — A unit of which the last syllable (1) must be the last syllable of a word, (2) may be – or 𝄐, (3) may end in consonant or vowel, and (4) must not be elided. Since many points in a sequence normally meet these conditions, there is often room for disagreement on the division of a sequence into verses. When there is responsion, the area of disagreement can be reduced by eliminating points which fail to meet the same conditions in both strophe and antistrophe.

word-end — A 'prepositive' (e.g. *καί*, *ἤ*, *ὡς*, the article, a preposition) is regarded as forming one word with the word that follows, and a postpositive (e.g. *γάρ*, *ἄν*, unemphatic *αὐτ-*, an enclitic) as forming one word with the word that precedes. For most (though not all) metrical purposes an elided word is not regarded as having an end.

Prosody

The basic rules of Comedy, as of Tragedy, are:

A long syllable is a syllable which contains (*a*) a long vowel or diphthong, or (*b*) a short vowel separated from the next vowel by more than one consonant-sound. A short syllable is a syllable which contains a short vowel not separated from the next vowel or separated from it by only one consonant-sound. Final ϵ, α, and ο (except in the definite article), and (in certain cases) ι are elided before an initial vowel. Initial α and ϵ commonly disappear ('prodelision') when the preceding word ends in a long vowel or diphthong. *καί*, *ὦ*, *ὅ*, *ἅ*, or the article may unite with a following initial vowel ('crasis') to form one long syllable. In certain expressions other final and initial vowels may unite ('synizesis'), e.g. *ἐγὼ οἶδα* > *ἐγᾦδα*.

Comedy differs from Tragedy in the following ways:

(i) Hiatus is common after *τί* (e.g. 21), *ὅτι* (e.g. 866), *περί* (e.g. 97), and interjections (e.g. 105 *ἤ*).

(ii) The infinitive ending -*αι* may be elided (e.g. 780 *καλεῖσθ'*).

(iii) Correption of a long vowel or diphthong within a word is common (e.g. 187 *οὑτοιί*, scanned – ∪ –); correption of a final syllable occurs (as in Tragedy) in lyrics, but also in anapaestic tetrameters (e.g. 321).

(iv) In spoken verse a short vowel separated from the next vowel by β, δ, γ, π, τ, κ, φ, θ, or χ + ρ or by π, τ, κ, φ, θ, and χ + λ, μ, or ν constitutes a short syllable; exceptions are normally explicable (on independent grounds) as parody of serious poetry.

(v) Initial ρ is treated as two consonant sounds (e.g. 344 *δὲ ῥῖνας*, scanned – – ∪).

NOTES ON THE APPARATUS CRITICUS

The purpose of the apparatus criticus is: first, to show what the manuscripts say, wherever a choice has been made between variant readings or an emendation has been printed in the text; and secondly, to show what emendations have been suggested where there are grounds for dissatisfaction with all the manuscripts. Many trivial errors and corrections have been passed over in silence.

The following symbols are used:

Π	one or other of the surviving fragments of ancient copies
R	the manuscript Ravennas 429
V	the manuscript Venetus Marcianus 474
p	consensus of those manuscripts which (*a*) date from the period 1261–1453 and (*b*) show few or no signs of Byzantine emendation
a	consensus of R, V, and **p**
p	one or more of the manuscripts subsumed under **p**
p	a reading which is known, or reasonably believed, to be a Byzantine emendation
z	an emendation made at any time from the beginning of the sixteenth century to the present day
Sch.	a reading incorporated in a scholion or explicitly cited by a scholiast
(Sch.)	a reading inferred from a scholion
test.	a reading found in another author's quotation from Aristophanes

ΥΠΟΘΕΣΕΙΣ

R contains no hypotheses; V contains seven, which are in many other manuscripts also. The three most important of the seven are given below.

HYPOTHESIS I

τοῦτο ταὐτόν ἐστι τῷ προτέρῳ, διεσκεύασται δὲ ἐπὶ μέρους, ὡς ἂν δὴ ἀναδιδάξαι μὲν αὐτὸ τοῦ ποιητοῦ προθυμηθέντος, οὐκέτι δὲ τοῦτο δι᾽ ἥνποτε αἰτίαν ποιήσαντος. καθόλου μὲν οὖν σχεδὸν παρὰ πᾶν μέρος γεγενημένη ⟨ἡ⟩ διόρθωσις ⟨. . .⟩. τὰ μὲν γὰρ περιῄρηται, τὰ δὲ παραπέπλεκται καὶ ἐν τῇ τάξει καὶ ἐν τῇ τῶν προσώπων διαλλαγῇ μετεσχημάτισται, ἃ δὲ ὁλοσχερῆ τῆς διασκευῆς τοιαῦτα ὄντα τετύχηκεν. αὐτίκα ἡ παράβασις τοῦ χοροῦ ἤμειπται, καὶ ὅπου ὁ δίκαιος λόγος πρὸς τὸν ἄδικον λαλεῖ, καὶ τελευταῖον ὅπου καίεται ἡ διατριβὴ Σωκράτους.

4 *γεγένηται ⟨ἡ⟩ z*

HYPOTHESIS II

αἱ πρῶται Νεφέλαι ἐδιδάχθησαν ἐν ἄστει ἐπὶ ἄρχοντος Ἰσάρχου, ὅτε Κρατῖνος μὲν ἐνίκα Πυτίνῃ, Ἀμειψίας δὲ Κόννῳ. δι᾽ ὅπερ Ἀριστοφάνης ἀπορριφθεὶς παραλόγως ᾠήθη δεῖν ἀναδιδάξας τὰς Νεφέλας τὰς δευτέρας καταμέμφεσθαι τὸ θέατρον. ἀτυχῶν δὲ πολὺ μᾶλλον καὶ ἐν τοῖς ἔπειτα οὐκέτι τὴν διασκευὴν εἰσήγαγεν. αἱ δὲ δεύτεραι Νεφέλαι ἐπὶ Ἀμεινίου ἄρχοντος.

HYPOTHESIS III

πρεσβύτης τις Στρεψιάδης ὑπὸ δανείων καταπονούμενος διὰ τὴν ἱπποτροφίαν τοῦ παιδὸς δεῖται τούτου φοιτήσαντος ὡς τὸν Σωκράτην μαθεῖν τὸν ἥττονα λόγον, εἴ πως δύναιτο τὰ ἄδικα λέγων ἐν τῷ δικαστηρίῳ τοὺς χρήστας νικᾶν καὶ μηδενὶ [τῶν δανειστῶν] μηδὲν ἀποδοῦναι. οὐ βουλομένου δὲ τοῦ μειρακίσκου, διαγνοὺς αὐτὸς ἐλθὼν μανθάνειν μαθητὴν τοῦ Σωκράτους ἐκκαλέσας τινὰ διαλέγεται. ἐκκυκληθείσης δὲ τῆς διατριβῆς οἵ τε μαθηταὶ κύκλῳ καθήμενοι πιναροὶ συνορῶνται καὶ αὐτὸς ὁ Σωκράτης ἐπὶ κρεμάθρας αἰωρούμενος καὶ ἀποσκοπῶν τὰ μετέωρα θεωρεῖται. μετὰ ταῦτα τελεῖ παραλαβὼν τὸν πρεσβύτην καὶ τοὺς νομιζομένους παρ' αὐτῷ θεούς, ἀέρα, προσέτι δὲ αἰθέρα καὶ νεφέλας, κατακαλεῖται. πρὸς δὲ τὴν εὐχὴν εἰσέρχονται νεφέλαι ἐν σχήματι χοροῦ, καὶ φυσιολογήσαντος οὐκ ἀπιθάνως τοῦ Σωκράτους ἀποστᾶσαι πρὸς τοὺς θεατὰς περὶ πλειόνων διαλέγονται. μετὰ δὲ ταῦτα ὁ μὲν πρεσβύτης διδασκόμενος ἐν τῷ φανερῷ τινὰ τῶν μαθημάτων γελωτοποιεῖ. καὶ ἐπειδὴ διὰ τὴν ἀμαθίαν ἐκ τοῦ φροντιστηρίου ἐκβάλλεται, διάγων πρὸς βίαν τὸν υἱὸν συνίστησι τῷ Σωκράτει. τούτου δὲ ἐξαγαγόντος αὐτῷ ἐν τῷ θεάτρῳ τὸν ἄδικον καὶ τὸν δίκαιον λόγον, διαγωνισθεὶς ὁ ἄδικος πρὸς τὸν δίκαιον λόγον παραλαβὼν αὐτὸν [ὁ ἄδικος λόγος] διδάσκει. κομισάμενος δὲ αὐτὸν ὁ πατὴρ ἐκπεπονημένον ἐπηρεάζει τοῖς χρήσταις καὶ ὡς κατωρθωκὼς εὐωχεῖ παραλαβών. γενομένης δὲ περὶ τὴν εὐωχίαν ἀντιλογίας πληγὰς λαβὼν ὑπὸ τοῦ παιδὸς βοὴν ἵστησι· καὶ καταλαλούμενος ὑπὸ τοῦ παιδός, ὅτι δίκαιον τοὺς πατέρας ὑπὸ τῶν υἱῶν ἀντιτύπτεσθαι, ὑπεραλγῶν διὰ τὴν πρὸς τὸν υἱὸν σύγκρουσιν ὁ γέρων κατασκάπτει καὶ ἐμπίπρησι τὸ φροντιστήριον τῶν Σωκρατικῶν. τὸ δὲ δρᾶμα τῶν πάνυ δυνατῶς πεποιημένων.

4–5 τῶν δανειστῶν secl. *z*   7 ἐκκυκληθείσης *z*: ἐκλυθείσης Vp
16 μαθημάτων p: μαθητῶν Vp   20 ὁ ἄδικος λόγος secl. *z*

ΤΑ ΤΟΥ ΔΡΑΜΑΤΟΣ ΠΡΟΣΩΠΑ

ΣΤΡΕΨΙΑΔΗΣ
ΦΕΙΔΙΠΠΙΔΗΣ
ΟΙΚΕΤΗΣ ΣΤΡΕΨΙΑΔΟΥ
ΜΑΘΗΤΗΣ ΣΩΚΡΑΤΟΥΣ Α′
ΣΩΚΡΑΤΗΣ
ΧΟΡΟΣ ΝΕΦΕΛΩΝ
Ο ΚΡΕΙΤΤΩΝ ΛΟΓΟΣ
Ο ΗΤΤΩΝ ΛΟΓΟΣ
ΧΡΗΣΤΗΣ Α′
ΧΡΗΣΤΗΣ Β′
ΜΑΘΗΤΗΣ ΣΩΚΡΑΤΟΥΣ Β′

ΜΑΡΤΥΣ κωφὸν πρόσωπον

ΝΕΦΕΛΑΙ

ΣΤΡΕΨΙΑΔΗΣ

ἰοὺ ἰού.
ὦ Ζεῦ βασιλεῦ, τὸ χρῆμα τῶν νυκτῶν ὅσον.
ἀπέραντον. οὐδέποθ' ἡμέρα γενήσεται;
καὶ μὴν πάλαι γ' ἀλεκτρυόνος ἤκουσ' ἐγώ.
οἱ δ' οἰκέται ῥέγκουσιν. ἀλλ' οὐκ ἂν πρὸ τοῦ.
ἀπόλοιο δῆτ', ὦ πόλεμε, πολλῶν οὕνεκα,
ὅτ' οὐδὲ κολάσ' ἔξεστί μοι τοὺς οἰκέτας.
ἀλλ' οὐδ' ὁ χρηστὸς οὑτοσὶ νεανίας
ἐγείρεται τῆς νυκτός, ἀλλὰ πέρδεται
ἐν πέντε σισύραις ἐγκεκορδυλημένος.
ἀλλ' εἰ δοκεῖ, ῥέγκωμεν ἐγκεκαλυμμένοι.
ἀλλ' οὐ δύναμαι δείλαιος εὕδειν δακνόμενος
ὑπὸ τῆς δαπάνης καὶ τῆς φάτνης καὶ τῶν χρεῶν
διὰ τουτονὶ τὸν υἱόν. ὁ δὲ κόμην ἔχων
ἱππάζεταί τε καὶ ξυνωρικεύεται
ὀνειροπολεῖ θ' ἵππους. ἐγὼ δ' ἀπόλλυμαι
ὁρῶν ἄγουσαν τὴν σελήνην εἰκάδας·
οἱ γὰρ τόκοι χωροῦσιν. ἅπτε παῖ λύχνον
κἄκφερε τὸ γραμματεῖον, ἵν' ἀναγνῶ λαβὼν
ὁπόσοις ὀφείλω καὶ λογίσωμαι τοὺς τόκους.
φέρ' ἴδω, τί ὀφείλω; δώδεκα μνᾶς Πασίᾳ.
τοῦ δώδεκα μνᾶς Πασίᾳ; τί ἐχρησάμην;
ὅτ' ἐπριάμην τὸν κοππατίαν. οἴμοι τάλας,
εἴθ' ἐξεκόπην πρότερον τὸν ὀφθαλμὸν λίθῳ.

21–2 *Οἰ.* δώδεκα et *Στ.* τοῦ (Sch.)

ΦΕΙΔΙΠΠΙΔΗΣ

Φίλων, ἀδικεῖς. ἔλαυνε τὸν σαυτοῦ δρόμον.

Στ. τοῦτ' ἐστὶ τουτὶ τὸ κακὸν ὅ μ' ἀπολώλεκεν·
ὀνειροπολεῖ γὰρ καὶ καθεύδων ἱππικήν.

Φε. πόσους δρόμους ἐλᾷ τὰ πολεμιστήρια;

Στ. ἐμὲ μὲν σὺ πολλοὺς τὸν πατέρ' ἐλαύνεις δρόμους.
ἀτὰρ τί χρέος ἔβα με μετὰ τὸν Πασίαν;
τρεῖς μναῖ διφρίσκου καὶ τροχοῖν Ἀμεινίᾳ.

Φε. ἄπαγε τὸν ἵππον ἐξαλίσας οἴκαδε.

Στ. ἀλλ' ὦ μέλ' ἐξήλικας ἐμέ γ' ἐκ τῶν ἐμῶν,
ὅτε καὶ δίκας ὤφληκα χἄτεροι τόκου
ἐνεχυράσεσθαί φασιν.

Φε. ἐτεόν, ὦ πάτερ,
τί δυσκολαίνεις καὶ στρέφει τὴν νύχθ' ὅλην;

Στ. δάκνει μέ τις δήμαρχος ἐκ τῶν στρωμάτων.

Φε. ἔασον ὦ δαιμόνιε καταδαρθεῖν τί με.

Στ. σὺ δ' οὖν κάθευδε. τὰ δὲ χρέα ταῦτ' ἴσθ' ὅτι
εἰς τὴν κεφαλὴν ἅπαντα τὴν σὴν τρέψεται.
φεῦ. 41a
εἴθ' ὤφελ' ἡ προμνήστρι' ἀπολέσθαι κακῶς 41b
ἥτις με γῆμ' ἐπῆρε τὴν σὴν μητέρα.
ἐμοὶ γὰρ ἦν ἄγροικος ἥδιστος βίος,
εὐρωτιῶν, ἀκόρητος, εἰκῇ κείμενος,
βρύων μελίτταις καὶ προβάτοις καὶ στεμφύλοις.
ἔπειτ' ἔγημα Μεγακλέους τοῦ Μεγακλέους
ἀδελφιδῆν ἄγροικος ὢν ἐξ ἄστεως,
σεμνήν, τρυφῶσαν, ἐγκεκοισυρωμένην.
ταύτην ὅτ' ἐγάμουν, συγκατεκλινόμην ἐγὼ

28 ἐλᾷς (Sch.?) 31 in. *Οἰ.* (Sch.) 35 ἐνεχυράσεσθαι (Sch.): ἐνεχυράσασθαι **a**

ὄζων τρυγός, τρασιᾶς, ἐρίων, περιουσίας,
ἡ δ' αὖ μύρου, κρόκου, καταγλωττισμάτων,
δαπάνης, λαφυγμοῦ, Κωλιάδος, Γενετυλλίδος.
οὐ μὴν ἐρῶ γ' ὡς ἀργὸς ἦν, ἀλλ' ἐσπάθα,
ἐγὼ δ' ἂν αὐτῇ θοἰμάτιον δεικνὺς τοδὶ
πρόφασιν ἔφασκον· ὦ γύναι, λίαν σπαθᾷς.

ΟΙΚΕΤΗΣ

ἔλαιον ἡμῖν οὐκ ἔνεστ' ἐν τῷ λύχνῳ.

Στ. οἴμοι. τί γάρ μοι τὸν πότην ἧπτες λύχνον;
δεῦρ' ἔλθ' ἵνα κλάῃς.

Οἰ. διὰ τί δῆτα κλαύσομαι;

Στ. ὅτι τῶν παχειῶν ἐνετίθεις θρυαλλίδων.
μετὰ ταῦθ', ὅπως νῷν ἐγένεθ' υἱὸς οὑτοσί,
ἐμοί τε δὴ καὶ τῇ γυναικὶ τἀγαθῇ,
περὶ τοὐνόματος δὴ 'ντεῦθεν ἐλοιδορούμεθα.
ἡ μὲν γὰρ ἵππον προσετίθει πρὸς τοὔνομα,
Ξάνθιππον ἢ Χαίριππον ἢ Καλλιππίδην,
ἐγὼ δὲ τοῦ πάππου 'τιθέμην Φειδωνίδην.
τέως μὲν οὖν ἐκρινόμεθ'· εἶτα τῷ χρόνῳ
κοινῇ ξυνέβημεν κἀθέμεθα Φειδιππίδην.
τοῦτον τὸν υἱὸν λαμβάνουσ' ἐκορίζετο·
"ὅταν σὺ μέγας ὢν ἅρμ' ἐλαύνῃς πρὸς πόλιν,
ὥσπερ Μεγακλέης, ξυστίδ' ἔχων—" ἐγὼ δ' ἔφην·
"ὅταν μὲν οὖν τὰς αἶγας ἐκ τοῦ φελλέως,
ὥσπερ ὁ πατήρ σου, διφθέραν ἐνημμένος—".
ἀλλ' οὐκ ἐπείθετο τοῖς ἐμοῖς οὐδὲν λόγοις,
ἀλλ' ἵππερόν μου κατέχεεν τῶν χρημάτων.
νῦν οὖν ὅλην τὴν νύκτα φροντίζων ὁδοῦ
μίαν ηὗρον ἀτραπὸν δαιμονίως ὑπερφυᾶ,
ἣν ἢν ἀναπείσω τουτονί, σωθήσομαι.

62 δὴ ταῦτ' p: δὴ 'νταῦθ' *z* 73 ἐπίθετο *p*

ἀλλ' ἐξεγεῖραι πρῶτον αὐτὸν βούλομαι.
πῶς δῆτ' ἂν ἥδιστ' αὐτὸν ἐπεγείραιμι; πῶς;
Φειδιππίδη, Φειδιππίδιον.
Φε. τί, ὦ πάτερ;
Στ. κύσον με καὶ τὴν χεῖρα δὸς τὴν δεξιάν.
Φε. ἰδού. τί ἐστιν;
Στ. εἰπέ μοι, φιλεῖς ἐμέ;
Φε. νὴ τὸν Ποσειδῶ τουτονὶ τὸν ἵππιον.
Στ. μή μοι γε τοῦτον μηδαμῶς τὸν ἵππιον·
οὗτος γὰρ ὁ θεὸς αἴτιός μοι τῶν κακῶν.
ἀλλ' εἴπερ ἐκ τῆς καρδίας μ' ὄντως φιλεῖς,
ὦ παῖ, πιθοῦ.
Φε. τί οὖν πίθωμαι δῆτά σοι;
Στ. ἔκτρεψον ὡς τάχιστα τοὺς σαυτοῦ τρόπους
καὶ μάνθαν' ἐλθὼν ἂν ἐγὼ παραινέσω.
Φε. λέγε δή, τί κελεύεις;
Στ. καί τι πείσει;
Φε. πείσομαι,
νὴ τὸν Διόνυσον.
Στ. δεῦρό νυν ἀπόβλεπε.
ὁρᾷς τὸ θύριον τοῦτο καὶ τοἰκίδιον;
Φε. ὁρῶ. τί οὖν τοῦτ' ἐστὶν ἐτεόν, ὦ πάτερ;
Στ. ψυχῶν σοφῶν τοῦτ' ἐστὶ φροντιστήριον.
ἐνταῦθ' ἐνοικοῦσ' ἄνδρες οἳ τὸν οὐρανὸν
λέγοντες ἀναπείθουσιν ὡς ἔστιν πνιγεύς,
κἄστιν περὶ ἡμᾶς οὗτος, ἡμεῖς δ' ἄνθρακες.
οὗτοι διδάσκουσ', ἀργύριον ἤν τις διδῷ,
λέγοντα νικᾶν καὶ δίκαια κἄδικα.

82 Στ. post εἰπέ μοι R 88 ἔκστρεψον RVp test. 95 ἐνταῦθα θακοῦσ' (Sch.)

Φε. εἰσὶν δὲ τίνες;
Στ. οὐκ οἶδ' ἀκριβῶς τοὔνομα.
μεριμνοφροντισταὶ καλοί τε κἀγαθοί.
Φε. αἰβοῖ, πονηροί γ', οἶδα. τοὺς ἀλαζόνας,
τοὺς ὠχριῶντας, τοὺς ἀνυποδήτους λέγεις,
ὧν ὁ κακοδαίμων Σωκράτης καὶ Χαιρεφῶν
Στ. ἢ ἤ, σιώπα. μηδὲν εἴπῃς νήπιον.
ἀλλ' εἴ τι κήδει τῶν πατρῴων ἀλφίτων,
τούτων γενοῦ μοι, σχασάμενος τὴν ἱππικήν.
Φε. οὐκ ἂν μὰ τὸν Διόνυσον εἰ δοίης γέ μοι
τοὺς Φασιανοὺς οὓς τρέφει Λεωγόρας.
Στ. ἴθ', ἀντιβολῶ σ', ὦ φίλτατ' ἀνθρώπων ἐμοί,
ἐλθὼν διδάσκου.
Φε. καὶ τί σοι μαθήσομαι;
Στ. εἶναι παρ' αὐτοῖς φασιν ἄμφω τὼ λόγω,
τὸν κρείττον', ὅστις ἐστί, καὶ τὸν ἥττονα.
τούτοιν τὸν ἕτερον τοῖν λόγοιν, τὸν ἥττονα,
νικᾶν λέγοντά φασι τἀδικώτερα.
ἢν οὖν μάθῃς μοι τὸν ἄδικον τοῦτον λόγον,
ἃ νῦν ὀφείλω διὰ σέ, τούτων τῶν χρεῶν
οὐκ ἂν ἀποδοίην οὐδ' ἂν ὀβολὸν οὐδενί.
Φε. οὐκ ἂν πιθοίμην· οὐ γὰρ ἂν τλαίην ἰδεῖν
τοὺς ἱππέας τὸ χρῶμα διακεκναισμένος.
Στ. οὐκ ἄρα μὰ τὴν Δήμητρα τῶν γ' ἐμῶν ἔδει
οὔτ' αὐτὸς οὔθ' ὁ ζύγιος οὔθ' ὁ σαμφόρας,
ἀλλ' ἐξελῶ σ' εἰς κόρακας ἐκ τῆς οἰκίας.
Φε. ἀλλ' οὐ περιόψεταί μ' ὁ θεῖος Μεγακλέης
ἄνιππον. ἀλλ' εἴσειμι, σοῦ δ' οὐ φροντιῶ.
Στ. ἀλλ' οὐδ' ἐγὼ μέντοι πεσών γε κείσομαι,
ἀλλ' εὐξάμενος τοῖσιν θεοῖς διδάξομαι

αὐτὸς βαδίζων εἰς τὸ φροντιστήριον.
πῶς οὖν γέρων ὢν κἀπιλήσμων καὶ βραδὺς
λόγων ἀκριβῶν σκινδαλάμους μαθήσομαι;
ἰτητέον. τί ταῦτ' ἔχων στραγγεύομαι
ἀλλ' οὐχὶ κόπτω τὴν θύραν; παῖ, παιδίον.

ΜΑΘΗΤΗΣ

βάλλ' εἰς κόρακας. τίς ἐσθ' ὁ κόψας τὴν θύραν;

Στ. Φείδωνος υἱὸς Στρεψιάδης Κικυννόθεν.

Μα. ἀμαθής γε νὴ Δί', ὅστις οὑτωσὶ σφόδρα
ἀπεριμερίμνως τὴν θύραν λελάκτικας
καὶ φροντίδ' ἐξήμβλωκας ἐξηυρημένην.

Στ. σύγγνωθί μοι· τηλοῦ γὰρ οἰκῶ τῶν ἀγρῶν.
ἀλλ' εἰπέ μοι τὸ πρᾶγμα τοὐξημβλωμένον.

Μα. ἀλλ' οὐ θέμις πλὴν τοῖς μαθηταῖσιν λέγειν.

Στ. λέγε νυν ἐμοὶ θαρρῶν· ἐγὼ γὰρ οὑτοσὶ
ἥκω μαθητὴς εἰς τὸ φροντιστήριον.

Μα. λέξω, νομίσαι δὲ ταῦτα χρὴ μυστήρια.
ἀνήρετ' ἄρτι Χαιρεφῶντα Σωκράτης
ψύλλαν ὁπόσους ἅλλοιτο τοὺς αὑτῆς πόδας.
δακοῦσα γὰρ τοῦ Χαιρεφῶντος τὴν ὀφρῦν
ἐπὶ τὴν κεφαλὴν τὴν Σωκράτους ἀφήλατο.

Στ. πῶς δῆτα διεμέτρησε;

Μα. δεξιώτατα.
κηρὸν διατήξας, εἶτα τὴν ψύλλαν λαβὼν
ἐνέβαψεν εἰς τὸν κηρὸν αὐτῆς τὼ πόδε,
κᾆτα ψυχείσῃ περιέφυσαν Περσικαί.
ταύτας ὑπολύσας ἀνεμέτρει τὸ χωρίον.

Στ. ὦ Ζεῦ βασιλεῦ, τῆς λεπτότητος τῶν φρενῶν.

148 τοῦτ' ἐμέτρησε V

Μα. τί δῆτ' ἄν, ἕτερον εἰ πύθοιο Σωκράτους
φρόντισμα;
Στ. ποῖον; ἀντιβολῶ, κάτειπέ μοι.
Μα. ἀνήρετ' αὐτὸν Χαιρεφῶν ὁ Σφήττιος
ὁπότερα τὴν γνώμην ἔχοι, τὰς ἐμπίδας
κατὰ τὸ στόμ' ᾄδειν ἢ κατὰ τοὐρροπύγιον.
Στ. τί δῆτ' ἐκεῖνος εἶπε περὶ τῆς ἐμπίδος;
Μα. ἔφασκεν εἶναι τοὔντερον τῆς ἐμπίδος
στενόν, διὰ λεπτοῦ δ' ὄντος αὐτοῦ τὴν πνοὴν
βίᾳ βαδίζειν εὐθὺ τοὐρροπυγίου·
ἔπειτα κοῖλον πρὸς στενῷ προσκείμενον
τὸν πρωκτὸν ἠχεῖν ὑπὸ βίας τοῦ πνεύματος.
Στ. σάλπιγξ ὁ πρωκτός ἐστιν ἄρα τῶν ἐμπίδων.
ὦ τρισμακάριος τοῦ διεντερεύματος.
ἦ ῥᾳδίως φεύγων ἂν ἀποφύγοι δίκην
ὅστις δίοιδε τοὔντερον τῆς ἐμπίδος.
Μα. πρῴην δέ γε γνώμην μεγάλην ἀφῃρέθη
ὑπ' ἀσκαλαβώτου.
Στ. τίνα τρόπον; κάτειπέ μοι.
Μα. ζητοῦντος αὐτοῦ τῆς σελήνης τὰς ὁδοὺς
καὶ τὰς περιφοράς, εἶτ' ἄνω κεχηνότος
ἀπὸ τῆς ὀροφῆς νύκτωρ γαλεώτης κατέχεσεν.
Στ. ἥσθην γαλεώτῃ καταχέσαντι Σωκράτους.
Μα. ἐχθὲς δέ γ' ἡμῖν δεῖπνον οὐκ ἦν ἑσπέρας.
Στ. εἶἑν. τί οὖν πρὸς τἄλφιτ' ἐπαλαμήσατο;
Μα. κατὰ τῆς τραπέζης καταπάσας λεπτὴν τέφραν,
κάμψας ὀβελίσκον, εἶτα διαβήτην λαβών,
ἐκ τῆς παλαίστρας θοἰμάτιον ὑφείλετο.

157 ἔχει p test. 161 διαλέπτου **p** 179 ἱμάτιον Sch. test.

Στ. τί δῆτ' ἐκεῖνον τὸν Θαλῆν θαυμάζομεν;
ἄνοιγ' ἄνοιγ' ἀνύσας τὸ φροντιστήριον
καὶ δεῖξον ὡς τάχιστά μοι τὸν Σωκράτη.
μαθητιῶ γάρ. ἀλλ' ἄνοιγε τὴν θύραν.

ὦ Ἡράκλεις, ταυτὶ ποδαπὰ τὰ θηρία;
Μα. τί ἐθαύμασας; τῷ σοι δοκοῦσιν εἰκέναι;
Στ. τοῖς ἐκ Πύλου ληφθεῖσι, τοῖς Λακωνικοῖς.
ἀτὰρ τί ποτ' εἰς τὴν γῆν βλέπουσιν οὑτοιί;
Μα. ζητοῦσιν οὗτοι τὰ κατὰ γῆς.
Στ. βολβοὺς ἄρα
ζητοῦσι. μή νυν τοῦτό γ' ἔτι φροντίζετε·
ἐγὼ γὰρ οἶδ' ἵν' εἰσὶ μεγάλοι καὶ καλοί.
τί γὰρ οἵδε δρῶσιν οἱ σφόδρ' ἐγκεκυφότες;
Μα. οὗτοι δ' ἐρεβοδιφῶσιν ὑπὸ τὸν Τάρταρον.
Στ. τί δῆθ' ὁ πρωκτὸς εἰς τὸν οὐρανὸν βλέπει;
Μα. αὐτὸς καθ' αὑτὸν ἀστρονομεῖν διδάσκεται.
ἀλλ' εἴσιθ', ἵνα μὴ 'κεῖνος ὑμῖν ἐπιτύχῃ.
Στ. μήπω γε μήπω γ', ἀλλ' ἐπιμεινάντων, ἵνα
αὐτοῖσι κοινώσω τι πραγμάτιον ἐμόν.
Μα. ἀλλ' οὐχ οἷόν τ' αὐτοῖσι πρὸς τὸν ἀέρα
ἔξω διατρίβειν πολὺν ἄγαν ἐστὶν χρόνον.

Στ. πρὸς τῶν θεῶν, τί γὰρ τάδ' ἐστίν; εἰπέ μοι.
Μα. ἀστρονομία μὲν αὑτηί.
Στ. τουτὶ δὲ τί;
Μα. γεωμετρία.
Στ. τοῦτ' οὖν τί ἐστι χρήσιμον;

185 δοκοῦσ' ἐοικέναι *p*: δοκοῦσιν ἐοικέναι Rp   186 τῆς Λακωνικῆς p
189 τοῦτό γ' ἔτι *z*: τοῦτό γε Rp: τοῦτ' ἔτι Vp: τουτογὶ *z*   192 γ' Vp
195 ὑμῖν (Sch.): ἡμῖν **a** test.   περιτύχῃ p

Μα. γῆν ἀναμετρεῖσθαι
Στ. πότερα τὴν κληρουχικήν;
Μα. οὔκ, ἀλλὰ τὴν σύμπασαν.
Στ. ἀστεῖον λέγεις·
τὸ γὰρ σόφισμα δημοτικὸν καὶ χρήσιμον.
Μα. αὕτη δέ σοι γῆς περίοδος πάσης. ὁρᾷς;
αἵδε μὲν Ἀθῆναι.
Στ. τί σὺ λέγεις; οὐ πείθομαι,
ἐπεὶ δικαστὰς οὐχ ὁρῶ καθημένους.
Μα. ὡς τοῦτ' ἀληθῶς Ἀττικὸν τὸ χωρίον.
Στ. καὶ ποῦ Κικυννῆς εἰσιν, οὑμοὶ δημόται;
Μα. ἐνταῦθ' ἔνεισιν. ἡ δέ γ' Εὔβοι', ὡς ὁρᾷς,
ἡδὶ παρατέταται μακρὰ πόρρω πάνυ.
Στ. οἶδ'· ὑπὸ γὰρ ἡμῶν παρετάθη καὶ Περικλέους.
ἀλλ' ἡ Λακεδαίμων ποῦ 'στίν;
Μα. ὅπου 'στίν; αὑτηί.
Στ. ὡς ἐγγὺς ἡμῶν. τοῦτο μεταφροντίζετε,
ταύτην ἀφ' ἡμῶν ἀπαγαγεῖν πόρρω πάνυ.
Μα. ἀλλ' οὐχ οἷόν τε.
Στ. νὴ Δί', οἰμώξεσθ' ἄρα.
φέρε τίς γὰρ οὗτος οὑπὶ τῆς κρεμάθρας ἀνήρ;
Μα. αὐτός.
Στ. τίς αὐτός;
Μα. Σωκράτης.
Στ. ὦ Σωκράτης.
ἴθ' οὗτος ἀναβόησον αὐτόν μοι μέγα.

214 ποῦ 'σθ'; *p* 215 μεταφροντίζετε (Sch.): μέγα φροντίζετε test.: πάνυ φροντίζετε **a** 217 *Στ.* ante νὴ Δί' *z*: post νὴ Δί' **a** 219 ὦ Σωκράτης *z*: ὦ Σώκρατες **a**

Μα. αὐτὸς μὲν οὖν σὺ κάλεσον· οὐ γάρ μοι σχολή.

Στ. ὦ Σώκρατες.
ὦ Σωκρατίδιον.

ΣΩΚΡΑΤΗΣ

τί με καλεῖς, ὦ 'φήμερε;

Στ. πρῶτον μὲν ὅτι δρᾷς, ἀντιβολῶ, κάτειπέ μοι.

Σω. ἀεροβατῶ καὶ περιφρονῶ τὸν ἥλιον.

Στ. ἔπειτ' ἀπὸ ταρροῦ τοὺς θεοὺς ὑπερφρονεῖς,
ἀλλ' οὐκ ἀπὸ τῆς γῆς, εἴπερ;

Σω. οὐ γὰρ ἄν ποτε
ἐξηῦρον ὀρθῶς τὰ μετέωρα πράγματα
εἰ μὴ κρεμάσας τὸ νόημα καὶ τὴν φροντίδα,
λεπτὴν καταμείξας εἰς τὸν ὅμοιον ἀέρα.
εἰ δ' ὢν χαμαὶ τἄνω κάτωθεν ἐσκόπουν,
οὐκ ἄν ποθ' ηὗρον· οὐ γὰρ ἀλλ' ἡ γῆ βίᾳ
ἕλκει πρὸς αὑτὴν τὴν ἰκμάδα τῆς φροντίδος.
πάσχει δὲ ταὐτὸ τοῦτο καὶ τὰ κάρδαμα.

Στ. πῶς φής;
ἡ φροντὶς ἕλκει τὴν ἰκμάδ' εἰς τὰ κάρδαμα;
ἴθι νυν κατάβηθ', ὦ Σωκρατίδιον, ὡς ἐμέ,
ἵνα με διδάξῃς ὧνπερ ἕνεκ' ἐλήλυθα.

Σω. ἦλθες δὲ κατὰ τί;

Στ. βουλόμενος μαθεῖν λέγειν·
ὑπὸ γὰρ τόκων χρήστων τε δυσκολωτάτων
ἄγομαι, φέρομαι, τὰ χρήματ' ἐνεχυράζομαι.

Σω. πόθεν δ' ὑπόχρεως σαυτὸν ἔλαθες γενόμενος;

226 περιφρονεῖς V   238 μ' ἐκδιδάξῃς Vp test.

Στ. νόσος μ' ἐπέτριψεν ἱππική, δεινὴ φαγεῖν.
ἀλλά με δίδαξον τὸν ἕτερον τοῖν σοῖν λόγοιν,
τὸν μηδὲν ἀποδιδόντα. μισθὸν δ' ὅντιν' ἂν
πράττῃ μ', ὀμοῦμαί σοι καταθήσειν τοὺς θεούς.

Σω. ποίους θεοὺς ὀμεῖ σύ; πρῶτον γὰρ θεοὶ
ἡμῖν νόμισμ' οὐκ ἔστι.

Στ. τῷ γὰρ ὄμνυτε;
[ἢ] σιδαρέοισιν, ὥσπερ ἐν Βυζαντίῳ;

Σω. βούλει τὰ θεῖα πράγματ' εἰδέναι σαφῶς
ἅττ' ἐστὶν ὀρθῶς;

Στ. νὴ Δί', εἴπερ ἐστί γε.

Σω. καὶ συγγενέσθαι ταῖς Νεφέλαισιν εἰς λόγους,
ταῖς ἡμετέραισι δαίμοσιν;

Στ. μάλιστά γε.

Σω. κάθιζε τοίνυν ἐπὶ τὸν ἱερὸν σκίμποδα.

Στ. ἰδού, κάθημαι.

Σω. τουτονὶ τοίνυν λαβὲ
τὸν στέφανον.

Στ. ἐπὶ τί στέφανον; οἴμοι, Σώκρατες,
ὥσπερ με τὸν Ἀθάμανθ' ὅπως μὴ θύσετε.

Σω. οὔκ, ἀλλὰ ταῦτα πάντα τοὺς τελουμένους
ἡμεῖς ποοῦμεν.

Στ. εἶτα δὴ τί κερδανῶ;

Σω. λέγειν γενήσει τρῖμμα, κρόταλον, παιπάλη.
ἀλλ' ἔχ' ἀτρεμεί.

Στ. μὰ τὸν Δί' οὐ ψεύσει γέ με·
καταπαττόμενος γὰρ παιπάλη γενήσομαι.

243 ἔτριψεν RVp 248–9 ἢ secl. *z*: ὄμνυτ'; ἢ *p* 258 πάντα ταῦτα p: πάντας ταῦτα *z* 261 ἀτρέμας p

Σω. εὐφημεῖν χρὴ τὸν πρεσβύτην καὶ τῆς εὐχῆς ἐπακούειν.
ὦ δέσποτ' ἄναξ, ἀμέτρητ' Ἀήρ, ὃς ἔχεις τὴν γῆν μετέωρον,
λαμπρός τ' Αἰθήρ, σεμναί τε θεαὶ Νεφέλαι βροντησικέραυνοι,
ἄρθητε, φάνητ', ὦ δέσποιναι, τῷ φροντιστῇ μετέωροι.

Στ. μήπω, μήπω γε, πρὶν ἂν τουτὶ πτύξωμαι, μὴ καταβρεχθῶ.
τὸ δὲ μηδὲ κυνῆν οἴκοθεν ἐλθεῖν ἐμὲ τὸν κακοδαίμον' ἔχοντα.

Σω. ἔλθετε δῆτ', ὦ πολυτίμητοι Νεφέλαι, τῷδ' εἰς ἐπίδειξιν·
εἴτ' ἐπ' Ὀλύμπου κορυφαῖς ἱεραῖς χιονοβλήτοισι κάθησθε,
εἴτ' Ὠκεανοῦ πατρὸς ἐν κήποις ἱερὸν χορὸν ἵστατε Νύμφαις,
εἴτ' ἄρα Νείλου προχοαῖς ὑδάτων χρυσέαις ἀρύτεσθε πρόχοισιν,
ἢ Μαιῶτιν λίμνην ἔχετ' ἢ σκόπελον νιφόεντα Μίμαντος·
ὑπακούσατε δεξάμεναι θυσίαν καὶ τοῖς ἱεροῖσι χαρεῖσαι.

ΧΟΡΟΣ

ἀέναοι Νεφέλαι, *στρ.*
ἀρθῶμεν φανεραὶ δροσερὰν φύσιν εὐάγητον
πατρὸς ἀπ' Ὠκεανοῦ βαρυαχέος
ὑψηλῶν ὀρέων κορυφὰς ἔπι
δενδροκόμους, ἵνα
τηλεφανεῖς σκοπιὰς ἀφορώμεθα
καρπούς τ' ἀρδομέναν ἱερὰν χθόνα
καὶ ποταμῶν ζαθέων κελαδήματα
καὶ πόντον κελάδοντα βαρύβρομον·
ὄμμα γὰρ αἰθέρος ἀκάματον σελαγεῖται

263 ὑπακούειν p 268 *μὴ κυνῆν* RVp test.: *μὴ κυνέην* z *κακοδαίμον'* Rp: *δύστηνον* Vp 272 *ἀρύτεσθε* test.: *ἀρύεσθε* a 274 *χαρεῖσαι* Rp: *φανεῖσαι* Vp 277 *εὐάητον* R 282 *κήπους* z *ἀρδομέναν θ'* Rp

μαρμαρέαισιν αὐγαῖς.
ἀλλ' ἀποσεισάμεναι νέφος ὄμβριον
ἀθανάτας ἰδέας ἐπιδώμεθα
τηλεσκόπῳ ὄμματι γαῖαν.

Σω. ὦ μέγα σεμναὶ Νεφέλαι, φανερῶς ἠκούσατέ μου καλέσαντος.
ᾔσθου φωνῆς ἅμα καὶ βροντῆς μυκησαμένης θεοσέπτου;

Στ. καὶ σέβομαί γ', ὦ πολυτίμητοι, καὶ βούλομαι ἀνταποπαρδεῖν
πρὸς τὰς βροντάς· οὕτως αὐτὰς τετραμαίνω καὶ πεφόβημαι.
κεἰ θέμις ἐστίν, νυνί γ' ἤδη, κεἰ μὴ θέμις ἐστί, χεσείω.

Σω. οὐ μὴ σκώψει μηδὲ ποήσεις ἅπερ οἱ τρυγοδαίμονες οὗτοι,
ἀλλ' εὐφήμει· μέγα γάρ τι θεῶν κινεῖται σμῆνος ἀοιδαῖς.

Χο. παρθένοι ὀμβροφόροι, ἀντ.
ἔλθωμεν λιπαρὰν χθόνα Παλλάδος, εὔανδρον γᾶν
Κέκροπος ὀψόμεναι πολυήρατον·
οὗ σέβας ἀρρήτων ἱερῶν, ἵνα
μυστοδόκος δόμος
ἐν τελεταῖς ἁγίαις ἀναδείκνυται·
οὐρανίοις τε θεοῖς δωρήματα,
ναοί θ' ὑψερεφεῖς καὶ ἀγάλματα,
καὶ πρόσοδοι μακάρων ἱερώταται
εὐστέφανοί τε θεῶν θυσίαι θαλίαι τε
παντοδαπαῖσιν ὥραις,
ἦρί τ' ἐπερχομένῳ Βρομία χάρις
εὐκελάδων τε χορῶν ἐρεθίσματα
καὶ μοῦσα βαρύβρομος αὐλῶν.

Στ. πρὸς τοῦ Διός, ἀντιβολῶ σε, φράσον, τίνες εἴσ', ὦ Σώκρατες, αὗται
αἱ φθεγξάμεναι τοῦτο τὸ σεμνόν; μῶν ἡρῷναί τινές εἰσιν;

287 μαρμαρέαις ἐν Rp : μαρμαρέαισιν ἐν p 289 ἀθανάταις ἰδέαις Vp 292 θεόσεπτον z 310 παντοδαπαῖσιν z: παντοδαπαῖς ἐν RVp: παντοδαπαῖσιν ἐν p

Σω. ἥκιστ', ἀλλ' οὐράνιαι Νεφέλαι, μεγάλαι θεαὶ ἀνδράσιν ἀργοῖς,
αἵπερ γνώμην καὶ διάλεξιν καὶ νοῦν ἡμῖν παρέχουσιν
καὶ τερατείαν καὶ περίλεξιν καὶ κροῦσιν καὶ κατάληψιν.

Στ. ταῦτ' ἄρ' ἀκούσασ' αὐτῶν τὸ φθέγμ' ἡ ψυχή μου πεπότηται
καὶ λεπτολογεῖν ἤδη ζητεῖ καὶ περὶ καπνοῦ στενολεσχεῖν
καὶ γνωμιδίῳ γνώμην νύξασ' ἑτέρῳ λόγῳ ἀντιλογῆσαι·
ὥστ' εἴ πως ἐστίν, ἰδεῖν αὐτὰς ἤδη φανερῶς ἐπιθυμῶ.

Σω. βλέπε νυν δευρὶ πρὸς τὴν Πάρνηθ'· ἤδη γὰρ ὁρῶ κατιούσας ἡσυχῇ αὐτάς.

Στ. φέρε ποῦ; δεῖξον.

Σω. χωροῦσ' αὗται πάνυ πολλαὶ
διὰ τῶν κοίλων καὶ τῶν δασέων, αὗται πλάγιαι.

Στ. τί τὸ χρῆμα;
ὡς οὐ καθορῶ.

Σω. παρὰ τὴν εἴσοδον.

Στ. ἤδη νυνὶ μόλις οὕτως.

Σω. νῦν γέ τοι ἤδη καθορᾷς αὐτάς, εἰ μὴ λημᾷς κολοκύνταις.

Στ. νὴ Δί' ἔγωγ'. ὦ πολυτίμητοι· πάντα γὰρ ἤδη κατέχουσιν.

Σω. ταύτας μέντοι σὺ θεὰς οὔσας οὐκ ᾔδεις οὐδ' ἐνόμιζες;

Στ. μὰ Δί', ἀλλ' ὁμίχλην καὶ δρόσον αὐτὰς ἡγούμην καὶ καπνὸν εἶναι.

Σω. οὐ γὰρ μὰ Δί' οἶσθ' ὁτιὴ πλείστους αὗται βόσκουσι σοφιστάς,
Θουριομάντεις, ἰατροτέχνας, σφραγιδονυχαργοκομήτας·
κυκλίων τε χορῶν ᾀσματοκάμπτας, ἄνδρας μετεωροφένακας,
οὐδὲν δρῶντας βόσκουσ' ἀργούς, ὅτι ταύτας μουσοποοῦσιν.

324 ἡσυχῇ z: ἡσύχως a 326 παρὰ Rp: πρὸς Vp οὕτως R: ὁρῶ Vp: ἀθρῶ p

9120095 C

Στ. ταῦτ᾽ ἄρ᾽ ἐποίουν "ὑγρᾶν Νεφελᾶν στρεπταίγλαν δάϊον ὁρμάν",
"πλοκάμους θ᾽ ἑκατογκεφάλα Τυφῶ" "πρημαινούσας τε θυέλλας",
εἶτ᾽ "ἀερίας διεράς" "γαμψούς τ᾽ οἰωνοὺς ἀερονηχεῖς"
"ὄμβρους θ᾽ ὑδάτων δροσερᾶν νεφελᾶν"· εἶτ᾽ ἀντ᾽ αὐτῶν κατέπινον
κεστρᾶν τεμάχη μεγαλᾶν ἀγαθᾶν κρέα τ᾽ ὀρνίθεια κιχηλᾶν.
Σω. διὰ μέντοι τάσδ᾽. οὐχὶ δικαίως;
Στ. λέξον δή μοι, τί παθοῦσαι,
εἴπερ νεφέλαι γ᾽ εἰσὶν ἀληθῶς, θνηταῖς εἴξασι γυναιξίν;
οὐ γὰρ ἐκεῖναί γ᾽ εἰσὶ τοιαῦται.
Σω. φέρε, ποῖαι γάρ τινές εἰσιν;
Στ. οὐκ οἶδα σαφῶς· εἴξασιν δ᾽ οὖν ἐρίοισιν πεπταμένοισιν,
κοὐχὶ γυναιξίν, μὰ Δί᾽, οὐδ᾽ ὁτιοῦν· αὗται δὲ ῥῖνας ἔχουσιν.
Σω. ἀπόκριναί νυν ἅττ᾽ ἂν ἔρωμαι.
Στ. λέγε νυν ταχέως ὅτι βούλει.
Σω. ἤδη ποτ᾽ ἀναβλέψας εἶδες νεφέλην κενταύρῳ ὁμοίαν
ἢ παρδάλει ἢ λύκῳ ἢ ταύρῳ;
Στ. νὴ Δί᾽ ἔγωγ᾽. εἶτα τί τοῦτο;
Σω. γίγνονται πάνθ᾽ ὅτι βούλονται· κᾆτ᾽ ἢν μὲν ἴδωσι κομήτην
ἄγριόν τινα τῶν λασίων τούτων, οἷόνπερ τὸν Ξενοφάντου,
σκώπτουσαι τὴν μανίαν αὐτοῦ κενταύροις ᾔκασαν αὑτάς.
Στ. τί γὰρ ἢν ἅρπαγα τῶν δημοσίων κατίδωσι Σίμωνα, τί δρῶσιν;
Σω. ἀποφαίνουσαι τὴν φύσιν αὐτοῦ λύκοι ἐξαίφνης ἐγένοντο.
Στ. ταῦτ᾽ ἄρα, ταῦτα Κλεώνυμον αὗται τὸν ῥίψασπιν χθὲς ἰδοῦσαι,
ὅτι δειλότατον τοῦτον ἑώρων, ἔλαφοι διὰ τοῦτ᾽ ἐγένοντο.

335 στραπταίγλαν *z* 337 τ᾽ *p*: om. **a** 343 γοῦν V test. 348 ὅτι Rp: ὅσα Vp

Σω. καὶ νῦν γ' ὅτι Κλεισθένη εἶδον, ὁρᾷς, διὰ τοῦτ' ἐγένοντο
γυναῖκες.
Στ. χαίρετε τοίνυν, ὦ δέσποιναι· καὶ νῦν, εἴπερ τινὶ κἄλλῳ,
οὐρανομήκη ῥήξατε κἀμοὶ φωνήν, ὦ παμβασίλειαι.
Χο. χαῖρ', ὦ πρεσβῦτα παλαιογενές, θηρατὰ λόγων φιλομούσων.
σύ τε, λεπτοτάτων λήρων ἱερεῦ, φράζε πρὸς ἡμᾶς ὅτι χρῄ-
ζεις·
οὐ γὰρ ἂν ἄλλῳ γ' ὑπακούσαιμεν τῶν νῦν μετεωροσοφιστῶν
πλὴν ἢ Προδίκῳ, τῷ μὲν σοφίας καὶ γνώμης οὕνεκα, σοὶ δὲ
ὅτι βρενθύει τ' ἐν ταῖσιν ὁδοῖς καὶ τὠφθαλμὼ παραβάλλεις
κἀνυπόδητος κακὰ πόλλ' ἀνέχει κἀφ' ἡμῖν σεμνοπροσωπεῖς.
Στ. ὦ Γῆ, τοῦ φθέγματος, ὡς ἱερὸν καὶ σεμνὸν καὶ τερατῶδες.
Σω. αὗται γάρ τοι μόναι εἰσὶ θεαί, τἄλλα δὲ πάντ' ἐστὶ φλύαρος.
Στ. ὁ Ζεὺς δ' ὑμῖν, φέρε, πρὸς τῆς Γῆς, Οὑλύμπιος οὐ θεός ἐστιν;
Σω. ποῖος Ζεύς; οὐ μὴ ληρήσεις. οὐδ' ἐστὶ Ζεύς.
Στ. τί λέγεις σύ;
ἀλλὰ τίς ὕει; τουτὶ γὰρ ἔμοιγ' ἀπόφηναι πρῶτον ἁπάντων.
Σω. αὗται δήπου· μεγάλοις δέ σ' ἐγὼ σημείοις αὐτὸ διδάξω.
φέρε, ποῦ γὰρ πώποτ' ἄνευ νεφελῶν ὕοντ' ἤδη τεθέασαι;
καίτοι χρῆν αἰθρίας ὕειν αὐτόν, ταύτας δ' ἀποδημεῖν.
Στ. νὴ τὸν Ἀπόλλω, τοῦτό γε τοι τῷ νυνὶ λόγῳ εὖ προσέφυσας.
καίτοι πρότερον τὸν Δί' ἀληθῶς ᾤμην διὰ κοσκίνου οὐρεῖν.
ἀλλ' ὅστις ὁ βροντῶν ἐστι φράσον, τοῦθ' ὅ με ποιεῖ τετραμαίνειν.
Σω. αὗται βροντῶσι κυλινδόμεναι.
Στ. τῷ τρόπῳ, ὦ πάντα σὺ τολμῶν;

364 σεμνὸν Rp: τερπνὸν Vp 366 ἡμῖν RVp 372 τοῦτό γε τοι δὴ τῷ νῦν z

Σω. ὅταν ἐμπλησθῶσ᾽ ὕδατος πολλοῦ κἀναγκασθῶσι φέρεσθαι
κατακριμνάμεναι πλήρεις ὄμβρου δι᾽ ἀνάγκην, εἶτα βαρεῖαι
εἰς ἀλλήλας ἐμπίπτουσαι ῥήγνυνται καὶ παταγοῦσιν.

Στ. ὁ δ᾽ ἀναγκάζων ἐστὶ τίς αὐτάς—οὐχ ὁ Ζεύς;—ὥστε φέρεσθαι;

Σω. ἥκιστ᾽, ἀλλ᾽ αἰθέριος δῖνος.

Στ. Δῖνος; τουτί μ᾽ ἐλελήθει,
ὁ Ζεὺς οὐκ ὤν, ἀλλ᾽ ἀντ᾽ αὐτοῦ Δῖνος νυνὶ βασιλεύων.
ἀτὰρ οὐδέν πω περὶ τοῦ πατάγου καὶ τῆς βροντῆς μ᾽ ἐδίδαξας.

Σω. οὐκ ἤκουσάς μου τὰς νεφέλας ὕδατος μεστὰς ὅτι φημὶ
ἐμπιπτούσας εἰς ἀλλήλας παταγεῖν διὰ τὴν πυκνότητα;

Στ. φέρε, τουτὶ τῷ χρὴ πιστεύειν;

Σω. ἀπὸ σαυτοῦ ᾽γώ σε διδάξω.
ἤδη ζωμοῦ Παναθηναίοις ἐμπλησθεὶς εἶτ᾽ ἐταράχθης
τὴν γαστέρα καὶ κλόνος ἐξαίφνης αὐτὴν διεκορκορύγησεν;

Στ. νὴ τὸν Ἀπόλλω, καὶ δεινὰ ποεῖ γ᾽ εὐθύς μοι καὶ τετάρακται,
χὤσπερ βροντὴ τὸ ζωμίδιον παταγεῖ καὶ δεινὰ κέκραγεν,
ἀτρέμας πρῶτον, παππὰξ παππάξ, κἄπειτ᾽ ἐπάγει παπαπαππάξ·
χὤταν χέζω, κομιδῇ βροντᾷ, παπαπαππάξ, ὥσπερ ἐκεῖναι.

Σω. σκέψαι τοίνυν ἀπὸ γαστριδίου τυννουτουὶ οἷα πέπορδας·
τὸν δ᾽ ἀέρα τόνδ᾽ ὄντ᾽ ἀπέραντον πῶς οὐκ εἰκὸς μέγα βροντᾶν;
ταῦτ᾽ ἄρα καὶ τὠνόματ᾽ ἀλλήλοιν, "βροντὴ" καὶ "πορδή", ὁμοίω.

Στ. ἀλλ᾽ ὁ κεραυνὸς πόθεν αὖ φέρεται λάμπων πυρί, τοῦτο δίδαξον,
καὶ καταφρύγει βάλλων ἡμᾶς, τοὺς δὲ ζῶντας περιφλεύει.
τοῦτον γὰρ δὴ φανερῶς ὁ Ζεὺς ἵησ᾽ ἐπὶ τοὺς ἐπιόρκους.

384 ὑγρότητα V 394 in. Στ. V 395 in. Στ. om. Vp
396 περιφλεύει z: περιφλύει Rp: περιφλέγει Vp

Σω. καὶ πῶς, ὦ μῶρε σὺ καὶ Κρονίων ὄζων καὶ βεκκεσέληνε,
εἴπερ βάλλει τοὺς ἐπιόρκους, δῆτ᾽ οὐχὶ Σίμων᾽ ἐνέπρησεν
οὐδὲ Κλεώνυμον οὐδὲ Θέωρον; καίτοι σφόδρα γ᾽ εἴσ᾽ ἐπίορκοι.
ἀλλὰ τὸν αὑτοῦ γε νεὼν βάλλει καὶ Σούνιον, ἄκρον Ἀθηνέων,
καὶ τὰς δρῦς τὰς μεγάλας, τί μαθών; οὐ γὰρ δὴ δρῦς γ᾽ ἐπιορκεῖ.

Στ. οὐκ οἶδ᾽· ἀτὰρ εὖ σὺ λέγειν φαίνει. τί γάρ ἐστιν δῆθ᾽ ὁ κεραυνός;

Σω. ὅταν εἰς ταύτας ἄνεμος ξηρὸς μετεωρισθεὶς κατακλεισθῇ,
ἔνδοθεν αὐτὰς ὥσπερ κύστιν φυσᾷ, κἄπειθ᾽ ὑπ᾽ ἀνάγκης
ῥήξας αὐτὰς ἔξω φέρεται σοβαρὸς διὰ τὴν πυκνότητα,
ὑπὸ τοῦ ῥοίβδου καὶ τῆς ῥύμης αὐτὸς ἑαυτὸν κατακάων.

Στ. νὴ Δί᾽ ἐγὼ γοῦν ἀτεχνῶς ἔπαθον τουτί ποτε Διασίοισιν.
ὀπτῶν γαστέρα τοῖς συγγένεσιν κᾆτ᾽ οὐκ ἔσχων ἀμελήσας,
ἡ δ᾽ ἄρ᾽ ἐφυσᾶτ᾽, εἶτ᾽ ἐξαίφνης διαλακήσασα πρὸς αὐτὼ
τὠφθαλμώ μου προσετίλησεν καὶ κατέκαυσεν τὸ πρόσωπον.

Χο. ὦ τῆς μεγάλης ἐπιθυμήσας σοφίας ἄνθρωπε παρ᾽ ἡμῶν,
ὡς εὐδαίμων ἐν Ἀθηναίοις καὶ τοῖς Ἕλλησι γενήσει
εἰ μνήμων εἶ καὶ φροντιστὴς καὶ τὸ ταλαίπωρον ἔνεστιν
ἐν τῇ ψυχῇ καὶ μὴ κάμνεις μήθ᾽ ἑστὼς μήτε βαδίζων
μήτε ῥιγῶν ἄχθει λίαν μήτ᾽ ἀριστᾶν ἐπιθυμεῖς
οἴνου τ᾽ ἀπέχει καὶ γυμνασίων καὶ τῶν ἄλλων ἀνοήτων
καὶ βέλτιστον τοῦτο νομίζεις, ὅπερ εἰκὸς δεξιὸν ἄνδρα,
νικᾶν πράττων καὶ βουλεύων καὶ τῇ γλώττῃ πολεμίζων.

Στ. ἀλλ᾽ εἵνεκά γε ψυχῆς στερρᾶς δυσκολοκοίτου τε μερίμνης
καὶ φειδωλοῦ καὶ τρυσιβίου γαστρὸς καὶ θυμβρεπιδείπνου,
ἀμέλει, θαρρῶν εἵνεκα τούτων ἐπιχαλκεύειν παρέχοιμ᾽ ἄν.

401 Ἀθηνέων z: Ἀθηναίων RVp test.: Ἀθηνῶν p 409 ὤπτων Vp test. 414 εἶ γὰρ μνήμων (Sch.) test. 416 μηδὲ ῥιγῶν . . . μηδ᾽ ἀριστᾶν z

Σω. ἄλλο τι δῆτ' οὐ νομιεῖς ἤδη θεὸν οὐδένα πλὴν ἅπερ ἡμεῖς,
τὸ Χάος τουτὶ καὶ τὰς Νεφέλας καὶ τὴν Γλῶτταν, τρία ταυτί;

Στ. οὐδ' ἂν διαλεχθείην γ' ἀτεχνῶς τοῖς ἄλλοις οὐδ' ἂν ἀπαντῶν,
οὐδ' ἂν θύσαιμ' οὐδ' ἂν σπείσαιμ' οὐδ' ἐπιθείην λιβανωτόν.

Χο. λέγε νυν ἡμῖν ὅτι σοι δρῶμεν θαρρῶν, ὡς οὐκ ἀτυχήσεις
ἡμᾶς τιμῶν καὶ θαυμάζων καὶ ζητῶν δεξιὸς εἶναι.

Στ. ὦ δέσποιναι, δέομαι τοίνυν ὑμῶν τουτὶ πάνυ μικρόν,
τῶν Ἑλλήνων εἶναί με λέγειν ἑκατὸν σταδίοισιν ἄριστον.

Χο. ἀλλ' ἔσται σοι τοῦτο παρ' ἡμῶν, ὥστε τὸ λοιπόν γ' ἀπὸ τουδὶ
ἐν τῷ δήμῳ γνώμας οὐδεὶς νικήσει πλείονας ἢ σύ.

Στ. μή μοι γε λέγειν γνώμας μεγάλας· οὐ γὰρ τούτων ἐπιθυμῶ,
ἀλλ' ὅσ' ἐμαυτῷ στρεψοδικῆσαι καὶ τοὺς χρήστας διολισθεῖν.

Χο. τεύξει τοίνυν ὧν ἱμείρεις· οὐ γὰρ μεγάλων ἐπιθυμεῖς.
ἀλλὰ σεαυτὸν παράδος θαρρῶν τοῖς ἡμετέροις προπόλοισιν.

Στ. δράσω ταῦθ' ὑμῖν πιστεύσας· ἡ γὰρ ἀνάγκη με πιέζει
διὰ τοὺς ἵππους τοὺς κοππατίας καὶ τὸν γάμον ὅς μ' ἐπέτριψεν.
νῦν οὖν [χρήσθων] ἀτεχνῶς ὅτι βούλονται
τουτὶ τό γ' ἐμὸν σῶμ' αὐτοῖσιν
παρέχω τύπτειν, πεινῆν, διψῆν,
αὐχμεῖν, ῥιγῶν, ἀσκὸν δείρειν,
εἴπερ τὰ χρέα διαφευξοῦμαι
τοῖς τ' ἀνθρώποις εἶναι δόξω
θρασύς, εὔγλωττος, τολμηρός, ἴτης,
βδελυρός, ψευδῶν συγκολλητής,
εὑρησιεπής, περίτριμμα δικῶν,
κύρβις, κρόταλον, κίναδος, τρύμη,

423 οὐ p : οὖν Vp : om. R   ἤδη Rp : εἶναι Vp   439 χρήσθων secl. *z*

μάσθλης, εἴρων, γλοιός, ἀλαζών,
κέντρων, μιαρός, στρόφις, ἀργαλέος,
ματιολοιχός.
ταῦτ' εἴ με καλοῦσ' ἀπαντῶντες,
δρώντων ἀτεχνῶς ὅτι χρῄζουσιν·
κεἰ βούλονται,
νὴ τὴν Δήμητρ' ἔκ μου χορδὴν
τοῖς φροντισταῖς παραθέντων.

Χο. λῆμα μὲν πάρεστι τῷδέ γ'
οὐκ ἄτολμον ἀλλ' ἕτοιμον.
ἴσθι δ' ὡς
ταῦτα μαθὼν παρ' ἐμοῦ κλέος οὐρανόμηκες
ἐν βροτοῖσιν ἕξεις.
Στ. τί πείσομαι;
Χο. τὸν πάντα χρόνον μετ' ἐμοῦ
ζηλωτότατον βίον ἀν-
θρώπων διάξεις.
Στ. ἆρά γε τοῦτ' ἄρ' ἐγώ ποτ'
ὄψομαι;
Χο. ὥστε γέ σου
πολλοὺς ἐπὶ ταῖσι θύραις
ἀεὶ καθῆσθαι,
βουλομένους ἀνακοινοῦ-
σθαί τε καὶ εἰς λόγον ἐλθεῖν
πράγματα κἀντιγραφὰς
πολλῶν ταλάντων,
ἄξια σῇ φρενὶ συμ-
βουλευσομένους μετὰ σοῦ.

451 ματτυολοιχός z   457 Χο. (Sch.) : Σω. **a**   463 Χο. (Sch.) : Σω. **a**   467 ἐπόψομαι test.   Χο. Sch.: om. R: Σω. **Vp**   471 λόγον (Sch.) : λόγους **a**

ἀλλ' ἐγχείρει τὸν πρεσβύτην ὅτιπερ μέλλεις προδιδάσκειν
καὶ διακίνει τὸν νοῦν αὐτοῦ καὶ τῆς γνώμης ἀποπειρῶ.

Σω. ἄγε δή, κάτειπέ μοι σὺ τὸν σαυτοῦ τρόπον,
ἵν' αὐτὸν εἰδὼς ὅστις ἐστὶ μηχανὰς
ἤδη 'πὶ τούτοις πρὸς σὲ καινὰς προσφέρω.
Στ. τί δέ; τειχομαχεῖν μοι διανοεῖ, πρὸς τῶν θεῶν;
Σω. οὔκ, ἀλλὰ βραχέα σου πυθέσθαι βούλομαι,
εἰ μνημονικὸς εἶ.
Στ. δύο τρόπω, νὴ τὸν Δία.
ἢν μέν γ' ὀφείληταί τι μοι, μνήμων πάνυ,
ἐὰν δ' ὀφείλω σχέτλιος, ἐπιλήσμων πάνυ.
Σω. ἔνεστι δῆτά σοι λέγειν ἐν τῇ φύσει;
Στ. λέγειν μὲν οὐκ ἔνεστ', ἀποστερεῖν δ' ἔνι.
Σω. πῶς οὖν δυνήσει μανθάνειν;
Στ. ἀμέλει, καλῶς.
Σω. ἄγε νυν ὅπως, ὅταν τι προβάλωμαι σοφὸν
περὶ τῶν μετεώρων, εὐθέως ὑφαρπάσει.
Στ. τί δαί; κυνηδὸν τὴν σοφίαν σιτήσομαι;
Σω. ἄνθρωπος ἀμαθὴς οὑτοσὶ καὶ βάρβαρος.
δέδοικά σ', ὦ πρεσβῦτα, μὴ πληγῶν δέει.
φέρ' ἴδω, τί δρᾷς ἤν τις σε τύπτῃ;
Στ. τύπτομαι,
κᾆπειτ' ἐπισχὼν ὀλίγον ἐπιμαρτύρομαι·
εἶτ' αὖθις ἀκαρῆ διαλιπὼν δικάζομαι.
Σω. ἴθι νυν κατάθου θοἰμάτιον.
Στ. ἠδίκηκά τι;

483 εἰ **a**: ἢ *z* 489 προβάλλωμαί σοι σοφὸν RV: προβάλω σοι σοφὸν *z*

Σω. οὔκ, ἀλλὰ γυμνοὺς εἰσιέναι νομίζεται.
Στ. ἀλλ' οὐχὶ φωράσων ἔγωγ' εἰσέρχομαι.
Σω. κατάθου. τί ληρεῖς;
Στ. εἰπὲ δή νυν μοι τοδί·
ἢν ἐπιμελὴς ὦ καὶ προθύμως μανθάνω,
τῷ τῶν μαθητῶν ἐμφερὴς γενήσομαι;
Σω. οὐδὲν διοίσεις Χαιρεφῶντος τὴν φύσιν.
Στ. οἴμοι κακοδαίμων, ἡμιθνὴς γενήσομαι.
Σω. οὐ μὴ λαλήσεις, ἀλλ' ἀκολουθήσεις ἐμοὶ
ἀνύσας τι δευρὶ θᾶττον.
Στ. εἰς τὼ χεῖρέ νυν
δός μοι μελιτοῦτταν πρότερον, ὡς δέδοικ' ἐγὼ
εἴσω καταβαίνων ὥσπερ εἰς Τροφωνίου.
Σω. χώρει. τί κυπτάζεις ἔχων περὶ τὴν θύραν;

Χο. ἀλλ' ἴθι χαίρων
τῆς ἀνδρείας εἵνεκα ταύτης.

εὐτυχία γένοιτο τἀν-
θρώπῳ ὅτι προήκων
εἰς βαθὺ τῆς ἡλικίας
νεωτέροις τὴν φύσιν αὑ-
τοῦ πράγμασιν χρωτίζεται
καὶ σοφίαν ἐπασκεῖ.

ὦ θεώμενοι, κατερῶ πρὸς ὑμᾶς ἐλευθέρως
τἀληθῆ, νὴ τὸν Διόνυσον τὸν ἐκθρέψαντά με.
οὕτω νικήσαιμί τ' ἐγὼ καὶ νομιζοίμην σοφὸς
ὡς ὑμᾶς ἡγούμενος εἶναι θεατὰς δεξιοὺς

520 νικήσαιμί τ' ἐγὼ z: νικήσαιμ' ἔγωγε **a**

καὶ ταύτην σοφώτατ' ἔχειν τῶν ἐμῶν κωμῳδιῶν
πρώτους ἠξίωσ' ἀναγεῦσ' ὑμᾶς, ἣ παρέσχε μοι
ἔργον πλεῖστον· εἶτ' ἀνεχώρουν ὑπ' ἀνδρῶν φορτικῶν
ἡττηθεὶς οὐκ ἄξιος ὤν. ταῦτ' οὖν ὑμῖν μέμφομαι
τοῖς σοφοῖς, ὧν οὕνεκ' ἐγὼ ταῦτ' ἐπραγματευόμην.
ἀλλ' οὐδ' ὧς ὑμῶν ποθ' ἑκὼν προδώσω τοὺς δεξιούς.
ἐξ ὅτου γὰρ ἐνθάδ' ὑπ' ἀνδρῶν, οὓς ἡδὺ καὶ λέγειν,
ὁ σώφρων τε χὼ καταπύγων ἄριστ' ἠκουσάτην,
κἀγώ, παρθένος γὰρ ἔτ' ἦν κοὐκ ἐξῆν πώ μοι τεκεῖν,
ἐξέθηκα, παῖς δ' ἑτέρα τις λαβοῦσ' ἀνείλετο,
ὑμεῖς δ' ἐξεθρέψατε γενναίως κἀπαιδεύσατε,
ἐκ τούτου μοι πιστὰ παρ' ὑμῶν γνώμης ἔσθ' ὅρκια.
νῦν οὖν Ἠλέκτραν κατ' ἐκείνην ἥδ' ἡ κωμῳδία
ζητοῦσ' ἦλθ', ἤν που 'πιτύχῃ θεαταῖς οὕτω σοφοῖς.
γνώσεται γάρ, ἤνπερ ἴδῃ, τἀδελφοῦ τὸν βόστρυχον.
ὡς δὲ σώφρων ἐστὶ φύσει σκέψασθ', ἥτις πρῶτα μὲν
οὐδὲν ἦλθε ῥαψαμένη σκύτινον καθειμένον
ἐρυθρὸν ἐξ ἄκρου, παχύ, τοῖς παιδίοις ἵν' ᾖ γέλως·
οὐδ' ἔσκωψεν τοὺς φαλακρούς, οὐδὲ κόρδαχ' εἵλκυσεν·
οὐδὲ πρεσβύτης ὁ λέγων τἄπη τῇ βακτηρίᾳ
τύπτει τὸν παρόντ', ἀφανίζων πονηρὰ σκώμματα·
οὐδ' εἰσῇξε δᾷδας ἔχουσ' οὐδ' "ἰοὺ ἰού" βοᾷ·
ἀλλ' αὑτῇ καὶ τοῖς ἔπεσιν πιστεύουσ' ἐλήλυθεν.
κἀγὼ μὲν τοιοῦτος ἀνὴρ ὢν ποητὴς οὐ κομῶ,
οὐδ' ὑμᾶς ζητῶ 'ξαπατᾶν δὶς καὶ τρὶς ταὔτ' εἰσάγων,
ἀλλ' αἰεὶ καινὰς ἰδέας εἰσφέρων σοφίζομαι
οὐδὲν ἀλλήλαισιν ὁμοίας καὶ πάσας δεξιάς·
ὃς μέγιστον ὄντα Κλέων' ἔπαισ' εἰς τὴν γαστέρα
κοὐκ ἐτόλμησ' αὖθις ἐπεμπηδῆσ' αὐτῷ κειμένῳ·
οὗτοι δ', ὡς ἅπαξ παρέδωκεν λαβὴν Ὑπέρβολος,
τοῦτον δείλαιον κολετρῶσ' ἀεὶ καὶ τὴν μητέρα.
Εὔπολις μὲν τὸν Μαρικᾶν πρώτιστον παρείλκυσεν

528 οὓς *z*: οἷς **a** 533 ὑμῶν *p*: ὑμῖν **a**

ἐκστρέψας τοὺς ἡμετέρους Ἱππέας κακὸς κακῶς,
προσθεὶς αὐτῷ γραῦν μεθύσην τοῦ κόρδακος οὕνεχ', ἣν
Φρύνιχος πάλαι πεπόηχ', ἣν τὸ κῆτος ἤσθιεν.
εἶθ' Ἕρμιππος αὖθις ἐποίησεν εἰς Ὑπέρβολον,
ἄλλοι τ' ἤδη πάντες ἐρείδουσιν εἰς Ὑπέρβολον,
τὰς εἰκοὺς τῶν ἐγχέλεων τὰς ἐμὰς μιμούμενοι.
ὅστις οὖν τούτοισι γελᾷ, τοῖς ἐμοῖς μὴ χαιρέτω.
ἢν δ' ἐμοὶ καὶ τοῖσιν ἐμοῖς εὐφραίνησθ' εὑρήμασιν,
εἰς τὰς ὥρας τὰς ἑτέρας εὖ φρονεῖν δοκήσετε.

ὑψιμέδοντα μὲν θεῶν στρ.
Ζῆνα τύραννον εἰς χορὸν
πρῶτα μέγαν κικλήσκω·
τόν τε μεγασθενῆ τριαίνης ταμίαν,
γῆς τε καὶ ἁλμυρᾶς θαλασ-
σης ἄγριον μοχλευτήν·
καὶ μεγαλώνυμον ἡμέτερον πατέρ'
Αἰθέρα σεμνότατον, βιοθρέμμονα πάντων·
τόν θ' ἱππονώμαν, ὃς ὑπερ-
λάμπροις ἀκτῖσιν κατέχει
γῆς πέδον, μέγας ἐν θεοῖς
ἐν θνητοῖσί τε δαίμων.

ὦ σοφώτατοι θεαταί, δεῦρο τὸν νοῦν προσέχετε·
ἠδικημέναι γὰρ ὑμῖν μεμφόμεσθ' ἐναντίον.
πλεῖστα γὰρ θεῶν ἁπάντων ὠφελούσαις τὴν πόλιν
δαιμόνων ἡμῖν μόναις οὐ θύετ' οὐδὲ σπένδετε,
αἵτινες τηροῦμεν ὑμᾶς. ἢν γὰρ ᾖ τις ἔξοδος
μηδενὶ ξὺν νῷ, τότ' ἢ βροντῶμεν ἢ ψακάζομεν.
εἶτα τὸν θεοῖσιν ἐχθρὸν βυρσοδέψην Παφλαγόνα
ἡνίχ' ᾑρεῖσθε στρατηγόν, τὰς ὀφρῦς ξυνήγομεν
κἀποοῦμεν δεινά, βροντὴ δ' ἐρράγη δι' ἀστραπῆς.
ἡ σελήνη δ' ἐξέλειπεν τὰς ὁδούς, ὁ δ' ἥλιος

τὴν θρυαλλίδ᾽ εἰς ἑαυτὸν εὐθέως ξυνελκύσας
οὐ φανεῖν ἔφασκεν ὑμῖν εἰ στρατηγήσοι Κλέων.
ἀλλ᾽ ὅμως εἵλεσθε τοῦτον· φασὶ γὰρ δυσβουλίαν
τῇδε τῇ πόλει προσεῖναι, ταῦτα μέντοι τοὺς θεούς,
ἅττ᾽ ἂν ὑμεῖς ἐξαμάρτητ᾽, ἐπὶ τὸ βέλτιον τρέπειν.
ὡς δὲ καὶ τοῦτο ξυνοίσει, ῥᾳδίως διδάξομεν.
ἢν Κλέωνα τὸν λάρον δώρων ἑλόντες καὶ κλοπῆς
εἶτα φιμώσητε τούτου τῷ ξύλῳ τὸν αὐχένα,
αὖθις εἰς τἀρχαῖον ὑμῖν, εἴ τι κἀξημάρτετε,
ἐπὶ τὸ βέλτιον τὸ πρᾶγμα τῇ πόλει ξυνοίσεται.

ἀμφί μοι αὖτε Φοῖβ᾽ ἄναξ *ἀντ.*
Δήλιε, Κυνθίαν ἔχων
ὑψικέρατα πέτραν·
ἥ τ᾽ Ἐφέσου μάκαιρα πάγχρυσον ἔχεις
οἶκον, ἐν ᾧ κόραι σε Λυ-
δῶν μεγάλως σέβουσιν·
ἥ τ᾽ ἐπιχώριος ἡμετέρα θεὸς
αἰγίδος ἡνίοχος, πολιοῦχος Ἀθάνα·
Παρνασσίαν θ᾽ ὃς κατέχων
πέτραν σὺν πεύκαις σελαγεῖ
Βάκχαις Δελφίσιν ἐμπρέπων
κωμαστὴς Διόνυσος.

ἡνίχ᾽ ἡμεῖς δεῦρ᾽ ἀφορμᾶσθαι παρεσκευάσμεθα,
ἡ Σελήνη ξυντυχοῦσ᾽ ἡμῖν ἐπέστειλεν φράσαι
πρῶτα μὲν χαίρειν Ἀθηναίοισι καὶ τοῖς ξυμμάχοις·
εἶτα θυμαίνειν ἔφασκε. δεινὰ γὰρ πεπονθέναι
ὠφελοῦσ᾽ ὑμᾶς ἅπαντας οὐ λόγοις ἀλλ᾽ ἐμφανῶς·
πρῶτα μὲν τοῦ μηνὸς εἰς δᾷδ᾽ οὐκ ἔλαττον ἢ δραχμήν,
ὥστε καὶ λέγειν ἅπαντας ἐξιόντας ἑσπέρας
"μὴ πρίῃ, παῖ, δᾷδ᾽, ἐπειδὴ φῶς Σεληναίης καλόν."

586 *στρατηγήσοι Π* Sch.: *στρατηγήσει* **a**

ἄλλα τ' εὖ δρᾶν φησιν, ὑμᾶς δ' οὐκ ἄγειν τὰς ἡμέρας
οὐδὲν ὀρθῶς, ἀλλ' ἄνω τε καὶ κάτω κυδοιδοπᾶν,
ὥστ' ἀπειλεῖν φησιν αὐτῇ τοὺς θεοὺς ἑκάστοτε,
ἡνίκ' ἂν ψευσθῶσι δείπνου κἀπίωσιν οἴκαδε
τῆς ἑορτῆς μὴ τυχόντες κατὰ λόγον τῶν ἡμερῶν.
κᾆθ' ὅταν θύειν δέῃ, στρεβλοῦτε καὶ δικάζετε,
πολλάκις δ' ἡμῶν ἀγόντων τῶν θεῶν ἀπαστίαν,
ἡνίκ' ἂν πενθῶμεν ἢ τὸν Μέμνον' ἢ Σαρπηδόνα,
σπένδεθ' ὑμεῖς καὶ γελᾶτ'· ἀνθ' ὧν λαχὼν Ὑπέρβολος
τῆτες ἱερομνημονεῖν κἄπειθ' ὑφ' ἡμῶν τῶν θεῶν
τὸν στέφανον ἀφῃρέθη· μᾶλλον γὰρ οὕτως εἴσεται
κατὰ σελήνην ὡς ἄγειν χρὴ τοῦ βίου τὰς ἡμέρας.

Σω. μὰ τὴν Ἀναπνοήν, μὰ τὸ Χάος, μὰ τὸν Ἀέρα,
οὐκ εἶδον οὕτως ἄνδρ' ἄγροικον οὐδαμοῦ
οὐδ' ἄπορον οὐδὲ σκαιὸν οὐδ' ἐπιλήσμονα,
ὅστις σκαλαθυρμάτι' ἄττα μικρὰ μανθάνων
ταῦτ' ἐπιλέλησται πρὶν μαθεῖν. ὅμως γε μὴν
αὐτὸν καλῶ θύραζε δεῦρο πρὸς τὸ φῶς.
ποῦ Στρεψιάδης; ἔξει τὸν ἀσκάντην λαβών;

Στ. ἀλλ' οὐκ ἐῶσί μ' ἐξενεγκεῖν οἱ κόρεις.

Σω. ἁνύσας τι κατάθου καὶ πρόσεχε τον νοῦν.

Στ. ἰδού.

Σω. ἄγε δή, τί βούλει πρῶτα νυνὶ μανθάνειν
ὧν οὐκ ἐδιδάχθης πώποτ' οὐδέν; εἰπέ μοι.
πότερον περὶ μέτρων ἢ περὶ ἐπῶν ἢ ῥυθμῶν;

Στ. περὶ τῶν μέτρων ἔγωγ'· ἔναγχος γάρ ποτε
ὑπ' ἀλφιταμοιβοῦ παρεκόπην διχοινίκῳ.

615 *φησὶν ὑμᾶς δ' οὐκ p* : *φησὶν ὑμᾶς κοὐκ* **a** : *φασινκουκ*[*Π* 624 *ἀφ' ἡμῶν* V 628 *οὐδαμοῦ Π*Vp test. : *οὐδένα* Rp 637 **Στ. οὐδέν. Σω.** *εἰπέ μοι* RV

Σω. οὐ τοῦτ' ἐρωτῶ σ', ἀλλ' ὅτι κάλλιστον μέτρον
ἡγεῖ, πότερον τὸ τρίμετρον ἢ τὸ τετράμετρον;
Στ. ἐγὼ μὲν οὐδὲν πρότερον ἡμιέκτεω.
Σω. οὐδὲν λέγεις, ὤνθρωπε.
Στ. περίδου νυν ἐμοὶ
εἰ μὴ τετράμετρόν ἐστιν ἡμιέκτεων.
Σω. εἰς κόρακας. ὡς ἄγροικος εἶ καὶ δυσμαθής.
ταχύ γ' ἂν δύναιο μανθάνειν περὶ ῥυθμῶν.
Στ. τί δέ μ' ὠφελήσουσ' οἱ ῥυθμοὶ πρὸς τἄλφιτα;
ω. πρῶτον μὲν εἶναι κομψὸν ἐν συνουσίᾳ,
ἐπαΐονθ' ὁποῖός ἐστι τῶν ῥυθμῶν
κατ' ἐνόπλιον, χὠποῖος αὖ κατὰ δάκτυλον.
Στ. κατὰ δάκτυλον; νὴ τὸν Δί', ἀλλ' οἶδ'.
Σω. εἰπὲ δή.
Στ. [τίς ἄλλος ἀντὶ τουτουὶ τοῦ δακτύλου;]
πρὸ τοῦ μέν, ἔτ' ἐμοῦ παιδὸς ὄντος, οὑτοσί.
Σω. ἀγρεῖος εἶ καὶ σκαιός.
Στ. οὐ γὰρ ᾠζυρὲ
τούτων ἐπιθυμῶ μανθάνειν οὐδέν.
Σω. τί δαί;
Στ. ἐκεῖν' ἐκεῖνο, τὸν ἀδικώτατον λόγον.
Σω. ἀλλ' ἕτερα δεῖ σε πρότερα τούτου μανθάνειν,
τῶν τετραπόδων ἅττ' ἐστὶν ὀρθῶς ἄρρενα.
Στ. ἀλλ' οἶδ' ἔγωγε τἄρρεν', εἰ μὴ μαίνομαι.
κριός, τράγος, ταῦρος, κύων, ἀλεκτρυών.
Σω. ὁρᾷς ἃ πάσχεις; τήν τε θήλειαν καλεῖς
ἀλεκτρυόνα κατὰ ταὐτὸ καὶ τὸν ἄρρενα.

647 τάχα δ' *p*   650 ἐπαΐειν θ' (Sch.): εἶτ' ἐπαΐειν **Vp**
653 secl. *z*   654 in. Στ. p   ἔτ' *p*: ἐπ' RVp: om. p

Στ. πῶς δή, φέρε;
Σω. πῶς; ἀλεκτρυὼν κἀλεκτρυών.
Στ. νὴ τὸν Ποσειδῶ. νῦν δὲ πῶς με χρὴ καλεῖν;
Σω. ἀλεκτρύαιναν, τὸν δ' ἕτερον ἀλέκτορα.
Στ. ἀλεκτρύαιναν; εὖ γε νὴ τὸν Ἀέρα·
ὥστ' ἀντὶ τούτου τοῦ διδάγματος μόνου
διαλφιτώσω σου κύκλῳ τὴν κάρδοπον.
Σω. ἰδοὺ μάλ' αὖθις, τοῦθ' ἕτερον. τὴν κάρδοπον
ἄρρενα καλεῖς θήλειαν οὖσαν.
Στ. τῷ τρόπῳ;
ἄρρενα καλῶ 'γὼ κάρδοπον;
Σω. μάλιστά γε,
ὥσπερ γε καὶ Κλεώνυμον.
Στ. πῶς δή; φράσον.
Σω. ταὐτὸν δύναταί σοι κάρδοπος Κλεωνύμῳ.
Στ. ἀλλ' ὦ 'γάθ', οὐδ' ἦν κάρδοπος Κλεωνύμῳ,
ἀλλ' ἐν θυείᾳ στρογγύλῃ γ' ἀνεμάττετο.
ἀτὰρ τὸ λοιπὸν πῶς με χρὴ καλεῖν;
Σω. ὅπως;
τὴν καρδόπην, ὥσπερ καλεῖς τὴν Σωστράτην.
Στ. τὴν καρδόπην θήλειαν;
Σω. ὀρθῶς γὰρ λέγεις.
Στ. ἐκεῖνο †δ' ἦν ἄν†· καρδόπη, Κλεωνύμη.
Σω. ἔτι δέ γε περὶ τῶν ὀνομάτων μαθεῖν σε δεῖ,
ἅττ' ἄρρεν' ἐστίν, ἅττα δ' αὐτῶν θήλεα.
Στ. ἀλλ' οἶδ' ἔγωγ' ἃ θήλε' ἐστίν.

664 *φέρ'; Σω. ὅπως;* z: *φέρε, πῶς; Σω.* z   679 *Σω.* z: om. **a** *ὀρθότερον λέγεις* **p**   680 *Στ.* om. RVp: *Σω.* *p*   *ἐκεῖνο δ' ἦν ἄν* susp. z: *ἐκεῖν' ἄρ' ἂν εἴη* z

Σω. εἰπὲ δή.
Στ. Λύσιλλα, Φίλιννα, Κλειταγόρα, Δημητρία.
Σω. ἄρρενα δὲ ποῖα τῶν ὀνομάτων;
Στ. μυρία.
Φιλόξενος, Μελησίας, Ἀμεινίας.
Σω. ἀλλ' ὦ πόνηρε, ταῦτά γ' ἔστ' οὐκ ἄρρενα.
Στ. οὐκ ἄρρεν' ὑμῖν ἐστιν;
Σω. οὐδαμῶς γ', ἐπεὶ
πῶς γ' ἂν καλέσειας ἐντυχὼν Ἀμεινίᾳ;
Στ. ὅπως ἄν; ὡδί· δεῦρο δεῦρ', Ἀμεινία.
Σω. ὁρᾷς; γυναῖκα τὴν Ἀμεινίαν καλεῖς.
Στ. οὔκουν δικαίως, ἥτις οὐ στρατεύεται;
ἀτὰρ τί ταῦθ' ἃ πάντες ἴσμεν μανθάνω;
Σω. οὐδὲν μὰ Δί', ἀλλὰ κατακλινεὶς δευρί—
Στ. τί δρῶ;
Σω. ἐκφρόντισόν τι τῶν σεαυτοῦ πραγμάτων.
Στ. μὴ δῆθ', ἱκετεύω, 'νταῦθά γ', ἀλλ' εἴπερ γε χρή,
χαμαί μ' ἔασον αὐτὰ ταῦτ' ἐκφροντίσαι.
Σω. οὐκ ἔστι παρὰ ταῦτ' ἄλλα.
Στ. κακοδαίμων ἐγώ.
οἵαν δίκην τοῖς κόρεσι δώσω τήμερον.
Χο. φρόντιζε δὴ καὶ διάθρει στρ.
πάντα τρόπον τε σαυτὸν
στρόβει πυκνώσας. ταχὺς δ', ὅταν εἰς ἄπορον
πέσῃς, ἐπ' ἄλλο πήδα
νόημα φρενός· ὕπνος δ' ἀπέ-
στω γλυκύθυμος ὀμμάτων.

688 ἡμῖν RVp 692 ὅστις **p** 696 'νταῦθά γ' *z*: σ' ἐνταῦθ' RVp: σ' ἐνθάδ' p 700 Χο. (Sch.): Σω. **a**

Στ. ἀτταταῖ ἀτταταῖ.

Χο. τί πάσχεις; τί κάμνεις;

Στ. ἀπόλλυμαι δείλαιος. ἐκ τοῦ σκίμποδος
δάκνουσί μ' ἐξέρποντες οἱ Κορίνθιοι,
καὶ τὰς πλευρὰς δαρδάπτουσιν
καὶ τὴν ψυχὴν ἐκπίνουσιν
καὶ τοὺς ὄρχεις ἐξέλκουσιν
καὶ τὸν πρωκτὸν διορύττουσιν,
καί μ' ἀπολοῦσιν.

Χο. μή νυν βαρέως ἄλγει λίαν.

Στ. καὶ πῶς; ὅτε μου
φροῦδα τὰ χρήματα, φρούδη χροιά,
φρούδη ψυχή, φρούδη δ' ἐμβάς,
καὶ πρὸς τούτοις ἔτι τοῖσι κακοῖς
φρουρᾶς ᾄδων
ὀλίγου φροῦδος γεγένημαι.

Σω. οὗτος τί ποιεῖς; οὐχὶ φροντίζεις;

Στ. ἐγώ;
νὴ τὸν Ποσειδῶ.

Σω. καὶ τί δῆτ' ἐφρόντισας;

Στ. ὑπὸ τῶν κόρεων εἴ μου τι περιλειφθήσεται.

Σω. ἀπολεῖ κάκιστ'.

Στ. ἀλλ' ὦ 'γάθ', ἀπόλωλ' ἀρτίως.

Χο. οὐ μαλθακιστέ' ἀλλὰ περικαλυπτέα.
ἐξευρετέος γὰρ νοῦς ἀποστερητικὸς
κἀπαιόλημ'.

708 *Χο.* Sch.: *Σω.* RVp: om. p 712 post 713 RV 716 *Χο.* (Sch.): *Σω.* **a** 727 *Χο.* *z*: *Σω.* **a**

Στ. οἴμοι τίς ἂν δῆτ' ἐπιβάλοι
ἐξ ἀρνακίδων γνώμην ἀποστερητρίδα;

Σω. φέρε νυν ἀθρήσω πρῶτον, ὅτι δρᾷ, τουτονί.
οὗτος, καθεύδεις;

Στ. μὰ τὸν Ἀπόλλω 'γὼ μὲν οὔ.

Σω. ἔχεις τι;

Στ. μὰ Δί' οὐ δῆτ' ἔγωγ'.

Σω. οὐδὲν πάνυ;

Στ. οὐδέν γε πλὴν ἢ τὸ πέος ἐν τῇ δεξιᾷ.

Σω. οὐκ ἐγκαλυψάμενος ταχέως τι φροντιεῖς;

Στ. περὶ τοῦ; σὺ γάρ μοι τοῦτο φράσον, ὦ Σώκρατες.

Σω. αὐτὸς ὅτι βούλει πρῶτος ἐξευρὼν λέγε.

Στ. ἀκήκοας μυριάκις ἁγὼ βούλομαι,
περὶ τῶν τόκων, ὅπως ἂν ἀποδῶ μηδενί.

Σω. ἴθι νυν καλύπτου, καὶ σχάσας τὴν φροντίδα
λεπτὴν κατὰ μικρὸν περιφρόνει τὰ πράγματα
ὀρθῶς διαιρῶν καὶ σκοπῶν.

Στ. οἴμοι τάλας.

Σω. ἔχ' ἀτρέμα· κἂν ἀπορῇς τι τῶν νοημάτων,
ἀφεὶς ἄπελθε, κᾆτα τῇ γνώμῃ πάλιν
κίνησον αὖθις αὐτὸ καὶ ζυγώθρισον.

Στ. ὦ Σωκρατίδιον φίλτατον.

Σω. τί, ὦ γέρον;

Στ. ἔχω τόκου γνώμην ἀποστερητικήν.

Σω. ἐπίδειξον αὐτήν.

737 ἐξευρεῖν **p** 744 κᾆτα τῇ γνώμῃ *z*: κᾆτα τὴν γνώμην **a**: καὶ κατὰ τὴν γνώμην *z*

Στ. εἰπὲ δή νυν μοι—
Σω. τὸ τί;
Στ. γυναῖκα φαρμακίδ᾽ εἰ πριάμενος Θετταλὴν
καθέλοιμι νύκτωρ τὴν σελήνην, εἶτα δὴ
αὐτὴν καθείρξαιμ᾽ εἰς λοφεῖον στρογγύλον
ὥσπερ κάτροπτον, κᾆτα τηροίην ἔχων.
Σω. τί δῆτα τοῦτ᾽ ἂν ὠφελήσειέν σ᾽;
Στ. ὅτι
εἰ μηκέτ᾽ ἀνατέλλοι σελήνη μηδαμοῦ,
οὐκ ἂν ἀποδοίην τοὺς τόκους.
Σω. ὁτιὴ τί δή;
Στ. ὁτιὴ κατὰ μῆνα τἀργύριον δανείζεται.
Σω. εὖ γ᾽. ἀλλ᾽ ἕτερον αὖ σοι προβαλῶ τι δεξιόν.
εἴ σοι γράφοιτο πεντετάλαντός τις δίκη,
ὅπως ἂν αὐτὴν ἀφανίσειας εἰπέ μοι.
Στ. ὅπως; ὅπως; οὐκ οἶδ᾽. ἀτὰρ ζητητέον.
Σω. μή νυν περὶ σαυτὸν εἶλλε τὴν γνώμην ἀεί,
ἀλλ᾽ ἀποχάλα τὴν φροντίδ᾽ εἰς τὸν ἀέρα
λινόδετον ὥσπερ μηλολόνθην τοῦ ποδός.
Στ. ηὕρηκ᾽ ἀφάνισιν τῆς δίκης σοφωτάτην,
ὥστ᾽ αὐτὸν ὁμολογεῖν σέ μοι.
Σω. ποίαν τινά;
Στ. ἤδη παρὰ τοῖσι φαρμακοπώλαις τὴν λίθον
ταύτην ἑόρακας, τὴν καλήν, τὴν διαφανῆ,
ἀφ᾽ ἧς τὸ πῦρ ἅπτουσι;
Σω. τὴν ὕαλον λέγεις;
Στ. ἔγωγε. [Σω.] φέρε, τί δῆτ᾽ ἄν, [Στ.] εἰ ταύτην λαβών,
ὁπότε γράφοιτο τὴν δίκην ὁ γραμματεύς,

769 Σω. et Στ. secl. *z*

ἀπωτέρω στὰς ὧδε πρὸς τὸν ἥλιον
τὰ γράμματ᾽ ἐκτήξαιμι τῆς ἐμῆς δίκης;
Σω. σοφῶς γε νὴ τὰς Χάριτας.
Στ. οἴμ᾽, ὡς ἥδομαι
ὅτι πεντετάλαντος διαγέγραπταί μοι δίκη.
Σω. ἄγε δὴ ταχέως τουτὶ ξυνάρπασον.
Στ. τὸ τί;
Σω. ὅπως ἀποστρέψαις ἂν ἀντιδικῶν δίκην,
μέλλων ὀφλήσειν, μὴ παρόντων μαρτύρων.
Στ. φαυλότατα καὶ ῥᾷστ᾽.
Σω. εἰπὲ δή.
Στ. καὶ δὴ λέγω.
εἰ πρόσθεν ἔτι μιᾶς ἐνεστώσης δίκης
πρὶν τὴν ἐμὴν καλεῖσθ᾽ ἀπαγξαίμην τρέχων.
Σω. οὐδὲν λέγεις.
Στ. νὴ τοὺς θεοὺς ἔγωγ᾽, ἐπεὶ
οὐδεὶς κατ᾽ ἐμοῦ τεθνεῶτος εἰσάξει δίκην.
Σω. ὑθλεῖς. ἄπερρ᾽. οὐκ ἂν διδαξαίμην σ᾽ ἔτι.
Στ. ὁτιὴ τί; ναί, πρὸς τῶν θεῶν, ὦ Σώκρατες.
Σω. ἀλλ᾽ εὐθὺς ἐπιλήθει σύ γ᾽ ἅττ᾽ ἂν καὶ μάθῃς.
ἐπεὶ τί νυνὶ πρῶτον ἐδιδάχθης; λέγε.
Στ. φέρ᾽ ἴδω, τί μέντοι πρῶτον ἦν; τί πρῶτον ἦν;
τίς ἦν ἐν ᾗ ματτόμεθα μέντοι τἄλφιτα;
οἴμοι, τίς ἦν;
Σω. οὐκ εἰς κόρακας ἀποφθερεῖ,
ἐπιλησμότατον καὶ σκαιότατον γερόντιον;

776 ἀποστρέψαιο (i.e. -ψαι᾽) *p* 783 διδάξαιμ᾽ ἄν *z*: διδάξαιμεν *z*
786 ἐδιδάσκου p

Στ. οἴμοι. τί οὖν δῆθ' ὁ κακοδαίμων πείσομαι;
ἀπὸ γὰρ ὀλοῦμαι μὴ μαθὼν γλωττοστροφεῖν.
ἀλλ' ὦ Νεφέλαι, χρηστόν τι συμβουλεύσατε.

Χο. ἡμεῖς μέν, ὦ πρεσβῦτα, συμβουλεύομεν,
εἴ σοι τις υἱός ἐστιν ἐκτεθραμμένος,
πέμπειν ἐκεῖνον ἀντὶ σαυτοῦ μανθάνειν.

Στ. ἀλλ' ἔστ' ἔμοιγ' υἱὸς καλός τε κἀγαθός·
ἀλλ' οὐκ ἐθέλει γὰρ μανθάνειν, τί ἐγὼ πάθω;

Χο. σὺ δ' ἐπιτρέπεις;

Στ. εὐσωματεῖ γὰρ καὶ σφριγᾷ,
κἄστ' ἐκ γυναικῶν εὐπτέρων καὶ Κοισύρας.
ἀτὰρ μέτειμί γ' αὐτόν· ἢν δὲ μὴ θέλῃ,
οὐκ ἔσθ' ὅπως οὐκ ἐξελῶ 'κ τῆς οἰκίας.
ἀλλ' ἐπανάμεινόν μ' ὀλίγον εἰσελθὼν χρόνον.

Χο. ἆρ' αἰσθάνει πλεῖστα δι' ἡ- *ἀντ.*
μᾶς ἀγάθ' αὐτίχ' ἕξων
μόνας θεῶν; ὡς ἕτοιμος ὅδ' ἐστὶν ἅπαντα δρᾶν ὅσ' ἂν κελεύῃς.
σὺ δ' ἀνδρὸς ἐκπεπληγμένου
καὶ φανερῶς ἐπηρμένου
γνοὺς ἀπολάψεις ὅτι πλεῖστον δύνασαι
ταχέως· φιλεῖ γάρ πως τὰ τοι-
αῦθ' ἑτέρᾳ τρέπεσθαι.

Στ. οὔτοι μὰ τὴν Ὁμίχλην ἔτ' ἐνταυθοῖ μενεῖς,
ἀλλ' ἔσθι' ἐλθὼν τοὺς Μεγακλέους κίονας.

Φε. ὦ δαιμόνιε, τί χρῆμα πάσχεις, ὦ πάτερ;
οὐκ εὖ φρονεῖς, μὰ τὸν Δία τὸν Ὀλύμπιον.

800 *καὶ* V: om. R: *τῶν* **p** test. 810 *ἀπολέψεις* Sch.: **ἀπολαύσαις** ***p***

Στ. ἰδού γ' ἰδοὺ Δί' Ὀλύμπιον. τῆς μωρίας·
τὸν Δία νομίζειν ὄντα τηλικουτονί.
Φε. τί δὲ τοῦτ' ἐγέλασας ἐτεόν;
Στ. ἐνθυμούμενος
ὅτι παιδάριον εἶ καὶ φρονεῖς ἀρχαϊκά.
ὅμως γε μὴν πρόσελθ', ἵν' εἰδῇς πλείονα,
καί σοι φράσω τι πρᾶγμ' ὃ [σὺ] μαθὼν ἀνὴρ ἔσει.
ὅπως δὲ τοῦτο μὴ διδάξεις μηδένα.
Φε. ἰδού. τί ἐστιν;
Στ. ὤμοσας νυνὶ Δία.
Φε. ἔγωγ'.
Στ. ὁρᾷς οὖν ὡς ἀγαθὸν τὸ μανθάνειν;
οὐκ ἔστιν, ὦ Φειδιππίδη, Ζεύς.
Φε. ἀλλὰ τίς;
Στ. Δῖνος βασιλεύει τὸν Δί' ἐξεληλακώς.
Φε. αἰβοῖ· τί ληρεῖς;
Στ. ἴσθι τοῦθ' οὕτως ἔχον.
Φε. τίς φησι ταῦτα;
Στ. Σωκράτης ὁ Μήλιος
καὶ Χαιρεφῶν, ὃς οἶδε τὰ ψυλλῶν ἴχνη.
Φε. σὺ δ' εἰς τοσοῦτον τῶν μανιῶν ἐλήλυθας
ὥστ' ἀνδράσιν πείθει χολῶσιν;
Στ. εὐστόμει
καὶ μηδὲν εἴπῃς φλαῦρον ἄνδρας δεξιοὺς
καὶ νοῦν ἔχοντας, ὧν ὑπὸ τῆς φειδωλίας
ἀπεκείρατ' οὐδεὶς πώποτ' οὐδ' ἠλείψατο
οὐδ' εἰς βαλανεῖον ἦλθε λουσόμενος· σὺ δὲ
ὥσπερ τεθνεῶτος καταλόει μου τὸν βίον.
ἀλλ' ὡς τάχιστ' ἐλθὼν ὑπὲρ ἐμοῦ μάνθανε.

819 *τὸ Δία z* *σ' ὄντα p*: *ὄντα σε p* 823 *τι* om. p *σὺ* secl. *z*

Φε. τί δ' ἂν παρ' ἐκείνων καὶ μάθοι χρηστόν τις ἄν;
Στ. ἄληθες; ὅσαπέρ ἐστιν ἀνθρώποις σοφά.
γνώσει δὲ σαυτὸν ὡς ἀμαθὴς εἶ καὶ παχύς.
ἀλλ' ἐπανάμεινόν μ' ὀλίγον ἐνταυθοῖ χρόνον.
Φε. οἴμοι· τί δράσω παραφρονοῦντος τοῦ πατρός;
πότερον παρανοίας αὐτὸν εἰσαγαγὼν ἕλω,
ἢ τοῖς σοροπηγοῖς τὴν μανίαν αὐτοῦ φράσω;
Στ. φέρ' ἴδω, σὺ τοῦτον τίνα νομίζεις; εἰπέ μοι.
Φε. ἀλεκτρυόνα.
Στ. καλῶς γε. ταυτηνὶ δὲ τί;
Φε. ἀλεκτρυόν'.
Στ. ἄμφω ταὐτό; καταγέλαστος εἶ.
μή νυν τὸ λοιπόν, ἀλλὰ τήνδε μὲν καλεῖν
ἀλεκτρύαιναν, τουτονὶ δ' ἀλέκτορα.
Φε. ἀλεκτρύαιναν; ταῦτ' ἔμαθες τὰ δεξιὰ
εἴσω παρελθὼν ἄρτι παρὰ τοὺς γηγενεῖς;
Στ. χἄτερά γε πόλλ'· ἀλλ' ὅτι μάθοιμ' ἑκάστοτε
ἐπελανθανόμην ἂν εὐθὺς ὑπὸ πλήθους ἐτῶν.
Φε. διὰ ταῦτα δὴ καὶ θοἰμάτιον ἀπώλεσας;
Στ. ἀλλ' οὐκ ἀπολώλεκ', ἀλλὰ καταπεφρόντικα.
Φε. τὰς δ' ἐμβάδας ποῖ τέτροφας, ὦ 'νόητε σύ;
Στ. ὥσπερ Περικλέης, εἰς τὸ δέον ἀπώλεσα.
ἀλλ' ἴθι, βάδιζ', ἴωμεν. εἶτα τῷ πατρὶ
πειθόμενος ἐξάμαρτε. κἀγώ τοι ποτὲ
οἶδ' ἑξέτει σοι τραυλίσαντι πιθόμενος.
ὃν πρῶτον ὀβολὸν ἔλαβον ἡλιαστικόν,
τούτου 'πριάμην σοι Διασίοις ἁμαξίδα.
Φε. ἦ μὴν σὺ τούτοις τῷ χρόνῳ ποτ' ἀχθέσει.

850 *κάλει* p 855 *ἂν* om. Vp *τῶν ἐτῶν* RVp

Στ. εὖ γ᾽ ὅτι ἐπείσθης.

δεῦρο δεῦρ᾽ ὦ Σώκρατες,
ἔξελθ᾽· ἄγω γάρ σοι τὸν υἱὸν τουτονὶ
ἄκοντ᾽ ἀναπείσας.

Σω. νηπύτιος γάρ ἐστ᾽ ἔτι
καὶ τῶν κρεμαστῶν οὐ τρίβων τῶν ἐνθάδε.

Φε. αὐτὸς τρίβων εἴης ἄν, εἰ κρέμαιό γε.

Στ. οὐκ εἰς κόρακας; καταρᾷ σὺ τῷ διδασκάλῳ;

Σω. ἰδοὺ κρέμαι᾽· ὡς ἠλίθιον ἐφθέγξατο
καὶ τοῖσι χείλεσιν διερρυηκόσιν.
πῶς ἂν μάθοι ποθ᾽ οὗτος ἀπόφευξιν δίκης
ἢ κλῆσιν ἢ χαύνωσιν ἀναπειστηρίαν;
καίτοι ταλάντου τοῦτ᾽ ἔμαθεν Ὑπέρβολος.

Στ. ἀμέλει δίδασκε. θυμόσοφός ἐστιν φύσει.
εὐθύς γε τοι παιδάριον ὂν τυννουτονὶ
ἔπλαττεν ἔνδον οἰκίας ναῦς τ᾽ ἔγλυφεν
ἁμαξίδας τε †σκυτίνας ἠργάζετο
κἀκ τῶν σιδίων βατράχους ἐποίει, πῶς δοκεῖς;
ὅπως δ᾽ ἐκείνω τὼ λόγω μαθήσεται,
τὸν κρείττον᾽, ὅστις ἐστί, καὶ τὸν ἥττονα,
ὃς τἄδικα λέγων ἀνατρέπει τὸν κρείττονα·
ἐὰν δὲ μή, τὸν γοῦν ἄδικον πάσῃ τέχνῃ.

Σω. αὐτὸς μαθήσεται παρ᾽ αὐτοῖν τοῖν λόγοιν·
ἐγὼ δ᾽ ἀπέσομαι.

Στ. τοῦτό νυν μέμνησ᾽, ὅπως
πρὸς πάντα τὰ δίκαι᾽ ἀντιλέγειν δυνήσεται.

869 κρεμαστῶν Sch.: κρεμαθρῶν **a** 872 κρέμαιο (i.e. -μαι᾽) ὡς *p*: κρέμαιό γ᾽ ὡς **a** 880 συκίνας *z* 883 f. secl. *z* 884 τἄδικ᾽ ἀνατρέπει λέγων *z* 887 in. Στ. p Στ. Sch.: om. **a** γοῦν Vp: δ᾽ οὖν p

Ο ΚΡΕΙΤΤΩΝ ΛΟΓΟΣ

χώρει δευρί· δεῖξον σαυτὸν
τοῖσι θεαταῖς καίπερ θρασὺς ὤν.

Ο ΗΤΤΩΝ ΛΟΓΟΣ

ἴθ' ὅποι χρῄζεις· πολὺ γάρ μᾶλλόν σ'
ἐν τοῖς πολλοῖσι λέγων ἀπολῶ.

Κρ. ἀπολεῖς σύ; τίς ὤν;
Ητ. λόγος.
Κρ. ἥττων γ' ὤν.
Ητ. ἀλλά σε νικῶ
τὸν ἐμοῦ κρείττω φάσκοντ' εἶναι.
Κρ. τί σοφὸν ποιῶν;
Ητ. γνώμας καινὰς ἐξευρίσκων.
Κρ. ταῦτα γὰρ ἀνθεῖ
διὰ τουτουσὶ τοὺς ἀνοήτους.
Ητ. οὔκ, ἀλλὰ σοφούς.
Κρ. ἀπολῶ σε κακῶς.
Ητ. εἰπέ, τί ποιῶν;
Κρ. τὰ δίκαια λέγων.
Ητ. ἀλλ' ἀνατρέψω ταῦτ' ἀντιλέγων·
οὐδὲ γὰρ εἶναι πάνυ φημὶ Δίκην.
Κρ. οὐκ εἶναι φῄς;
Ητ. φέρε γάρ, ποῦ 'στίν;
Κρ. παρὰ τοῖσι θεοῖς.
Ητ. πῶς δῆτα Δίκης οὔσης ὁ Ζεὺς
οὐκ ἀπόλωλεν τὸν πατέρ' αὑτοῦ
δήσας;

889 etc. *Κρ.* et *Ητ.* *z*: *Δι.* et *Αδ.* **a**

Κρ. αἰβοῖ, τουτὶ καὶ δὴ
χωρεῖ τὸ κακόν. δότε μοι λεκάνην.
Ητ. τυφογέρων εἶ κἀνάρμοστος.
Κρ. καταπύγων εἶ κἀναίσχυντος.
Ητ. ῥόδα μ' εἴρηκας.
Κρ. καὶ βωμολόχος.
Ητ. κρίνεσι στεφανοῖς.
Κρ. καὶ πατραλοίας.
Ητ. χρυσῷ πάττων μ' οὐ γιγνώσκεις.
Κρ. οὐ δῆτα πρὸ τοῦ γ', ἀλλὰ μολύβδῳ.
Ητ. νῦν δέ γε κόσμος τοῦτ' ἐστὶν ἐμοί.
Κρ. θρασὺς εἶ πολλοῦ.
Ητ. σὺ δέ γ' ἀρχαῖος.
Κρ. διὰ σὲ δὲ φοιτᾶν
οὐδεὶς ἐθέλει τῶν μειρακίων.
καὶ γνωσθήσει ποτ' Ἀθηναίοις
οἷα διδάσκεις τοὺς ἀνοήτους.
Ητ. αὐχμεῖς αἰσχρῶς.
Κρ. σὺ δέ γ' εὖ πράττεις.
καίτοι πρότερόν γ' ἐπτώχευες,
Τήλεφος εἶναι Μυσὸς φάσκων
ἐκ πηριδίου
γνώμας τρώγων Πανδελετείους.
Ητ. ὤμοι σοφίας—
Κρ. ὤμοι μανίας—
Ητ. ἧς ἐμνήσθης.
Κρ. τῆς σῆς πόλεως θ'
ἥτις σε τρέφει
λυμαινόμενον τοῖς μειρακίοις.

918 καὶ p: om. RVp   925–6 sic RV: 925_1–926_1 925_2–926_2 p

Ητ. οὐχὶ διδάξεις τοῦτον Κρόνος ὤν.

Κρ. εἴπερ γ' αὐτὸν σωθῆναι χρὴ
καὶ μὴ λαλιὰν μόνον ἀσκῆσαι.

Ητ. δεῦρ' ἴθι, τοῦτον δ' ἔα μαίνεσθαι.

Κρ. κλαύσει, τὴν χεῖρ' ἢν ἐπιβάλλῃς.

Χο. παύσασθε μάχης καὶ λοιδορίας.
ἀλλ' ἐπίδειξαι
σύ τε τοὺς προτέρους ἅττ' ἐδίδασκες,
σύ τε τὴν καινὴν
παίδευσιν, ὅπως ἂν ἀκούσας σφῷν
ἀντιλεγόντοιν κρίνας φοιτᾷ.

Κρ. δρᾶν ταῦτ' ἐθέλω.

Ητ. κἄγωγ' ἐθέλω.

Χο. φέρε δή, πότερος λέξει πρότερος;

Ητ. τούτῳ δώσω·
κᾆτ' ἐκ τούτων ὧν ἂν λέξῃ
ῥηματίοισιν καινοῖς αὐτὸν
καὶ διανοίαις κατατοξεύσω,
τὸ τελευταῖον δ', ἢν ἀναγρύζῃ,
τὸ πρόσωπον ἅπαν καὶ τὠφθαλμὼ
κεντούμενος ὥσπερ ὑπ' ἀνθρηνῶν
ὑπὸ τῶν γνωμῶν ἀπολεῖται.

Χο. νῦν δείξετον τὼ πισύνω στρ.
τοῖς περιδεξίοισιν
λόγοισι καὶ φροντίσι καὶ
γνωμοτύποις μερίμναις

936 γε RV 940 πότερος ΠR: τίς **Vp** πρότερος *z*: πρότερον Rp: πρότερον (vel -ρος) ὑμῶν Vp

ὁπότερος αὐτοῖν ἀμεί-
νων λέγων φανήσεται.
νῦν γὰρ ἅπας ἐνθάδε κίν-
δυνος ἀνεῖται σοφίας,
ἧς πέρι τοῖς ἐμοῖς φίλοις
ἐστὶν ἀγὼν μέγιστος.

ἀλλ᾽ ὦ πολλοῖς τοὺς πρεσβυτέρους ἤθεσι χρηστοῖς στεφανώ-
σας,
ῥῆξον φωνὴν ᾗτινι χαίρεις καὶ τὴν σαυτοῦ φύσιν εἰπέ.

Κρ. *λέξω τοίνυν τὴν ἀρχαίαν παιδείαν ὡς διέκειτο,*
ὅτ᾽ ἐγὼ τὰ δίκαια λέγων ἤνθουν καὶ σωφροσύνη 'νενόμιστο.
πρῶτον μὲν ἔδει παιδὸς φωνὴν γρύξαντος μηδέν᾽ ἀκοῦσαι·
εἶτα βαδίζειν ἐν ταῖσιν ὁδοῖς εὐτάκτως εἰς κιθαριστοῦ
τοὺς κωμήτας γυμνοὺς ἁθρόους, κεἰ κριμνώδη κατανείφοι.
εἶτ᾽ αὖ προμαθεῖν ᾆσμ᾽ ἐδίδασκεν τὼ μηρὼ μὴ ξυνέχοντας,
ἢ "Παλλάδα περσέπολιν δεινάν" ἢ "τηλέπορόν τι
βόαμα",
ἐντειναμένους τὴν ἁρμονίαν ἣν οἱ πατέρες παρέδωκαν.
εἰ δέ τις αὐτῶν βωμολοχεύσαιτ᾽ ἢ κάμψειέν τινα καμπὴν
οἵας οἱ νῦν, τὰς κατὰ Φρῦνιν ταύτας τὰς δυσκολοκάμ-
πτους,
ἐπετρίβετο τυπτόμενος πολλὰς ὡς τὰς Μούσας ἀφανίζων.
ἐν παιδοτρίβου δὲ καθίζοντας τὸν μηρὸν ἔδει προβαλέσθαι
τοὺς παῖδας, ὅπως τοῖς ἔξωθεν μηδὲν δείξειαν ἀπηνές·
εἶτ᾽ αὖ πάλιν αὖθις ἀνιστάμενον συμψῆσαι καὶ προνοεῖσθαι
εἴδωλον τοῖσιν ἐρασταῖσιν τῆς ἥβης μὴ καταλείπειν.
ἠλείψατο δ᾽ ἂν τοὐμφαλοῦ οὐδεὶς παῖς ὑπένερθεν τότ᾽ ἄν,
ὥστε

953–4 *ὁπότερος αὐτοῖν ἀμείνων λέγων z*: *ὁπότερος αὐτοῖν λέγων ἀμείνων* **a**: *λέγων ἀμείνων πότερος z* 954 *γενήσεται* V 963 *μηδὲν* RV test. 964 *κιθαριστὰς* RV 965 *κρημνώδη Π*Vp test. 966 *ξυνέχοντα* R 975 *ἀνισταμένους Π*p test.

τοῖς αἰδοίοισι δρόσος καὶ χνοῦς ὥσπερ μήλοισιν ἐπήνθει.
οὐδ' ἂν μαλακὴν φυρασάμενος τὴν φωνὴν πρὸς τὸν ἐραστὴν
αὐτὸς ἑαυτὸν προαγωγεύων τοῖν ὀφθαλμοῖν ἐβάδιζεν.
οὐδ' ἀνελέσθαι δειπνοῦντ' ἐξῆν κεφάλαιον τῆς ῥαφανῖδος,
οὐδ' ἄννηθον τῶν πρεσβυτέρων ἁρπάζειν οὐδὲ σέλινον,
οὐδ' ὀψοφαγεῖν οὐδὲ κιχλίζειν οὐδ' ἴσχειν τὼ πόδ' ἐναλλάξ.

Ητ. ἀρχαῖά γε καὶ Διπολιώδη καὶ τεττίγων ἀνάμεστα
καὶ Κηκείδου καὶ Βουφονίων.

Κρ. ἀλλ' οὖν ταῦτ' ἐστὶν ἐκεῖνα
ἐξ ὧν ἄνδρας Μαραθωνομάχας ἡμὴ παίδευσις ἔθρεψεν.
σὺ δὲ τοὺς νῦν εὐθὺς ἐν ἱματίοισι διδάσκεις ἐντετυλίχθαι,
ὥστε μ' ἀπάγχεσθ' ὅταν ὀρχεῖσθαι Παναθηναίοις δέον αὐτοὺς
τὴν ἀσπίδα τῆς κωλῆς προέχων ἀμελῇ τις Τριτογενείης.
πρὸς ταῦτ', ὦ μειράκιον, θαρρῶν ἐμὲ τὸν κρείττω λόγον αἱροῦ.
κἀπιστήσει μισεῖν ἀγορὰν καὶ βαλανείων ἀπέχεσθαι,
καὶ τοῖς αἰσχροῖς αἰσχύνεσθαι κἂν σκώπτῃ τίς σε φλέγεσθαι,
καὶ τῶν θάκων τοῖς πρεσβυτέροις ὑπανίστασθαι προσιοῦσιν,
καὶ μὴ περὶ τοὺς σαυτοῦ γονέας σκαιουργεῖν, ἄλλο τε μηδὲν
αἰσχρὸν ποιεῖν ὅτι τῆς Αἰδοῦς μέλλεις τἄγαλμ' †ἀναπλήσειν†·
μηδ' εἰς ὀρχηστρίδος εἰσᾴττειν, ἵνα μὴ πρὸς ταῦτα κεχηνὼς
μήλῳ βληθεὶς ὑπὸ πορνιδίου τῆς εὐκλείας ἀποθραυσθῇς,
μηδ' ἀντειπεῖν τῷ πατρὶ μηδὲν μηδ' Ἰαπετὸν καλέσαντα
μνησικακῆσαι τὴν ἡλικίαν ἐξ ἧς ἐνεοττοτροφήθης.

Ητ. εἰ ταῦτ', ὦ μειράκιον, πείσει τούτῳ, νὴ τὸν Διόνυσον
τοῖς Ἱπποκράτους υἱέσιν εἴξεις καί σε καλοῦσι βλιτομάμμαν.

981 οὐδ' ἂν ἑλέσθαι RVp test. 982 ἄννηθον *z*: ἄνηθον RVp test.: ἂν ἄνηθον p 985 Κηδείδου *z* 989 κωλῆς **a**: αἰδοῦς test. 995 ἀναπλήσσειν *p*: ἀναπλάσσειν *p*: ἀμαλάπτειν *z* 999 τῆς ἡλικίας *z*

Κρ. ἀλλ' οὖν λιπαρός γε καὶ εὐανθὴς ἐν γυμνασίοις διατρίψεις,
οὐ στωμύλλων κατὰ τὴν ἀγορὰν τριβολεκτράπελ', οἷάπερ οἱ νῦν,
οὐδ' ἑλκόμενος περὶ πραγματίου γλισχραντιλογεξεπιτρίπτου,
ἀλλ' εἰς Ἀκαδήμειαν κατιὼν ὑπὸ ταῖς μορίαις ἀποθρέξει
στεφανωσάμενος καλάμῳ λευκῷ μετὰ σώφρονος ἡλικιώτου,
σμίλακος ὄζων καὶ ἀπραγμοσύνης καὶ λεύκης †φυλλοβολούσης†,
ἦρος ἐν ὥρᾳ, χαίρων ὁπόταν πλάτανος πτελέᾳ ψιθυρίζῃ.
ἢν ταῦτα ποῇς ἁγὼ φράζω
καὶ πρὸς τούτοις προσέχῃς τὸν νοῦν
ἕξεις αἰεὶ
στῆθος λιπαρόν, χροιὰν λαμπράν,
ὤμους μεγάλους, γλῶτταν βαιάν,
πυγὴν μεγάλην, πόσθην μικράν·
ἢν δ' ἅπερ οἱ νῦν ἐπιτηδεύῃς,
πρῶτα μὲν ἕξεις
χροιὰν ὠχράν, ὤμους μικρούς,
στῆθος λεπτόν, γλῶτταν μεγάλην,
κωλῆν μικράν, ψήφισμα μακρόν,
καί σ' ἀναπείσει τὸ μὲν αἰσχρὸν ἅπαν
καλὸν ἡγεῖσθαι, τὸ καλὸν δ' αἰσχρόν,
καὶ πρὸς τούτοις τῆς Ἀντιμάχου
καταπυγοσύνης ἀναπλήσει.

Χο. ὦ καλλίπυργον σοφίαν ἀντ.
κλεινοτάτην ἐπασκῶν,
ὡς ἡδύ σου τοῖσι λόγοις
σῶφρον ἔπεστιν ἄνθος.

1005 καταθρέξεις V: ὑποθρέξει p 1007 φυλλοκομούσης z 1010 πρὸς τούτοισιν ἔχῃς z: τούτοισιν προσέχῃς z 1012 χροιὰν λευκὴν RVp 1017 μικρούς **a**: λευκούς Sch.: λεπτούς Sch. 1019 κωλῆν μικράν z: πυγὴν μικράν (μεγάλην V), κωλῆν μεγάλην **a**

εὐδαίμονες ἄρ' ἦσαν οἱ ζῶντες τότε.
πρὸς τάδε σ', ὦ κομψοπρεπῆ μοῦσαν ἔχων,
δεῖ σε λέγειν τι καινόν, ὡς
ηὐδοκίμηκεν ἀνήρ.
δεινῶν δέ σοι βουλευμάτων ἔοικε δεῖν πρὸς αὐτόν,
εἴπερ τὸν ἄνδρ' ὑπερβαλεῖ καὶ μὴ γέλωτ' ὀφλήσεις.

Ητ. καὶ μὴν πάλαι 'γὼ 'πνιγόμην τὰ σπλάγχνα κἀπεθύμουν
ἅπαντα ταῦτ' ἐναντίαις γνώμαισι συνταράξαι.
ἐγὼ γὰρ ἥττων μὲν λόγος δι' αὐτὸ τοῦτ' ἐκλήθην
ἐν τοῖσι φροντισταῖσιν, ὅτι πρώτιστος ἐπενόησα
τοῖσιν νόμοις καὶ ταῖς δίκαις τἀναντί' ἀντιλέξαι.
καὶ τοῦτο πλεῖν ἢ μυρίων ἔστ' ἄξιον στατήρων,
αἱρούμενον τοὺς ἥττονας λόγους ἔπειτα νικᾶν.
σκέψαι δὲ τὴν παίδευσιν ᾗ πέποιθεν, ὡς ἐλέγξω,
ὅστις σε θερμῷ φησι λοῦσθαι πρῶτον οὐκ ἐάσειν.
καίτοι τίνα γνώμην ἔχων ψέγεις τὰ θερμὰ λουτρά;
Κρ. ὁτιὴ κάκιστόν ἐστι καὶ δειλὸν ποεῖ τὸν ἄνδρα.
Ητ. ἐπίσχες· εὐθὺς γάρ σε μέσον ἔχω λαβὼν ἄφυκτον.
καί μοι φράσον· τῶν τοῦ Διὸς παίδων τίν' ἄνδρ' ἄριστον
ψυχὴν νομίζεις, εἰπέ, καὶ πλείστους πόνους πονῆσαι;
Κρ. ἐγὼ μὲν οὐδέν' Ἡρακλέους βελτίον' ἄνδρα κρίνω.
Ητ. ποῦ ψυχρὰ δῆτα πώποτ' εἶδες Ἡράκλεια λουτρά;
καίτοι τίς ἀνδρειότερος ἦν;
Κρ. ταῦτ' ἐστί, ταῦτ', ἐκεῖνα
ἃ τῶν νεανίσκων ἀεὶ δι' ἡμέρας λαλούντων
πλῆρες τὸ βαλανεῖον ποιεῖ κενὰς δὲ τὰς παλαίστρας.

1028 ἄρ' ἦσαν *p*: δ' ἦσαν ἄρ' RVp: δ' ἄρ' ἦσαν p   1029 τότε *z*: τότ' ἐπὶ τῶν προτέρων **a**   1030 πρὸς τάδε σ' *z*: πρὸς οὖν τάδ' **a**   1036 πάλαι 'γὼ 'πνιγόμην *z*: ἔγωγ' ἐπνιγόμην RV: πάλαι (vel πάλ' vel πάλαι γ') ἔγωγ' ἐπνιγόμην **p**   1040 τοῖσιν RV: καὶ τοῖς p: καὶ τοῖσι p   1046 δειλὸν ποεῖ τὸν ἄνδρα *p*: δειλότατον ποεῖ τὸν ἄνδρα **a**: δειλότατον ἄνδρα ποιεῖ *z*

Ητ. εἶτ' ἐν ἀγορᾷ τὴν διατριβὴν ψέγεις, ἐγὼ δ' ἐπαινῶ.
εἰ γὰρ πονηρὸν ἦν, Ὅμηρος οὐδέποτ' ἂν ἐποίει
τὸν Νέστορ' ἀγορητὴν ἄν, οὐδὲ τοὺς σοφοὺς ἅπαντας.
ἄνειμι δῆτ' ἐντεῦθεν εἰς τὴν γλῶτταν, ἣν ὁδὶ μὲν
οὔ φησι χρῆναι τοὺς νέους ἀσκεῖν, ἐγὼ δέ φημι.
καὶ σωφρονεῖν αὖ φησὶ χρῆναι, δύο κακὼ μεγίστω.
ἐπεὶ σὺ διὰ τὸ σωφρονεῖν τῷ πώποτ' εἶδες ἤδη
ἀγαθόν τι γενόμενον; φράσον, καί μ' ἐξέλεγξον εἰπών.

Κρ. πολλοῖς. ὁ γοῦν Πηλεὺς ἔλαβε διὰ τοῦτο τὴν μάχαιραν.

Ητ. μάχαιραν; ἀστεῖόν γε κέρδος ἔλαβεν ὁ κακοδαίμων.
Ὑπέρβολος δ' οὑκ τῶν λύχνων πλεῖν ἢ τάλαντα πολλὰ
εἴληφε διὰ πονηρίαν, ἀλλ' οὐ μὰ Δί' οὐ μάχαιραν.

Κρ. καὶ τὴν Θέτιν γ' ἔγημε διὰ τὸ σωφρονεῖν ὁ Πηλεύς.

Ητ. κᾆτ' ἀπολιποῦσά γ' αὐτὸν ᾤχετ'· οὐ γὰρ ἦν ὑβριστὴς
οὐδ' ἡδὺς ἐν τοῖς στρώμασιν τὴν νύκτα παννυχίζειν·
γυνὴ δὲ σιναμωρουμένη χαίρει. σὺ δ' εἶ Κρόνιππος.
σκέψαι γάρ, ὦ μειράκιον, ἐν τῷ σωφρονεῖν ἅπαντα
ἅνεστιν, ἡδονῶν θ' ὅσων μέλλεις ἀποστερεῖσθαι·
παίδων, γυναικῶν, κοττάβων, ὄψων, πότων, καχασμῶν.
καίτοι τί σοι ζῆν ἄξιον, τούτων ἐὰν στερηθῇς;
εἶέν. πάρειμ' ἐντεῦθεν εἰς τὰς τῆς φύσεως ἀνάγκας.
ἥμαρτες, ἠράσθης, ἐμοίχευσάς τι, κᾆτ' ἐλήφθης.
ἀπόλωλας· ἀδύνατος γὰρ εἶ λέγειν. ἐμοὶ δ' ὁμιλῶν
χρῶ τῇ φύσει, σκίρτα, γέλα, νόμιζε μηδὲν αἰσχρόν.
μοιχὸς γὰρ ἢν τύχῃς ἁλούς, τάδ' ἀντερεῖς πρὸς αὐτόν,
ὡς οὐδὲν ἠδίκηκας· εἶτ' εἰς τὸν Δί' ἐπανενεγκεῖν,
κἀκεῖνος ὡς ἥττων ἔρωτός ἐστι καὶ γυναικῶν·
καίτοι σὺ θνητὸς ὢν θεοῦ πῶς μεῖζον ἂν δύναιο;

Κρ. τί δ' ἢν ῥαφανιδωθῇ πιθόμενός σοι τέφρᾳ τε τιλθῇ;
ἕξει τινὰ γνώμην λέγειν τὸ μὴ εὐρύπρωκτος εἶναι;

1066 ἀλλὰ μὰ Δί' οὐ *p*: ἀλλ' οὐ μὰ Δία *z* 1067 γ' RVp: δ' p
1073 κιχλισμῶν Vp 1084 τίνα p

Ητ. ἢν δ' εὐρύπρωκτος ᾖ, τί πείσεται κακόν;
Κρ. τί μὲν οὖν ἂν ἔτι μεῖζον πάθοι τούτου ποτέ;
Ητ. τί δῆτ' ἐρεῖς, ἢν τοῦτο νικηθῇς ἐμοῦ;
Κρ. σιγήσομαι. τί δ' ἄλλο;
Ητ. φέρε δή μοι φράσον,
συνηγοροῦσιν ἐκ τίνων;
Κρ. ἐξ εὐρυπρώκτων.
Ητ. πείθομαι.
τί δαί; τραγῳδοῦσ' ἐκ τίνων;
Κρ. ἐξ εὐρυπρώκτων.
Ητ. εὖ λέγεις.
δημηγοροῦσι δ' ἐκ τίνων;
Κρ. ἐξ εὐρυπρώκτων.
Ητ. ἆρα δῆτ'
ἔγνωκας ὡς οὐδὲν λέγεις;
καὶ τῶν θεατῶν ὁπότεροι πλείους σκόπει.
Κρ. καὶ δὴ σκοπῶ.
Ητ. τί δῆθ' ὁρᾷς;
Κρ. πολὺ πλείονας, νὴ τοὺς θεούς,
τοὺς εὐρυπρώκτους. τουτονὶ
γοῦν οἶδ' ἐγὼ κἀκεινονὶ
καὶ τὸν κομήτην τουτονί.
Ητ. τί δῆτ' ἐρεῖς;
Κρ. ἡττήμεθ'. ὦ κινούμενοι,
πρὸς τῶν θεῶν δέξασθέ μου θοἰμάτιον, ὡς
ἐξαυτομολῶ πρὸς ὑμᾶς.

1088 *Αδ.* (i.e. *Ητ.*) τί δ' ἄλλο φέρε RV   1093 δημηγοροῦσι δ' R: δημαγωγοῦσι δ' **p**: καὶ δημαγωγοῦσ' *p* (1090–4 om. V)   1102 *Δι.* (i.e. *Κρ.*) *Φειδ.* V   *Φε.* ὦ p   1103 *Φε.* p

Ητ. τί δῆτα; πότερα τοῦτον ἀπάγεσθαι λαβὼν
βούλει τὸν υἱόν, ἢ διδάσκω σοι λέγειν;
Στ. δίδασκε καὶ κόλαζε καὶ μέμνησ' ὅπως
εὖ μοι στομώσεις αὐτόν, ἐπὶ μὲν θάτερα
οἷον δικιδίοις, τὴν δ' ἑτέραν αὐτοῦ γνάθον
στόμωσον οἵαν εἰς τὰ μείζω πράγματα.
Ητ. ἀμέλει, κομιεῖ τοῦτον σοφιστὴν δεξιόν.
Φε. ὠχρὸν μὲν οὖν οἶμαί γε καὶ κακοδαίμονα.

Χο. χωρεῖτέ νυν. οἶμαι δὲ σοὶ
ταῦτα μεταμελήσειν.

τοὺς κριτὰς ἃ κερδανοῦσιν, ἤν τι τόνδε τὸν χορὸν
ὠφελῶσ' ἐκ τῶν δικαίων, βουλόμεσθ' ἡμεῖς φράσαι.
πρῶτα μὲν γάρ, ἢν νεᾶν βούλησθ' ἐν ὥρᾳ τοὺς ἀγρούς,
ὕσομεν πρώτοισιν ὑμῖν, τοῖσι δ' ἄλλοις ὕστερον.
εἶτα τὸν καρπὸν τεκούσας ἀμπέλους φυλάξομεν,
ὥστε μήτ' αὐχμὸν πιέζειν μήτ' ἄγαν ἐπομβρίαν.
ἢν δ' ἀτιμάσῃ τις ἡμᾶς θνητὸς ὢν οὔσας θεάς,
προσεχέτω τὸν νοῦν πρὸς ἡμῶν οἷα πείσεται κακά,
λαμβάνων οὔτ' οἶνον οὔτ' ἄλλ' οὐδὲν ἐκ τοῦ χωρίου.
ἡνίκ' ἂν γὰρ αἵ τ' ἐλαῖαι βλαστάνωσ' αἵ τ' ἄμπελοι,
ἀποκεκόψονται· τοιαύταις σφενδόναις παιήσομεν.
ἢν δὲ πλινθεύοντ' ἴδωμεν, ὕσομεν καὶ τοῦ τέγους
τὸν κέραμον αὐτοῦ χαλάζαις στρογγύλαις συντρίψομεν.
κἂν γαμῇ ποτ' αὐτὸς ἢ τῶν ξυγγενῶν ἢ τῶν φίλων,
ὕσομεν τὴν νύκτα πᾶσαν, ὥστ' ἴσως βουλήσεται
κἂν ἐν Αἰγύπτῳ τυχεῖν ὢν μᾶλλον ἢ κρῖναι κακῶς.

1105 *Ητ.* (Sch.) (Hyp.): *Σω.* **a** 1108 *θατέραν* p Sch. 1109 *οἷον* (Sch.) *p*: *οἵαν* **a** 1112 *Στ.* RVp *οἶμαί γε* **p**: *ἔγωγε* RV 1113 *Χο. p*: *Φε.* RV: *Σω.* p: om. p *χώρει* RVp *Φε. οἶμαι p* 1116 *ἡμεῖς* RVᴅ: *ὑμῖν* p 1128 *ἢ τῶν φίλων* **a**: *τις ἢ φίλων z*

Στ. πέμπτη, τετράς, τρίτη· μετὰ ταύτην δευτέρα·
εἶθ' ἣν ἐγὼ μάλιστα πασῶν ἡμερῶν
δέδοικα καὶ πέφρικα καὶ βδελύττομαι,
εὐθὺς μετὰ ταύτην ἔσθ' ἕνη τε καὶ νέα.
πᾶς γάρ τις ὀμνύς, οἷς ὀφείλων τυγχάνω,
θείς μοι πρυτανεῖ' ἀπολεῖν μέ φησι κἀξολεῖν.
κἀμοῦ μέτριά τε καὶ δίκαι' αἰτουμένου,
"ὦ δαιμόνιε, τὸ μέν τι νυνὶ μὴ λάβῃς,
τὸ δ' ἀναβαλοῦ μοι, τὸ δ' ἄφες", οὔ φασίν ποτε
οὕτως ἀπολήψεσθ', ἀλλὰ λοιδοροῦσί με
ὡς ἄδικός εἰμι, καὶ δικάσεσθαί φασί μοι.
νῦν οὖν δικαζέσθων. ὀλίγον γάρ μοι μέλει,
εἴπερ μεμάθηκεν εὖ λέγειν Φειδιππίδης.
τάχα δ' εἴσομαι κόψας τὸ φροντιστήριον.
παῖ, ἠμί, παῖ, παῖ.

Σω. Στρεψιάδην ἀσπάζομαι.

Στ. κἄγωγέ σ'. ἀλλα τουτονὶ πρῶτον λαβέ.
χρὴ γὰρ ἐπιθαυμάζειν τι τὸν διδάσκαλον.
καί μοι τὸν υἱόν, εἰ μεμάθηκε τὸν λόγον
ἐκεῖνον, εἴφ', ὃν ἀρτίως εἰσήγαγες.

Σω. μεμάθηκεν.

Στ. εὖ γ', ὦ παμβασίλει' Ἀπαιόλη.

Σω. ὥστ' ἀποφύγοις ἂν ἥντιν' ἂν βούλῃ δίκην.

Στ. κεἰ μάρτυρες παρῆσαν ὅτ' ἐδανειζόμην;

Σω. πολλῷ γε μᾶλλον, κἂν παρῶσι χίλιοι.

Στ. βοάσομαι τἄρα τὰν ὑπέρτονον
βοάν. ἰώ, κλάετ' ὦ 'βολοστάται,
αὐτοί τε καὶ τἀρχαῖα καὶ τόκοι τόκων.
οὐδὲν γὰρ ἄν με φλαῦρον ἐργάσαισθ' ἔτι,

1137 κἀμοῦ μέτριά τε *p*: ἐμοῦ μέτριά τε **a**: ἐμοῦ τε (vel δὲ) μέτρια *z*

οἷος ἐμοὶ τρέφεται
τοῖσδ' ἐνὶ δώμασι παῖς
ἀμφήκει γλώττῃ λάμπων,
πρόβολος ἐμός, σωτὴρ δόμοις, ἐχθροῖς βλάβη,
λυσανίας πατρῴων μεγάλων κακῶν·
ὃν κάλεσον τρέχων ἔνδοθεν ὡς ἐμέ.
ὦ τέκνον, ὦ παῖ, ἔξελθ' οἴκων,
ἄϊε σοῦ πατρός.

Σω. ὅδ' ἐκεῖνος ἀνήρ.

Στ. ὦ φίλος, ὦ φίλος.

Σω. ἄπιθι λαβών.

Στ. ἰὼ ἰώ, τέκνον.

ἰοῦ ἰοῦ.
ὡς ἥδομαί σου πρῶτα τὴν χροιὰν ἰδών.
νῦν μέν γ' ἰδεῖν εἶ πρῶτον ἐξαρνητικὸς
κἀντιλογικός, καὶ τοῦτο τοὐπιχώριον
ἀτεχνῶς ἐπανθεῖ, τὸ "τί λέγεις σύ;" καὶ δοκεῖν
ἀδικοῦντ' ἀδικεῖσθαι, καὶ κακουργοῦντ', οἶδ' ὅτι.
ἐπὶ τοῦ προσώπου τ' ἐστὶν Ἀττικὸν βλέπος.
νῦν οὖν ὅπως σώσεις μ', ἐπεὶ κἀπώλεσας.

Φε. φοβεῖ δὲ δὴ τί;

Στ. τὴν ἕνην τε καὶ νέαν.

Φε. ἕνη γάρ ἐστι καὶ νέα τις ἡμέρα;

Στ. εἰς ἣν γε θήσειν τὰ πρυτανεῖά φασί μοι.

Φε. ἀπολοῦσ' ἄρ' αὔθ' οἱ θέντες. οὐ γάρ ἐσθ' ὅπως
μί' ἡμέρα γένοιτ' ἂν ἡμέραι δύο.

Στ. οὐκ ἂν γένοιτο;

1161 *βλάβη* RVp: *ἀνιαρός* p 1165 *Σω.* RVp 1169 *λαβών* *z*: *λαβὼν τὸν υἱόν σου* RV: *σὺ λαβών* **p**: *συλλαβών* *p* 1176 secl. *z* 1179 *τίς* Vp 1182 *ἡμέρα* R

Φε. πῶς γάρ, εἰ μή περ γ' ἅμα
αὐτὴ γένοιτ' ἂν γραῦς τε καὶ νέα γυνή.
Στ. καὶ μὴν νενόμισταί γ'.
Φε. οὐ γὰρ οἶμαι τὸν νόμον
ἴσασιν ὀρθῶς ὅτι νοεῖ.
Στ. νοεῖ δὲ τί;
Φε. ὁ Σόλων ὁ παλαιὸς ἦν φιλόδημος τὴν φύσιν.
Στ. τουτὶ μὲν οὐδέν πω πρὸς ἕνην τε καὶ νέαν.
Φε. ἐκεῖνος οὖν τὴν κλῆσιν εἰς δύ' ἡμέρας
ἔθηκεν, εἴς γε την ἕνην τε καὶ νέαν,
ἵν' αἱ θέσεις γίγνοιντο τῇ νουμηνίᾳ.
Στ. ἵνα δὴ τί τὴν ἕνην προσέθηκεν;
Φε. ἵν', ὦ μέλε,
παρόντες οἱ φεύγοντες ἡμέρᾳ μιᾷ
πρότερον ἀπαλλάττοινθ' ἑκόντες· εἰ δὲ μή,
ἕωθεν ὑπανιῷντο τῇ νουμηνίᾳ.
Στ. πῶς οὐ δέχονται δῆτα τῇ νουμηνίᾳ
ἀρχαὶ τὰ πρυτανεῖ', ἀλλ' ἕνῃ τε καὶ νέᾳ;
Φε. ὅπερ οἱ προτένθαι γὰρ δοκοῦσί μοι παθεῖν·
ὅπως τάχιστα τὰ πρυτανεῖ' ὑφελοίατο,
διὰ τοῦτο προυτένθευσαν ἡμέρᾳ μιᾷ.
Στ. εὖ γ'. ὦ κακοδαίμονες, τί κάθησθ' ἀβέλτεροι,
ἡμέτερα κέρδη τῶν σοφῶν, ὄντες λίθοι,
ἀριθμός, πρόβατ' ἄλλως, ἀμφορῆς νενησμένοι;
ὥστ' εἰς ἐμαυτὸν καὶ τὸν υἱὸν τουτονὶ
ἐπ' εὐτυχίαισιν ᾀστέον μοὐγκώμιον.
"μάκαρ ὦ Στρεψίαδες
αὐτός τ' ἔφυς, ὡς σοφός,

1184 γένοιτο γραῦς p test. 1192 προσέθηκ' (i.e. -θηχ') *p*
1198 ποεῖν RVp

χοῖον τὸν υἱὸν τρέφεις",
φήσουσι δή μ' οἱ φίλοι χοἰ δημόται
ζηλοῦντες ἡνίκ' ἂν σὺ νι-
κᾷς λέγων τὰς δίκας.
ἀλλ' εἰσάγων σε βούλομαι πρῶτον ἑστιᾶσαι.

ΧΡΗΣΤΗΣ Α'

εἶτ' ἄνδρα τῶν αὑτοῦ τι χρὴ προϊέναι;
οὐδέποτέ γ', ἀλλὰ κρεῖττον εὐθὺς ἦν τότε
ἀπερυθριᾶσαι μᾶλλον ἢ σχεῖν πράγματα,
ὅτε τῶν ἐμαυτοῦ γ' ἕνεκα νυνὶ χρημάτων
ἕλκω σε κλητεύσοντα, καὶ γενήσομαι
ἐχθρὸς ἔτι πρὸς τούτοισιν ἀνδρὶ δημότῃ.
ἀτὰρ οὐδέποτέ γε τὴν πατρίδα καταισχυνῶ
ζῶν, ἀλλὰ καλοῦμαι Στρεψιάδην—

Στ. τίς οὑτοσί;

Χρ. —εἰς τὴν ἕνην τε καὶ νέαν.

Στ. μαρτύρομαι
ὅτι εἰς δύ' εἶπεν ἡμέρας. τοῦ χρήματος;

Χρ. τῶν δώδεκα μνῶν, ἃς ἔλαβες ὠνούμενος
τὸν ψαρὸν ἵππον.

Στ. ἵππον; οὐκ ἀκούετε;
ὃν πάντες ὑμεῖς ἴστε μισοῦνθ' ἱππικήν.

Χρ. καὶ νὴ Δί' ἀποδώσειν γ' ἐπώμνυς τοὺς θεούς.

Στ. μὰ τὸν Δί' οὐ γάρ πω τότ' ἐξηπίστατο
Φειδιππίδης μοι τὸν ἀκατάβλητον λόγον.

Χρ. νῦν δὲ διὰ τοῦτ' ἔξαρνος εἶναι διανοεῖ;

1208 ἐκτρέφεις p 1212 εἰσαγαγών p 1214 etc. χρηστής z: δανειστής Rp: Πασίας δανειστής Vp 1228 τὸ χρέος ante Στ. RVp μὰ τὸν Δί' p: μὰ Δί' a οὐ δῆτ' οὐ γάρ πω τότ' (vel πώποτ') p

Στ. τί γὰρ ἄλλ' ἂν ἀπολαύσαιμι τοῦ μαθήματος;
Χρ. καὶ ταῦτ' ἐθελήσεις ἀπομόσαι μοι τοὺς θεοὺς
ἵν' ἂν κελεύσω 'γώ σε;
Στ. τοὺς ποίους θεούς;
Χρ. τὸν Δία, τὸν Ἑρμῆν, τὸν Ποσειδῶ.
Στ. νὴ Δία,
κἂν προσκαταθείην γ', ὥστ' ὀμόσαι, τριώβολον.
Χρ. ἀπόλοιο τοίνυν ἕνεκ' ἀναιδείας ἔτι.
Στ. ἁλσὶν διασμηχθεὶς ὄναιτ' ἂν οὑτοσί.
Χρ. οἴμ' ὡς καταγελᾷς.
Στ. ἓξ χοᾶς χωρήσεται.
Χρ. οὔτοι μὰ τὸν Δία τὸν μέγαν καὶ τοὺς θεοὺς
ἐμοῦ καταπροίξει.
Στ. θαυμασίως ἥσθην θεοῖς,
καὶ Ζεὺς γελοῖος ὀμνύμενος τοῖς εἰδόσιν.
Χρ. ἦ μὴν σὺ τούτων τῷ χρόνῳ δώσεις δίκην.
ἀλλ' εἴτ' ἀποδώσεις μοι τὰ χρήματ' εἴτε μή,
ἀπόπεμψον ἀποκρινάμενος.
Στ. ἔχε νυν ἥσυχος·
ἐγὼ γὰρ αὐτίκ' ἀποκρινοῦμαί σοι σαφῶς.
Χρ. τί σοι δοκεῖ δράσειν; ἀποδώσειν σοι δοκεῖ;
Στ. ποῦ 'σθ' οὗτος ἀπαιτῶν με τἀργύριον; λέγε,
τουτὶ τί ἐστι;
Χρ. τοῦθ' ὅτι ἐστί; κάρδοπος.
Στ. ἔπειτ' ἀπαιτεῖς ἀργύριον τοιοῦτος ὤν;
οὐκ ἂν ἀποδοίην οὐδ' ἂν ὀβολὸν οὐδενὶ
ὅστις καλέσειε "κάρδοπον" τὴν καρδόπην.

1243 *ἀλλ' εἴτε γ'* p *μοι* om. RVp 1246 *Μαρτ.* p Sch. *Μαρ. ἀπο-* Vp Sch.

Χρ. οὐκ ἄρ᾽ ἀποδώσεις;

Στ. οὐχ ὅσον γ᾽ ἔμ᾽ εἰδέναι.
οὔκουν ἀνύσας τι θᾶττον ἀπολιταργιεῖς
ἀπὸ τῆς θύρας;

Χρ. ἄπειμι· καὶ τοῦτ᾽ ἴσθ᾽, ὅτι
θήσω πρυτανεῖ᾽, ἢ μηκέτι ζῴην ἐγώ.

Στ. προσαποβαλεῖς ἄρ᾽ αὐτὰ πρὸς ταῖς δώδεκα.
καίτοι σε τοῦτό γ᾽ οὐχὶ βούλομαι παθεῖν
ὁτιὴ ᾽κάλεσας εὐηθικῶς "τὴν κάρδοπον".

ΧΡΗΣΤΗΣ Β′

ἰώ μοι μοι.

Στ. ἔα·
τίς οὑτοσί ποτ᾽ ἔσθ᾽ ὁ θρηνῶν; οὔ τι που
τῶν Καρκίνου τις δαιμόνων ἐφθέγξατο;

Χρ. τί δ᾽, ὅστις εἰμί, τοῦτο βούλεσθ᾽ εἰδέναι;
ἀνὴρ κακοδαίμων.

Στ. κατὰ σεαυτόν νυν τρέπου.

Χρ. ὦ σκληρὲ δαῖμον· ὦ τύχαι θραυσάντυγες
ἵππων ἐμῶν· ὦ Παλλάς, ὥς μ᾽ ἀπώλεσας.

Στ. τί δαί σε Τληπόλεμός ποτ᾽ εἴργασται κακόν;

Χρ. μὴ σκῶπτέ μ᾽, ὦ τᾶν, ἀλλά μοι τὰ χρήματα
τὸν υἱὸν ἀποδοῦναι κέλευσον ἅλαβεν,
ἄλλως τε μέντοι καὶ κακῶς πεπραγότι.

Στ. τὰ ποῖα ταῦτα χρήμαθ᾽;

Χρ. ἁδανείσατο.

Στ. κακῶς ἄρ᾽ ὄντως εἶχες, ὥς γ᾽ ἐμοὶ δοκεῖς.

1254 *καίτοι γ᾽ ἴσθ᾽* p 1260 *τίς ἐσθ᾽ ὁ θρηνῶν οὗτος* RV
1269 *γε* RVp

Χρ. ἵππους γ᾽ ἐλαύνων ἐξέπεσον νὴ τοὺς θεούς.
Στ. τί δῆτα ληρεῖς ὥσπερ ἀπ᾽ ὄνου καταπεσών;
Χρ. ληρῶ, τὰ χρήματ᾽ ἀπολαβεῖν εἰ βούλομαι;
Στ. οὐκ ἔσθ᾽ ὅπως σύ γ᾽ αὐτὸς ὑγιαίνεις.
Χρ. τί δαί;
Στ. τὸν ἐγκέφαλον ὥσπερ σεσεῖσθαί μοι δοκεῖς.
Χρ. σὺ δὲ νὴ τὸν Ἑρμῆν προσκεκλήσεσθαί γ᾽ ἐμοί,
εἰ μὴ ᾽ποδώσεις τἀργύριον.
Στ. κάτειπέ νυν·
πότερα νομίζεις καινὸν αἰεὶ τὸν Δία
ὕειν ὕδωρ ἑκάστοτ᾽, ἢ τὸν ἥλιον
ἕλκειν κάτωθεν ταὐτὸ τοῦθ᾽ ὕδωρ πάλιν;
Χρ. οὐκ οἶδ᾽ ἔγωγ᾽ ὁπότερον, οὐδέ μοι μέλει.
Στ. πῶς οὖν ἀπολαβεῖν τἀργύριον δίκαιος εἶ,
εἰ μηδὲν οἶσθα τῶν μετεώρων πραγμάτων;
Χρ. ἀλλ᾽ εἰ †σπανίζεις τἀργυρίου μοι τὸν τόκον
ἀπόδοτε†.
Στ. τοῦτο δ᾽ ἔσθ᾽, ὁ τόκος, τί θηρίον;
Χρ. τί δ᾽ ἄλλο γ᾽ ἢ κατὰ μῆνα καὶ καθ᾽ ἡμέραν
πλέον πλέον τἀργύριον αἰεὶ γίγνεται
ὑπορρέοντος τοῦ χρόνου;
Στ. καλῶς λέγεις.
τί δῆτα; τὴν θάλατταν ἔσθ᾽ ὅτι πλείονα
νυνὶ νομίζεις ἢ πρὸ τοῦ;
Χρ. μὰ Δί᾽, ἀλλ᾽ ἴσην.
οὐ γὰρ δίκαιον πλείον᾽ εἶναι.

1273 *ἀπὸ νοῦ* Sch. 1285 *ἀλλ᾽ εἰ σπανίζετ᾽ ἀργυρίου, τὸν γοῦν τόκον* z 1286 *ἀπόδος* **p**: *ἀπόδος γε* *p*

Στ. κᾆτα πῶς
αὕτη μέν, ὦ κακόδαιμον, οὐδὲν γίγνεται
ἐπιρρεόντων τῶν ποταμῶν πλείων, σὺ δὲ
ζητεῖς ποῆσαι τἀργύριον πλέον τὸ σόν;
οὐκ ἀποδιώξει σαυτὸν ἀπὸ τῆς οἰκίας;
φέρε μοι τὸ κέντρον.

Χρ. ταῦτ' ἐγὼ μαρτύρομαι.

Στ. ὕπαγε. τί μέλλεις; οὐκ ἐλᾷς, ὦ σαμφόρα;

Χρ. ταῦτ' οὐχ ὕβρις δῆτ' ἐστίν;

Στ. ἄξεις; ἐπιαλῶ
κεντῶν ὑπὸ τὸν πρωκτόν σε τὸν σειραφόρον.
φεύγεις; ἔμελλόν σ' ἆρα κινήσειν ἐγὼ
αὐτοῖς τροχοῖς τοῖς σοῖσι καὶ ξυνωρίσιν.

Χο. οἷον τὸ πραγμάτων ἐρᾶν φλαύρων· ὁ γὰρ στρ.
γέρων ὅδ' ἐρασθεὶς
ἀποστερῆσαι βούλεται
τὰ χρήμαθ' ἁδανείσατο.
κοὐκ ἔσθ' ὅπως οὐ τήμερον
λήψεταί τι πρᾶγμ' ὃ τοῦ-
τον ποήσει τὸν σοφι-
στὴν ὧν πανουργεῖν ἤρξατ' ἐξαίφνης †τι κακὸν λαβεῖν†.
οἶμαι γὰρ αὐτὸν αὐτίχ' εὑρήσειν ὅπερ ἀντ.
πάλαι ποτ' ἐζήτει,
εἶναι τὸν υἱὸν δεινόν οἱ
γνώμας ἐναντίας λέγειν
τοῖσιν δικαίοις, ὥστε νι-

1296 ἀποδιώξει *z*: ἀποδιώξεις **a** ἐκ τῆς RVp 1297 *Μάρτυς* p
1298 *Μάρτ.* Sch. *Μάρτ.* ante οὐκ ἐλᾷς Sch. *σαμφόρα* **p**: *Πασία* RV
1299 ᾄξεις *z* 1308 *τι* om. RVp 1310*b* *κακὸν λαβεῖν τι z*:
καλόν γ' ὄνασθαι z 1312 *ἐπεζήτει* RVp: *ἐπῄτει z*: *ἐπῄει z*

κἂν ἅπαντας, οἷσπερ ἂν
ξυγγένηται, κἂν λέγῃ
παμπόνηρ'. ἴσως δ' ἴσως
βουλήσεται
κἄφωνον αὐτὸν εἶναι.

Στ. ἰοὺ ἰού.
ὦ γείτονες καὶ ξυγγενεῖς καὶ δημόται,
ἀμυνάθετέ μοι τυπτομένῳ πάσῃ τέχνῃ.
οἴμοι κακοδαίμων τῆς κεφαλῆς καὶ τῆς γνάθου.
ὦ μιαρέ, τύπτεις τὸν πατέρα;
Φε. φήμ', ὦ πάτερ.
Στ. ὁρᾶθ' ὁμολογοῦνθ' ὅτι με τύπτει;
Φε. καὶ μάλα.
Στ. ὦ μιαρὲ καὶ πατραλοῖα καὶ τοιχωρύχε.
Φε. αὖθίς με ταὐτὰ ταῦτα καὶ πλείω λέγε.
ἆρ' οἶσθ' ὅτι χαίρω πόλλ' ἀκούων καὶ κακά;
Στ. ὦ λακκόπρωκτε.
Φε. πάττε πολλοῖς τοῖς ῥόδοις.
Στ. τὸν πατέρα τύπτεις;
Φε. κἀποφανῶ γε νὴ Δία
ὡς ἐν δίκῃ σ' ἔτυπτον.
Στ. ὦ μιαρώτατε,
καὶ πῶς γένοιτ' ἂν πατέρα τύπτειν ἐν δίκῃ;
Φε. ἔγωγ' ἀποδείξω καί σε νικήσω λέγων.
Στ. τουτὶ σὺ νικήσεις;
Φε. πολύ γε καὶ ῥᾳδίως.
ἑλοῦ δ' ὁπότερον τοῖν λόγοιν βούλει λέγειν.
Στ. ποίοιν λόγοιν;

Φε. τὸν κρείττον' ἢ τὸν ἥττονα.

Στ. ἐδιδαξάμην μέντοι σε νὴ Δί', ὦ μέλε,
τοῖσιν δικαίοις ἀντιλέγειν, εἰ ταῦτά γε
μέλλεις ἀναπείσειν, ὡς δίκαιον καὶ καλὸν
τὸν πατέρα τύπτεσθ' ἐστὶν ὑπὸ τῶν υἱέων.

Φε. ἀλλ' οἴομαι μέντοι σ' ἀναπείσειν, ὥστε γε
οὐδ' αὐτὸς ἀκροασάμενος οὐδὲν ἀντερεῖς.

Στ. καὶ μὴν ὅτι καὶ λέξεις ἀκοῦσαι βούλομαι.

Χο. σὸν ἔργον, ὦ πρεσβῦτα, φροντίζειν ὅπῃ στρ.
τὸν ἄνδρα κρατήσεις,
ὡς οὗτος, εἰ μή τῳ 'πεποίθειν, οὐκ ἂν ἦν
οὕτως ἀκόλαστος.
ἀλλ' ἔσθ' ὅτῳ θρασύνεται· δῆλόν ⟨γε τοι⟩
τὸ λῆμα τἀνθρώπου.

ἀλλ' ἐξ ὅτου τὸ πρῶτον ἤρξαθ' ἡ μάχη γενέσθαι
ἤδη λέγειν χρὴ πρὸς χορόν· πάντως δὲ τοῦτο δράσεις.

Στ. καὶ μὴν ὅθεν γε πρῶτον ἠρξάμεσθα λοιδορεῖσθαι
ἐγὼ φράσω. 'πειδὴ γὰρ εἱστιώμεθ', ὥσπερ ἴστε,
πρῶτον μὲν αὐτὸν τὴν λύραν λαβόντ' ἐγὼ 'κέλευσα
ᾆσαι Σιμωνίδου μέλος, τὸν Κριόν, ὡς ἐπέχθη.
ὁ δ' εὐθέως ἀρχαῖον εἶν' ἔφασκε τὸ κιθαρίζειν
ᾄδειν τε πίνονθ', ὡσπερεὶ κάχρυς γυναῖκ' ἀλοῦσαν.

Φε. οὐ γὰρ τότ' εὐθὺς χρῆν σ' ἀράττεσθαί τε καὶ πατεῖσθαι,
ᾄδειν κελεύονθ', ὡσπερεὶ τέττιγας ἑστιῶντα;

1347 'πεποίθειν *z*: πεποίθει Rp: πέποιθεν Vp 1349 γε add. *p* τοι add. *z* 1350 λῆμα *z*: λῆμ' ἐστὶ **a** 1359 ἀράττεσθαι *z*: ἄρα τύπτεσθαι Rp: ἀλλὰ τύπτεσθαι Vp

Στ. τοιαῦτα μέντοι καὶ τότ' ἔλεγεν ἔνδον, οἷάπερ νῦν,
καὶ τὸν Σιμωνίδην ἔφασκ' εἶναι κακὸν ποιητήν.
κἀγὼ μόλις μέν, ἀλλ' ὅμως, ἠνεσχόμην τὸ πρῶτον.
ἔπειτα δ' ἐκέλευσ' αὐτὸν ἀλλὰ μυρρίνην λαβόντα
τῶν Αἰσχύλου λέξαι τί μοι. κᾆθ' οὗτος εὐθὺς εἶπεν·
"ἐγὼ γὰρ Αἰσχύλον νομίζω πρῶτον ἐν ποιηταῖς—
ψόφου πλέων, ἀξύστατον, στόμφακα, κρημνοποιόν."
κἀνταῦθα πῶς οἴεσθέ μου τὴν καρδίαν ὀρεχθεῖν;
ὅμως δὲ τὸν θυμὸν δακὼν ἔφην· "σὺ δ' ἀλλὰ τούτων
λέξον τι τῶν νεωτέρων, ἅττ' ἐστὶ τὰ σοφὰ ταῦτα."
ὁ δ' εὐθὺς ἦγ' Εὐριπίδου ῥῆσίν τιν', ὡς ἐκίνει
ἀδελφός, ὦ 'λεξίκακε, τὴν ὁμομητρίαν ἀδελφήν.
κἀγὼ οὐκέτ' ἐξηνεσχόμην, ἀλλ' εὐθέως ἀράττω
πολλοῖς κακοῖς καἰσχροῖσι. κᾆτ' ἐντεῦθεν, οἷον εἰκός,
ἔπος πρὸς ἔπος ἠρειδόμεσθ'· εἶθ' οὗτος ἐπαναπηδᾷ,
κἄπειτ' ἔφλα με κἀσπόδει κἄπνιγε κἀπέτριβεν.

Φε. οὔκουν δικαίως, ὅστις οὐκ Εὐριπίδην ἐπαινεῖς,
σοφώτατον;

Στ. σοφώτατόν γ' ἐκεῖνον, ὦ—τί σ' εἴπω;
ἀλλ' αὖθις αὖ τυπτήσομαι.

Φε. νὴ τὸν Δί', ἐν δίκῃ γ' ἄν.

Στ. καὶ πῶς δικαίως; ὅστις ὦ 'ναίσχυντέ σ' ἐξέθρεψα
αἰσθάνομενός σου πάντα τραυλίζοντος, ὅτι νοοίης.
εἰ μέν γε βρῦν εἴποις, ἐγὼ γνοὺς ἂν πιεῖν ἐπέσχον·
μαμμᾶν δ' ἂν αἰτήσαντος, ἧκόν σοι φέρων ἂν ἄρτον·
κακκᾶν δ' ἂν οὐκ ἔφθης φράσας, κἀγὼ λαβὼν θύραζε
ἐξέφερον ἂν καὶ προυσχόμην σε. σὺ δέ με νῦν ἀπάγχων,
βοῶντα καὶ κεκραγόθ' ὅτι
χεζητιῴην, οὐκ ἔτλης
ἔξω 'ξενεγκεῖν, ὦ μιαρέ,

1371 ἦγ' z: ᾖσ' Rp: ᾖσεν Vp 1373 εὐθέως ἀράττω Π: εὐθὺς ἐξαράττω **a** 1376 κἀπέθλιβεν RV

θύραζέ μ', ἀλλὰ πνιγόμενος
αὐτοῦ 'πόησα κακκᾶν.

Χο. οἶμαί γε τῶν νεωτέρων τὰς καρδίας ἀντ.
πηδᾶν ὅτι λέξει.
εἰ γὰρ τοιαῦτά γ' οὗτος ἐξειργασμένος
λαλῶν ἀναπείσει,
τὸ δέρμα τῶν γεραιτέρων λάβοιμεν ἂν
ἀλλ' οὐδ' ἐρεβίνθου.

σὸν ἔργον, ὦ καινῶν ἐπῶν κινητὰ καὶ μοχλευτά,
πειθώ τινα ζητεῖν, ὅπως δόξεις λέγειν δίκαια.

Φε. ὡς ἡδὺ καινοῖς πράγμασιν καὶ δεξιοῖς ὁμιλεῖν
καὶ τῶν καθεστώτων νόμων ὑπερφρονεῖν δύνασθαι.
ἐγὼ γὰρ ὅτε μὲν ἱππικῇ τὸν νοῦν μόνῃ προσεῖχον,
οὐδ' ἂν τρί' εἰπεῖν ῥήμαθ' οἷός τ' ἦν πρὶν ἐξαμαρτεῖν·
νυνὶ δ', ἐπειδή μ' οὑτοσὶ τούτων ἔπαυσεν αὐτός,
γνώμαις δὲ λεπταῖς καὶ λόγοις ξύνειμι καὶ μερίμναις,
οἶμαι διδάξειν ὡς δίκαιον τὸν πατέρα κολάζειν.
Στ. ἵππευε τοίνυν νὴ Δί', ὡς ἔμοιγε κρεῖττόν ἐστιν
ἵππων τρέφειν τέθριππον ἢ τυπτόμενον ἐπιτριβῆναι.
Φε. ἐκεῖσε δ' ὅθεν ἀπέσχισάς με τοῦ λόγου μέτειμι,
καὶ πρῶτ' ἐρήσομαί σε τουτί· παῖδά μ' ὄντ' ἔτυπτες;
Στ. ἔγωγέ σ', εὐνοῶν τε καὶ κηδόμενος.
Φε. εἰπὲ δή μοι,
οὐ κἀμὲ σοὶ δίκαιόν ἐστιν εὐνοεῖν ὁμοίως
τύπτειν τ', ἐπειδήπερ γε τοῦτ' ἔστ' εὐνοεῖν, τὸ τύπτειν;
πῶς γὰρ τὸ μὲν σὸν σῶμα χρὴ πληγῶν ἀθῷον εἶναι,
τοὐμὸν δὲ μή; καὶ μὴν ἔφυν ἐλεύθερός γε κἀγώ.

1401 τὸν νοῦν μόνῃ z: τὸν νοῦν μόνον R: τὸν νοῦν μου V: μόνῃ τὸν νοῦν p

"κλάουσι παῖδες, πατέρα δ' οὐ κλάειν δοκεῖς;"
φήσεις νομίζεσθαι σὺ παιδὸς τοῦτο τοὔργον εἶναι·
ἐγὼ δέ γ' ἀντείποιμ' ἂν ὡς δὶς παῖδες οἱ γέροντες.
εἰκός τε μᾶλλον τοὺς γέροντας ἢ νέους τι κλάειν,
ὅσῳπερ ἐξαμαρτάνειν ἧττον δίκαιον αὐτούς.

Στ. ἀλλ' οὐδαμοῦ νομίζεται τὸν πατέρα τοῦτο πάσχειν.

Φε. οὔκουν ἀνὴρ ὁ τὸν νόμον θεὶς τοῦτον ἦν τὸ πρῶτον,
ὥσπερ σὺ κἀγώ, καὶ λέγων ἔπειθε τοὺς παλαιούς;
ἧττόν τι δῆτ' ἔξεστι κἀμοὶ καινὸν αὖ τὸ λοιπὸν
θεῖναι νόμον τοῖς υἱέσιν, τοὺς πατέρας ἀντιτύπτειν;
ὅσας δὲ πληγὰς εἴχομεν πρὶν τὸν νόμον τεθῆναι,
ἀφίεμεν, καὶ δίδομεν αὐτοῖς προῖκα συγκεκόφθαι.
σκέψαι δὲ τοὺς ἀλεκτρυόνας καὶ τἄλλα τὰ βοτὰ ταυτί,
ὡς τοὺς πατέρας ἀμύνεται· καίτοι τί διαφέρουσιν
ἡμῶν ἐκεῖνοι, πλήν γ' ὅτι ψηφίσματ' οὐ γράφουσιν;

Στ. τί δῆτ', ἐπειδὴ τοὺς ἀλεκτρυόνας ἅπαντα μιμεῖ,
οὐκ ἐσθίεις καὶ τὴν κόπρον κἀπὶ ξύλου καθεύδεις;

Φε. οὐ ταὐτόν, ὦ τᾶν, ἐστίν, οὐδ' ἂν Σωκράτει δοκοίη.

Στ. πρὸς ταῦτα μὴ τύπτ'· εἰ δὲ μή, σαυτόν ποτ' αἰτιάσει.

Φε. καὶ πῶς;

Στ. ἐπεὶ σὲ μὲν δίκαιός εἰμ' ἐγὼ κολάζειν,
σὺ δ', ἢν γένηταί σοι, τὸν υἱόν.

Φε. ἢν δὲ μὴ γένηται,
μάτην ἐμοὶ κεκλαύσεται, σὺ δ' ἐγχανὼν τεθνήξεις.

Στ. ἐμοὶ μέν, ὦνδρες ἥλικες, δοκεῖ λέγειν δίκαια,
κἄμοιγε συγχωρεῖν δοκεῖ τούτοισι τἀπιεικῆ·
κλάειν γὰρ ἡμᾶς εἰκός ἐστ', ἢν μὴ δίκαια δρῶμεν.

1415 fin. Στ. τιὴ τί δή (vel sim.) p 1416 σὺ RVp: γε p 1418 μάλιστα Vp νέους z: τοὺς νέους Rp: τοὺς νεωτέρους Vp 1431 καθίζεις p test. 1436 τεθνήξεις z: τεθνήξει a test.

Φε. σκέψαι δὲ χἀτέραν ἔτι γνώμην.

Στ. ἀπὸ γὰρ ὀλοῦμαι.

Φε. καὶ μὴν ἴσως γ' οὐκ ἀχθέσει παθὼν ἃ νῦν πέπονθας.

Στ. πῶς δή; δίδαξον γὰρ τί μ' ἐκ τούτων ἐπωφελήσεις.

Φε. τὴν μητέρ' ὥσπερ καὶ σὲ τυπτήσω.

Στ. τί φής, τί φὴς σύ;
τοῦθ' ἕτερον αὖ μεῖζον κακόν.

Φε. τί δ' ἢν ἔχων τὸν ἥττω
λόγον σε νικήσω λέγων
τὴν μητέρ' ὡς τύπτειν χρεών;

Στ. τί δ' ἄλλο γ' ἤ, ταῦτ' ἢν ποῇς,
οὐδέν σε κωλύσει σεαυτὸν ἐμβαλεῖν
εἰς τὸ βάραθρον μετὰ Σωκράτους
καὶ τὸν λόγον τὸν ἥττω;

ταυτὶ δι' ὑμᾶς, ὦ Νεφέλαι, πέπονθ' ἐγώ,
ὑμῖν ἀναθεὶς ἅπαντα τἀμὰ πράγματα.

Χο. αὐτὸς μὲν οὖν σαυτῷ σὺ τούτων αἴτιος,
στρέψας σεαυτὸν εἰς πονηρὰ πράγματα.

Στ. τί δῆτα ταῦτ' οὔ μοι τότ' ἠγορεύετε,
ἀλλ' ἄνδρ' ἄγροικον καὶ γέροντ' ἐπήρατε;

Χο. ἡμεῖς ποοῦμεν ταῦθ' ἑκάστοθ', ὅντιν' ἂν
γνῶμεν πονηρῶν ὄντ' ἐραστὴν πραγμάτων,
ἕως ἂν αὐτὸν ἐμβάλωμεν εἰς κακόν,
ὅπως ἂν εἰδῇ τοὺς θεοὺς δεδοικέναι.

Στ. ὤμοι, πονηρά γ', ὦ Νεφέλαι, δίκαια δέ·
οὐ γάρ με χρῆν τὰ χρήμαθ' ἁδανεισάμην

1442 ὠφελήσεις p: ἔτ' ὠφελήσεις z 1447 ἤ, ταῦτ' ἢν z: ἢν ταυτὶ Rp: ἢν ταύτην V: ἢν ταῦτα p 1458 ἡμεῖς RV: ἀεὶ p ὅντιν' ἂν z: ὅταν τινὰ RVp: ἄν τιν' οὖν p

ἀποστερεῖν. νῦν οὖν ὅπως, ὦ φίλτατε,
τὸν Χαιρεφῶντα τὸν μιαρὸν καὶ Σωκράτη
ἀπολεῖς μετ' ἐμοῦ 'λθών, οἳ σὲ κἄμ' ἐξηπάτων.

Φε. ἀλλ' οὐκ ἂν ἀδικήσαιμι τοὺς διδασκάλους.

Στ. ναὶ ναί, καταιδέσθητι πατρῷον Δία.

Φε. ἰδού γε Δία πατρῷον. ὡς ἀρχαῖος εἶ.
Ζεὺς γάρ τις ἐστίν;

Στ. ἐστίν.

Φε. οὐκ ἔστ', οὔκ, ἐπεὶ
Δῖνος βασιλεύει, τὸν Δί' ἐξεληλακώς.

Στ. οὐκ ἐξελήλακ', ἀλλ' ἐγὼ τοῦτ' ᾠόμην
διὰ τουτονὶ τὸν δῖνον. ὤμοι δείλαιος,
ὅτε καὶ σὲ χυτρεοῦν ὄντα θεὸν ἡγησάμην.

Φε. ἐνταῦθα σαυτῷ παραφρόνει καὶ φληνάφα.

Στ. οἴμοι παρανοίας. ὡς ἐμαινόμην ἄρα
ὅτ' ἐξέβαλον καὶ τοὺς θεοὺς διὰ Σωκράτη.
ἀλλ', ὦ φίλ' Ἑρμῆ, μηδαμῶς θύμαινέ μοι,
μηδέ μ' ἐπιτρίψῃς, ἀλλὰ συγγνώμην ἔχε
ἐμοῦ παρανοήσαντος ἀδολεσχίᾳ.
καί μοι γενοῦ ξύμβουλος, εἴτ' αὐτοὺς γραφὴν
διωκάθω γραψάμενος, εἴθ' ὅτι σοι δοκεῖ.
ὀρθῶς παραινεῖς οὐκ ἐῶν δικορραφεῖν
ἀλλ' ὡς τάχιστ' ἐμπιμπράναι τὴν οἰκίαν
τῶν ἀδολεσχῶν. δεῦρο δεῦρ', ὦ Ξανθία,
κλίμακα λαβὼν ἔξελθε καὶ σμινύην φέρων,
κἄπειτ' ἐπαναβὰς ἐπὶ τὸ φροντιστήριον
τὸ τέγος κατάσκαπτ', εἰ φιλεῖς τὸν δεσπότην,

1470 *τίς* p : *τί* RV 1480 *παρανομήσαντος* RVp 1482 **Ἑρμ.** *εἴθ'* V

ἕως ἂν αὐτοῖς ἐμβάλῃς τὴν οἰκίαν.
ἐμοὶ δὲ δᾷδ' ἐνεγκάτω τις ἡμμένην.
κἀγώ τιν' αὐτῶν τήμερον δοῦναι δίκην
ἐμοὶ ποήσω, κεἰ σφόδρ' εἴσ' ἀλαζόνες.

ΜΑΘΗΤΗΣ Α'

ἰοὺ ἰού.

Στ. σὸν ἔργον, ὦ δᾴς, ἱέναι πολλὴν φλόγα.
Μα. ἄνθρωπε, τί ποεῖς;
Στ. ὅτι ποῶ; τί δ' ἄλλο γ' ἢ
διαλεπτολογοῦμαι ταῖς δοκοῖς τῆς οἰκίας;

ΜΑΘΗΤΗΣ Β'

οἴμοι· τίς ἡμῶν πυρπολεῖ τὴν οἰκίαν;

Στ. ἐκεῖνος οὗπερ θοἰμάτιον εἰλήφατε.
Μα. ἀπολεῖς, ἀπολεῖς.
Στ. τοῦτ' αὐτὸ γὰρ καὶ βούλομαι,
ἢν ἡ σμινύη μοι μὴ προδῷ τὰς ἐλπίδας
ἢ 'γὼ πρότερόν πως ἐκτραχηλισθῶ πεσών.
Σω. οὗτος, τί ποιεῖς ἐτεόν, οὑπὶ τοῦ τέγους;
Στ. ἀεροβατῶ καὶ περιφρονῶ τὸν ἥλιον.
Σω. οἴμοι τάλας δείλαιος, ἀποπνιγήσομαι.
Μα. ἐγὼ δὲ κακοδαίμων γε κατακαυθήσομαι.

1495 Οἰκ. R: Ξανθ. V 1497 Σω. RVp 1499 in. Σω. RVp 1503 Οἰ. R: Ξανθ. οἰκ. V 1504 Χαιρεφῶν p 1505 Χαιρεφῶν p

Στ. τί γὰρ μαθόντες τοὺς θεοὺς ὑβρίζετε
καὶ τῆς σελήνης ἐσκοπεῖσθε τὴν ἕδραν;
δίωκε, παῖε, βάλλε, πολλῶν οὕνεκα,
μάλιστα δ' εἰδὼς τοὺς θεοὺς ὡς ἠδίκουν.

Χο. ἡγεῖσθ' ἔξω· κεχόρευται γὰρ μετρίως τό γε τήμερον
ἡμῖν.

1507 ἐσκοπεῖσθον p 1508 Ἑρμ. RV

COMMENTARY

(A) **1–125.** STREPSIADES AT HOME

(i) **1–78.** *Strepsiades recounts his troubles*

There is a door in the centre of the skene. Two frames of wood and canvas are brought in, fitted together, and placed against the left-hand end of the skene; the frame which faces us has a door in it; a third frame is placed horizontally from the top of this façade to the top of the skene, to represent a roof, and is tied or nailed in place. Then a wooden screen, in which there is a small closed door, is carried in and placed obliquely in front of the wood-and-canvas house, concealing from us the façade of the house. The men who have carried the screen in remain behind it, and we do not see them.

From the other side of the theatre two beds are carried in and placed in front of the skene, somewhat to the right of the central door. In each bed there is a person covered with blankets. The men who have carried the beds in go away. The play begins.

The fact that there are two people lying in their beds suggests that it is night. One of the two remains motionless. The other tosses and turns with increasing violence, and finally sits upright with a gesture of despair. We see from his mask that he is an old man.

He is going to deliver a soliloquy, in which the situation and its antecedents will be expounded to us. At no point, however, are we explicitly addressed as an audience; the speaker begins by verbalizing the emotions which he feels, and the transition from emotional reaction to pure narrative is effected subtly, with a renewed outburst of emotion at 41 ff. The participation of the slave (18 ff., 56 ff.) and the dreams and temporary awakening of the other sleeper (25 ff.) interrupt and enliven what would otherwise be an abnormally prolonged soliloquy. The other man's presence, even when he is asleep, also makes it possible for some of the information which we need to be given as words addressed to him, not to us.

Acharnians similarly begins with a soliloquy, but that is shorter and less detailed. In *Knights* 40 ff., *Wasps* 54 ff., *Peace* 50 ff., and *Birds* 30 ff. Ar. adopts a different technique, making one character step out of the play to tell us the situation after our interest and curiosity have been aroused by lively dialogue and action.

We infer from the old man's words in 5 ff. that he is the head of a household, and from 8 that the other sleeper is his son; this is confirmed at 14. We learn the son's name at 67, but not the old man's until 134.

1 ff. tell us that the dramatic time is shortly before first light, and 5 ff. that the place of the action is the old man's own house. If we think of the two men as sleeping in the same room, we may wonder why the father is not sleeping with his wife, and the son in a separate room. The temperature in the theatre at the Dionysia does not make us think at once of people sleeping out of doors to keep cool, and line 10 shows that we are not to imagine the weather as hot. There is, in fact, no point in speculating what spatial relation between father's bed and son's bed in the dramatic situation is represented by the relation of the two beds in the theatre.

We do not know until 134 ff. whether we are to think of the house as being in the city or in the country.

1 ἰοὺ ἰού: The opening words are characteristic. *Knights* too opens with a cry of distress and *Acharnians* with an emphatic statement of distress.

2 τὸ χρῆμα . . . ὅσον: = *ὅσον* (exclamatory) ⟨*ἐστί*⟩ . . . The singular *χρῆμα* is extremely restricted in Attic; most often, *τὸ χρῆμα* with a genitive occurs in exclamations which express a reaction to size, numbers, goodness or badness. **τῶν νυκτῶν:** Since the plural *νύκτες* is used with reference to an unspecified number of nights but occasionally with reference to one night only (e.g. Pl. *Prt.* 310 C *ἔπειτά μοι λίαν πόρρω ἔδοξε τῶν νυκτῶν εἶναι*), it is probable that we should take the exclamation of distress as referring to this night, not as implying that the old man has habitually lain awake at night.

5 οἱ δ' οἰκέται: His mood changes from the disgruntlement of insomnia to anger against his slaves. *οἰκέται* = 'slaves', not the whole household; in Lys. vii. 16 *οἰκέται* and *θεράποντες* are synonyms. **ἀλλ' οὐκ ἄν:** '⟨They⟩ wouldn't ⟨have been⟩ . . .'; cf. 108 and p. xxxii.

6 ἀπόλοιο . . . 7 οἰκέτας: During the Peloponnesian War, with Megara and Boiotia both hostile and a Peloponnesian army ravaging Attica at times, ill-treated slaves had far better opportunities to desert than in peace-time. The two slaves in the first scene of *Knights* timorously contemplate desertion (21 ff.) as a way of escape from their intolerable fellow slave, and in *Peace* 451 it is assumed that 'a slave ready to desert' is one of the beneficiaries of war. No doubt the 'servant problem' was a regular talking-point among Attic householders, but it was a real enough problem, as later events showed; by the time that the Peloponnesian force established at Dekelia in 413 had been active for some months Athens was the poorer by 20,000 slaves, through capture and desertion together (Thuc. vii. 27. 5). **ὅτ':** *ὅτε* often = *νῦν γάρ*, like 'when' in English; cf. 34 and 717. **κολάσ':** Cf. p. xxxviii.

8 οὐδ': The point is: '<I am awake> but *he* is *not*.' **χρηστός**: This heavy sarcasm, rare in comedy (but cf. 61, 647), is common in oratory; cf. Dem. xviii. 130 *οἱ χρηστοὶ πρέσβεις οὗτοι*.

9 πέρδεται: The assumptions of Old Comedy (cf. 734 n.) make 'fart' almost a synonym for 'sleep' (cf. *Ach.* 256), but farting is also associated with lively insouciance, e.g. *Wasps* 1305 *ἐσκίρτα, 'πεπόρδει, κατεγέλα* ~ *Clouds* 1078 *σκίρτα, γέλα, κτλ.* This passage combines both ideas to suggest sleeping without a care in the world. One further consideration is that Old Comedy exploits to the utmost the humorous potentialities of the bowels (e.g. 157 ff., 169 ff., 293 ff., 373, 386 ff., 1384 ff.).

10 ἐγκεκορδυλημένος: Probably 'swathed'; but the etymology is controversial.

11 ἀλλ' εἰ δοκεῖ: 'Well, all right, then . . .'; seeing that his son isn't going to lose any sleep, the old man acquiesces grudgingly.

He wraps himself up and lies still for a moment. Then he begins to toss again, with increasing exaggeration, until he flings back the blankets and sits up. He may perhaps swing his legs over the side of the bed, as if giving up all further hope of sleep. As vase-paintings show, Greeks commonly sat on beds with their legs horizontal, either propped up on cushions and one elbow or raising one knee and grasping it; but the old man will soon (18 ff.) read his account-book, for which he will need both hands.

12 δακνόμενος: Coupled with 'I can't sleep' this suggests vermin, but 13 shows that the biting (as often, e.g. *Ach.* 1) is metaphorical.

13 φάτνης: *δαπάνης* tells us that he is worried by debt; *φάτνης* tells us what kind of debt; and 14 shows that his son's passion for horses is the trouble.

14 κόμην: Long hair was characteristic of (*a*) unworldly men, careless of their appearance (cf. 836 and perhaps 332), and (*b*) fastidious, well-to-do young men. It was therefore characteristic of those who served as cavalry, for only the rich could afford to maintain horses. The chorus of cavalrymen in *Knights* 580 says *μὴ φθονεῖθ' ἡμῖν κομῶσι*. Anyone who wore long hair but was not otherwise unkempt or dirty could be regarded as 'giving himself airs'; cf. 348, 545, and 1100.

15 ξυνωρικεύεται: *συνωρίς* is a racing-chariot drawn not (as normally) by four horses but by two. *συνωρικεύεσθαι* implies a hypothetical *συνωρικός*, 'having to do with' (hence 'skilled at' or 'knowledgeable in') 'racing with pairs'. Verbs in *-εύεσθαι* commonly denote ways of life or behaviour, e.g. 970 *βωμολοχεύσαιτ'*.

17 ὁρῶν . . . 18 χωροῦσιν: The interest on loans was reckoned by the month, as we are told explicitly in 756; cf. Dem. xxxvii. 4 f., where 150 drachmai a month are the interest on a loan of 150 mnai. Creditors, therefore, although especially pressing at the end of the year, would also want to collect the money owed to them at the end of each month. The Attic months were alternately of 29 and 30 days and (unlike our months) were normally in step with the moon (cf. 615 ff. n.); hence the old man speaks of the moon where we would say 'it's the last part of the month'. As well as εἰκάς, the plural εἰκάδες can mean 'the 20th', as in the dating formula μετ' εἰκάδας, which first appears in 334/3, but I do not think that the meaning 'the twenties' can be excluded here. χωρεῖν is often 'move on', 'move forward' (cf. 906 f.); in this case 'mount up'.

18 ἅπτε: He calls to a slave, who comes out of the skene while 19 f. are being spoken. This slave, at any rate, is not 'still snoring'.

19 κἄκφερε: He uses the word appropriate not to bringing something from one room to another within a real house but to bringing it out of the skene into sight of the audience. **γραμματεῖον**: We cannot be sure of the form and material of this, but it was probably a number of wooden tablets with waxed surfaces; a more durable object than a sheet or roll of papyrus, and more economical in that it could be used afresh if all the debts were ever paid off. Ar. fr. 157 says 'they ate the wax from their *γραμματεῖα*'. **ἵν' ἀναγνῶ λαβών**: 'so that I may take it and read ...'. Cf. 149; superfluous *λαβών* is abundant in comedy.

He takes the book from the slave, who stands behind him holding the lamp (the Scholiast says that the slave reads aloud to him, but no MS. assigns 21 to 31 to the slave, and this method of production does not quite suit *φέρ' ἴδω, τί ὀφείλω;*). The play is being acted in daylight; is the lamp really alight? If so, it must go out between 31 and 56, and neither earlier nor later; but that should not be beyond the wit of a producer.

20 καὶ λογίσωμαι τοὺς τόκους: It would be tedious if he did, and he is not allowed to go that far; cf. 56 n.

21 Πασίᾳ: Cf. p. xviii.

22 τοῦ: sc. *ὀφείλω*. In inscriptions which record expenditure on public works the object or service for which a sum is paid is commonly put in the genitive. **τί ἐχρησάμην**: Not 'why did I borrow it?' ((LSJ), for although *χρῶ* = 'lend' is normal Attic prose language, *χρῶμαι* = 'borrow' is not; rather 'What use did I make of it?' Cf. *Knights* 1183 *καὶ τί* (= 'how', 'what ... for') *τούτοις χρήσομαι τοῖς ἐντέροις;*

23. He remembers the answer and gives it. **κοππατίαν**: There existed a breed of horses which it was customary to brand, as a guarantee of pedigree, with the letter Ϙ (*koppa*) and another, *σαμφόρας*, branded with M (not *mu*, but *san*, the Corinthian *s*); cf. 123 and 1298. This branding was still customary when the scholion on this line was composed. Brands appear on the hindquarters of horses on early Attic vases. As for the price, in Lys. viii. 10 a horse seems to have been deposited as security for a loan of 12 mnai, but the situation is obscure; Is. v. 43 implies that a horse worth only 3 mnai was of poor quality.

24 ἐξεκόπην: Ar.'s puns are seldom sophisticated, and this pun on *-κοπ-* is one of his feeblest. **πρότερον**: i.e. 'I would sooner have lost my eye (= one of my eyes).'

25. The young man cries out in his sleep; he is dreaming that he is in a race and that one of his competitors is 'cutting in'.

27 ὀνειροπολεῖ: So he has already told us (16); cf. *Peace* 58 ff., where the slave has just said that Trygaios keeps on crying out *ὦ Ζεῦ, τί ποτε βουλεύει ποεῖν;* and we hear Trygaios' voice: *ὦ Ζεῦ, τί δρασείεις ποθ' ἡμῶν τὸν λεών;* Here, however, we can make something dramatically more effective out of the repetition, as if the old man were saying, 'He *does* dream, you see . . .' or 'I *told* you he dreams . . .'

28 ἐλᾷ: A rider *ἐλαύνει*, and so does the driver of a chariot; but the rider's horse *ἐλαύνεται*, and we should expect the passive to be used of the chariot too; but in 1298 *ἐλᾷς* is spoken as if to a horse, and here it is easier to take the chariots as the subject of the verb, representing the men in them, than to assume an unidentified 'he' as the (single) driver of a succession of chariots. Cf. Hdt. v. 113. 1, 'after the treachery of the Kurians the war-chariots of the Salaminians also at once did the same as the Kurians.' **πολεμιστήρια**: The use of chariots in warfare was a thing of the remote past, but 'war-chariots' were used for racing; cf. 69 n.

29 ἐμὲ μέν: Cf. p. xxxii.

30 ἀτὰρ τί χρέος ἔβα με: The forms *χρέος* and *ἔβα*, instead of *χρέως* and *ἔβη*, as well as the syntax of *με*, show that these words are a quotation from serious poetry (cf. p. xxxiii), and the Scholiast cites *τί χρέος ἔβα δῶμα* from Euripides, but without naming the play. Needless to say, the meaning 'debt' is imported by Ar. and does not belong to the tragic original; in tragedy *τί χρέος* is little more than *τί*.

32. The young man, still dreaming, gives an order to his groom. The situation to which the order is appropriate is precisely that of Ischomachos in Xen. *Oec.* 11. 18, 'I go for a ride, imitating as closely as possible the kind of riding which is unavoidable in war . . . and when this is done, *ὁ παῖς ἐξαλίσας τὸν ἵππον οἴκαδε ἀπάγει*.'

34 ὅτε . . . 35 φασιν: 'For now' (= *ἤδη γάρ*: cf. 7 n.) 'I have lost lawsuits ⟨brought by some of my creditors⟩ and other ⟨creditors⟩ say that they will have securities taken for ⟨the⟩ interest ⟨which I owe⟩.' **ἐνεχυράσεσθαι**: If a man failed to pay a debt (of any kind) to which he had been judged liable by a lawcourt, securities (*ἐνέχυρα*) could be taken from him to the value of his debt. But the old man's distinction between 'I have lost lawsuits' and 'others' shows that he is referring now to creditors who lent him money on condition that they could take securities *τόκου* (cf. 22, 1223), i.e. as a substitute for the interest due. A similar attitude to the difference between capital and interest is shown in 1285 f. Of course it was open to a creditor to lend without any such contractual agreement; it was equally open to him to lend only *ἐπ' ἐνεχύρῳ*.

35 ἑτεόν . . . 36 ὅλην: The young man wakes up for a moment and expostulates. On *ἑτεόν* cf. p. xxxii.

37 δήμαρχος: 'I'm being bitten by a bug' would be a common answer to 'Why are you tossing and turning?' 'Demarch' comes as a surprise, but the rest of the line, *ἐκ τῶν στρωμάτων*, is appropriate to bugs, not demarchs. I know of no other example of an 'unexpected' joke in the form A–B–A. Each deme appointed a demarch annually as its chief officer; he had the custody of the official list of members of the deme. We know that he was responsible for exacting the rents on land leased by the deme to individuals and for making inventories of the property of condemned men, and it is a fair inference from this passage that he had the authority to enforce the surrender of securities by a debtor to a private creditor. Harpokration says; 'That the demarchs took securities is shown by Ar.' (in a lost play)—but we do not know how plainly it was shown.

39. The young man goes back to sleep.

40 τρέψεται: Sons inherited their fathers' debts.

41*b* εἴθ' ὤφελ': Tragic colouring; cf. Eur. *Med.* 1. **προμνήστρι'**: Mixing of the sexes before marriage was limited in Greece, and the marriageable daughters of prosperous families (where slaves did the shopping) would not often be seen or talked to (except surreptitiously) by the unmarried men of other households. In such a society old women have an important part to play as matchmakers, describing to a bachelor the attractions of a girl whom he cannot himself see, and it is surprising that we hear so little about their activity. Plato and Xenophon speak of it in a way which takes it for granted as a social phenomenon.

42 γῆμ': Cf. p. xxxviii.

46 Μεγακλέους τοῦ Μεγακλέους: A real Megakles son of Megakles was one of the Treasurers of Athena in 428/7, but it is most unlikely that Ar. means us to think of his fictitious hero as married to the niece of an actual person. The whole point is that 'Megakles' is in itself a grandiloquent name, like 'Algernon Fortescue' (Athenian names beginning with *Μεγα-* are not common), and in particular is a name borne in earlier days by several members of the wealthy and distinguished Alkmeonidai. It was comparatively rare for a father to give his own name to his son (cf. 65 n.), but a few did—Alkibiades among them. On Strepsiades' marriage cf. p. xvii.

47 ἐξ ἄστεως: The phrase functions as an adjective, 'a city ⟨girl⟩', just as a demotic may be indifferently an adjective or an *ἐκ*-phrase.

48 σεμνήν: In 315, 365, and 570 the relation of *σεμνός* to *σέβειν* is prominent, and the word is commonly used of gods; the derogatory sense, 'arrogant', 'pretentious', is implied in 363 *σεμνοπροσωπεῖς*. But applied to a woman the meaning is almost 'classy'; cf. *Eccl.* 617, where *αἱ σεμναί* are contrasted with *αἱ φαυλότεραι καὶ σιμότεραι*. **ἐγκεκοισυρωμένην**: Koisyra (cf. 800) figured in folklore as a *grande dame*, and we do not know her origin; in *Ach.* 614 *ὁ Κοισύρας* designates an aristocratic type, not an identifiable individual. Ancient commentators made a variety of assertions in the belief (which may be correct) that (*a*) she was a real person, (*b*) she was somehow connected with the Alkmeonidai, and (*c*) she came from Eretria.

49 ταύτην ὅτ' ἐγάμουν: 'When I wedded her'. **συγκατεκλινόμην**: Bride and bridegroom were both present at the banquet which preceded the journey of the bride from her father's house, and the guests at a banquet *συγκατακλίνονται* in order to eat and drink. But given Hdt. ii. 181. 2, 'whenever Amasis lay with her (*ξυγκλίνοιτο*) he became impotent' it seems more likely that the old man is speaking of the marriage-bed than of the marriage-feast.

50 ὄζων: The first three items are precise and familiar smells; *περιουσίας* gives much more latitude to the imagination. Similarly in 51 f. the first item is specific, but the remainder (especially 52) can only be regarded as 'smells' by association. Cf. 398 and 1007 n.

51 κρόκου: *κροκωτός* (i.e. dyed with saffron) was a woman's best dress, worn on ceremonial occasions and when she wanted to attract and stimulate her husband. 'Scent, saffron, and tongue-kisses'—the third item determines the associations of the first two—carry the implication that sex was more important to an idle, rich woman than to a hard-working farmer's wife.

52 Κωλιάδος: Aphrodite Kolias had a sanctuary on the promontory of that name, in the deme Anaphlystos, and women gathered *ἐπὶ Κωλιάδα* for a festival. **Γενετυλλίδος**: A 'woman's goddess' (Hesychios), also mentioned in *Lys.* 2. In *Thesm.* 130 we find the plural (*ὦ πότνιαι Γενετυλλίδες*)—there too associated with seductive kissing —and Pausanias locates the 'goddesses named Genetyllides' with Aphrodite Kolias.

53 οὐ μὴν ἐρῶ γ': 'But, for all that, I won't say . . .' **ἐσπάθα**: One meaning of *σπάθη* is the blade used to pack the threads together in the normal Greek upright loom. Weaving was the characteristic activity of the good housewife. If, following the suggestion of 51 f., we take *σπαθᾶν* as a slang word (not attested elsewhere) for sexual intercourse we spoil the joke of 54 f., to which 53 is only a lead.

54 ἄν: Cf. English 'I would say . . .' = 'I was accustomed to say'.

55 πρόφασιν: 'As a reason ⟨for saying what I did⟩ . . .' **λίαν σπαθᾷς**: Excessive use of the blade packs the thread too tight and is therefore extravagant. Hence *σπαθᾶν* is used metaphorically of extravagance. If the old man holds up part of his himation to show us that it is threadbare (because he is now impoverished), the joke is that his wife's metaphorical *λίαν σπαθᾶν* has had the opposite result from literal *λίαν σπαθᾶν*.

56 ἔλαιον . . . λύχνῳ: Cf. 20 n. It is, of course, dramatically necessary that the old man's recital of his debts should be curtailed; we are left to imagine that there are many more. **ἡμῖν:** Slave and master are engaged in a joint enterprise, one holding the lamp and the other reading by it.

57 γάρ: Cf. p. xxxii. **πότην:** The joke is commonplace, but we do not know who made it first. **ἧπτες:** The imperfect is surprising. The old man must be looking at the act of lighting the lamp from the point of view of the slave when the command *ἅπτε* (18) was given; hence also *ἐνετίθεις* in 59.

58 κλάῃς: *κλάειν*, like *οἰμώζειν* (e.g. 217) implies 'with pain, at a beating'; we look at the relationship from the other end and say (e.g.) 'I'll knock your block off!' **διὰ τί:** No doubt the slave in fact keeps out of range, and runs indoors at 59.

59 τῶν: sc. 'one of . . .'

60 ὅπως: Here 'when'.

61 τἀγαθῇ: Sarcastic (cf. 8 n.), in that it is a way of expressing his bitterness against his wife's pretensions.

62 δὴ 'ντεῦθεν: This makes good sense (for *ἐντεῦθεν* = 'then', 'next', cf. 1075, 1374); on the metre, cf. p. xxxvi. We should expect *ἐντεῦθεν δή*, but *δή* sometimes comes before the word with which it is associated.

63 ἡ μέν . . . 67 Φειδιππίδην: The aspect of the verbs is important: 'she was for adding' (imperfect) '"hippos" to the name, ⟨naming him⟩ . . ., while I was for giving him the name' (imperfect) 'Pheidonides . . .'; then, lit., 'we tried to get the question decided', i.e. 'we argued', but eventually 'we named him' (aorist) 'Pheidippides'. Cf. 152, 582 ff., 629. The syntactical relation of 64 to 63 is not easily defined, but presents no problem of intelligibility. **ἵππον:** A quoted word is something declined in conformity with the syntactical structure of the containing sentence, e.g. *Birds* 58 *οὐκ ἀντὶ τοῦ παιδός σε χρῆν ἐποποῖ καλεῖν*, 'Oughtn't you to have called out "*ἐποποῖ*" instead of "*παῖ*"?' **Ξάνθιππον κτλ.:** Xanthippos was the name of Perikles' father and of one of his sons; otherwise it was rare, and thus has much the same associations as 'Megakles' (but cf. 1070 n.). 'Chairippos', on the other hand, is common. **τοῦ πάππου:** Grandfather's name was actually 'Pheidon', as we learn at 134. The practice of naming a man after his father's father was extremely common, as many known genealogies testify. **κοινῇ ξυνέβημεν:** 'we came to an agreement.' **Φειδιππίδην:** We have actual examples of this name from Thera in

VII and Eretria in III; and it is an alternative to 'Philippides' in stories of the Athenian who took the message from Marathon to Sparta.

69 πόλιν: Not riding from country to city in a chariot, but taking part in the Panathenaic procession to the Akropolis (*πόλις* normally, without the article, in Classical Attic); cf. the chariots on the north frieze of the Parthenon.

70 Μεγακλέης: Cf. 46. On the form, cf. p. xxxi. **ξυστίδ'**: According to the Scholiast *ξυστίς* is a saffron-dyed himation 'worn by charioteers, to this day, and kings in tragedy use it too'. It is often represented in art, as (e.g.) on the north frieze of the Parthenon (cf. 69 n.).

71 φελλέως: The same phrase occurs in *Ach.* 273, in an incident imagined as typical of country life. The usage of the word in fourth-century mine-leases shows that it denotes a type of land. Whether it was ever a proper name, 'a rocky district of Attica' (LSJ, following the Scholiast) is very doubtful.

72 ἐνημμένος: ~ *ἐνάπτεσθαι.*

73 ἐπείθετο: On the metre cf. p. xxxvi. *οὐκ ἐπείθετο* (not *οὐκ ἐπίθετο*) occurs in *Wasps* 117 and 746; *οὐκ ἐπίθετο* is not found in Ar.

74 ἵππερον: Meant to remind us of *ἴκτερος*, 'jaundice', which plainly cannot have been a 'technical term' (for if it was, what did laymen call jaundice?), though it happens now to be found only in the medical writers; cf. *ὕδερος*, 'dropsy' and 243, 1276 nn. **κατέχεεν**: Not 'he infected my property' (*ἀναπιμπλάναι* and *καταπιμπλάναι* are used of infection), but the word has physiological associations; cf. *Wasps* 7, 'Sleep *καταχεῖται* over my eyes.'

75 ὁδοῦ: 'A way out', 'a means ⟨of dealing with the situation⟩'. For *φροντίζειν c. gen.* cf. 125; but it is much commoner with negatives than positives.

76 ἀτραπόν: Commonly something smaller than *ὁδός*.

77 ἤν . . . τουτονί: 'And if I persuade him of this . . .'; cf. Thuc. ii. 21. 1 *χρήμασι πεισθῆναι τὴν ἀναχώρησιν. ἀναπείθειν* is used especially of persuading someone contrary to his inclinations (e.g. 868) or his existing standards (e.g. 1019) or opinions (e.g. 96, 1340).

(ii) **79–125**. *Strepsiades tries to persuade Pheidippides*

79 πῶς . . . πῶς: Cf. the old man's agonized attempt to answer a question in 787 ff. **ἥδιστ'**: 'In the way least disagreeable to him'.

80 Φειδιππίδιον: For the wheedling diminutive cf. 132 and 222 f.

The old man gets off his bed, puts on his slippers (we do not know at what point he has put on his himation; possibly he was sleeping in it) and approaches his son's bed. **τί, ὦ πάτερ**: Pheidippides wakes and sits up.

81 κύσον . . . δεξιάν: In *Frogs* 754 f., when Xanthias recognizes a kindred spirit in Pluton's slave, he says *ἔμβαλέ μοι τὴν δεξιὰν καὶ δὸς κύσαι καὐτὸς κύσον, καί μοι φράσον κτλ.* But the clasping of the right hand is not an expression of affection, greeting, or farewell; it is also a pledge of good faith. Strepsiades wants from his son a solemn assurance of affection (82) which will induce obedience (86 f.).

82 ἰδού: Pheidippides gets out of bed and does what has been asked of him, saying *ἰδού* (cf. 635) as he does so. He puts on his himation and sandals. **φιλεῖς**: *φιλεῖν* is used of a relationship which can exist between any two people, irrespective of age or sex, including people who also desire each other sexually; it is the strongest word available in Greek for the love of parents and children (e.g. Eur. *Alc.* 302), and shades off through 'be fond of' and 'like' to a minimal emotional content in 'be wont to'.

83 τουτονί: *οὗτος* (like 'this' in modern colloquial English) can be used with reference to people or things not visible to the speaker or hearer; cf. 296, 971, and 1369. *οὑτοσί* may well have been used in this way in Ar.'s time, but it is hard to prove; 1427 *τὰ βοτὰ ταυτί* is not metrically guaranteed, and *Lys.* 1168 is complicated by *double entendre*. Later, there is no doubt: e.g. Dem. xxiii. 211 *Αἰγινήτας τουτουσί . . .* 212 *Μεγαρέας τουτουσί.* The Scholiast remarks that *οὗτος* is often used superfluously in oaths, e.g. *μὰ τοῦτον τὸν Ἀσκληπιόν*, but suggests that Pheidippides' oath is different in that he actually has a statue of Poseidon indoors (*ἔνδον*), to which he is referring, though we cannot see it. This scholion is the product of a theory about statues in the theatre, but the theory may not be well grounded. Later (1478 ff.) we shall see that a herm stands besides Strepsiades' door, and there are strong grounds for believing that a *dinos* stood beside Socrates' door (1472 ff. and p. xi); why should there not be a statue of Poseidon also beside Strepsiades' door? **ἵππιον**: Poseidon Hippios is the god naturally invoked by the horsy Pheidippides; so too the chorus of cavalrymen in *Knights* 551 begins the ode of the parabasis with an invocation *ἵππι' ἄναξ Πόσειδον*.

84 μή μοι γε κτλ.: sc. *ὄμνυε* or *λέγε*. Cf. 433 and p. xxxii.

85 αἴτιος: He does not mean that Poseidon bears him malice, but that the god's sphere of interest is the cause of his troubles. ↓

88 ἔκτρεψον: According to the Scholiast *ἐκστρέφειν* is used of turning clothes inside out, to make them last longer. This suits *ἐκστρέψας* in 554 very well, but it will not do here, for what is wanted of Pheidippides is a change or reversal of direction. The variant *ἔκτρεψον*, which is in any case well suited to *τρόπους*, gives this sense; cf. 813.

89 μάνθαν' ἐλθών: 'Go and learn . . .'; but *where* Pheidippides is to go matters, and the *ἃ ἄν* clause should not be dissociated from *ἐλθών*.

↓ 87 πίθωμαι: rhetorical deliberative (aorist) subjunctive

91 δεῦρο: The two men move further over towards the screen which is across the left-hand side of the skene (cf. p. xi). At some point between now and 125 the beds are removed from the theatre.

92 θύριον: Strepsiades points towards the door in the screen, but it is not the special nature of this door which accounts for the diminutive. In *Thesm.* 26 Euripides points to Agathon's door with the words *ὁρᾷς τὸ θύριον τοῦτο;* and that is probably the permanent central door of the skene, through which Agathon will shortly be 'rolled out' on the theatrical trolley. The diminutive, here and in *Thesm.*, is persuasive (cf. 80); the speaker is going to ask for a favour.

93 ἐτεόν: Cf. 35 and p. xxxii.

94 ψυχῶν: Souls are insubstantial and, as we shall see (198 f., 593 f.), the philosophers are not 'real men' but pale and feeble. This is the point of *Birds* 1553 ff., where Socrates *ψυχαγωγεῖ* and Chairephon appears 'from below' when Peisandros comes, like Odysseus, to the edge of the underworld *δεόμενος ψυχὴν ἰδεῖν*. Cf. p. xx. **σοφῶν**: *σοφία* in Ar., and in the fifth century generally, most commonly denoted an active, creative skill or artistry, for which knowledge, practice, and native wit are all required. Hence *σοφός* means 'accomplished', 'discriminating' (535), 'highly educated', 'brilliant', 'inventive', 'ingenious'; it is often applied, as a term of high praise, to poets. It seldom means 'wise' in the sense implied by the English 'you acted wisely', but it comes close to that when used of men skilled in dealing with people and situations (e.g. 1057). Nowhere in this play does it have a sense intended by the speaker to be derogatory; cf. 331, 520, 522, 772, 895, 1370, 1377. **φροντιστήριον**: *φροντίς* and *φροντίζειν* were already common words. *φροντιστής* (266, cf. 101 n.) and *φροντιστήριον* first appear in this play; they owe something to *δικαστής* and *δικαστήριον*, but something also to nouns in *-της* denoting specialized craftsmen (cf. 1397 n.).

96 ἀναπείθουσιν: '⟨On the subject of⟩ the sky ⟨try to⟩ persuade ⟨us, against established opinion,⟩ by argument . . .' On the order, cf. 145 and 1115; on *ἀναπείθειν*, cf. 77 n.; and on *λέγοντες*, cf. 954. **πνιγεύς**: The idea that 'the air as a whole is, in its shape, more like a *πνιγεύς* than anything' is attributed to Meton in *Birds* 1000 f. *πνιγεύς* ('choker') is a roughly hemispherical cover used in baking bread; it is heated by being placed over a heap of burning charcoal, and the charcoal is then replaced by dough and heaped round the outside of the cover. According to the Scholiast the comparison of the sky to a *πνιγεύς* was made by Hippon, who had been (before this play) ridiculed for it by Kratinos, and perhaps we need look no further than Kratinos for Ar.'s source. Diogenes of Apollonia (*flor. c.* 440), however, thought of the stars as perforations of some kind in a solid covering, and Hippon is linked with Diogenes on a point of embryological doctrine; on the relation between Diogenes and this play cf. also 230, 264 nn.

97 ἄνθρακες: 'And we are the charcoal (sc. which is normally in a *πνιγεύς*)'. Cf. 492, 558, 1372 nn.

98 ἀργύριον: Cf. 876, 1146 f. nn. and p. xix.

99 νικᾶν: Used of winning a lawsuit or an argument or 'carrying the day' in a deliberative body; cf. 115 and 432 n. **καὶ δίκαια κἄδικα:** These words belong to *λέγοντα νικᾶν* as a whole, and should be regarded as object of the participle *or* of the verb.

101 μεριμνοφροντισταί: On *φροντιστής* cf. 94 n. *μέριμνα* (cf. 420, 952) is characteristic of serious poetry and a favourite word of Empedokles in the sense 'philosophical thought'. Eur. *Med.* 1225 f. puts into the mouth of a messenger a gratuitous attack on *τοὺς σοφοὺς δοκοῦντας εἶναι καὶ μεριμνητὰς λόγων*, but it is not clear what type of intellectual he has in mind. The word is not common in prose; Xenophon uses it unselfconsciously, but Pl. *Rep.* 607 C *οἱ λεπτῶς μεριμνῶντες* has a sarcastic ring and may be a quotation. **καλοί τε κἀγαθοί:** Applied in Ar. to persons (except in *Frogs* 1236), this virtually = *χρηστός*, a general word of commendation; sometimes 'excellent' (in the plural, rather like 'good men and true'), in *Wasps* 1256 'decent' or 'nice', and elsewhere the opposite of *πονηρός*. It implies 'of noble birth' or 'wealthy' when the speaker regards nobility or wealth as criteria of excellence, and no doubt many rich and noble men regarded only their own peers as *καλοί τε κἀγαθοί*, but that is not the same as saying that the term objectively denotes a social category.

102 αἰβοῖ . . . 103 λέγεις: *αἰβοῖ* expresses disgust (e.g. 829), even nausea (906). For *γε* cf. 1462. Punctuate after *οἶδα* (cf. 213): 'I know ⟨them⟩! You mean those . . .' The repeated article conveys scorn; it can express other emotions too, including fear. **ἀλαζόνας:** Aristotle defines *ἀλαζών* as a man who claims a respect which he does not deserve, and this accords well with the passages of Ar. in which the word is used (e.g. 449). **ὠχριῶντας:** The intellectual is characteristically pale, because of his indoor life (cf. 120, 1112), but a 'normal' man is expected to be sunburnt, either, if poor, through long hours of work on the farm or, if rich, through outdoor sports (cf. 120). Cf. p. xx. **ἀνυποδήτους:** Cf. 363.

104 Χαιρεφῶν: In Pl. *Ap.* 20 E Socrates calls him *ἐμὸς ἑταῖρος ἐκ νέου*: on his 'hidden' role in the play cf. p. xxx. ↓

105 νήπιον: Almost 'don't talk like a baby!' *νήπιος* is not usual in comic dialogue, but cf. 868.

106 εἴ τι κήδει: A form of appeal used also in *Ach.* 1028. **ἀλφίτων:** 'Meal', coarse-ground and usually barley, the staple cereal of the time, of which *μᾶζαι* were made, here symbolizes (as in 648) 'livelihood', like 'daily bread'.

↓ 104 κακοδαίμων: could be 'jinks' here (χρουσούζης)

107 τούτων: The *μεριμνοφροντισταί*.

108 οὐκ ἄν: Cf. 5 n. and p. xxxii. **εἰ δοίης γε**: We need '*Even* if you gave me . . .', and *εἰ . . . γε* in fact has this sense in *Ach.* 966 *οὐκ ἂν μὰ Δί'* (sc. 'give him a share') *εἰ δοίη γέ μοι τὴν ἀσπίδα.*

109 Φασιανούς: Some ancient commentators thought that Pheidippides is referring to a breed of horse, but the evidence for the meaning 'pheasants' is overwhelming. They may have been bred more for show than for consumption, like the peacocks kept by one Pyrilampes and greatly admired about this date. **Λεωγόρας**: A member of a wealthy and aristocratic family, connected by marriage with Perikles, and father of the orator Andokides.

110 ὦ φίλτατ' ἀνθρώπων ἐμοί: *ἀνθρώπων* is so commonly added to superlatives that the expression is not as powerfully emotive as we might at first think, but the addition of *ἐμοί* gives it a hint of paratragedy; cf. Soph. *El.* 1126 *ὦ φιλτάτου μνημεῖον ἀνθρώπων ἐμοί.*

112 ἄμφω . . . 118 οὐδενί: On the personification of the *λόγοι* in this passage cf. p. xxiii. **ὅστις ἐστί**: 'No matter what it is', i.e. 'on any subject' or 'in any given case'. This makes rather better sense than to suppose that the old rogue is expressing scorn of 'the right' or that he is so unaccustomed to being in the right that its nature is mysterious to him (cf. 1370). **τἀδικώτερα**: The comparative is often used of one of a pair of opposites even when the other is not specified; cf. *νεώτερος* (515, 1370) and *πρεσβύτερος* (959, 993).

115. Cf. 99 n.

117 τούτων: This picks up *ἅ*.

120 διακεκναισμένος: Cf. 103 n.

121 οὐκ ἄρα . . . ἔδει: 'All right, then . . . you won't eat ⟨anything⟩ of mine!'

122 ζύγιος: In a racing-team of four horses (cf. 1407) the two in the middle are *ζύγιοι*, the two on the outside *σειραφόροι* (1300). **σαμφόρας**: Cf. 23 n., 1298.

124 ὁ θεῖος Μεγακλέης: Cf. 46 n., 70.

125 εἴσειμι: Pheidippides goes into the door of Strepsiades' house.

(B) 126–262. STREPSIADES MEETS SOCRATES

(i) 126–83. *Strepsiades and the student*

By now thoroughly worked up (121 ff.), Strepsiades takes the bold decision to go and learn from Socrates, and marches towards the door of the school. Half-way there he is overwhelmed with misgivings about his own inadequacy (129 f.). Then he summons up his courage again and knocks on the door (131 f.).

126 ἀλλ' οὐδ' ἐγὼ μέντοι: The point of *οὐδ'* is '*I*'ll take a strong line, too!' On *μέντοι* cf. p. xxxii. **πεσὼν γε κείσομαι**: The ubiquity of wrestling as a sport would have made this a more vivid metaphor to the Greeks than (e.g.) 'I won't lie down under it!' is to us. It suggests 'I've been thrown, but I'll jump up again.' Cf. 551.

127 εὐξάμενος τοῖσιν θεοῖς: 'I will utter a prayer and then . . .' is an example of 'performative utterance'; the word *εὐξάμενος* constitutes the prayer. Cf. Pl. *Rep.* 432 C *ἕπου, ἦν δ' ἐγώ, εὐξάμενος μετ' ἐμοῦ.—ποιήσω ταῦτα, ἀλλὰ μόνον, ἦ δ' ὅς, ἡγοῦ.* **διδάξομαι**: Simply 'I will be taught'; cf. Eur. *Andr.* 739 *διδάξω καὶ διδάξομαι λόγους. διδαχθήσομαι* does not exist in Attic.

129 οὖν: 'But if I do that . . .' **κἀπιλήσμων**: Socrates' pupils need a good memory (414, 483)—an obvious requirement of the *φιλόσοφος*—and, as we shall see, forgetfulness is one of Strepsiades' besetting weaknesses: 629 ff., 785 ff., 854 f.

130 σκινδαλάμους: Probably 'slivers'; cf. English 'hair-splitting'.

131 τί ταῦτ' ἔχων στραγγεύομαι: 'Why do I keep on hanging back like this?' *ταῦτ'* is used as in *Ach.* 385 *τί ταῦτα στρέφει;* 'What is all this evasion?' *ἔχων* = 'keeping on' (intr.) almost always follows the finite verb (e.g. 509) but the insertion of *ταῦτα* between *τί* and the verb affects the order.

132 ἀλλ' οὐχί: 'Instead of . . .' **παῖ, παιδίον**: Strepsiades knocks on the door. One does not expect the master or mistress of a Greek household to open the door; hence the cry assumes that a slave is within earshot.

133. The man who opens the door to Strepsiades and later tells him about the school and shows him round it shares the philosophical enthusiasms of the school and is obviously an 'initiate' (140 ff.). In these respects he resembles the slave of Agathon in *Thesm.* 37 ff., who talks his master's poetic language, and the slave of Euripides in *Ach.* 396 ff. But he is nowhere called a slave; his opening words are coarsely abusive (133), he behaves with authority (195 ff., 221) and is treated by Strepsiades with deference (138, 200; on 217, *v.* n.). It is therefore pretty certain that the ancient commentators were right in regarding him as a student of philosophy. The school seems to have no slaves—in 1145 Socrates himself comes in response to *παῖ, ἡμί, παῖ, παῖ*—and this suits philosophical poverty; but it also suits the particular humorous development which Ar. has in mind, just as it suits him dramatically to make Herakles answer his own door in *Frogs* 38.

134. The fullest answer that an Athenian can give to the question 'Who are you?': name, father's name, and demotic. We have been given an indication already (65) of the father's name, though not an exact one; we now learn our hero's name for the first time. In other plays we have to wait just as long or longer; in *Birds* the names of Peisetairos and Euelpides are first given in 644 f. In ordinary life it seems that either the patronymic or the demotic could be specified, according to which, in any given case, rendered identification easier; cf. Pl. *Lys.* 203 A, 'I met Hippothales the son of Hieronymos and Ktesippos of the deme Paiania.' Specification of both is formal and often (though by no means always) observable in state documents. The name 'Strepsiadas' is found in a Theban family celebrated by Pindar, and 'Strepsippidas' at Lebadeia in III. Ar.'s name for his hero is determined by the old man's desperation (36 *στρέφει*) and desire to pervert justice (434 *στρεψοδικῆσαι*, 450 *στρόφις*: cf. 1455). The location of the deme Kikynna is not known; but Strepsiades lives 'far off in the country' (138, cf. 210 n.). The deme belonged to the phyle Akamantis; to judge from the infrequency of its occurrence in documentary inscriptions it was not large.

136 ἀπεριμερίμνως: Cf. 101 n. **λελάκτικας**: Whether Strepsiades has really kicked at the door—and whether Athenians (urban or rustic) commonly did so—is hard to say. Probably the humour of the passage lies in the opposite direction; Strepsiades knocked timidly, and is now cowering before the hyperbolically expressed anger of the strange-looking person who has flung the door open. Cf. Karion's attempted bullying of Hermes in *Wealth* 1101, 'Was it you knocking at the door *οὑτωσὶ σφόδρα*?' (as above, 135).

137 ἐξήμβλωκας: In Plato's *Theaetetus* Socrates describes himself as a 'midwife' who brings to birth the ideas of others; the ideas of those who leave his company too soon 'miscarry'. But if this was a metaphor used by the real Socrates and well known, it is remarkable that we do not encounter it elsewhere in Plato or Xenophon. I suspect that Ar. gives this comic metaphor to the student because he has presented Strepsiades to us as a man whose life has been spent among sheep and goats (45, 71), creatures who miscarry easily when frightened by loud noises. Hence Strepsiades is interested to hear about the *φροντίς* which has miscarried.

138 τῶν ἀγρῶν: 'A long way off *in* the country'; cf. *πόρρω c. gen.* The line is a parody of Euripides.

140 οὐ θέμις: That is to say, contrary to rules prescribed, or at least sanctioned, by a god. The expressions *οὐ θέμις* and *οὐ θεμιτόν* are particularly used of divulging secrets to those who have not gone through rites of initiation (cf. 143) or do not belong to a given sex, family, or nationality. Cf. 295.

141 οὑτοσί: 'Here I am, and I've come . . .'; cf. 324 (where *αὑται* corresponds to the English adverb 'there').

143 μυστήρια: The analogy between initiation into mysteries and instruction in difficult subjects is exploited more fully in 254 ff.

(especially 258 *τελουμένους*). The Platonic Socrates also exploits it light-heartedly in *Tht.* 155 E ('Look round carefully to make sure none of the uninitiated can overhear! They're the people who don't believe in the existence of anything they can't grasp in their fists . . .') and seriously in *Smp.* 209 E.

The student comes forward, closing the door behind him; cf. 184 n. and p. xi.

144 ἀνήρετ' . . . 145 πόδας: The construction *ἀνήρετο . . . ψύλλαν ὁπόσους κτλ.* = *ἀνήρετο . . . ὁπόσους ψύλλα κτλ.* is normal (cf. 95 f., 1115 f.); but this instance is unusual in that the controlling verb has two accusatives, *Χαιρεφῶντα* and *ψύλλαν*, of different reference. **ψύλλαν:** Diogenes and Demokritos are known to have been interested in the physiology of animals, fishes, and insects.

146 δακοῦσα . . . 147 ἀφήλατο: The Scholiast alleges that Chairephon had massive eyebrows and Socrates a bald head. On the latter statement cf. p. xviii; on the former, we have no evidence. Reference to portrait-masks is irrelevant, because Chairephon does not appear in the play. Perhaps the comic philosopher, unkempt and dirty, was visualized as having a mass of hair all over his head and face; cf. 836.

148 πῶς δῆτα διεμέτρησε: It is often alleged that Greek intellectuals did not experiment, and it is true that they often said things which simple experiments could have confirmed or refuted; but we do in fact hear occasionally of experiments, and it is important that Ar. makes Strepsiades say 'How did he measure it?', *not* 'Did Chairephon know?' **δεξιώτατα:** *δεξιότης* is a quality of which Ar. boasts in the exercise of his own art (548), and he flatters his audience by calling them *δεξιοί* (521, 527); it is nowhere intended by the speaker to have any derogatory overtones (cf. 418, 428).

149 εἶτα: Cf. p. xxxii. Cf. After writing the check, he then tore it up ↓

150 τὼ πόδε: We regard insects, including fleas, as having six legs. Ar. may have regarded a flea as having two legs (the long back legs) and four arms. It is unlikely, however, that Ar. knew or cared enough about zoology to distinguish between insects, which are all six-legged, and (e.g.) eight-legged arthropods such as spiders; being accustomed to use *πούς* (like *σκέλος*) more often in the dual than the plural, he gave priority to ordinary usage.

151 ψυχείσῃ: It was the wax, after it had been removed from the flea's feet, that needed to cool, not the flea itself, but the run of the rest of the line inhibits any reader or hearer (unless he is also a commentator) from raising any objection to the text, and it is prudent for the commentator to be guided by what he hears in his mind's ear as he imagines himself sitting in the theatre. **Περσικαί:** Worn by women; men wore *Λακωνικαί*. We do not know how they differed from each

↓ or: After he wrote ... up. Cf. also Modern Greek: Αφου εγραψε την επιταγη, μετα την εσκισε. or: Αφου πρωτα εγραψε ...

other or from other types of footwear. The feminine plural noun underlying both terms is *ἐμβάδες* (cf. 719, 858).

152 ἀνεμέτρει: The point of the imperfect may be that the laborious process was still going on when Strepsiades caused it to 'miscarry'; but this is a heavy weight to put on an imperfect tense when the joke about miscarriage is over and done with. **χωρίον**: Mathematicians, from Plato (e.g. *Meno* 82 B) onwards, meant by this an area or two-dimensional figure. Ar. here means (LSJ is wrong) a linear distance; the word is therefore more likely a colloquial term for 'space ⟨between⟩ . . .' than a technical term. Cf. *Il.* iii. 315, where *χῶρον . . . διεμέτρεον* refers to pacing the distance between two adversaries.

153 τῆς λεπτότητος: The earliest datable instance of *λεπτός* in the sense 'subtle', '⟨intellectually⟩ refined' is Eur. *Med.* 529 (cf. *Hipp.* 923 *λεπτουργεῖς*). It is naturally a recurrent word in this play (cf. 230 ff., 320, 359), and is freely used by Ar. thereafter.

154 τί δῆτ' ἄν . . . εἰ: (sc. if you are so impressed by the experiment with the flea) 'What would ⟨you say⟩ if . . .', implying 'How much more impressed you would be!' Cf. p. xxxii.

156 Σφήττιος: Sphettos was a large deme, belonging to the phyle Akamantis; its location is uncertain. We have no other evidence for the deme of Chairephon and cannot be sure that he is not given a false demotic here for the sake of a weak pun on *σφήξ*, 'wasp', to suit the entomological context. A fictitious character can be allocated a demotic for the sake of a pun, e.g. *Lys.* 852 *Παιονίδης Κινησίας*: and a real character may be given a false nationality (830 'Socrates the Melian', *v.* n.) or a false patronymic, e.g. *Ach.* 1131 'Lamachos, son of Gorgasos' (a reference to the Gorgon's head on his shield [574 al.], though he was actually son of Xenophanes). But whether Chairephon came from Sphettos or not, the addition of the demotic strikes an odd note when he has already been mentioned twice; elsewhere, we learn a man's demotic at the same time as we first learn his name. The answer to this problem may lie in the formation, at an early date, of a certain type of orally transmitted anecdote about the wisdom, wit, or prescience of famous men: 'When so-and-so asked him . . ., he replied . . .' The Socrates of the pseudo-Platonic *Theages* tells stories of this kind about himself, and much of Xen. *Mem.* iii consists of such anecdotes, e.g. 10. 6, 'He once went into the house of Kleiton the sculptor, and in conversation with him said . . .' Many of Xenophon's anecdotes do not name the interlocutor, but begin (e.g.) 'Once, when someone was angry . . .', 'When someone else said . . .' This is certainly an old form, and a form which increasingly prevailed in collections of anecdotes and apophthegmata from early Hellenistic times; Diogenes Laertius offers us a great concentration of them. When the virtues of a wise man were being advertised during his own lifetime and in the society to which he belonged, it was more natural to give the story added point by specifying, as precisely as possible, the person who could testify to the truth of the story. I suggest that in adding *ὁ Σφήττιος* to the name of Chairephon Ar. is parodying a contemporary form of oral anecdote and making the student, as it were, 'say his piece' in praise of his teacher; in production, we should make the student take a deep breath, look over Strepsiades' head, and speak as if he were addressing a larger audience.

157 f. We do not know whether anyone seriously believed that a gnat's hum was produced through its anus (Aristotle did not), but the idea suits the comic preoccupation with excretion (cf. 9 n.).

163 κοῖλον . . . 164 πνεύματος: Lit., '⟨Since it is a⟩ hollow ⟨place⟩ adjoining (a) narrow ⟨one⟩'. We know little about the study of sound in the fifth century (Archytas, who was interested in it, was a generation younger than Ar.), but Alkmaion had already explained hearing as made possible by the entry of air through a comparatively narrow passage into a cavity (*κενός, κοῖλος*) within the ear.

165 σάλπιγξ: The Greek trumpet, unlike ours, had a chamber at the end of the tube, the maximum diameter of this chamber being slightly larger than that of the exit from it.

166 διεντερεύματος: *ἐντερεύειν* is used of a fishmonger gutting fish. By *δι-* Ar. means to suggest words which imply perspicacity or thoroughness, e.g. *διειδέναι* (168) and *διερευνᾶν*.

167 ἦ ῥᾳδίως . . . 168 ἐμπίδος: What would be sarcasm in the mouth of a more sophisticated character is naïve enthusiasm on the part of Strepsiades, as he shows by his own inconsequential arguments in 1247 ff., 1283 ff. **φεύγων ἂν ἀποφύγοι:** Strepsiades uses *φεύγειν* in its legal sense, 'being a defendant', and both the aorist aspect (cf. 63, 65, 67, 580 ~ 587) and the prefix *ἀπο-* combine to give *ἀποφυγεῖν* the sense 'succeed in getting off'. Cf. *Ach.* 177 *φεύγοντ' ἐκφυγεῖν*, 'escape by flight'.

169 δέ γε: In the dialogue of Ar. and Plato *δέ γε* often picks up the thread after another speaker has put in a remark.

170 ἀσκαλαβώτου: The creature called *ἀσκαλαβώτης* here and (several times) in Aristotle is no doubt the same as that which is portrayed (with the helpful label *ΑΣΚΑΛΑΒΟΣ*) on a Corinthian vase. The same creature is called *γαλεώτης* in 173 f. Dialectal difference in the naming of species is common enough, but that the same speaker in one and the same context should use two different names for the same species is hardly credible. The obvious conclusion is that one name is more specific than the other, and we would expect the one which comes first to be the less specific; a story beginning 'He was bitten by a snake' and containing the statement 'there was a cobra in his bed' sounds more plausible than it does if we interchange 'snake' and 'cobra'. Aristotle in fact uses *ἀσκαλαβώτης* in a very general sense, but names *ἀσκαλαβῶται* and *σαῦραι* ('lizards') separately; this fact, in conjunction with the picture on the Corinthian vase, indicates that *ἀσκαλαβώτης* means 'gecko', and since more than one species of gecko is found in Greece *γαλεώτης* can be the name of a species.

171 ὁδούς: The plural is natural, since the moon does not follow the same track every night (cf. also 584).

172 περιφοράς: This is the earliest surviving example of *περιφορά* in an astronomical context, but it would be surprising if it was not already an established term. The *περιφοραί* of the moon are the ways in which it is apparently carried round, according to an ascertainable but complicated scheme, by the revolving sky; its *ὁδοί* are its own paths from horizon to horizon, which it follows within the limits of those *περιφοραί*. **εἶτ'**: Cf. p. xxxii.

173 ὀροφῆς: 'Ceiling' in *Wasps* 1215, where the scene imagined is indoors; but Socrates must go outside to look at the moon, so 'roof' here. (The articles *ὀροφή* and *ὄροφος* in LSJ are confusing.) **νύκτωρ**: Almost '—and it was night, of course—'; a reminder that Socrates could not see what was coming to him. **γαλεώτης**: Cf. 170 n.

174 ἥσθην: Strepsiades has guffawed, and now says why; cf. 1240.

175 δέ γ': The student ignores Strepsiades' reaction and goes on to another anecdote in praise of Socrates' intelligence. Cf. 169 n.

176 εἶέν: Here 'Well, well!', expressing surprised interest and leading on to a question. **τἄλφιτ'**: Cf. 106 n. *πρός* is 'to deal with the problem of'. **ἐπαλαμήσατο**: The word sounds poetic, and in *Ach.* 659 it occurs in a close adaptation of Euripides, but the context in *Peace* 94 is less obviously paratragic, and the point of putting a high-sounding word into Strepsiades' mouth at this moment is not clear, unless its juxtaposition with the down-to-earth *πρὸς τἄλφιτα* is judged humorous enough. Given *παλάμη* in *Wasps* 645 and Hdt., and *παλαμᾶσθαι* in Xen., we may suspect that they were not strikingly poetic in Ar.'s time, but part of a common Ionic–Attic vocabulary which was increasingly shed—in accordance with the normal processes of linguistic change—in the fourth century. There are other examples.

177 τέφραν: Socrates starts as a cook does with *ἄλφιτα*; but it is ash that he sprinkles, for instead of dinner the students are to have a geometry lesson. Socrates uses for this purpose a spit which in happier circumstances would be used for roasting meat. The ancients often drew their diagrams not on papyrus (unless they were composing a treatise for circulation) but on wax or in dust or sand (on the ground, or, as here, on a table). Cf. Cic. *Tusc.* v. 64 *a puluere et radio*.

178 εἶτα: Cf. p. xxxii. **διαβήτην**: 'Taking it ⟨to serve as⟩ a pair of compasses'. Compasses are used by Meton in *Birds* 1003 and mentioned among carpenter's tools in Plato.

179 ἐκ τῆς παλαίστρας κτλ.: It is tolerably clear that the purpose of stealing the himation is to sell it and buy food. The point may be simply that Socrates' high-minded diversion of the students' interest from their empty bellies to the abstractions of geometry did not last long, and he had recourse to the crudest remedy. The stealing of clothes and property from baths, wrestling-schools, and gymnasia was a well-known category of crime, severely punished; Socrates later in the play makes Strepsiades part with his clothes (497 ff., 856 ff., 1498), and the idea of Socrates as a surreptitious thief of vessels at a party appears in Eupolis. The problem lies in the definite articles: '*the* wrestling-school' (there were many at Athens) and '*the* himation'; we could rid ourselves of the latter article by emendation (Demetrios' quotation has *ἱμάτιον*, but as he runs the line together with 149 he must have been quoting from memory), but not of the former. The Platonic Socrates frequented wrestling-schools, but they belong to a way of life alien to that of the Aristophanic Socrates (cf. 417, 1054), and we are not to imagine that the students have a wrestling-school on the premises. Possibly 'he stole his himation from the wrestling-school' was a colloquial expression meaning 'he's not to be trusted' or 'he hasn't a penny to his name', and the joke lies in the incorporation of such an expression in an actual narrative. Another possibility is a malicious story already told against Socrates and known to Ar. Or again, the student may be referring to a *fourberie* (of which he is rather proud) as if his hearer must know of the incident already; cf. the definite article in similar reminiscences in *Wasps* 236 ff., 1201 f.

180 Θαλῆν: Thales was the only intellectual immortalized (hence *ἐκεῖνον*, 'that ⟨famous⟩') in folklore. He was believed (Hdt. i. 74. 2) to have foretold the solar eclipse of 585, and there were anecdotes which cast him in the role of the 'absent-minded professor'. When Meton speaks in *Birds* Peisetairos claims (1009), 'The man's a Thales!'

181 ἄνοιγ': Strepsiades' mood of naïve enthusiasm is raised to fever-pitch; cf. 167 f. n. **ἀνύσας:** Cf. p. xxxii.

183 μαθητιῶ: The form of the word is meant to remind us of urgent physical needs; cf. 1387 *χεζητιῴην*. This reinforces the tone of Strepsiades' demand.

(ii) **184–99.** *Strepsiades encounters the other students*

The student wheels round with an expansive gesture towards the screen which has hitherto concealed the left-hand third of the skene. This screen is now moved away and out of the theatre, along the left *eisodos*, by the men who have been concealed behind it. Its removal reveals to us

(i) a door into the skene itself (195 ff. n., 505 ff., 1493 ff.), beside which stands, instead of the customary herm and other statues (cf. 83, 1478 nn.), a cup on a column (1473 f. n.), (ii) at least two groups of students, each group containing at least two members (187, 191), (iii) three large pieces of apparatus (200, 201, 206), and (iv) a bed, on which there is a chaplet and a receptacle containing flour (254, 255 f., 261 f.). We do not yet see Socrates suspended in the air (218 n.).

184 ὦ Ἡράκλεις: A normal reaction (sometimes without *ὦ*, sometimes with *ὦναξ* instead) to a sudden, extraordinary, or frightening sight. **θηρία**: Not quite as hostile as it sounds; cf. 1286. Rather 'what on *earth* are these creatures?' than 'what kind of *animals* are these?'

185 τῷ σοι δοκοῦσιν εἰκέναι: The question is an artificial 'feed' for the joke in 186 (cf. 501 f. n.), but less artificial to a Greek than to us, because of the use of *εἰκόνες* in popular humour (cf. 559 n.) and the formality of their expression, 'I liken you to . . .'

186 τοῖς Λακωνικοῖς: The Spartans captured on Sphakteria, off Pylos, in the summer of 425 were kept at Athens until the spring of 421. Spartans did not often surrender, and the prisoners remained as lasting a boost to the morale of Athens as a blow to that of Sparta; presumably they were pale and emaciated after two years of captivity. *Λακωνικοί* (Thucydides and other historians say *Λακεδαιμόνιοι*, and so do all inscribed documents) is normal in comedy (e.g. *Peace* 212); cf. *Ach.* 830 *θάρρει Μεγαρικέ*. The variant *τῆς Λακωνικῆς* would be oddly pedantic in comic dialogue, especially with reference to a famous recent event; the corruption was caused by identity of pronunciation of *η* and *οι* in late Greek and by the familiarity of expressions such as *ἐς Μεθώνην τῆς Λακωνικῆς* (Thuc. ii. 25. 1) in historians and commentators.

187 ἐς τὴν γῆν: Not bending right down, like the students of 191 f., but in an attitude of deep thought.

188 βολβούς: Pl. *Rep.* 372 C reckons *βολβοί* and *λάχανα* as the staple cooked vegetables of an agrarian community; like many Greek vegetables, they were gathered, not cultivated.

191 γάρ: Cf. p. xxxii. **ἐγκεκυφότες**: They must have their heads almost on the ground, to provide a sufficient contrast with 187 and give point to the joke of 193.

192 δ': *δέ* in an answer of this kind often repeats the *δέ* of the question. Cf. Pl. *Cra.* 398 C *ὁ δὲ δὴ "ἥρως" τί ἂν εἴη; — τοῦτο δ' οὐ πάνυ χαλεπὸν ἐννοῆσαι*. The variant *γ'* is a banalization of this rare idiom. **ἐρεβοδιφῶσιν . . . Τάρταρον**: In Hesiod Tartaros is one of the primary beings (with Chaos, Earth, and Eros) and one of the extremities of the cosmos, but Erebos is a child of Chaos and less remote. Similarly in Hom. *Il.* xvi. 327 Erebos is simply the dark realm of Hades and the dead. The distinction is not observed in *Birds* 691 ff. Hesiod might

↓ 187 ἀτάρ: but, yet; (also marks rapid transition).

have found 'they are scrutinizing Erebos under Tartaros' strange; Ar.'s audience would not.

193 τί . . . βλέπει: 'Because their heads are down' would be the simple answer; but the line is a 'feed'. *πρωκτός* is 'anus' (cf. 165, 1300 n.), not 'buttocks', and the superficial resemblance between anus and eye makes *βλέπει* more vivid.

195 εἴσιθ': i.e. *εἴσιτε*. The fact that the action is taking place in the theatre in the open air is recognized and utilized in the dramatic situation, regardless of the shortness of the time since we had to imagine that Strepsiades was being allowed *into* the school. **ὑμῖν**: Implied by the Scholiast (*μὴ . . . εὕρῃ ὑμᾶς*), and obviously right (*ἡμῖν* MSS.); the student guide himself is not afraid of being caught outside by Socrates (221), and he tells Strepsiades that it is wrong for 'them' (198 f.), not 'us', to stay outside. Confusion between *ἡμεῖς* and *ὑμεῖς* is universal in medieval texts. We do not yet see Socrates suspended in the air; cf. 218 n.

196 μήπω . . . 197 ἐμόν: In real life Strepsiades would want to put his problem to Socrates (cf. 182), but the lines are a 'feed'. **ἵνα | αὐτοῖσι**: This is a striking 'enjambement'.

(iii) **200–21.** *Strepsiades is shown the equipment of the school*

200. Strepsiades now begins to look at the objects and apparatus lying about. **γάρ**: Cf. p. xxxii.

201 ἀστρονομία: The text leaves the nature of these objects to our imagination, and in imagining what Ar. would have presented to his audience as 'astronomy' we must guard against anachronism. Big star-maps are an obvious possibility, but in view of what the Greeks did know and could measure in Ar.'s time instruments for accurate sighting and alignment, coupled with accurate time-measurement, must also have existed. Astronomy was among the subjects taught by Hippias of Elis and had long been one of the main subjects of scientific speculation; the Socrates of Plato (*Rep.* 528 E ff.) and Xenophon (*Mem.* iv. 7. 4 ff.) is unsympathetic towards empirical astronomical observation.

202 γεωμετρία: Rulers, set-squares, and compasses (cf. 177 f.), and possibly also sighting instruments. **τί**: 'For what?', 'in what way?'; cf. 22 n.

203 ἀναμετρεῖσθαι: It is doubtful whether Ar. believed, or intended his audience to believe, that the interest of the sophists in geometry was wholly due to the practical purpose which the etymology of the word indicates. Strepsiades has asked 'What is the *use* of it?' and gets a fair answer, which is also the answer needed to introduce the joke about cleruchies. The Platonic (*Rep.* 526 DE) and Xenophontean

(*Mem.* iv. 7. 2 f.) Socrates do not speak with one voice on the intellectual value of geometry. **κληρουχικήν**: When Athens defeated the revolt of Mytilene in 427 she confiscated Mytilenean land and allocated it (*κλῆρος*, 'allotment') to a large number of Athenian citizens; this was not a novelty, for she had taken a similar measure against Chalkis at the end of the sixth century.

204 ἀστεῖον: *ἀστεῖος* is to *ἀστικός* rather as 'urbane' is to 'urban', but of much wider application than 'urbane'; commonly 'attractive', 'agreeable', 'inviting', 'charming'. (The sense 'witty', *pace* LSJ, is totally absent here; there is nothing 'witty' about *οὔκ, ἀλλὰ τὴν σύμπασαν*.) Cf. 1064.

205 σόφισμα: Essentially, an exercise of *σοφία* (cf. 94 n.). But a derogatory sense was gaining ground in Ar.'s time: cf. *Birds* 431, where it is coupled with terms of abuse. **δημοτικόν**: Strepsiades thinks that 'geometry' is some (magical?) device for distributing all the land in the world gratis to Athenian citizens like himself.

206 περίοδος: Hdt. v. 49 relates how Aristagoras of Miletos displayed at Sparta in 499 'a bronze plaque on which a *περίοδος* of the whole earth had been inscribed, with all the sea and the rivers'. The earliest Greek map may have been constructed by Anaximandros; certainly the idea of a map of the known world was not a novelty to Ar.'s audience.

208 δικαστάς: The joke against the Athenians' insistence on trying cases, both domestic and imperial, by large juries is a standby of Ar.; cf. the whole plot of *Wasps*. In general, ridicule of Athenian weaknesses, and even the coarsest vilification of the audience, are characteristic of Old Comedy. Cf. 494 ff., 520, 587 ff., 1096 ff., and 1172 ff.

209 ὡς: Cf. *Ach.* 335 *ὡς ἀποκτενῶ*, 'I swear' (or 'I can assure you') 'I'll kill him!'

210 καὶ ποῦ: *καί* with an interrogative indicates surprise, often coloured with indignation; cf. 717. **Κικυννῆς**: Cf. 134 n. Since membership of a deme was hereditary through one's father, we might have expected men bearing the demotic *Κικυννεύς* to be distributed throughout Attica by Ar.'s time; but even eighty years later a speaker can tell a jury that the majority of members of the deme Halimus live in the deme itself (Dem. lvii. 10). In 1322 Strepsiades cries for immediate help to 'neighbours, relations, and demesmen'.

212 παρατέταται: Euboia is much longer than it is wide, and in such a case *τείνειν* means 'lay' or 'put' (not 'stretch' in the sense 'make longer'); it also lies *παρά* the coast of Attica and Boiotia. The term occurs in geographical information given by Hdt., and there is no reason to see here the mathematical sense of *παρατείνειν* which is found (only) in Pl. *Meno* 87 A.

213 παρετάθη: The English idiom 'laid out' closely corresponds. **ἡμῶν . . . καὶ Περικλέους**: The cities of Euboia revolted from Athens in 446 and were reduced by an Athenian force of which Perikles was the (or a) commander. When Strepsiades says 'us' he means not simply 'Athens', but his own generation; as he is now an old man, we are to imagine him as having fought in the Euboian campaign. For the expression 'by us and Perikles' cf. Thuc. v. 3. 4, 'Kleon and the Athenians erected trophies . . . and enslaved the women and children of Torone.'

215 **ὡς . . . 216 πάνυ**: Rather as he thought of geometrical instruments as a means of turning all the world's land into land which could be appportioned to Athenian citizens, Strepsiades thinks of a map as a magical means of bringing places nearer together or further apart, and he naturally wants Sparta removed as far away as possible. **μεταφροντίζετε**: This is implied by the scholion *μεταβουλεύεσθε* and supported by *μέγα φρ-* in the *Suda*. It gives a positive joke (the coining of a word) and is far preferable to the repetition of *πάνυ*, for which it is hard to see any stylistic or theatrical reason.

217 **νὴ Δί'**: In the MSS., part of the student's utterance; but with *οὐχ οἷόν τε* we would want *μά*, not *νή*, and if we emended to *μά* further emendation would be needed to make the line scan. In view of *Wasps* 1506 *νὴ Δί' ᾠψώνηκ' ἄρα* there is no doubt that *νὴ Δί'* should be assigned to Strepsiades. **οἰμώξεσθ' ἄρα**: Strepsiades' rapid swing from servility to petulant threats of violence is in character; cf. 57 f., 121 ff. and p. xv.

218 **φέρε . . . ἀνήρ**: While the audience's attention is held by the noise and movement of 217, the theatrical crane swings Socrates out above the heads of Strepsiades and the student; he is in a basket (cf. 226 n.) hooked on to the end of a rope, and is gazing up at the sky. The appearance of the students at 184 was enough to go on with, and 195 makes better sense if Socrates is not visible then. **γάρ**: Cf. p. xxxii.

219 **αὐτός**: 'The master.' *αὐτὸς ἔφα* was a formula used to introduce sayings attributed to Pythagoras, but *αὐτός* is more familiar in domestic contexts, e.g. Men. *Sam.* 41 ff. *ἔνδον ἐστὶν αὐτός* and *αὐτὴ καλεῖ, τίτθη, σε*. Cf. the Latin *ipse*. **ὦ Σωκράτης**: The MSS. have *ὦ Σώκρατες*. If this is right, then either (i) Strepsiades calls out to Socrates, Socrates takes no notice, and Strepsiades hopes that the student can attract his attention more effectively, or (ii) Strepsiades, awestruck, invokes Socrates as one would a god, without necessarily expecting an answer 'Yes, Strepsiades?'; cf. 293 *καὶ σέβομαί γ', ὦ πολυτίμητοι*. The student's words 'call him yourself' (221) would rather favour interpretation (ii). But *ὦ Σωκράτης* is preferable; cf. Pl. *Phdr.* 227 c *ὦ* (*sic* edd.) *γενναῖος* (Socrates, on hearing Phaidros' summary of Lysias' argument) and Men. *Epitr.* 720 f. *τίς ἐσθ' ὁ κόπτων τὴν θύραν; ὦ* (= 'Ah, I see it is . . .') *Σμικρίνης . . . ἥκων*.

220 οὗτος: 'You', addressed to the student. This mode of address is not confined to calling from a distance.

221. The student goes through the door of the school.

(iv) **222–62.** *Socrates accepts Strepsiades as a pupil*

223 Σωκρατίδιον: Cf. 80 n. **ὦ 'φήμερε**: *ἐφήμερος*, 'creature of a day' is highly poetic (*Birds* 687 *ἐφημέριοι* is in epic parody), and pretentious as a mode of address. Socrates is looking down on Strepsiades as a god might look down from Olympos on a mortal.

224 πρῶτον μέν: Cf. p. xxxii.

225 ἀεροβατῶ: The word is no doubt coined for the occasion by Ar.; it is, in fact, the earliest attested verb in *-βατεῖν*. Given *ναυβάτης* and the poetic *ἱπποβάτης* and *ὀρεσσιβάτης*, it is meant to suggest 'the air is the medium in which I move.' **περιφρονῶ**: Socrates means 'think *about*', as 741 *περιφρόνει τὰ πράγματα* shows; but Ar. gives him the word (it can mean 'despise') for the sake of the joke in 226.

226 ἀπὸ ταρροῦ: The usual ancient interpretation was that *ταρρός* here means a bar such as hens perch on. If this is right, Socrates is sitting or standing on a horizontal bar or plank, steadying himself by holding on to ropes which go from each end of the bar to a hook suspended from the crane. Yet *ταρρός* normally means 'rack' (*Od.* ix. 219, Theokr. 11. 37), 'mat', 'row of oars', later 'wing', 'eyelashes'—almost anything, that is, which is composed of units parallel and close together; and the Scholiast says 'plaiting of osier'. It seems most likely Socrates is sitting comfortably in a sling formed by attaching a rope from each corner of a mat to the hook on the end of a rope. To that extent we can speak of him as sitting in a 'basket'; but that does not mean that a Greek would have called a modern shopping-basket *ταρρός*. **τοὺς θεούς**: The sun is, of course, a god to Strepsiades. **ὑπερφρονεῖς**: The variant *περιφρονεῖς* spoils the joke, and in any case *φ|ρ* is prosodically objectionable (cf. p. xxxviii). Strepsiades treats Socrates as physically above the divine beings who are the object of his study, and this is one reason for *ὑπερ-*; but also, *περιφρονεῖν* has something of the flavour of *περιορᾶν*, 'regard as unimportant', and *ὑπερφρονεῖν* is always (intr.) 'be proud' or (tr.) 'depise', as in 1400 *τῶν νόμων . . . ὑπερφρονεῖν*. The English 'look down on' is a suitable translation here.

227 εἴπερ: 'If that's what you're doing', not 'if you must'. The nearest parallel in comedy is *Frogs* 38 f. *ὡς κενταυρικῶς ἐνήλαθ', ὅστις* (sc. *ἦν*). **γάρ**: 'No, because . . .'

228 μετέωρα: Fundamental to Ar.'s portrait of Socrates (cf. 333, 360, 1284 and p. xix), and the point on which he is directly challenged by Pl. *Ap.* 19 BC, 26 DE.

229 εἰ μή: 'Except by . . .'. **νόημα**: Usually '*a* thought' or 'idea', but used by the philosophical poets in an abstract sense; in Xenophanes *δέμας* and *νόημα* are contrasted, and Empedokles said 'the blood around the human heart is *νόημα*'.

230 λεπτήν . . . 233 φροντίδος: Aischylos used *ἰκμάς* of the liquid content which distinguishes the living body from the 'withered' ghost, and Socrates' words transfer this concept to the plane of mental activity, but the underlying 'doctrine' is different. Diogenes of Apollonia believed not only that air, *λεπτομερέστατον* of all substances, is a god endowed with life and intelligence (cf. Socrates' prayer, 264), but also that the soul, which is *λεπτότατον* in every living creature, is air differing in density, humidity, and temperature from species to species and from individual to individual. Perception is the movement of air within the body by air without; thinking, the activity of 'clean, dry air', is impaired by moisture (*ἰκμάς*). Animals are inferior to men in thought (*διάνοια*) because 'they breathe air from the earth'; Diogenes had to devise a special explanation for the inferiority of birds. Cf. the principle of 'perception of like by like' in Parmenides and Empedokles. **οὐ γὰρ ἀλλ'**: Given *Frogs* 58, 'Don't make fun of me, brother; *οὐ γὰρ ἀλλ'* I'm in a bad way', it is hard to draw sharp distinctions between *οὐ γὰρ ἀλλά, καὶ γάρ*, and *γάρ τοι*. **ἕλκει**: Diogenes, as part of an explanation of magnetism, held the theory that bronze and iron ingest and secrete moisture (*ἰκμάς*), and thought this proved by their rusting when smeared with vinegar. Magnetic pyrites, 'drier and earthier' than iron, draws (*ἕλκει*) iron towards itself in order to ingest the surplus moisture of iron. Diogenes' general theory was that moisture 'finds its own level'. Ar. plainly has some idea of Diogenes' theories; how far his audience had, is another question and not, on present evidence, answerable, for the comic effect is adequate if they merely recognize the *kind* of terms in which intellectuals talk. If Ar. had been a doxographer summarizing Diogenes and not a comic poet ridiculing him, he would have said the opposite of what he says in 232 f., for loss of moisture from soul to earth would increase the efficiency of thought, not impair it.

234 κάρδαμα: We have no other evidence for Diogenes' use of 'cress' as an illustration, but this passage is itself evidence not to be taken lightly. Cf. 148 n.; and Diogenes said something about plants in connection with cognition.

235 πῶς φῄς . . . 236 κάρδαμα: The total misunderstanding of a scientific argument by an ignorant man is an obvious form of humour. So in *Thesm.* 19, when Euripides has expounded how 'Aither in the beginning . . . devised the eye in imitation of the sun's orb, and bored the ears as a funnel for hearing', his old relative says 'Because of the funnel, then, aren't I to hear or see?'—and there, as here, the joke is dropped once it has been made.

241 ἄγομαι, φέρομαι: One ἄγει the cattle and slaves of an enemy (and him too, for enslavement, if one can catch him), and φέρει his portable goods. But ἄγειν καὶ φέρειν is used as a set phrase, as in Hecuba's cry (Eur. *Tro.* 310) ἀγόμεθα φερόμεθα. **ἐνεχυράζομαι:** Having described the legally justified threats of his creditors at first in highly rhetorical terms, Strepsiades now descends to sober fact; cf. 35 n.

243 νόσος: Cf. 74 n. Strepsiades speaks like a patient describing his symptoms to a doctor. **δεινὴ φαγεῖν:** Horses eat a lot, and Pheidippides' indulgence has eaten up Strepsiades' livelihood; but the terminology is doubly appropriate, since diseases too 'consume' or 'devour' the sufferer. Philoktetes in Soph. *Phil.* 313 speaks of himself as βόσκων τὴν ἀδηφάγον νόσον.

245 ἀποδιδόντα: i.e. which enables the person who uses it to escape repaying his debts. We do not need to think here of the personification of the λόγοι, for Greek can use verbs in a 'causative' sense much more freely than English; cf. 770 and 782.

246 ὀμοῦμαι κτλ.: 'I'll swear to you by the gods that I'll put it down' (i.e. 'pay it').

247 ποίους: Without the article, a scornful exclamation, not a question (contrast 1233); cf. 367. **πρῶτον:** Cf. p. xxxii.

248 νόμισμ': In Classical prose always 'currency', 'coinage'; but though not a synonym of νόμος, its affinity is obvious, and we could translate 'Gods aren't current coin with us.' **τῷ γὰρ ὄμνυτε:** 'Why, what do you use for oaths?', not 'What do you swear *by*?'; note τοὺς θεούς in 246, and cf. 1232.

249 [ἦ] σιδαρέοισιν: The inhabitants of Byzantion, unlike most Greek states in the fifth century, used an iron coinage, and Attic writers refer to it by its local (Doric) name, σιδᾱρέοι. ἦ gives the line one syllable too many. In a Thoman MS. it appears at the end of 248, necessitating the elision ὄμνυτ'; but Ar. does not elsewhere end a line with a prepositive interrogative immediately after a pause, and deletion of the word is preferable. It was probably interpolated through mistaken scansion of σιδαρέοισιν as -δᾰ-. Deletion of ἦ leaves us with two successive questions, of which the second is not introduced by any interrogative word; for this cf. 481, *Ach.* 612 f., and *Birds* 1203 (all of which have τί in the first of the two questions).

251 εἴπερ ἐστί γε: 'If, that is, it is really possible'. Cf. 322, 'εἴ πως ἐστίν, I want to see them now with my own eyes.' It would be inappropriate for Strepsiades at this moment to express doubts about the existence or validity of the supernatural world which Socrates promises to reveal to him.

254 κάθιζε: The 'initiation' of Strepsiades (cf. 140 n.) now begins. The process includes (1) enthronement (254 f.), (2) coronation with a chaplet (255 ff.), and (3) baptism (260 ff.). For (1) and (3) parallels in initiation rites are known, notably Demosthenes' description (xviii. 259) of the assistance given by Aischines to his mother, who (Demosthenes alleges) initiated people into a cult from which, no doubt, they believed themselves to derive some advantage: 'purifying the initiates and wiping them off' (*ἀπομάττων*) 'with the (sc. prescribed) clay and bran and raising them up (*ἀνιστάς*) from their purification' (evidently they had been sitting or lying down) 'and telling them to say . . .'. Enthronement was part of the initiation rites of the Corybantic cult, as Pl. *Euthd.* 277 D shows, referring to dancing round the initiate *ὅταν τὴν θρόνωσιν ποιῶσιν*. The chaplet is an element not attested in our evidence for initiations, but (see below) Ar. has a good comic reason for introducing it. **σκίμποδα**: This was one of the objects revealed by the 'opening' of the school; cf. 184 n. How a *σκίμπους* differed from other kinds of bed we do not know, but everything (including the squalid discomfort of the school) combines to suggest that it was not luxurious. Plato's Socrates slept on one at home (*Prt.* 310 C). Since Plato (*Euthd.*) refers to dancing round the seated initiate, it is possible that Socrates now prances absurdly round Strepsiades.

255 τουτονί: Socrates now picks up from the bed a chaplet, which (for comic effect) we should imagine made of the ugliest and untidiest wild plants.

256 ἐπὶ τί στέφανον: Chaplets were worn on so many festive and ceremonial occasions that in real life there would be no grounds for apprehensiveness if one were told 'Put on this chaplet'—especially when a process plainly leading to one's own initiation had begun. But Ar. consistently makes Strepsiades apprehensive (as in 129 f., 506 ff.) and wishes also to achieve comic incongruity by making him resemble certain characters in legend who were offered as human sacrifices. Vase-paintings do not show animal victims wearing chaplets, but Iphigeneia is crowned before her sacrifice by Kalchas in Eur. *Iph. Aul.* 1567: *κρᾶτά τ' ἔστεψεν κόρης*.

257 ὥσπερ με . . . θύσετε; The postpositive *με*, object of *θύσετε*, gravitates to a position after the leading word in the clause, as in *Wasps* 363 f. *ὥσπερ με γαλῆν . . . τηροῦσιν*. **τὸν Ἀθάμανθ'**: Sophokles, in one of his two plays called *Athamas*, represented Athamas as standing at the altar of Zeus, wearing a chaplet, about to be offered as a sacrificial victim—a predicament from which he was rescued by Herakles. Phrixos and Helle were the children of Athamas, ruler of Boiotia, and of the goddess Nephele. Athamas also married (or seduced) the mortal Ino. Ino by a trick contrived to ensure that the crops did not grow, and when Athamas sent to Delphi to seek a remedy Ino corrupted the envoys, and they reported that Phrixos must be sacrificed to Zeus. Nephele, however, rescued Phrixos and Helle by means of the golden ram. It is not quite clear how Athamas himself came to the altar, but Hdt. vii. 197. 3, although he locates these events at Halos in Thessaly, gives what he calls 'the local story', and makes Athamas' grandson (not Herakles) his rescuer, perhaps provides the essential clue in saying that the people intended to sacrifice Athamas as a *καθαρμός*, an expiatory sacrifice, at the behest of an oracle. Possibly Nephele turned against her husband the weapon which Ino had used against their children. The fact that the mother of Phrixos and Helle was named Nephele may have given Ar. the idea for the joke; whether or not he expected his audience to notice that depends on how fresh either tragedy was in their memory, and we do not know their dates.

258. 'No, no, we do all this to those who are being initiated.'

260 τρῖμμα: This (~ *τρίβειν*, cf. 447 and 870 n.) implies 'practised'. **κρόταλον:** 'Castanet' is an obvious slang term for a fluent talker; cf. 448 ff., and Eur. *Cycl.* 104, where Silenos speaks of Odysseus as *κρόταλον* and is reproved for discourtesy. **παιπάλη:** 'Fine flour' has the same point as *λεπτός*: cf. 444 ff. and *Birds* 430 f. *πυκνότατον κίναδος, σόφισμα, κύρμα, τρῖμμα, παιπάλημ' ὅλον.*

261 ἀλλ' ἔχ' ἀτρεμεί: Socrates is now sprinkling Strepsiades with material from a receptacle on the bed (cf. 184–99 n.), and the old man is fidgeting.

262 καταπαττόμενος: καταπάττειν 'sprinkle'.

(C) 263–509. STREPSIADES MEETS THE CLOUDS

This section of the play combines (i) the *πάροδος*, the entry of the Chorus, which in this play is in a form unique among Ar.'s plays, and (ii) an argument in which Socrates gives Strepsiades elementary instruction in Sophistic doctrines and beats down his objections. This second element corresponds to that part of *Wasps* (546 ff., especially 648 ff.) in which Bdelykleon beats down the defences of Philokleon, and to *Birds* 460 ff., where Peisetairos wins over the birds; it differs, however, in that, although Socrates has to meet opposition from Strepsiades on the intellectual level, he does not have to bring about any change of disposition, and the Chorus is well disposed from the start. Hence, despite its formal resemblances to the *ἀγῶνες* of *Wasps* and *Birds*, its mood is different; Socrates' efforts to convince Strepsiades on questions of doctrine are balanced by Strepsiades' own efforts to demonstrate his acceptability as a student; the true *ἀγωνία* is Strepsiades'.

(i) 263–74. *Socrates' invocation*

Socrates looks up at the sky, raises his arms, and intones a prayer in a voice of exaggerated solemnity. The invocation contains many of the features of actual prayer: (i) The call for silence (263). (ii) The list of deities, in the form A B *τε* (264 f.); cf. 563 ff., 595 ff. The fact that three gods are named is not as significant here as in certain other circumstances; cf. 1234 n. (iii) The request to the gods to 'appear' (266) and 'come' (269). (iv) The list, in the form *εἴτε . . . εἴτε . . .*, of the places where the god might be at the moment of prayer. (v) The request that the god shall 'accept the sacrifice' (274, *v.* n.) and 'rejoice in the rites'.

263 εὐφημεῖν: *εὐφημεῖτε* was the call for silence uttered before a public prayer or ceremony. In comic verse, it may be represented by *εὐφημεῖν χρή*. Socrates' use of the formula with reference to an audience of one ('the old man') has rather the effect of standing back and addressing a couple of friends loudly as 'ladies and gentlemen!' **ἐπακούειν:** When A prays to B or calls upon him, B, if well disposed, *ὑπακούει*: cf. 274 *ὑπακούσατε* and 360. If C is within earshot, C *ἐπακούει*. Textual variation is common, as here.

264 ὦ δέσποτ' . . . 265 βροντησικέραυνοι: Here Socrates' gods are Aer, Aither, and Clouds (cf. 253); in 365 they are the Clouds alone, and in 423 f. Void, Clouds, and Tongue; in 627 he swears by Breath, Void, and Aer. On *ἀήρ* cf. 230 n. *αἰθήρ* is treated as a god in 570 (*v.* n.). In archaic poetry *αἰθήρ* is what lies above and beyond the medium in which we live, between this medium and the sky; knowing better than the Greeks what 'sky' is, we have no word for *αἰθήρ*. The distinction between *ἀήρ* and *αἰθήρ* is not always made consistently either by philosophers or by poets, though Pl. *Phd.* 111 AB makes one. **μετέωρον:** The belief that the earth maintained a position of equilibrium in the centre of the universe was as old as Anaximandros, and Anaximenes was the first to make *ἀήρ* the medium which supports it (cf. Pl. *Phd.* 99 B). Diogenes' doctrine that the earth is round and *ἠρεισμένη ἐν τῷ μέσῳ* (cf. Pl. loc. cit. *ὁ δέ . . . βάθρον* [sc. *τῇ γῇ*] *τὸν ἀέρα ὑπερείδει*) belongs to this tradition.

267 τουτί: Strepsiades pulls his himation up over his head.

268 τὸ δέ . . . ἔχοντα: An exclamation of indignation at his own improvidence; cf. 819. *κυνῆν* is object of *μηδέ . . . ἔχοντα*.

269 πολυτίμητοι: One of the commonest epithets in invocations and exclamations. **ἐπίδειξιν:** i.e. to display yourselves to Strepsiades; the terminology belongs to rhetoric, not religion.

270 'Ολύμπου: The first four of the five places specified go round from the north anti-clockwise; from the fourth, Lake Maiotis, to the fifth, Mt. Mimas, we go back from north-east to east. It is doubtful whether the sequence represents the order in which a Greek thought of the 'points of the compass'. Olympos is named first because that is where one would expect gods to be, and the mountain is apt to be covered by clouds; the 'gardens of Ocean' come second, because they are at the ends of the earth, like the Ethiopians (*Il.* i. 423 f.), the Hyperboreans, and the Isles of the Blessed, all favoured by the gods; and the Nile third, because of current interest in theories about rain and the Nile flood (272 n.).

271 πατρός: In 569 f. Aither is the Clouds' father; but Okeanos, child of Earth and Sky in Hesiod, was father of all rivers and of 'three thousand daughters', and he has as good a title to *πατήρ* as Zeus. **κήποις**: The gardens of the Hesperides, fruit-trees 'beyond Ocean' and 'at the ends of the earth' (Hesiod). Herodotos thought of Ocean not as a river encircling the earth but as a sea lying west from the Mediterranean. The location of the supernatural gardens in the west was clearly established by Ar.'s time (Eur. *Hipp.* 742 ff.). **ἵστατε**: When *χορός* is its object, *ἱστάναι* = 'bring into being'; cf. Dem. xxi. 51 *τοὺς χορούς . . . καὶ τοὺς ὕμνους τῷ θεῷ ποιεῖτε* ~ ibid. *χοροὺς ἱστάναι* (in both, the state, as deciding on the content of festivals, is the subject). In *Birds* 217 ff. Apollo *θεῶν ἵστησι χορούς* by playing his lyre. We are meant to think of the clouds as taking the initiative in the singing and dancing in which both they and the nymphs participate.

272 Νείλου προχοαῖς: From early times a stock expression for the Nile Delta, Lower Egypt. Diogenes, as a contribution to speculation about the summer-flooding of the Nile, argued that the sun drew up water vapour from land and sea and that the Nile was augmented by subterranean water which rushed into it to compensate for the process of desiccation; cf. 1279 ff. Since the dative is not accompanied by a preposition, the translation '*for* the Nile Delta' has been suggested; but the language here is elevated, and that makes all the difference. I question whether Ar. would have been at once so accurate and so allusive as is suggested; and surely the audience, with the exception of some individual who happened to have a precise recollection of Diogenes' argument, would have taken the dative in a locative sense. No solution is wholly satisfactory, but it is easier to believe that Ar. regarded the clouds as (somehow, invisibly) drawing their moisture during the winter from the 'surplus' produced by the Nile in summer. **χρυσέαις**: Naturally golden, since the clouds are divine; so in Hesiod Zeus sends Iris to bring water of Styx *ἐν χρυσέῃ προχόῳ*.

273 Μαιῶτιν: The Sea of Azov. **Μίμαντος**: Mimas, a mountain on the ↓ peninsula of Erythrai, is 'windy' in *Od.* iii. 172, 'rocky' in the *Hymn to Apollo*. 'Snowy' is something of an exaggeration.

274 θυσίαν: There is none; but there normally would be on the occasion for so elaborate a prayer (cf. *Peace* 974 ff. *ὦ σεμνοτάτη βασίλεια θεά . . . δέξαι θυσίαν τὴν ἡμετέραν*), and the formula has 'taken charge'. **χαρεῖσαι**: Another important element in prayer; cf. *Thesm.* 977 ff.

↓ Arrowsmith: Mimas is a mountain on the coast of Ionia.

Ἑρμῆν . . . ἄντομαι . . . ἐπιγελάσαι προθύμως ταῖς ἡμετέραισι χαρέντα χορείαις.

(ii) **275–90.** *Strophe*

The Chorus sings both the strophe and the antistrophe while still approaching the orchestra, and does not enter the orchestra until 326. We may wonder whether its singing was fully audible to the audience, and, if not, whether this contributed at all to the failure of the original play.

In addition to normal metrical responsion, strophe and antistrophe respond in vocabulary and in sound. Note especially the placing of **ἀρθῶμεν** in 276 and **ἔλθωμεν** in 299; these two words are the kernel of the Chorus's response to Socrates' prayers ἄρθητε (266) and ἔλθετε (269). The other obvious elements of linguistic responsion are 277 εὐάγητον ∼ 300 εὔανδρον γᾶν, 283 κελαδήματα ∼ 306 καὶ ἀγάλματα and 287 μαρμαρέαισιν αὐγαῖς ∼ 310 παντοδαπαῖσιν ὥραις. This phenomenon is common in tragedy, especially, but not exclusively, in lamentation.

(1) 275 ∼ 98
– ⏑ ⏑ – ⏑ ⏑ –

(2) 276 f. ∼ 99 f.
– – – | ⏑ ⏑ – | ⏑ ⏑ – ⏑ ⏑ | – – – – |

(3) 278–86 ∼ 301–9
– ⏑ ⏑ – ⏑ ⏑ – | ⏑ ⏑ – ⏑ ⏑ |
– ⏖ – ⏗ – | ⏑ ⏑ – | ⏑ ⏑ – ⏑ ⏑ – | ⏑ ⏑ |
– ⏑ ⏑ – | ⏑ ⏑ – | ⏑ ⏑ – ⏑ ⏑ |
– ⏖ – ⏑ ⏑ – | ⏗ – ⏑ ⏑ |
– ⏗ – ⏑ ⏑ – | ⏑ ⏑ – ⏑ ⏑ |
– ⏖ – | ⏑ ⏑ – ⏑ ⏑ – ⏑ ⏑ |
– ⏑ ⏑ – ⏑ ⏑ – ⏑ ⏑ – | ⏑ ⏑ – ⏔ ||

(4) 287 ∼ 310
– ⏑ ⏑ – ⏑ | – – |

(5) 288–90 ∼ 311–13
– ⏑ ⏑ – ⏑ ⏑ – | ⏑ ⏑ – ⏑ ⏑ |
– ⏑ ⏑ – ⏑ ⏑ – | ⏑ ⏑ – ⏑ ⏑ |
– – ⏑ ⏑ – ⏑ ⏑ | – – |

(1) is a dactylic hemiepes. (2) is a dactylic hexameter. (3) is a sequence of thirty-one lyric dactyls, grouped by word-end 4+6+4+4+4+4+5. Lyric dactyls occur also in 569 f. ∼ 601 f., but are uncommon in comedy. In 569 f. ∼ 601 f., as in *Birds* 250 ff. and 1748 ff., they belong to an invocation. The end of each group is not verse-end; note correption of **-ται** in 304 and 307. (4) is an aristophanean (*ch ba*). For this clausula

to a sequence of lyric dactyls cf. Eur. *Alc.* 591 f. ~ 600 f. (5) is a sequence of eight lyric dactyls followed by a paroemiac; alternatively (but less in accord with (2) and (3)), dactylic hemiepes + anapaestic trimeter + dactylic trimeter. Cf. Soph. *Oed. Tyr.* 171 f. ~ 182 f. – ⏑ ⏑ – ⏑ ⏑ – ⏑ ⏑ – ⏑ ⏑ | × – ⏑ ⏑ – ⏑ ⏑ – ⏑ ⏑ – ⏓.

On lyric alpha cf. p. xxxi.

275 ἀέναοι: Simply 'eternal'; the etymological connection with *νάειν* = 'flow' was increasingly lost to sight.

276/7 ἀρθῶμεν . . . φύσιν: For the syntax cf. the epigram cited in Thuc. vi. 59. 3, *οὐκ ἤρθη νοῦν ἐς ἀτασθαλίην*, and *ἐξεκόπην* in 24 above. *ἀρθῆναι* is not always 'be raised' (by an external agency), but often 'rise' (e.g. 266). *φύσις* here is physical appearance, as in 503. **εὐάγητον**: This variant, 'bright', 'shining', not *εὐάητον*, is required; *ἀῆναι*, 'blow', does not produce any known instances of *ἄητος* or compound *-άητος*. *εὐᾱγής* = *εὐαυγής*, and *εὐάγητος* is to *εὐαγής* as *ἀμάθητος* (Phrynichos Comicus) is to *ἀμαθής*.

281 τηλεφανεῖς σκοπιάς: The clouds have already said that they will descend on to the mountain-tops (279 f.). One might prefer an internal accusative here. *σκοπιά*, however, is not a *nomen actionis* but = 'vantage-point' (e.g. Hdt. v. 13. 1, on which LSJ is misleading), usually a mountain-top or hill-top. Hence the hill-tops are part of the terrestrial scene upon which the clouds will look.

282 καρπούς τ' ἀρδομέναν ἱερὰν χθόνα: Most MSS. have *θ'* also after *ἀρδομέναν*, but this makes *καρπούς* curiously bald and isolated, by contrast with all the other items in strophe and antistrophe alike. 'The land which has its crops watered' is preferable; again, cf. 24 and 276/7 n. Any land or city can be described as *ἱερός* in so far as gods are worshipped there and it is under their protection.

285 ὄμμα γὰρ αἰθέρος: A poetic cliché.

289 ἀθανάτας ἰδέας: Probably genitive singular; conceivably accusative plural, since both constructions occur with words meaning 'take away from'; but the plural might suggest, inappropriately, that every cloud was permanently different in appearance from every other.

(iii) **291–7.** *Reactions to the Strophe*

292 μυκησαμένης: The Scholiast suggests that a theatrical machine, *βροντεῖον*, was used at 290 to imitate thunder, and obviously both Socrates' words and Strepsiades' reply would be inappropriate if the Chorus had sung faintly and sweetly; but the music, by *crescendo* and *diminuendo* on low notes, could give the desired impression, and after what has been sung in 288 we do not want to suggest to the audience an imminent downpour.

293 καὶ σέβομαί γ': Picking up -σεπ-: 'I *do* revere it.' Pl. *Phd.* 74 D is similar: . . . ἢ ἐνδεῖ τι . . .; — καὶ πολύ γε ἐνδεῖ. **πολυτίμητοι**: Cf. 269 n., 328.

293 βούλομαι . . . 295 χεσείω: Cf. 9 n.

296 τρυγοδαίμονες: Obviously 'comedians', a humorous distortion of τραγ-, as in *Ach.* 499 τρυγῳδίαν ποῶν, blended with the disparaging κακοδαίμων. **οὗτοι**: Cf. 83 n.

297 κινεῖται: 'Is on the move'. **σμῆνος**: 'Swarm', an eccentric term for a company of deities; in Kratinos σοφιστῶν σμῆνος is derogatory. **ἀοιδαῖς**: ἀοι- for ᾠ- is pretentious, in anapaestic dialogue; but cf. Kratinos, καὶ Πολυμνήστει' ἀείδει (= ᾄδει) μουσικήν τε μανθάνει.

(iv) **298–313.** *Antistrophe*

In the strophe the Chorus sang 'Let us visit the earth'; now they sing 'Let us visit Attica.'

299 λιπαράν: Like ἰοστέφανος, a stock epithet of Athens. Pindar uses λιπαρός of many other places also, including Egypt.

300 εὔανδρον . . . 301 πολυήρατον: With these *laudes Atticae* cf. Soph. *Oed. Col.* 668–719 and Eur. *Med.* 824–45. 'Land of Kekrops' is a stock term.

302 σέβας . . . 304 ἀναδείκνυται: They give pride of place to the Eleusinian Mysteries (ἀρρήτων = 'not to be divulged', and ἵνα = 'where', as normally in inscriptions of the time), because possession of this cult gave Athens an international standing in religion comparable with that of Delphi and Olympia. The Scholiast notes also the connection between rain and the growth of crops, and suggests that Demeter and Iacchos are the deities of whom the Clouds would think first.

305 οὐρανίοις: sc. 'there are', the force of which extends to the end of the antistrophe. The Scholiast points out an antithesis between θεοὶ οὐράνιοι and Demeter and Persephone, θεαὶ χθόνιαι (cf. Hdt. vi. 134. 1 f.), whose province has been described in 302–4.

310 παντοδαπαῖσιν ὥραις: A recurrent element in praise of Attica is its piety, as manifested in the number and magnificence of its sacrifices, processions, and festivals. πρόσοδοι virtually = πομπαί, 'processions'; cf. Dem. xviii. 86 θυσίας τοῖς θεοῖς καὶ προσόδους ~ 216 θυσίαι καὶ πομπαὶ τοῖς θεοῖς.

311 ἦρι . . . 313 αὐλῶν: The City Dionysia (8–13 Elaphebolion) naturally earns special mention. **ἐρεθίσματα**: 'Provocations' seems odd to us, but all artistic events at the Dionysia were competitive; it was alien to the Greeks to pretend that one is not elated by victory and humiliated by defeat, and competitors were not expected to show a sporting generosity to each other. Cf. Ar. on the subject of his rivals (524 f., 551 ff.).

(v) **314–411.** *Socrates explains the Clouds to Strepsiades*

315 σεμνόν: The relation of the word to *σεβ-* is prominent here; cf. 48 n. **ἡρῷναι:** In the fifth century *ἥρως* was above all one of the great figures of the Trojan and Theban wars, and these were worshipped with prayer and sacrifices; there are exceptional cases, such as the worship of the founder of a colony even during his lifetime, which led to a debasement of the term *ἥρως* in Hellenistic times. *ἡρῷναι* were such as Helen and Penelope.

316 ἀργοῖς: Ar. makes Socrates speak out of character and from the standpoint of the Attic farmer, to whom work is necessarily physical; cf. 332.

317 γνώμην: Here abstract: 'intelligence', 'judgement'. **διάλεξιν:** Ar. is coining words, here with a predilection for the formative *-σις*.

318 τερατείαν: Ar. would probably have classed much of Herodotos as *τερατεία*, the relation or exposition of the marvellous and unusual, and would not have drawn a firm distinction between fairy-tales and speculation on natural phenomena. **περίλεξιν:** Cf. 317 n. **κροῦσιν καὶ κατάληψιν:** Both 317 f. and Strepsiades' response show that these words refer to techniques of argument. The passage must be taken in conjunction with *Knights* 1377 ff., where affected young men are portrayed as discussing Phaiax's oratorical gifts and coining words in *-ικός*: *καὶ γνωμοτυπικὸς καὶ σαφὴς καὶ κρουστικὸς καταληπτικός τ' ἄριστα τοῦ θορυβητικοῦ*. *κρούειν* is 'strike' (an audience with a telling point, or an opponent with an argument which discomfits him). In Pl. *Tht.* 154 E and *Prt.* 336 C *κρούειν* and *ἐκκρούειν* are used metaphorically of verbal argument, in the former case with an elaborate build-up of the metaphor. *καταλαμβάνειν* is 'check' (an unfavourable reaction from the audience or an argument in which an opponent trusts); in the sense 'grasp', 'comprehend' the word is not Classical. Both terms are used of the playing of musical instruments, and their application to rhetorical criticism must have been secondary.

319 ταῦτ' ἄρ': 'So that's why ...'; cf. 335, 353, and 394 n.

320 λεπτολογεῖν: Cf. 153 n. **καπνοῦ:** Appropriate because of its resemblance to clouds (cf. 330), but already established as a derogatory term; cf. Eur. *Hipp.* 954 *πολλῶν γραμμάτων ... καπνούς*. **στενολεσχεῖν:** Modelled on *ἀδολεσχεῖν* (cf. 1480 n.). *στενός* here is rather like *λεπτός* (cf. 153 n.), 'finicky'; in Pl. *Grg.* 497 C Kallikles says to Socrates contemptuously: *ἐρώτα δὴ σὺ τὰ σμικρά τε καὶ στενὰ ταῦτα.*

321 νύξασ': Cf. 318 n. on *κροῦσιν*.

323 Πάρνηθ': Anyone who stands in the theatre in the sanctuary of Dionysos at Athens and looks towards Parnes will find that the Akropolis looms over him and blocks the view. But we should not infer from this that the play was composed for performance in some other theatre; the action represented occurs at some unspecified place in Attica, and almost anywhere except under the shadow of the Akropolis one can point to clouds gathering over Parnes. Probably Ar. intended the actor to compromise with theatrical conditions by pointing, not too precisely, past the east or west end of the Akropolis.

324 αὗται: Cf. 141 n.

325 κοίλων . . . δασέων: The clouds are imagined as blotting out Parnes from the tops downwards, filling the re-entrants and covering the wooded slopes. **πλάγιαι**: 'Approaching from the side' takes account of the actual position of the Chorus in the theatre, made even more explicit in 326.

326 εἴσοδον: Now the Chorus is entering the orchestra, via what we (but not Ar.; cf. *Birds* 296) call the *parodos* (a word first attested in connection with theatrical buildings at Eretria in III in.). Strepsiades' exaggerated short-sightedness is possibly introduced by Ar. as a lead into this humorous rupture of dramatic illusion. **οὕτως**: *ὁρῶ* does not scan, and *ἀθρῶ*, prosodically undesirable (cf. p. xxxviii), is an obvious ancient or medieval emendation. *οὕτως* refers to Strepsiades' stance and peering gesture.

328 πολυτίμητοι: Cf. 219, 293 nn.

330 καπνόν: The variant *σκιάν* does not scan, for its second syllable is long.

331 σοφιστάς: *σοφιστής* in Ar.'s time could still be used as a synonym of *σεσοφισμένος*, 'skilled in an art'; cf. 547. The word was applied to great poets and musicians, seers and sages. The practitioner of an art is normally also a teacher of apprentices, and in Eur. *Hipp.* 921 that implication of *σοφιστής* is necessary. Our passage may be the earliest example of the sense 'teacher of undesirable or superfluous accomplishments'. But Plato and Xenophon represent the word as used by and of teachers of rhetoric such as Protagoras in the 430s.

332 Θουριομάντεις: The Athenian foundation of Thurioi (between 446 and 443) was no doubt an occasion for much divination and prophecy, like the dispatch of the Sicilian Expedition in 415. So too a pedlar of oracles is one of the nuisances with which Peisetairos has to deal at the founding of Nephelokokkygia in *Birds* 959–91. **ἰατροτέχνας**: Whether Ar. intends a condemnation of doctors as a whole or only of the writers of medical theory is uncertain. The analogy of *χειροτέχνης*, 'craftsman', suggests the former, but *τέχνη* is so wide a word that distinctions should not be pressed too hard. Medical theory of the time certainly took account of astronomy and meteorology, and the boundary between medicine and philosophy might often be uncertain. **σφραγιδονυχαργοκομήτας**: *-αργο-* (cf. 316 n.) and *-κομήτας* (cf. 14 n.) are plain enough. *σφραγίς* is 'seal' (commonly set in a ring), and *ὄνυξ* can mean the gem 'onyx'. This was used in signet-rings, and if that is the meaning here *σφραγιδονυχαργοκομῆται* are well-to-do, fashionable idlers who wear valuable rings. But they are keeping odd company, and we should consider the commoner meaning of *ὄνυξ*, 'fingernail'; the reference is then to unkempt creatures, like the Socratics, whose only 'seal' is the marks they can make on wax with their nails. Ar., I think, intends a pun, and Socrates can make the point clear by a gesture with his forefinger.

333 κυκλίων τε χορῶν: In Ar. fr. 149 (from *Gerytades*) Kinesias the dithyrambic poet (cf. *Birds* 1372–1409) represents *κύκλιοι χοροί*, distinguished from tragedy and comedy. **ᾀσματοκάμπτας**: On *καμπή* cf. 969, 971 nn. **μετεωροφένακας**: Trygaios on his return from Olympos tells his slave that he saw 'two or three souls of *διθυραμβοδιδάσκαλοι*' up in the sky (*Peace* 829), and Kinesias in *Birds* 1372 ff. sings all the time of flying through the air. Perhaps the metaphor of flying (not unknown to earlier poets) was overdone by the fifth-century dithyrambic poets with reference to the practice of their own art.

334 βόσκουσ': Picking up *βόσκουσι* from 331; cf. *Thesm.* 498 *οὐδ' ἐκεῖν' εἴρηκέ πω, ὡς . . .* 501 *οὐκ εἴρηκέ πω.* **μουσοποοῦσιν**: Here, and in what follows, the types of *σοφισταί* mentioned in 332 are ignored.

335 ταῦτ' ἄρ' . . . 338 νεφελᾶν: Strepsiades cites 'dithyrambic' expressions (with lyric alpha and first declension genitive plural in *-ᾶν*), one of which (335 *στρεπταίγλαν*) is attributed by the Scholiast to a known poet, Philoxenos of Kythera; if our other evidence for him is true he cannot have composed dithyrambs by the time of the revision of *Clouds*, let alone by 423. **στρεπταίγλαν**: *αἴγλη* meant (*inter alia*) 'bracelet'; *στρεπτός* = 'plaited', 'twisted', or, as a noun, 'collar or bracelet of twisted metal'. *στρεπταίγλα δάϊος ὁρμά* is a possible description of the zigzag lightning which flashes between storm-cloud and earth. For the form of the adjective, implying masc. *στρεπταίγλᾱς*, cf. *Knights* 1181 *ἡ Γοργολόφα* ~ *Ach.* 567 *γοργολόφα* (masc. voc.) *φανείς*.

336 Τυφῶ: The hundred-headed Typhos (Typhoeus, conflated at an early date with Typhaon) was buried beneath the earth (*Il.* ii. 782 ff.), but Hesiod thinks of him as generating the storm-winds, and in the tragic poets *τυφώς* is certainly a violent wind.

337 γαμψούς τ': The connective, offered only by one MS, is needed (as in 336 and 338), unless *γαμψοὺς κτλ.* is in apposition, a metaphorical description of the same phenomenon (clouds or storms) as *ἀερίας διεράς*.

338 ἀντ' αὐτῶν . . . 339 κιχηλᾶν: The reference may be to the entertainment given by the choregos to the dithyrambic chorus (cf. *Ach.* 1155 f. on choregos and comic chorus); no doubt the poet would be invited, in return for what Ar. must have regarded as creative effort hardly comparable with that of a dramatist. But it is also a stock joke, dating from the days when Simonides, Pindar, and Bacchylides were invited to the courts of tyrants and wealthy families, to treat lyric poets as parasites. This is implied by *Birds* 904–57, where the poet who has composed *μέλη . . . κύκλια . . . κατὰ τὰ Σιμωνίδου* (917 ff.) in honour of Nephelokokkygia comes in the hope that Peisetairos will understand *Πινδάρειον ἔπος* (939) and reward him. Strepsiades caricatures the language of lyric poetry by overdoing *-ᾶν*. *καταπίνειν* is often used of swallowing food. Thrushes were a standard delicacy.

340 μέντοι: Cf. p. xxxii.

342 ἐκεῖναί γ': sc. the clouds with which he is familiar.

343 δ' οὖν: 'Anyway', implying 'although I don't *know*, I can tell you what they *look* like', is better sense than the variant *γοῦν*, which would be appropriate if Strepsiades had offered a positive opinion and were now adducing partial evidence for it.

344 ῥῖνας: The joke is mysterious; the Scholiast suggests that the Chorus wore masks with grotesque noses—but why?

345 ἀπόκριναί νυν: Socrates, in true tutorial style, leads Strepsiades towards the answer.

347 παρδάλει: One would not have thought that the Greeks were familiar with leopards, but a large spotted feline appears in school scenes on Attic red-figure vase-paintings. Leopards were, of course, (like centaurs) familiar motifs in sculpture. **εἶτα τί τοῦτο**: 'Well, what about it?' or 'What does that mean?'

348 ὅτι: Cf. Eur. *Ion* 232 f. *πάντα θεᾶσθ' ὅτι καὶ θέμις ὄμμασι*. With *βούλεσθαι*, *ὅτι* *c. ind.* occurs where we might have expected *ὅτι ἄν* *c. subjv.*; cf. 439. **κᾆτ'**: 'And so . . .' **κομήτην**: Cf. 14 n. The Scholiast states that an individual named Kleitos is under attack here; this information presumably comes from a compiler of *κωμῳδούμενοι* who found Kleitos ridiculed in some other play both for long hair and for the habits of the *ἄγριοι* in 349.

349 ἀγρίων: The statement of the Scholiast that men exceptionally addicted to pederasty were called *ἄγριοι* is supported by Aischin. i. 52 (on the habits of Timarchos): 'these *ἄγριοι* . . . in whose houses he has been welcomed'. **λασίων**: Whether or not a hairy body was popularly believed to be a sign of the pederast, or merely characteristic of 'the son of Xenophantos', we do not know. **τὸν Ξενοφάντου**: One Hieronymos, according to the Scholiast; and a man of that name is ridiculed in *Ach.* 388 ff. as having *σκοτοδασυπυκνότριχά τιν' Ἄϊδος κυνῆν*, probably a mass of hair overshadowing his face.

350 μανίαν: 'Craze' rather than 'perversion'; cf. pp. xxv f. **κενταύροις**: Centaurs were notoriously hybristic and indiscriminately indulgent to their appetites. 'Centaurs' was one of many slang terms for over-enthusiastic pederasts.

351 Σίμωνα: Cf. 399. The statement of the Scholiast that he was *σοφιστής* is probably a guess.

352 ἐγένοντο: The aorist, as often, generalizes about past and present alike.

353 Κλεώνυμον: The hapless Kleonymos was alleged to have 'thrown away his shield', sc. in order to run away from a battle and save his skin, and he was never allowed to forget it: cf. *Knights* 1372, *Wasps* 19, *Peace* 1295 ff., and *Birds* 1473 ff. To call a man *ῥίψασπις* was actionable slander (Lys. x. 1 ff.), but Kleonymos perhaps found it imprudent, impracticable, or undignified (cf. Lys. x. 2) to prosecute Ar.

354 ἔλαφοι: Proverbially timid; cf. *Il.* ii. 225.

355 Κλεισθένη: The stock effeminate of Old Comedy: cf. *Birds* 829 ff. and *Frogs* 426 ff. It appears from *Ach.* 117 ff. and *Knights* 1373 f. that (no doubt through an endocrine disorder) he found it hard to grow a beard.

356 χαίρετε: A formal greeting; cf. 358 and 609. **εἴπερ τινὶ κἄλλῳ**: A formula of entreaty, similar to the common *εἴ ποτε* / *καὶ νῦν*.

359 λεπτοτάτων: Cf. 153 n. **λήρων**: Ar. associates *λῆρος* with Socrates also in *Frogs* 1497. **ἱερεῦ**: Whereas a normal priest administers ritual, sacrifice, and prayer Socrates worships his false gods by devoting himself to 'subtle nonsense'.

361 Προδίκῳ . . . σοὶ δέ: The humorous point is that Prodikos was the most distinguished intellectual of the time and an elegant writer acceptable even to men of such conservative tastes as Xenophon (*Mem.* ii. 1. 21), whereas Socrates could be regarded as a pretentious parasite and no artist. Saying 'you and Prodikos' to him is rather like saying 'you and Einstein' to a journalist-astrologer.

362 βρενθύει . . . παραβάλλεις: This description was accepted by Plato (*Smp.* 221 B) as applicable to Socrates' bearing in the retreat from Delion in 424.

363 κἀνυπόδητος: Cf. 103.

364 σεμνόν: Cf. 48 n. The variant *τερπνόν*, appropriate to food (*Ach.* 881), music (*Eccl.* 889), and sex (*Lys.* 553), is ill assorted with *ἱερόν* and *τερατῶδες*: the voice of the clouds scared Strepsiades in 293 ff. and is *σεμνός* in 315.

365 μόναι: Socrates goes back on this in 424.

366 ὑμῖν: If *ἡμῖν* were right, Strepsiades would already be identifying himself with the school, which seems wrong at this stage. On *ἡμ-* / *ὑμ-* cf. 195 n.

367 ποῖος: Cf. 247 n. **οὐδ' ἐστὶ Ζεύς**: Possibly *οὐδέ* here = *οὐ γάρ*, but better sense is given by 'Zeus doesn't even exist' (cf. 902), sc. much less act.

368 πρῶτον: Cf. p. xxxii.

369 αὗται δήπου: There seems to be no true parallel to this apparently impatient *δήπου*, '*They* do, of course!', but *δήπου*, often diffident, can be used when the speaker is actually confident, and Socrates may be using a bland tutorial ploy: 'Well, there's no alternative, is there?'

370 πώποτ' . . . ἤδη: 'Ever yet'.

371 χρῆν: sc. if you were right in thinking that it is Zeus who rains. **αἰθρίας ὕειν αὐτόν:** The variant *αἰθρίας οὔσης*, which would necessitate deletion of *αὐτόν*, is not required: (cf. *Birds* 1089 *χειμῶνος* ~ *Knights* 883 *χειμῶνος ὄντος*), and there is a positive advantage to Socrates' argument in retaining *αὐτόν*. The argument is of scientific type, but very crude, for it leaves open the hypothesis that clouds are simply the instrument of Zeus; but it perhaps exploits an ingrained feeling that Zeus is the sky and that clouds intervene between us and the sky.

372 τῷ νυνὶ λόγῳ: Strepsiades means 'what you were saying a moment ago' (cf. 825) rather than 'the argument you are in the middle of expounding'. **προσέφυσας:** The word seems to be similarly used in Aisch. *Supp*. 276, but the interpretation of that line is not straightforward.

373 διὰ κοσκίνου οὐρεῖν: Whether this was a traditional joke told to Attic children or a comic idea of Ar., we do not know.

374 τοῦθ' ὅ: '—That's the thing that . . .'

376 ἐμπλησθῶσ' . . . 378 παταγοῦσιν: Speculation on the cause of thunder and lightning goes back at least to Anaximandros. Herakleitos attributed thunder to the interaction of winds and clouds; Anaxagoras came nearest to what Socrates is now propounding, that thunder is a 'collision of clouds'. **ἀνάγκην:** Prominent as a cosmological principle in the fifth-century philosophers. They did not all mean the same thing by it; it could (and can) be regarded either as a set of rules laid down by the gods or as a chain of cause and effect implicit in the material world. Socrates is represented (cf. 405) as inclined to the latter interpretation. Strepsiades unwittingly asks the right question.

379 ὥστε: When an infinitive depends on a verb, there is no rigid rule on the presence or absence of *ὥστε*.

380 δῖνος: Empedokles believed that the sky rotates at high speed round the earth, and he used the word *δίνη*, but the connections in which he used it are far from clear. It was Anaxagoras who made the rotation of the universe the first act of Mind, from which the diverse elements in the universe came into being, but he used *περιχωρεῖν* and *περιχώρησις*. Diogenes may have adopted the theory of primeval and continuing rotation, and there are slight indications that he did, but we do not know what he called it. Rotation was fundamental to the atomists, and Demokritos used the word *δῖνος*, as did Antiphon. Ar.'s audience would have been familiar with *δίνη*, 'rotation', 'whirling', but *δῖνος* to them meant a certain type of vessel; that humorous possibility, however, is reserved until 1472 ff., and here a different one is exploited in Strepsiades' reply.

381 ὁ Ζεὺς οὐκ ὤν: Lit., 'this fact (*τουτί*) had escaped my notice, ⟨I mean⟩ Zeus ⟨had escaped my notice⟩ not existing.' The use of substantival subjects throughout, without recourse to infinitives or subject-clauses, makes the following *ἀλλ'* intractable in literal translation, though natural enough in proper translation: '. . . ⟨I mean,⟩ that Zeus does not exist, but Dinos rules . . .' **Δῖνος**: The word suggests to Strepsiades that someone connected with Zeus (*Δι-*) has overthrown Zeus as ruler just as Zeus overthrew Kronos; cf. 1471. *-ῖνος* occurs in well-known proper names, e.g. *Φιλῖνος*, and Sophron used *παλλακῖνος* in the sense 'son of a concubine'.

382 οὐδέν πω: Socrates has in fact offered an adequate explanation, but Strepsiades wants the evidence (385), and Ar. is leading up to a lengthy joke about excretion; cf. 295.

383: = *οὐκ ἤκουσάς μου ὅτι φημὶ τὰς νεφέλας κτλ.*

385 τῷ: 'On what grounds?', 'by what argument?' **ἀπὸ σαυτοῦ**: The attempt to group phenomena as alike in mechanism and differing only in scale is a reasonable scientific and philosophical procedure (cf. Eryximachos and Diotima in Pl. *Smp.*, especially in 186 AB ~ 188 AB and 207 A ff.).

386 Παναθηναίοις: A great public festival (the 'small' Panathenaia was held annually, the 'great' Panathenaia every four years) included the sacrificing of many animals, and was therefore an occasion for overeating of meat and soup. Each colony and ally of Athens was required to provide a cow for sacrifice at the Great Panathenaia.

387 κλόνος: Used in epic and lyric of the turmoil of battle, and never in Classical prose, but it reappears in late Hellenistic literature in the sense '⟨physical⟩ agitation', and it may have been a recognized medical term (ctr. 74 n.); we get a glimpse of the scale of medical terminology in Ar.'s day from the reference in Thuc. ii. 49. 3 to 'all the evacuations of bile which have been named by the doctors'.

388 δεινὰ ποεῖ: 'Grumbles', 'is angry'; cf. 583.

390 παππάξ . . . 391 παπαπαππάξ: Possibly Strepsiades puts his tongue between his lips and blows rhythmically, a sound for which no alphabet makes adequate provision. **ἐπάγει**: 'Steps up' the pace.

394 ταῦτ' ἄρα . . . ὁμοίω: Everywhere else in Ar. initial *ταῦτ' ἄρα* signals a change of speaker (e.g. 319, 335), and in 353 above, though the sense does not compel us to posit a change, it makes sense and nearly all the MSS. exhibit it. Here only a minority of MSS. gives this crude etymology to Strepsiades. It is as surprising that Strepsiades should etymologize as it is right that Socrates should do so, for etymology was an interest of the sophists. There is a possible defence of *ταῦτ' ἄρα* in continuous speech; in *Birds* 486 *διὰ ταῦτ' ἄρα* exactly = *ταῦτ' ἄρα*, and in *Thesm.* 166 *διὰ τοῦτ' ἄρα* is a continuation of one speaker. *βροντή* and *πορδή* are not much alike; but metathesis of *ρ* is a recurrent phenomenon in most Greek dialects, and *βροντή* may have been commonly pronounced *βορ(ν)τή*.

396 καί: The thread of the *πόθεν*-question is picked up again. **ζῶντας περιφλεύει**: Either 'singes them alive' (and, perhaps, kills them), whereas one normally singes only the carcass of an animal, or 'singes them ⟨and leaves them⟩ alive'. The latter gives a better antithesis to *καταφρύγει*.

397 ἐπιόρκους: In societies which use writing sparingly (cf. 777 n.) and have few techniques for establishing guilt or innocence, the oath is of supreme importance, and perjury an especially heinous crime, visited with divine vengeance; the thunderbolt is Zeus' weapon against all who offend him. Strepsiades makes himself vulnerable to counter-argument by saying *φανερῶς*.

398 Κρονίων: The festival *Κρόνια* was celebrated shortly before the Panathenaia. Since Kronos reigned before Zeus, his name was used colloquially to mean 'old-fashioned'; cf. 1070. **ὄζων**: Cf. 50 n. **βεκκεσέληνε**: Hdt. ii. 2 gives one version of a famous story: Psammetichos, king of Egypt, wishing to discover the aboriginal language of mankind, isolated two infants from all contact with human speech, and the first word they uttered, at the sight of the man who brought them food, was *βέκ(κ)ος*, the Phrygian for 'bread'. Herodotos refers to other versions (2. 5), and another is in fact found in the Scholiast. Either *βεκκε-* alludes to some version of this story, or we do not know to what it alludes. As for *-σέληνε*, it can be related to the epithet *προσέληνοι*, used of the Arkadians, 'who are said to have been living even before the Moon' (Ap. Rhod.).

399 δῆτ': The wide separation of this connective postpositive from the beginning of its clause, and its position immediately after a subordinate clause, are unique. If it were any other postpositive we should be justified in rejecting it in favour of the repeated *πῶς* offered by many MSS. Repetition is a common phenomenon in a lengthy question; cf. *τί* in 351. But the use of *δῆτα* may possibly be influenced by the epic mobile adverb *δή*, often in initial position; cf. 62 n. **Σίμων'**: Cf. 351 n.

400 Κλεώνυμον: Cf. 353 n. **Θέωρον**: Presumably the man represented unflatteringly in *Ach.* 134 ff. as an ambassador to the Odrysian king.

401 τὸν αὑτοῦ γε νεών: The reference is not necessarily to any particular one of the many temples of Zeus or to any particularly disastrous occasion. **Σούνιον**: The temple of Athena stands on the promontory. **Ἀθηνέων**: The fact that many MSS. have *Ἀθηναίων* and the rest *Ἀθηνῶν* suggests that Ar. is quoting *Od.* iii. 278 in the original dialect. Cf. 614, 989 n.

402 τί μαθών: MSS. here, as often elsewhere, are divided between *μαθών* and *παθών*, but both expressions are intelligible: 'What was the idea of . . .?' or 'What put it into his head to . . .?', and 'What made him . . .?' **οὐ γὰρ δὴ δρῦς γ'**: 'For certainly . . . not . . .'

403 οὐκ οἶδ': An Athenian determined to defend traditional belief might argue: (1) Punishment can be delayed, and a perjurer's son or descendant may be struck by lightning. (2) An innocent man struck is paying the penalty for an ancestor's perjury. But we do not know how traditionalists explained the striking of temples. Perhaps they believed that Zeus showed his displeasure at human wickedness by hurling thunderbolts at random, rather as in *Il.* xvi. 384 ff. he rains on everyone when angered by injustice. **τί γάρ ἐστιν δῆθ'**: 'Well, then, what . . .?'; *γάρ* is used when one possible answer to a question has been eliminated.

404 εἰς ταύτας . . . 407 κατακάων: Anaximandros and Anaximenes regarded thunder and lightning alike as caused by the bursting of wind out of dense cloud, the lightning being the sudden contrast with the blackness of the cloud. Leukippos seems to have followed this explanation. Anaxagoras, however, introduced friction as a cause of lightning, explaining it as *ἔκτριψις νεφῶν*; similarly Demokritos, as *σύγκρουσις νεφῶν*. Diogenes' explanation is obscure; we do not find anywhere precisely the explanation given here by Socrates. A society which has to produce light and warmth the hard way might be expected to understand more readily than ours how heat and flame can be a product of rapid friction. **ὑπ' ἀνάγκης**: Cf. 377 n. **σοβαρός**: sometimes 'overbearing': here 'carrying all before it'.

408 Διασίοισιν: A festival of great importance to the Athenians. Festivals of this kind were evidently an occasion for parties for relations and friends.

409 κᾆτ': Cf. pp. xxxi f.

(vi) **412–56.** *The Clouds accept Strepsiades*

The Chorus's address to Strepsiades was taken out of context by the source of Diogenes Laertios ii. 27 and converted into a complimentary address to Socrates (a good example of what Bertrand Russell called 'one of those reckless lies in which respectable people are wont to indulge in the interests of virtue') by (i) substituting *δικαίως* for *παρ' ἡμῶν* in 412, thus cutting the cord that ties the passage to the play; (ii) converting *εἰ μνήμων εἶ* into *εἰ γὰρ μνήμων* in 414, and *μή* and *μήτε* into *οὐ* and *οὔτε* throughout 415 f.; (iii) substituting *ἀδηφαγίας* for *γυμνασίων* in 417; (iv) stopping at the end of 417.

413 καὶ τοῖς Ἕλλησι: 'And the ⟨other⟩ Greeks', in effect, 'the rest of the world'; cf. Lys. xxi. 10 *τῶν Ἑλλήνων ἄριστος* = 'the best *anywhere*'.
414 μνήμων: Cf. 129 n.
415 μήθ' ἑστὼς μήτε βαδίζων: The point is 'whatever you are doing'. Cf. *Od.* xvii. 157 f. *ὡς ἦ τοι Ὀδυσεὺς ἤδη ἐν πατρίδι γαίῃ ἥμενος ἢ ἕρπων* and Aisch. *Eum.* 292 ff. (Orestes' call to Athena) *εἴτε χώρας ἐν τόποις Λιβυστικῆς . . . τίθησιν ὀρθὸν ἢ κατηρεφῆ πόδα.*
416 μήτε . . . μήτ': Emendation to *μηδέ . . . μηδ'* is very tempting, to achieve co-ordination with *μή* in 415 and isolate *μήθ' ἑστὼς μήτε βαδίζων*, but *τ'* in 417 makes us think twice.
417 ἀνοήτων: Probably to be taken (cf. *μῶρος*) as a euphemistic allusion to sexual pleasure.
418 εἰκός: sc. *νομίζειν*. **δεξιόν**: Cf. 148 n.
419 βουλεύων: Normally in Attic the active = 'be a member of the Council', the middle = 'deliberate'; but in poetry the active is commonly synonymous with the middle.
422 παρέχοιμ' ἄν: sc. *ἐμαυτόν*: cf. Pl. *Tht.* 191 A *παρέξομεν* (sc. *ἡμᾶς αὐτούς*) . . . *χρῆσθαι ὅτι ἂν βούληται.*
423 ἄλλο τι δῆτ' οὐ νομιεῖς: In Plato we often find a question, of a kind which we would colour by 'surely', beginning with *ἄλλο τι ἤ* or (more commonly) *ἄλλο τι*: and the latter is often followed by *οὖν*, e.g. *Rep.* 337 C *ἄλλο τι οὖν καὶ σὺ οὕτω ποιήσεις;* But δῆτ' *οὖν* (which many MSS. have here) is unparalleled except as a variant in Eur. *Med.* 1290, where *οὐ* makes better sense than *οὖν*.
424 Χάος: Chaos is the primeval being in early cosmogonies but also means 'space', 'the void'. **Γλῶτταν**: As a deity, *Γλῶττα* merits a capital, according to our printing conventions. **τρία ταυτί**: The point is, '*only* three, and no more'; cf. Thuc. vi. 73. 1, where, after discarding their college of fifteen generals because of the disadvantages of *πολυαρχία*, the Syracusans elect 'Hermokrates and Herakleides and Sikanos, *τούτους τρεῖς*'. On a different point in the number three cf. 1234 f. n.
425 γ': *οὐδέ . . . γε* is simply the negative of *καί . . . γε.*
427 δρῶμεν: Subjunctive, of 'deliberative' type; hence 'Tell us—don't be afraid—what we are to do for you.' **ἀτυχήσεις**: sc. your request.
428 θαυμάζων: Showing respect by action, not simply feeling it; cf. Eur. *El.* 84 (Orestes to Pylades) *μόνος δ' Ὀρέστην τόνδ' ἐθαύμαζες φίλων.*
429 πάνυ μικρόν . . . 430 ἄριστον: The joke seems naïve, but the effect of surprise can be exploited if the actor utters 429 in a wheedling tone and suddenly flames into excitement in 430. **ἑκατὸν σταδίοισιν**: As we say 'by a hundred miles'. τὸ στάδιον, οἱ στάδιοι or τὰ στάδια: 100 ὀργυιαί = 600 Gk feet = 606 3/4 English feet = c. 1/8 of a Roman mile.

432 γνώμας . . . νικήσει: δῆμος here = 'Assembly', as normally in legal and political language (e.g. ἔδοξε τῇ βουλῇ καὶ τῷ δήμῳ, the normal prescript of a decree). When a man makes or supports a proposal in the Assembly he gives his γνώμη, and γνώμην νικᾶν = 'propose a motion which is then carried'. Cf. 99 n.

433 μή μοι γε λέγειν: Either (i) 'Don't ⟨talk⟩ to me about speaking on important proposals', or (ii) 'Please don't talk about . . . proposals.' In (i) the imperative is understood, as in 84 (*v.* n.), and in (ii) the infinitive λέγειν has an imperatival sense, as it certainly has in (e.g.) 850. Cf. 1352 n. (i) is more probable, because of the formulaic nature of μή μοι γε and because the undeniable examples of the imperatival infinitive in Ar. are all positive.

434 ὅσ': 'Enough for . . .' **στρεψοδικῆσαι**: Not chosen solely to fit Strepsiades' name; it recurs in *Birds* 1468 στρεψοδικοπανουργία.

435 ἱμείρεις: Somewhat grandiloquent language.

436 προπόλοισιν: 'Ministers' of a deity. The plural suggests that we are meant to think not only of Socrates but also of Chairephon and of such other students as are in a position to instruct a newcomer.

439 νῦν οὖν . . . 442 δείρειν: Strepsiades' extravagant self-surrender is echoed humorously by Socrates and Ktesippos in Pl. *Euthd.* 285 C, where they profess their willingness to be boiled or flayed by Dionysodoros if only he will make good men of them. **[χρήσθων]**: if this word is retained, then (i) 439–56 contain one ⏑⏑ – too many or too few (cf. p. xxxv), (ii) unless we can plausibly interpolate a word scanning ⏑⏑ – before ὅτι, the coincidence of word-end and a metron-end, normal in anapaestic sequences of this type, is largely eliminated, and (iii) there is asyndeton between . . . βούλονται and τουτὶ κτλ. Deletion of χρήσθων is thus necessary, and the sense is not impaired: 'Now, then, I hand over my person to them ⟨to treat⟩ absolutely as they like.' **ὅτι βούλονται**: Cf. 348. **τύπτειν κτλ.**: The subject of the verbs does not stay the same throughout; it is as if one said 'For beatings, for hunger', etc. **αὐχμεῖν**: The word is used of dry (because unanointed) skin; cf. 920. **ἀσκὸν δείρειν**: Cf. Solon (not speaking for himself), 'I wouldn't mind . . . if I could be tyrant of Athens for just one day, being flayed afterwards ⟨and my skin used⟩ as a wine-skin.' This character was 'selling his body' as Faust 'sold his soul'; Strepsiades, on the other hand, will endure suffering now in the hope of reward later.

443 εἴπερ κτλ.: 'If I am going to escape ⟨as I wish . . .⟩' or '. . . ⟨as seems possible⟩ . . .'; cf. 1035 εἴπερ . . . ὑπερβαλεῖ, 'If you are going to surpass ⟨as you hope⟩ . . .'

444 τοῖς τ' ἀνθρώποις: 'The world', 'other people'; cf. *Peace* 98 τοῖς τ' ἀνθρώποισι φράσον σιγᾶν, 'Tell everyone to be quiet.'

445 θρασύς . . . 451 ματιολοιχός: This is a catalogue of abusive terms used against a man who is a tricky opponent in lawsuits, as is plain from 452. Some of these terms are frequent in Attic literature (not always—e.g. ἴτης—with a pejorative sense), and they may all have been current in Ar.'s time, but the evidence does not tell us whether (e.g.) εὔγλωττος was really used as a term of abuse. Some, e.g. εὑρησιεπής and ματιολοιχός, sound more like comic inventions. We can see why (e.g.) γλοιός and κέντρων should be abusive; it is not so easy to see why (e.g.) τρύμη and μάσθλης should be. **συγκολλητής**: συγκολλᾶν suggests the turning of skill to malicious ends. **περίτριμμα**: The point is 'worn smooth by practice'; cf. Dem. xviii. 217 (on Aischines) σπερμολόγος, περίτριμμ' ἀγορᾶς. **κύρβις**: The law code of Athens in the early sixth century was in part inscribed on κύρβεις (possibly components of a wall), and the point of calling a man κύρβις would be that (unlike peaceable citizens, who avoided litigation) he knew the details of the law too well. **κρόταλον**: Cf. 260 n. **τρύμη**: The Scholiast says 'drill' or 'bore'. *Eccl.* 337 ἐκτετρύπηκεν λαθοῦσά μ' ἔνδοθεν is perhaps related; the idea is that of a person whose comings and goings one cannot stop. **μάσθλης**: Cf. *Knights* 269 (the knights replying to Kleon's claim that he has been their friend) ὡς δ' ἀλαζών, ὡς δὲ μάσθλης· εἶδες οἷ' ὑπέρχεται ὥσπερεὶ γέροντας ἡμᾶς κτλ. **εἴρων**: 'Deceitful' in pretending to be innocent when one is up to mischief. εἰρωνεία approximates to 'making excuses', 'pleading inability'; to Aristotle it lies on one side of truth, as ἀλαζονεία does on the other, but he recognizes its attractive side, and specifically mentions the εἰρωνεία of Socrates, whom Plato represents as using affectation of intellectual inadequacy as a dialectic tool. **ἀλαζών**: Cf. 102 n. **κέντρων**: Coupled with μαστιγίας in a fragment of Sophokles. **ἀργαλέος**: This word, common in epic and elegiac poetry, seems to have acquired a colloquial flavour in Attic; its absence from the lyrics of tragedy is striking, and it is uncommon in fourth-century prose, but Ar. uses it both in lyrics and in dialogue. **ματιολοιχός**: The Scholiast alleges μάτιον τὸ ἐλάχιστον εἰώθασι λέγειν, and it may well be one of the many colloquial words of which we catch only a glimpse, but the Scholiast betrays uncertainty by mentioning alternative theories, one of which connects the word (impossibly) with μάταιος and the other with the measure which is called (in Roman Egypt!) μάτιον.

452 καλοῦσ': Future; cf. 443 n. **ἀπαντῶντες**: In Dem. xxxvi. 45 the meaning is '<even> people whom one does not know'.

453 δρώντων: sc. Socrates and his associates; cf. 436.

455 ἔκ μου: Enclitic pronouns are not normally governed by prepositions, but πρός με is common enough, (not always metrically guaranteed), and μου after περί is guaranteed in *Wasps* 1358 ταῦτ' οὖν περί μου δέδοικε μὴ διαφθαρῶ.

456 φροντισταῖς: All those in the school, including themselves.

(vii) **457–75.** *Lyric dialogue*

For lyric dialogue between chorus and actor cf. *Ach.* 929–39 ~ 941–51 and *Knights* 111–50. Passages in which the choral utterances are in lyric metres, the actor's in the metres of spoken dialogue, are also common.

In the MSS. the interlocutor of Strepsiades in this scene is Socrates. But the Scholiast says of 467 *νῦν ὁ Σωκράτης λέγει· μᾶλλον δὲ ὁ χορός· εἴωθε γὰρ μετὰ τὸ ᾆσαι ἐπάγειν δίστιχα, ὡς ἂν ᾄδῃ τὸ "ἀλλ' ἐγχείρει"*. This scholion combines (i) a judgement by one ancient commentator, implying that 457–62 and 463–5 were not sung by Socrates, and (ii) a correction of this by a second ancient commentator, who pointed out that 476 f., a *κατακελευσμός*, i.e. encouragement to a character to speak, are characteristic of a chorus which has just concluded a lyric utterance. This second observation is correct; it is supported by 959 f., 1034 f., 1351 f., 1397 f. *κατακελευσμοί* are normally in the same metre as the dialogue which follows them, but there are exceptions: *Peace* 357 ff., *Birds* 637 f.

The sense of 457 and 463 suits the Chorus, not Socrates (*v.* nn.). The attribution to Socrates may have started from misinterpretation of 459 and 460 f. (*v.* nn.).

(1) 457 f. – ∪ – ∪ – ∪ – ∪ – ∪ – ∪ – ∪ – ⌒ |
(2) 459–61 – ∪ – – ∪ ∪ – ∪ ∪ – ∪ ∪ – ∪ ∪ – ⌒ |
(3) 462 – ∪ – ∪ – – |
(4) 463 ∪ – ∪ – – – ∪ ∪ – ∪ ∪ – |
(5) 464 f. – – ∪ ∪ – ∪ ∪ – – – ∪ – – |
(6) 466 f. – ∪ ∪ – ∪ ∪ – ∪ – ∪ ∪ – ∪ ∪ – |
(7) 468 f. – – ∪ ∪ – ∪ ∪ – × – ∪ – – |
(8) 470 f. – ∪ ∪ – ∪ ∪ – – – ∪ ∪ – ∪ ∪ – – |
(9) 472 f. – ∪ ∪ – ∪ ∪ – – – ∪ – – |
(10) 474 f. – ∪ ∪ – ∪ ∪ – – – ∪ ∪ – ∪ ∪ – |

The whole passage is dactylo-epitrite, of which the basic units are – ∪ – and – ∪ ∪ – ∪ ∪ –. These units may be separated by a syllable, and an extra syllable may come at the beginning or end of a verse. The dactylic unit may be extended, as in (2). (3) is an ithyphallic, *cr ba*, which occurs as a clausula to a dactylo-epitrite sequence in *Knights* 1273 ~ 99 and elsewhere in drama.

457 λῆμα: A typical comment by a chorus on the speech or action of a character; cf. 1350.

459 ἴσθι: The switch from comment on Strepsiades to direct address is more abrupt, but characteristic, like the dactylo-epitrites, of encomiastic poetry. Cf. especially Pi. *Ol.* 6. 8 *ἴστω γάρ . . . Σωστράτου υἱός* (i.e. Hagesias) . . . 12 *Ἁγησία, τὶν δ' αἶνος ἑτοῖμος* and *Nem.* 2. 3 *ὅδ' ἀνήρ* (i.e. Timodemos) . . . 14 *ὦ Τιμόδημε, σὲ δ' ἀλκὰ κτλ.*

460 f. παρ' ἐμοῦ: For the Chorus's use of the first person singular (a comic chorus is free to speak of itself as one person or as many) cf. 463 and 957. Though Socrates and his associates (cf. 436) will be the instructors, the Clouds are the source of wisdom (cf. 412 *παρ' ἡμῶν*), it is they who decide that Strepsiades shall be instructed (cf. 431, 435), and Strepsiades' excited anapaests are addressed to them, not to Socrates, as is clear from 439 f. and 453 ff.

461 οὐρανόμηκες: The concept is Homeric: *Il.* viii. 192 *κλέος οὐρανὸν ἵκει.*

463 τί πείσομαι: 'What will happen to me?'—hopeful, not apprehensive; cf. *εὖ πάσχειν.* **τὸν πάντα χρόνον**: The expression has associations with treaties, contracts, and leases (cf. our 'in perpetuity') and is not as poetic as we might have thought. **μετ' ἐμοῦ**: Strepsiades is not going to live with Socrates—it is his own door, not the door of the school, which will be thronged by clients (467 ff.)—but he will live 'with' the Clouds because he will worship them and they will protect and inspire him to return. Cf. Ariphron's hymn to Health: *Ὑγίεια βροτοῖσι πρεσβίστα μακάρων, μετὰ σεῦ ναίοιμι τὸ λειπόμενον βιοτᾶς, σὺ δέ μοι πρόφρων ξυνείης.*

464 ἀνθρώπων: Cf. 110 n.

466 ἆρά γε . . . ἄρ': The combination of particles is unparalleled, but they are wholly intelligible separately; *ἆρά γε* introduces a question, and *ἄρα* turns the question into a demand for a promise.

470 βουλομένους . . . 475 μετὰ σοῦ: We have a choice between treating *πράγματα . . . ταλάντων* (i) as object of *ἀνακοινοῦσθαι . . . ἐλθεῖν* or (ii) as object of *συμβουλευσομένους*, *ἄξια* being appositional. The difficulties of (i) are: (*a*) *ἀνακοινοῦσθαι* is normally intransitive in Attic; but cf. Hdt. iv. 48. 3 *ἀνακοινοῦται τῷ Ἴστρῳ τὸ ὕδωρ*, 'it contributes its water to the Danube.' (*b*) If *ἀνακοινοῦσθαι* is transitive it must, as it were, 'jump over' *εἰς λόγον ἐλθεῖν*: but this is possible; cf. Dem. xxi. 208 *ἐξαιτήσεσθαι καὶ λιπαρήσειν παρ' ὑμῶν αὐτόν* and 612 n. below. In (ii) there is no difficulty in making *ἄξια* appositional; cf. Xen. *An.* i. 4. 8 *τέκνα καὶ γυναῖκας . . . φρουρούμενα.* The real difficulty is that *συμβουλεύεσθαι* is also normally intransitive—that is to say, it can govern a neuter adjective or pronoun, but not a substantive. Neither interpretation is free from linguistic abnormality, but (i) seems to me to divide the sentence in a way that gives better balance. **πράγματα**: The word has the overtone 'troubles', as commonly in *πράγματα παρέχειν*, etc. (e.g. 1216). **κἀντιγραφάς**: *ἀντιγραφή* is not simply 'counter-indictment', i.e. an indictment brought against someone who has indicted oneself, but 'charge (or counter-charge, or counter-affirmation) in a contested case'. **πολλῶν ταλάντων**: 'Involving vast sums of money'; cf. 1065 n. **ἄξια σῇ φρενί**: In 1074 *τί σοι ζῆν ἄξιον* is (lit.) 'in what way is it worth while (profitable, satisfactory) for you to live?' 'Worth while for your intelligence', which is not quite the same as 'worthy of your intelligence', implies both that it is the intellect which is concerned in these consultations and that they will be lucrative for Strepsiades. **μετὰ σοῦ**: The construction is a cross between the normal *συμβουλεύεσθαί τινι* and (e.g.) Pl. *Rep.* 400 B *μετὰ Δάμωνος βουλευσόμεθα.* In general, compound verbs in *συν-* take a dative, which in later Greek is replaced by *μετά c. gen.* There are, however, some early examples of the later usage, e.g. *Lys.* 1221 *μετὰ σοῦ ξυνταλαιπωρήσομεν.* 'To consult your intelligence with you', treating Strepsiades' *φρήν* as an entity distinguishable from him, is theoretically possible, but I doubt whether Ar. could expect his audience to take the words in this sense.

(viii) **476 f.**

Anapaestic tetrameters; cf. p. xxxv.

476 ἐγχείρει κτλ.: 'Embark on teaching the old man what you're going to teach him.' **προδιδάσκειν**: Not entirely the appropriate word for the questions which Socrates is going to put, but it would be rash to suggest that *προδιδάσκειν* could convey the sense *ποιεῖν πρὶν διδάσκειν.* Like *προμαθεῖν* in 966, *προδιδάσκειν* simply = 'teach', because teaching precedes the practice of what is taught.

(ix) **478–509.** *Socrates 'interviews' Strepsiades*

480 'πὶ τούτοις: 'Given this knowledge', 'on this basis'.

481 τειχομαχεῖν: *μηχανάς . . . προσφέρω* naturally suggests to Strepsiades battering-rams and similar engines. The metaphor is not used by Socrates in Plato or Xenophon.

483 εἰ μνημονικὸς εἶ: '⟨To see⟩ if ⟨, for example,⟩ you have a good memory'. Cf. 658 f. 'You have to learn a lot of other things first, ⟨for example⟩ the right form of the names of male animals.'

485 σχέτλιος: It is uncertain whether we should punctuate before or after this word.

487 ἀποστερεῖν δ' ἔνι: 'But I can *cheat*!' It is far-fetched to see a pun on *λέγειν* and *ἐρεῖν* and to print *ἀποστ-ερεῖν*. Strepsiades knows what end he wants and what he is prepared to do, but knows also his own technical incapacity to achieve that end.

488 ἀμέλει, καλῶς: Strepsiades must give some such (unchallenged) assurance if we are to pass on to the next joke without delay.

489 προβάλωμαι: All MSS. have the middle, but (*a*) in 757 the active = 'set a problem', and Plato's usage agrees; the point might be that Socrates will formulate a problem for his own consideration and Strepsiades will show his brightness by jumping in and solving it before Socrates can; (*b*) the active is used of throwing food to dogs, birds, or the audience, and Strepsiades' reply (491) shows that he has understood Socrates in this sense. Could he make such a reply to *προβάλωμαι*? If not, we must emend to *προβάλω σοι*. But *ὑφαρπάσει* (490) is enough for Strepsiades, and we cannot express ourselves with confidence about actives and middles in this play; cf. 368 (*ἀπόφηναι* where we expect *ἀπόφηνον*) and 783 n.

490 ὑφαρπάσει: Pl. *Euthd.* 300 D uses this of a speaker 'jumping in' to make a point before the person addressed can reply. Neither *ἁρπάζειν* nor its compounds are used by Plato and Xenophon of an eager pupil giving a prompt answer.

491 κυνηδόν: Because an animal or a bird of prey *ἁρπάζει* food thrown to it or left unguarded.

492 ἅνθρωπος: Almost certainly Ar. intended 'This man is stupid' (hence *ἅν-*; cf. 97), not 'This is a stupid man' (*ἄν-*); cf. *Frogs* 652 *ἅνθρωπος ἱερός*.

493 μὴ πληγῶν δέει: Socrates thinks of Strepsiades as a Greek school-master thought of a stupid boy. Whether Ar. intended indicative *δέει* or subjunctive *δέῃ* is uncertain; manuscript evidence on *-ει/-ῃ* is valueless.

494. Now Socrates wonders how far he can go.

494 τύπτομαι . . . 496 δικάζομαι: Strepsiades is something of a coward, as we have already had reason to suspect, and does not return blow for blow. He cries out *μαρτύρομαι* (like the Second Creditor when threatened [1297]), but after 'waiting a bit', so that he can exaggerate what has happened and go to court with a more impressive case. His promptitude in litigation (*ἀκαρῆ* stresses this; cf. *Wealth* 244 *ἐν ἀκαρεῖ χρόνου*, 'in a moment') is perhaps a reminder of the stock joke against Athenians (cf. 208 n.).

497 ἠδίκηκά τι: Strepsiades thinks that Socrates is going to beat him. Socrates' motive is in fact to make away with the himation; cf. 179 and 856.

498 γυμνούς: Not necessarily, or even probably, stark naked. *γυμνός* in *Lys.* 1020 refers to the absence of the outer garment *ἐξωμίς* (1021 ~ 622). **νομίζεται**: 'It is customary', 'it is the rule'; cf. 1185, 1420.

499 φωράσων: Under Attic law, if A believed that B had in his house articles belonging to A, he was entitled to enter B's house and look for them, on condition, as appears from this passage, that he wore no garment in which he could smuggle the article in and 'plant' it on B.

500 εἰπέ . . . 504 γενήσομαι: An artificial question designed solely to lead up to the joke in 504. On Chairephon cf. 104 n. On *φύσις* cf. 277.

507 μελιτοῦτταν . . . 508 Τροφωνίου: Near Lebadeia in Boiotia there was a cave visited by those who wished to obtain oracular responses from the hero Trophonios. It was customary for those consulting the oracle to placate with honey-cakes the snakes which lived in the cave, just as a honey-cake was put out for the 'great snake' believed in early fifth-century Athens to inhabit the Akropolis. For *εἰς Τροφωνίου*, 'into Trophonios' ⟨place⟩', cf. 964, 973.

509 κυπτάζεις: The word is not simply 'bend down ⟨and peer⟩' but carries a strong suggestion of being active, busy, even up to no good.

Strepsiades fearfully tiptoes through the door of the school and Socrates stalks in after him.

(D) 510–626. PARABASIS

(i) 510–17. *κομμάτιον*: *Valediction*

(*a*) **510 f.** The formula *ἀλλ' ἴθι χαίρων* plays the same part in other plays at the beginning of the parabasis and in *Ach.* 1143, where Dikaiopolis goes out of sight and the chorus sings. Normally, however, the anapaestic rhythm continues for the whole of the *κομμάτιον*, whereas here it gives place to lyrics.

(*b*) **512–17.** The metrical analysis is:

(1) 512 f.	– ∪ ∪ – ∪ – ∪ – – ∪ ∪∪ ∪ – –
(2) 514	– ∪ ∪ – – ∪ ∪ –
(3) 515 f.	∪ – ∪ – – ∪ ∪ – – – ∪ – – – ∪ –
(4) 517	– ∪ ∪ – ∪ – –

(1) is an iambo-choriambic tetrameter: *ch ia* (choriambic dimeter) + *cr ba* (ithyphallic). Note the resolution (*ὅτι*) and the correption of -*πῳ*. (2) is a choriambic dimeter: *ch ch.* (3) is an iambo-choriambic tetrameter: *ia ch* (choriambic dimeter) + *ia ia* (iambic dimeter). (4) is an aristophanean: *ch ba.* Cf. 287 ~ 310 nn.

515 νεωτέροις: The meaning '⟨appropriate to the⟩ young', normal in Ar., is uppermost here too, for contrast with 514; but *νεώτερος* also has sinister associations with violence and revolution.

515 f. τὴν φύσιν αὑτοῦ: For the exceptional divorce of the reflexive genitive from the article cf. 905 *τὸν πατέρ' αὑτοῦ*.
517 σοφίαν ἐπασκεῖ: Cf. 1025.

(ii) **518–62.** *Parabasis proper*

The first person singular throughout is the poet; the role of the Chorus as clouds is discarded. In *Ach.* 628 ff., *Knights* 507 ff., *Wasps* 1015 ff., *Peace* 734 ff., the chorus praises the poet in the third person, but in none of these cases does it have to change its character in order to do so, and in *Knights* 507–9 a fictitious separation of the chorus from the poet is deliberately emphasized.

The metre is eupolidean; cf. p. xxxvi. Ar. does not use this metre elsewhere in his extant plays, though other comic poets do. It may owe its name to frequency in Eupolis, or possibly he was the author of the earliest datable play in which Hellenistic metricians found it.

519 ἐκθρέψαντα: A god *τρέφει* a human being whom he cherishes and favours; cf. 463 n. and the epic adjective *διοτρεφής*, used of kings and warriors. As a comic poet, whose work is produced at festivals of Dionysos, Ar. naturally regards Dionysos as his special deity (cf. Pl. *Smp.* 177 E: 'Aristophanes, whose entire concern is with Dionysos and Aphrodite'), and the point of *ἐκ-* is that Dionysos has looked after him from childhood (cf. 795).
520 οὕτω: Lit., 'thus may I win . . . as (521 *ὡς*) . . . I thought it right (523 *ἠξίωσ'*) . . . ', i.e. 'If I did not think it right . . ., may I not win!', a strong assertion of 'I thought it right.' Cf. *Thesm.* 469 f., 'For I too— *οὕτως ὀναίμην τῶν τέκνων*—hate that man!' The poet has no inhibitions about declaring his desire to win first prize; cf. 1115 ff. **σοφός:** Cf. 94 n.
521 δεξιούς: Cf. 148 n.
522. Cf. 94 n.
523 πρώτους . . . ἀναγεῦσ': *ἀναγεύειν* occurs only here. The meanings of the prefix *ἀνα-* are so varied that if *ἀναγεύειν* was a word in general currency we can only admit that we do not know what it meant, and if Ar. coined it for this occasion we cannot know (and I do not see how his audience could know) what he intended. *ἀνα-* sometimes means 'back' (e.g. *ἀναχωρεῖν*) or 'afresh', 'for the second time'. If it means that in *ἀναγεύειν*, Ar. is saying: 'I have thought it right to present my play again to you—the play over which I took more trouble ⟨in 423⟩ than any other, in spite of which ⟨trouble⟩ I was defeated ⟨in 423⟩ . . .' If, on the other hand, *ἀναγεύειν* is akin to *ἀνοιγνύναι*, *ἀναδεικνύναι* (cf. 304), etc., which express the idea of display and revelation, the whole sentence can refer to 423. We may

well ask how Ar. could speak of giving his audience the first taste of the play (*πρώτους*), as if it had been open to him to put on in some other state a comedy about contemporary Athenian life. Tragic poets sometimes put on plays elsewhere (e.g. Aischylos in Sicily), and Euripides' *Andromache*, which was not performed at Athens, may have been performed at Argos shortly before Ar. wrote this parabasis. Ar. would therefore be pretending humorously that he could have done likewise had he wished—as one might say to a child 'Now here's a very special treat for you!' in giving him something which one would have given him in any case.

524 φορτικῶν: The usual term of contempt used by a comic poet of his rivals.

528 ἐξ ὅτου . . . 529 ἠκουσάτην: The reference is to Ar.'s first play, *Banqueters*, performed in 427 (*ἐνθάδ'* = in the theatre). It contained a good young man and a bad one (they are *ὁ σώφρων* and *ὁ καταπύγων*); in a quotation from it we have a dialogue between an old man and his impudent son, somewhat reminiscent of *Clouds* 1399 ff., the son abusing his father in terms which the father characterizes as reflecting current rhetorical jargon. This community of theme with *Clouds*—old education and new, tradition and rhetoric, and the relations between father and son—helps to explain why Ar. expected *Clouds* to succeed. **οὓς ἡδὺ καὶ λέγειν:** *οἷς* (MSS.) is senseless. It cannot mean 'even to speak to whom is a pleasure', for (*a*) *λέγω σοι* means 'I tell you', not 'I converse with you' or 'I speak in your presense', and (*b*) with what could 'speaking' be contrasted? If a man said of a pretty girl, 'It is a pleasure even to speak to her', the point would be obvious (and similarly, if a Greek said it of a handsome boy), but we are concerned here with grown men whose judgement on plays matters to the poet. 'Who enjoy speaking also' would be a distorted way of implying that those who liked *Banqueters* did not hesitate to praise it in talking to others, and an equally distorted way of saying (even if Ar. had wished to say such a thing) that *Banqueters* appealed especially to talkative men (men who enjoy speaking, not men who are necessarily good speakers). Sense is restored by the emendation *οὕς*. *λέγειν c. acc.* = 'speak of', 'mention' (cf. 103 and 768), and Ar.'s point is: 'It is agreeable ⟨to me now⟩ even to mention them ⟨let alone to know them personally and hear their praise⟩.' Cf. Hesiod, *ἡδὺ δὲ καὶ τὸ πυθέσθαι ὅσα θνητοῖσιν ἔνειμαν ἀθάνατοι* and Pl. *Phdr.* 240 D *ἃ καὶ λόγῳ ἐστὶν ἀκούειν οὐκ ἐπιτερπές*. **σώφρων:** The word is applied to those who refrain from breaking moral or social rules for gratification of their own ambitions or desires; hence 'disciplined', 'prudent', 'modest', 'chaste'. **καταπύγων:** The word, as is clear from its etymology (∼ *πυγή*) originally meant a man who practises anal coitus, but (like English 'bugger') came to be a general term of abuse or contempt; cf. *Lys.* 137 *ὦ παγκατάπυγον θἠμέτερον* (sc. *τὸ θῆλυ*) *ἅπαν γένος* and fr. 130, where *καταπυγοσύνη* = 'worthless rubbish'.

530 κἀγώ . . . 532 κἀπαιδεύσατε: Ar. did not act as *διδάσκαλος* for his earliest plays, and *Knights* in 424 was the first which he himself *ἐδίδαξεν*. Whether there was a statutory minimum age for *κωμῳδοδιδάσκαλοι* (as there was [e.g.] for speaking in the Assembly) and he did not attain that age until 424, or whether he did not feel sufficient confidence in his own capabilities, we do not know; but *Wasps* in 422 and *Birds* in 414 were put on respectively *διὰ Φιλωνίδου* and *διὰ Καλλιστράτου*, from which it follows that youth is not a necessary explanation of Ar.'s giving *Banqueters* to someone else. He speaks of himself metaphorically as an unmarried girl who had a baby and (in accordance with a common Greek custom) left it to die in open country; another girl found it (as so often happens to foundlings in Greek stories) and it has been looked after in the household (the Athenian people, in their role as audience) to which she brought it. **παρθένος**: Not 'virgin', but 'unmarried'; hence *οὐκ ἐξῆν* is not 'it was impossible' but 'it was contrary to the rules'. **ἦν**: *ἦν* = *ἦ* is metrically guaranteed in (e.g.) Eur. *Ion* 280.

533 ἐκ τούτου . . . ὅρκια: *ἐκ τούτου* picks up *ἐξ ὅτου* (528). *ὅρκια* (of which *πιστά* is the stock epithet in epic) are the objects over which oaths are taken. *πιστά* are 'pledges' which one can 'give and receive'. If A *πιστὰ λαμβάνει παρά* B, B is making a promise to A; cf. Xen. *An.* ii. 3. 26 *ἔξεστιν ὑμῖν πιστὰ λαβεῖν παρ' ἡμῶν ἦ μὴν φιλίαν παρέξειν ὑμῖν τὴν χώραν*. If *παρ' ὑμῖν* is right, lit., 'there are for me pledges of judgement in your keeping', then *Banqueters*, 'brought up' by the audience, must be the 'pledge'; but Ar. is complaining as a man complains when a promise made to him has not been kept. The point is that the judgement passed by the audience on *Banqueters* is, in his eyes, a pledge *given to him* of equally favourable judgement (*γνώμη*) in the future. Hence it is necessary to adopt *παρ' ὑμῶν* from one late MS.

534 Ἠλέκτραν . . . 536 βόστρυχον: *κατά* here virtually = 'like', 'in the manner of'. In the version of the story of Elektra and Orestes portrayed by Aischylos in *Choephori*—and *ἐκείνην* assumes that 'the' story of Elektra is known to the audience—(i) Orestes returns secretly from exile, puts a lock of hair on Agamemnon's tomb, (ii) Elektra, sent to the tomb with offerings by Klytaimestra, and hoping—but hardly daring to admit her hopes to herself—for Orestes' return, is thunderstruck to find the hair, which she recognizes as being like her own. Unlike Ar.'s play, which has come to the theatre (but cf. pp. xxix f.) in the hope of finding there the approbation which his earlier play found, Elektra does not 'go seeking' (it is Orestes who seeks her), but the essential point of the comparison is that Elektra waited with desperate longing for some news or sign of the return of one whom she had known and loved long ago, one who would reinstate her and rescue her from humiliation; and a sign of favourable reaction from the audience is the 'lock' which will revive Ar.'s hopes. ἤν = 'to see if . . .', 'in the hope that . . .'.

538 οὐδέν . . . 539 γέλως: In Ar.'s time the comic actor playing a male role commonly (perhaps invariably) wore artificial genitals of abnormal size. But Ar. is not saying that his revised play has discarded this conventional item of dress; he is claiming (in keeping with 540 ff.) that he disdains certain humorous ideas which other poets have used. The punctuation of *ἐρυθρὸν ἐξ ἄκρου παχύ* is doubtful (cf. 1202 n.): (i) 'red at the end ⟨and⟩ thick ⟨at the end⟩', (ii) 'red at the end ⟨and⟩ thick ⟨sc. throughout⟩', or (iii) 'red ⟨sc. throughout⟩ ⟨and⟩ thick at the end'? The third interpretation would accord with occasional representations of herms on red-figure vases, but on a Classical herm the penis is erect, and Ar. is speaking of a leather penis 'hanging down' (538). This is reconcilable with the first or second interpretations on the assumption that the comic poets sometimes represented a circumcised penis; indeed, this is the only assumption which makes sense of both 'hanging down' and 'red at the end', because the alternative, an inflamed foreskin, is not particularly humorous even to *τὰ παιδία*. Circumcision was not practised by the Greeks at all, but they knew of it as a barbarian custom, owned circumcised slaves, and exploited its humorous potentialities.

540 φαλακρούς: It appears from *Peace* 771 that Ar. himself was somewhat bald (perhaps he only had an abnormally high hairline), but he could take a joke against himself; cf. 545 n. **κόρδαχ'**: The *κόρδαξ* was an undignified dance characteristic of comedy; cf. 555 and Theophr. *Char.* 6. 3 (where dancing the *κόρδαξ* when neither drunk nor a member of a comic chorus is a product of *ἀπόνοια*). *ἕλκειν* is used by a lively dancer, with reference to his own movements, in *Peace* 328; contrast the point of 553 below.

541 πρεσβύτης . . . 542 σκώμματα: The Scholiast offers three possible references for Ar.'s criticism: Eupolis' *Προσπάλτιοι*, Hermippos in general, or the actor Hermon. **τἄπη**: *ἔπος* is an utterance considered in its formal aspect; here, therefore, 'the lines' (of the play), 'the verses'. Cf. 544, and *Frogs* 801 and 1410 (both referring to tragic iambic trimeters). It was only later that *ἔπος* became specially applied to the dactylic hexameter (whence *ἐπικός*, 'epic'). **τὸν παρόντ'**: 'Whoever is there', on stage. **ἀφανίζων**: 'Concealing' by noisy slapstick the poor quality of the verbal humour.

543 οὐδ' εἰσῆξε . . . βοᾷ: sc. 'this play'. The claim is notoriously untrue of the finale of *Clouds* as we have it, but Ar. is simply making, in somewhat rhetorical form, the claim that his play (as it was when *this* passage was written; cf. p. xxix) does not rely on noise or violence for its comic effect.

544 ἔπεσιν: Cf. 541 n.

545 ἀνήρ: This forms part of a single expression with *ποητής*. **οὐ κομῶ**: Cf. 14 n.; and Ar.'s baldness (540 n.) gives additional point.

546 δὶς καὶ τρίς: In revising *Clouds* Ar. would seem to be doing just this; but the following lines show that he is criticizing his rivals for writing ostensibly different plays on the same themes.

547 καινάς: Ar. was ready to adopt a conservative standpoint, for comic purposes, towards tragedy and philosophy, but in his own craft he prided himself on his innovations. It was not for nothing that Kratinos described a *κομψὸς θεατής* as *ὑπολεπτολόγος γνωμοδιώκτης εὐριπιδαριστοφανίζων*. **σοφίζομαι**: 'I practise my art'; cf. 94 n.

549 μέγιστον . . . γαστέρα: The reference is to the sustained and virulent attack on Kleon in *Knights*, when his political power was indeed at its peak; cf. 581 ff.

550 οὐκ ἐτόλμησ': 'I was not so shameless as to . . .' **κειμένῳ**: 'When he was down'.

551 παρέδωκεν λαβήν: Cf. 126 n. **Ὑπέρβολος**: We first hear of him in *Ach.* 846 f., and *Peace* 681 represents him (Kleon being dead by then) as the most influential speaker in the Assembly. Both Ar. and Thucydides are hostile to him, as to Kleon. Ostracized in 417/16, he was murdered at Samos in 411.

552 κολετρῶσ': The Scholiast offers 'hit in the belly' (probably an inference from 549) and 'trample, as olives are trampled'. The latter is supported by *κελέτρα* as the name of a rural fixed object (an olive-press?) in an inscription from Larissa. (Hesychios, however, interprets *κέλετρον* as 'fishing-net'.) **μητέρα**: Cf. 557 n.; in politics and comedy alike an opponent's mother was not spared slander and ridicule, as we see from (e.g.) Dem. xviii. 130.

553 Εὔπολις: An exact contemporary of Ar. His first play was produced in 429, and he died (at sea) before the end of the Peloponnesian War, though not long before. **Μαρικᾶν**: The play was produced at the Lenaia of 421. 'Marikas' represented Hyperbolos (Quintil. i. 10. 8), but the point of the name is obscure. Herodian calls it a 'barbarian name'. The stem *Μαρι-* does not appear among slave-names at Athens, but Hesychios records *μαρίς* as a Cretan word for 'sow', and if this word was widely distributed and known to the Athenians it may be relevant, for the pig was the symbol of uncouth ignorance (cf. LSJ s.v. *ὗς* I. 3) and Marikas *nihil se ex musicis scire nisi litteras confitetur* (Quintil., loc. cit). **παρείλκυσεν**: If Ar. had wished to be polite, he would have said *εἰσήγαγεν*: both *παρ-* (common in words meaning 'corrupt', 'deceive', 'mistake', etc.) and *ἕλκειν* are meant to give the impression that Eupolis' play was incompetent, dishonest, and unwelcome.

554 ἐκστρέψας: The Scholiast on 88 points out that the word is used of turning a garment inside-out in order to double its life, and that is appropriate here (though not in 88, *v.* n.). Eupolis apparently retorted that he helped Ar. to write *Knights* and 'made him a present of it'. **κακὸς κακῶς**: In these expressions sometimes the adverb intensifies the adjective, sometimes vice versa; cf. *Knights* 188 f. *οὐδὲ μουσικὴν ἐπίσταμαι πλὴν γραμμάτων, καὶ ταῦτα μέντοι κακὰ κακῶς* and *Ach.* 253 f. *ὅπως τὸ κανοῦν καλὴ καλῶς οἴσεις.*

555 γραῦν μεθύσην: Possibly Hyperbolos' mother. Drunkenness was a stock joke against women. **κόρδακος**: Cf. 540 n.

556 Φρύνιχος . . . ἤσθιεν: Phrynichos was an older contemporary of Ar. The play to which Ar. refers included a burlesque of Andromeda threatened (note the imperfect *ἤσθιεν*) by the sea-monster, a theme which lent itself to comic treatment, as in *Thesm.* 1010 ff. **πάλαι**: With a perfect tense, surprising at first sight; but a play, once written, continues in circulation as a text, and cf. Soph. *Phil.* 1030 *τέθνηχ' ὑμῖν πάλαι.*

557 Ἕρμιππος: A rather older contemporary of Ar.; he won his first victory at the City Dionysia in 436/5. The play in which Hermippos ridiculed Hyperbolos was *Ἀρτοπωλίδες*, in which one character represented Hyperbolos' mother.

558 ἄλλοι τ' ἤδη πάντες: Plato Com. wrote a *Hyperbolos*. I suspect that Ar. intended *ἄλλοι* = *οἱ ἄλλοι* (cf. 97 n.), as he normally says *τἄλλα πάντα* (e.g. 365). **εἰς Ὑπέρβολον**: The repetition strengthens Ar.'s expression of tedium; cf. Hor. *Sat.* i. 6. 45 f. *nunc ad me redeo libertino patre natum, quem rodunt omnes libertino patre natum.*

559 εἰκούς: = *εἰκόνας*. In the extant plays, this can only be the *εἰκών* of *Knights* 864 ff., where Kleon is compared with an eel-fisher who stirs up the mud. No doubt another poet, applying the image to Hyperbolos, made more of it, and Ar. was sensitive to this theft of his own joke. *εἰκόνες* seem to us a rather frigid kind of humour (our traditional riddles of the form 'Why is A like B?' play on words, not things), but the Greeks regarded them highly; 185 f. and 500 ff.

562 εἰς: 'In' is *εἰς* when the reference is to the future, and often *ἐκ* when the reference is to the past; cf. Thuc. vi. 71. 2 'with the intention of attacking *ἐς τὸ ἔαρ*'.

(iii) **563–74.** *Ode*

The ode is divided into four periods by distinct pauses in sense, and the antode (595–606), which responds metrically, is divided in sense at the same points.

(1) 563 ~ 595	–⏑⏑–		⏑–⏑–|	
(2) 564 ~ 596	–⏑⏑–		⏑–⏑–|	
(3) 565 ~ 597	–⏑⏑–		⏑––|	
(4) 566 ~ 598	–⏑⏑–		⏑–⏑–	–⏑⏑–|
(5) 567 f. ~ 599 f.	–⏑|⏑–		⏑–⏑–	–|⏑⏑– ⏑–⏒||
(6) 569 f. ~ 601 f.	–⏑⏑	–⏑⏑|	–⏑⏑	–|⏑⏑
	–⏑⏑|	–⏑⏑	–|⏑⏑	–⏑⏑ ––|
(7) 571 f. ~ 603 f.	––⏑–		–⏑⏑–	––|–– –|⏑⏑–|
(8) 573 ~ 605	–⏓–⏑⏑|–⏑–|			
(9) 574 ~ 606	–––⏑⏑––|			

(1) and (2) are choriambic dimeters of the form *ch ia*. (3) is an aristophanean, *ch ba*. (4) is a choriambic trimeter of the form *ch ia ch*. (5) is a choriambic tetrameter of the form choriambic dimeter (*ch ia*)+aristophanean (*ch ba*). (6) is a sequence of nine lyric dactyls. On this metre cf. p. 99. (7) is a choriambic tetrameter of the form *ia ch* –––– *ch*. (8) is a glyconic, and (9) a pherecratean. The central passage of lyric dactyls recalls the unusually elevated parodos and gives a comparable elevation to the ode.

The Chorus, as at the same point in the parabasis of *Knights*, invites the gods to its dance. Ode and antode together may be summarized: 'Come, Zeus, Poseidon, Athena . . .' Such an invitation to a festival or celebration is fully in accord with Greek practice and sentiment. It is notable that the Chorus resumes its role as clouds (Aither is 'our father', 569), and does not simply sing as a chorus of Athenians at a festival. The maintenance of dramatic role is necessarily less obtrusive in *Knights*, where the chorus represents Athenian cavalrymen.

The form of invocation is a serious one, not peculiar to comedy or even characteristic of it; we find it in Aisch. *Sept.* 116 ff., where the chorus calls upon gods to avert an enemy attack.

Poseidon, Helios, and Artemis are not named outright in this song, but are identified by their attributes. The names of Athena (602) and Dionysos (606) are delayed until their characterizations are complete, and Zeus and Aither are partially characterized before they are named. This elaborate allusive reference is common in epic and serious lyric poetry (especially Pindar); Ar. has exaggerated it. By contrast, in *Knights* Poseidon and Athena, the only two deities invoked, are named outright in the first verse of ode and antode respectively.

563–4 θεῶν Ζῆνα τύραννον: 'Zeus, . . . ruler of the gods'.

566 ταμίαν: Poseidon is '*ταμίας* of the trident' because it is he who decides when to use it to cause earthquakes and tidal waves. Cf. Soph. *Ant.* 1154 *τὸν ταμίαν* (sc. *ἀγαθῶν*) *Ἴακχον*.

568 ἄγριον: 'Savage', an appropriate word for rough seas, is strong language when used of the god.

570 βιοθρέμμονα πάντων: They are not exactly philosophizing, for the ordinary Greek recognized that the life of plants and animals depends on the weather, but the treatment of Aither as a god does not appear in the fifth century, outside this play, except in two quotations from Euripides: 'treat Aither as Zeus' and 'parent of men and gods'——an idea facilitated by the role of the sky as progenitor in mythological and quasi-philosophical cosmogony.

571 ἱππονώμαν: Cf. Eur. *Hipp.* 1399; there being no Attic prose words in *-νώμης*, Ar. did not 'Atticize' artificially a word no doubt known to him only from poetry. Cf. 278, 597.

(iv) **575–94.** *Epirrhema*

The Chorus now addresses the audience as clouds, deities, speaking to the citizens of Athens and giving political advice relevant to the date at which the original version of the play was produced (cf. p. xxix).

Normally, as here, the metre of the epirrhema is the trochaic tetrameter catalectic (e.g. *Ach.* 676 ff.). Normally, too, its matter is (in the broad sense) political, its standpoint critical, and it is spoken by the chorus-leader in character; cf. *Ach.* 676, 'We old men criticize the city.'

579 ἔξοδος: The dispatch of a military force, often on a small scale and only for a few days.

580 μηδενὶ ξὺν νῷ: The ordinary soldier, whose standpoint Old Comedy adopts, commonly regards his generals and their orders as half-witted. **τότ' . . . ψακάζομεν:** Thunder and rain, like earth-tremors, signified that the gods disapproved (for their own inscrutable reasons) of the enterprise, and sometimes it was abandoned, if this was practicable. In *Ach.* 170 f. Dikaiopolis brings about the dissolution of the Assembly by pretending that it is coming on to rain. It appears from *Ach.* 1073 ff., however, that snow did not necessarily take precedence over military requirements.

581 βυρσοδέψην Παφλαγόνα: Kleon, the 'Paphlagonian slave' of *Knights* 2 (etc.), and a 'tanner', as in *Knights* 44, because Kleon made his living from tanneries. The radical democracy of late fifth-century Athens retained a strong tendency to elect wealthy aristocrats to high office (many offices, of course, were filled by lot, not by election), and it was possible for the comic poets to sneer at *novi homines*.

582 ᾑρεῖσθε: The imperfect is important, cf. 63 n.; Clouds, Sun, and Moon tried to stop the process, but (587) failed. Kleon was elected as one of the ten generals for 424/3; at least in the fourth century (we cannot be sure about the fifth) the elections were held 'on a day of favourable omens after the sixth prytany' (Aristotle) and this would normally be in late February or early March.

583 βροντή . . . ἀστράπης: Taken from Sophocles.

584 ἡ σελήνη . . . 586 Κλέων: There was an eclipse of the moon on 29 Oct. 425 and an eclipse of the sun on 21 March 424. Ar., writing the play in the latter part of 424 (and this epirrhema belongs to the original version, for it treats Kleon as still alive), can hardly have regarded *both* eclipses as occurring 'when you were electing Kleon general', and it is better sense to suppose that he means what he says: that at the time when the elections were due the weather was unusually bad, the moon 'started to fade out of her path' (untrue, but topical; on the plural *ὁδούς* cf. 172 n.) and the sun, growing dim (as the sun does in bad weather) 'threatened that he would not shine' (hardly verifiable, but also topical).

587 φασί . . . 589 τρέπειν: Cf. 208 n. *Eccl.* 743 ff. refers to the same comforting belief, as *λόγος . . . τις . . . τῶν γεραιτέρων*.

590 τοῦτο: The election of Kleon.

591 λάρον: Cf. *Knights* 956 *λάρος κεχηνὼς ἐπὶ πέτρας δημηγορῶν*, 'a gull with gaping beak, making a speech on a rock'. **δώρων:** '(Accepting) bribes'. It was a standard assumption of ancient politics—and, for all we know, often justified—that one's adversaries were corrupt.

592 φιμώσητε . . . αὐχένα: A disagreeable way of imprisoning a man, by putting his hands, feet, and head each through a hole in a board.

593 τἀρχαῖον: 'As they were', not necessarily a long time ago; cf. *Knights* 1387 *μακάριος εἰς τἀρχαῖα δὴ καθίσταμαι*. **εἴ τι κἀξημάρτετε:** 'Any mistake that you *did* make'.

(v) **595–606.** *Antode*

595 ἀμφί μοι . . . ἄναξ: A poem of Terpander began *ἀμφί μοι αὖτις* (*αὖτε*?) *ἄνακτα*, a formula followed by dithyrambic poets; it serves to introduce a multiple invocation, and no imperatives are addressed to the gods invoked.

596 Κυνθίαν: Kynthos is the rocky height (106 m.) on Delos, and Delos was comparable with Delphi as a centre of the cult of Apollo.

597 ὑψικέρατα πέτραν: The phrase is Pindar's.

599 f. Λυδῶν: The great temple of Artemis at Ephesos was a focus of Lydian as well as Greek worship; Kroisos had contributed to its building.

602 αἰγίδος ἡνίοχος: The phrase suggests that the goddess travels by flapping the aigis, which (in sculpture and vase-paintings) she wears like a short cape. Cf. Aisch. *Eum.* 403 f. *ἦλθον . . . πτερῶν ἄτερ ῥοιβδοῦσα κόλπον αἰγίδος*. **πολιοῦχος:** A stock epithet of Athena (cf. *Knights* 581) in the dedications on the Akropolis. **Ἀθάνα:** Possible forms of her name are the epic *Ἀθήνη* and *Ἀθηναίη*, the lyric and dramatic (even in dialogue) *Ἀθάνα*, and the normal Attic *Ἀθηναία* or *Ἀθηνᾶ*. On the dedications Ἀθήνη occurs sporadically, Ἀθάνα once, and the hybrid Ἀθαναία once.

603 Παρνασσίαν: It sounds for a moment as if we are coming back to Apollo; but the song is rounded off with Dionysos (cf. 311 ff.), who was the god of Delphi during the three winter months. The running of the maenads over the ridges of Parnassos, carrying torches, is mentioned in Soph. *Ant.* 1125 ff. and Eur. *Ion* 714 ff.

606 κωμαστής: *κωμῳδία* gives the word a special appropriateness; cf. the chorus in *Thesm.* 989 *ἐγὼ δὲ κώμοις σε* (sc. Dionysos) *φιλοχόροισι μέλψω.*

(vi) **607–626.** *Antepirrhema*

The Chorus again addresses the audience in character. The antepirrhema is in the same metre as the epirrhema, and has the same number (twenty) of verses. This identity of antepirrhema with epirrhema in character, metre, and size is found also in other plays.

608 ἐπέστειλεν . . . 610 πεπονθέναι: 'Charged us, first of all, to salute' (*φράσαι χαίρειν* = *φράσαι* "*χαίρετε*") 'the Athenians and their allies; then she said she was angry, for ⟨she said⟩ she has been very badly treated . . .'

612 δραχμήν: One could hardly say *ὠφελῶ σε δραχμήν*, but the accusative is made possible by the preceding internal accusative *ἔλαττον*.

614 πρίῃ: Some MSS. have *πρίω*, but the aorist imperative in a prohibition, whether one is cajoling a master or giving orders to a slave, has no parallel in comedy (*Thesm.* 870 is a parody of Sophokles). **Σεληναίης:** An ancient fragment has *σεληνα*]*ιας*, but since *Σεληναίη* (found in Empedokles) is in any case a grandiloquent name for the moon there is no reason why it should not be made (humorously) to sound more grandiloquent by retaining the epic form. Two Akropolis dedications use *Ἀθηναίη* even when nothing else in them is 'epicized'. Cf. 989.

620 δικάζετε: Cf. 208 n. The lawcourts were shut on festival days.

622 τὸν Μέμνον' ἢ Σαρπηδόνα: The gods mourn Memnon because he was the son of Dawn, and killed at Troy. Sarpedon was a son of Zeus and 'dearest of men' to him; Zeus wished that he could save him from death at the hands of Patroklos (*Il.* xvi. 431 ff.), and had his body miraculously conveyed by Sleep and Death to his native land (ibid. 666 ff.). For the article with the first of two co-ordinated nouns but not with the second cf. 104, 1418, and 1465.

623 ἀνθ' ὧν . . . 625 ἀφῃρέθη: Each state which was a member of the Delphic Amphiktyony sent to its meetings representatives called *ἱερομνήμονες*: the Athenian representatives were appointed by lot, hence λαχών. How 'we, the gods' 'took away Hyperbolos' chaplet (which he was wearing as a badge of ceremonial office) we do not know; perhaps by blowing it off at an embarrassing moment. **κἄπειθ'**: Cf. p. xxxii.

626 κατὰ σελήνην: Cf. 17 n. It seems that recently (but we do not know whether the antepirrhema belongs to the original play or the revised version) there had been intercalations of days which temporarily put the month out of step with the moon. Evidence that either Athens or Sparta (or both) was out of step at the time of the original play is provided by Thuc. iv. 118 f., where the 14th of a month at Athens (118. 11) = the 12th at Sparta (119. 1).

(E) 627–888. STREPSIADES AS A PUPIL

(i) 627–99. *Socrates tries to teach Strepsiades metre and grammar*

Socrates comes out of the school alone, expressing his exasperation.

627 μὰ τὴν Ἀναπνοήν: Of the three deities by which he swears (cf. 1234 n.) we have already encountered Chaos (424 *v.* n.) and Aer (264); 'Breath' or 'Breathing' is new to us; cf. 814. It would be interesting to know whether the work attributed to Pythagoras, beginning with the words *οὐ μὰ τὸν ἀέρα τὸν ἀναπνέω*, was already in circulation in Ar.'s time.

628 οὕτως . . . οὐδαμοῦ: *οὕτως* qualifies the adjectives which follow, and *οὐδαμοῦ* reinforces *οὐκ εἶδον*.

629 σκαιόν: Coupled with *ἀπαίδευτος* in *Wasps* 1183, and with *ἀναίσθητος* in Dem. xviii. 120; it is the opposite of *δεξιός* (cf. 148 n.) in *Wasps* 1265 f.

630 ὅστις . . . 631 μαθεῖν: Almost (but it is heavy-handed in English) 'for he . . . *trying to learn* . . . has forgotten them before he has *succeeded in learning* them'; cf. 63 n., 582. **ταῦτ' ἐπιλέλησται**: For the demonstrative in the main clause, referring to something in the preceding participial clause, cf. 591 f.

633 ἕξει: When a question is asked with a *negatived* future, it is equivalent to a command (e.g. 1296); a *positive* future sometimes occurs when a command is expected, and we cannot always be sure whether it is a question or not. Probably it is a statement when the sentence is long and the style serious (cf. 811 n.), a question when the sentence is short and the tone lively, as here and in 1299. **τὸν ἀσκάντην**: Cf. 254 n.

634 οὐκ ἐῶσί μ': The joke is akin to the traditional modern joke about ripe cheese walking. Strepsiades emerges, carrying the bed.

635 ἰδού: Cf. 82. Strepsiades puts down the bed in a central position, but does not yet lie on it; cf. 694 n.

637 οὐδέν: This is not Strepsiades' answer, ignored by Socrates; the dramatic point is spoiled if Strepsiades says at this stage that he does not want to learn anything new. He does want to learn (738 f.) *τὸν ἄδικον λόγον*.

638. The difference between *μέτρον* and *ῥυθμός* is best explained by saying that an iambic tetrameter and a trochaic tetrameter (cf. p. xxxvi) differ *ῥυθμῷ* but not *μέτρῳ*, whereas an iambic trimeter and an iambic tetrameter differ *μέτρῳ* but not *ῥυθμῷ*. **ἐπῶν**: Hardly 'verses' here (cf. 541 n.), because when both the 'measure' and the 'rhythm' of a verse have been identified the formal classification of that verse is complete. After 'measures' (639–46) and 'rhythms' (647–54) Socrates goes on (658 ff.) to linguistic questions, the first of which is 'which creatures are *ὀρθῶς* masculine?' Therefore Ar. probably intends by *ἐπῶν* 'words', as in Hdt. ii. 30. 1, 'their name is *asmakh* and this *ἔπος* means . . .'. Pl. *Phdr.* 267 C ascribes *ὀρθοέπειά τις* to Protagoras.

640. Strepsiades, as a farmer, was possibly selling *ἄλφιτα*, not buying it. 'I was cheated to the extent of two choinikes.'

641 ὅτι: 'What . . .' or 'which . . .'

642 τὸ τρίμετρον ἢ τὸ τετράμετρον: When we first meet these and similar words they are plainly adjectives, e.g. Hdt. i. 47. 2 *ἐν ἑξαμέτρῳ τόνῳ*, lit. 'in six-measure metrical form' (cf. 968 n.); this can be abbreviated to *ἐν ἑξαμέτρῳ*, which is not quite 'in a hexameter'. The only 'three-measure ⟨verse⟩' in common use was the iambic trimeter; Hdt. i. 174. 5 quotes verses uttered *ἐν τριμέτρῳ τόνῳ*, and they are iambic trimeters. What Aristotle calls the 'four-measure ⟨verse⟩' is plainly the trochaic tetrameter. Whether Ar. has in mind the iambic tetrameter or the trochaic tetrameter, or either to the exclusion of the other, is not easily determined; but since the iambic tetrameter was confined to Comedy, whereas the trochaic tetrameter was not uncommon in the dialogue of Tragedy, the obvious aesthetic comparison is between the iambic trimeter and the trochaic tetrameter.

643. 'I ⟨regard⟩ nothing ⟨as⟩ superior to the half-hekteus.'

644 οὐδὲν λέγεις: 'You're talking nonsense'; cf. 781 (the same point) and 1095, 'there's nothing in your argument.' **περίδου**: lit., 'bet for me ⟨to see⟩ if a half-hekteus is not four-measured', i.e. 'I bet you that . . . is . . .'

645 τετράμετρον: 1 *μέδιμνος* = 6 *ἑκτεῖς*: 1 *ἑκτεύς* = 8 *χοίνικες*: hence 4 *χοίνικες* = 1 *ἡμιεκτέων*, approximately 4,350 cubic centimeters.

646 ὡς: Exclamatory, 'How . . .!'

647 ταχύ γ' ἄν: For this sarcastic expression cf. Dem. xxi. 209 *ταχύ γ' ἂν χαρίσαιντο, οὐ γάρ;*, 'they'd be so quick to show him favours, don't you think?' There is no exact parallel in comedy (but cf. 8 n.). **ῥυθμῶν**: Cf. 638 n.

648. Note that it is Strepsiades who takes the initiative in pursuing the subject of rhythm. **πρός**: Here almost 'to get'.

649 κομψόν: 'Discriminating' or 'accomplished'. **συνουσίᾳ**: *συνουσία* can refer to a drinking-party (cf. English 'we have company tonight' = 'we are giving a party tonight'), but it can also refer to any other kind of meeting or association.

650 τῶν ῥυθμῶν: Perhaps sc. of the songs sung at the party.

651 κατ' ἐνόπλιον . . . δάκτυλον: Pl. *Rep.* 400 B mentions (but does not explain) both *δάκτυλος* and *ἐνόπλιός τις σύνθετος* (sc. *ῥυθμός*) among the technical terms used by Damon in the time of Socrates. The expression *ἐνόπλιος ῥυθμός* occurs also in Xenophon; *δάκτυλος*, as a metrical term, does not recur in Classical Greek. In Hellenistic metricians it usually means – ⏑ ⏑, but Aristoxenos defines the *δακτυλικὸν γένος* of 'feet' as *ἐν ἴσῳ λόγῳ*. It is perilous to interpret Ar. in the light of later technical works, and even more so to interpret him in the light of modern definitions. Possibly Ar. included under rhythms *κατὰ δάκτυλον* all types of verse made up of the units – ⏕ or ⏕ –, and under *κατ' ἐνόπλιον* all those in which a division of the verse into such units is not possible without 'remainder'; another possibility is that he meant by *δάκτυλος* – ⏕ – ⏕ – and by *ἐνόπλιος* ⏕ – ⏕ – ⏕ – –.

652 εἰπὲ δή . . . 654 οὑτοσί: 'Well, tell me then!', as in 683 (following Strepsiades' confident *ἀλλ' οἶδ' ἔγωγε*) and 778. Either 653 or 654 would be a possible humorous answer; together they do not constitute a possible answer, because there is no adversative particle linking 654 to 653 and no room for its introduction by conjecture, and no type of asyndeton of which 654 would be a recognizable example. Plainly at 653 Strepsiades holds up a finger, and at 654 he extends his middle finger in a vulgar gesture made by Greek boys. I suggest that the two lines are ancient alternatives, such as we find in *Frogs* 1431 f.:

> *οὐ χρὴ λέοντος σκυμνὸν ἐν πόλει τρέφειν·* 1431a (om. testimonia)
> *μάλιστα μὲν λέοντα μὴ 'ν πόλει τρέφειν·* 1431b (om. some MSS.)
> *ἢν δ' ἐκτραφῇ τις, τοῖς τρόποις ὑπηρετεῖν.* 1432

654 is a more pungent joke than 653 and therefore to be preferred. *μέν* does little more than emphasize *πρὸ τοῦ* (cf. 732 and *ἐγὼ μέν* in 643), implying an antithesis between then and now which need not be made more explicit. It cannot (in Attic) mean 'but'.

655 οὐ γάρ: Strepsiades rebuts the suggestion that he is to blame; almost 'No, I'm not, I just don't want . . .'

656 τί δαί: Cf. *Wasps* 1211 f., 'Is that how you want me to lie?'—'Oh, no!'— *πῶς δαί;* (= 'How, then?'). Ctr. 1275 below.

659 τῶν τετραπόδων . . . 661 ἀλεκτρυών: Socrates says that Strepsiades must learn '⟨e.g.⟩ which of the ⟨domestic⟩ animals are rightly ⟨called by⟩ masculine ⟨names⟩.' Strepsiades assumes that he is being asked a simpler question, whether he can distinguish male from female animals; and, not surprisingly, having visualized three which have names unlike those of the females, he goes on to visualize a male dog (*κύων* means both 'dog' and 'bitch', but that does not matter, because he is not thinking about *words*) and then a male fowl, which is not *τετράπους* but is naturally thought of in the same context. It is possible that in actual Attic usage *τετράπους*, despite its etymology, included domestic fowls. **ὀρθῶς**: Cf. 638 n. Protagoras expatiated on the genders of nouns, as part of *ὀνομάτων ὀρθότης*.

662 ὁρᾷς ἃ πάσχεις . . . 663 ἄρρενα: Socrates does not mean 'You have just used the same word for male and female' (as the Athenians did, in the case of *ἀλεκτρυών*) but 'You have just used for the male a word which, as we all know, is used by the ignorant for the female also.'

664 Σω. πῶς: Cf. *Peace* 847 *πόθεν δ' . . .; — πόθεν; ἐκ τοὐρανοῦ*. Emendation to *φέρ'. Σω. ὅπως;* (cf. 677) is unnecessary. Nor need we suspect that Ar. divided the line between the speakers after the second *πῶς*, so that Strepsiades asks *πῶς δή; φέρε πῶς* (cf. *Lys.* 574 *πῶς δή; φέρ' ἴδω*); for the position of *φέρε* cf. *Frogs* 993 *σὺ δὲ τί φέρε πρὸς ταῦτα λέξεις;*

666 ἀλεκτρύαιναν . . . ἀλέκτορα: Whereas *ἀλεκτρύαινα* is coined for the occasion, on the analogy of *θεράπαινα*, 'slave-girl', and *λέαινα*, 'lioness', *ἀλέκτωρ*, 'cock', was already established.

669 διαλφιτώσω: 'I'll fill your trough with flour right round.' **κάρδοπον**: A trough or tray in which dough was kneaded. On *ἄλφιτα* cf. 106 n.

672 μάλιστά γε . . . 673 Κλεώνυμον: On Kleonymos cf. 353 n. For the repeated *γε* cf. 696.

674 δύναται: *δύνασθαι* in the sense 'mean' is attested as early as Herodotos, but Ar. means something less precise: '⟨The word⟩ "*κάρδοπος*" has ⟨in one respect⟩ the same power (worth, value) as ⟨the name⟩ "*Κλεώνυμος*" '—because it is a word which sounds like the name of a male but denotes something female.

675 ὦ 'γάθ': Used both in encouragement and (as here) in expostulation (cf. 726). *μάττεσθαι* is 'knead', 'make dough' (cf. 788).

676 ἀνεμάττετο: The middle *ἀναμάττεσθαι* does not occur elsewhere in Classical Greek, nor does it refer in Hellenistic Greek to kneading dough. The past tenses show that Kleonymos is being ridiculed not for some general characteristic which he still possesses but for something which he did on an occasion, or during a period, which Ar. expects his audience to identify. This occasion is probably related to whatever underlies *Knights* 1292 ff., where Kleonymos is ridiculed for bestial greed, bad manners, and sponging. It is hard not to feel that 'he kneaded his dough in a round mortar' is more than a mere reference to gross habits or to poverty; what is the point of 'round', and of the prefix ἀν-? One would expect ἀναμάττεσθαι (lit., 'knead up for oneself'), like δέφεσθαι, to denote male masturbation, in which case the 'round mortar' would be the two hands. Strepsiades can make the metaphor fully intelligible by gesture. For masturbation as a humorous topic cf. 734; it is improbable that the Greeks attached moral significance to it, but it could be ridiculed on much the same basis as manifestations of hunger and poverty.

678 τὴν Σωστράτην: This is a common name among women, and if Ar. means to ridicule one Sostratos for effeminacy, he has not made it easy for the audience to see the joke.

679 ὀρθῶς γὰρ λέγεις: 'Yes, that's right.' The variant *ὀρθότερον λέγεις* is a banalization of this idiomatic *γάρ*.

680 ἐκεῖνο †δ' ἦν ἄν†: The forward reference of *ἐκεῖνο* is normal, but the oddity of the words has not been noticed. If Strepsiades speaks the line, we expect him to express his realization of the correct form, "*καρδόπη*". δ' has no place in such an utterance. *ἄρ' ἦν* or *ἦν ἄρα* would be possible, though not exactly appropriate, for it implies 'that's what it was all the time, if only I had known'; Strepsiades might, of course, be looking at his lesson in that light. On the other hand, if Socrates speaks the line, δ' is intelligible, but *ἦν ἄν* not at all; we expect Socrates to speak dogmatically, not tentatively, and still less as if he had just realized something. Suspicion of the text is increased by the fact that, although *ἦν ἄν* in the sense 'it must be' or 'it is, I suppose' has affinities with *εἴη ἄν* 'must have been' or 'were, I think', no one has yet pointed to a clear parallel; certainly the idiom *ἐβουλόμην ἄν* has nothing in common with it semantically. Observing the instability of *ἄρα* in the MSS. (it is often corrupted to *ἄν*), and having strong grounds for believing δ' interpolated with *ἄρ'* in 1028 (*v.* n.), I suspect that Ar. may have written *ἐκεῖν' ἄρ' ἂν εἴη* or *ἐκεῖνο τἄρ' ἦν*. *τἄρα* is used elsewhere when the speaker is communicating something which he regards as new to the hearer, and Strepsiades might put the discovery of *Κλεωνύμη* into this category. In any case I think that it is Strepsiades who speaks this line.

681 περὶ τῶν ὀνομάτων: Not, as so often (cf. 638 n.), 'words', but 'names' in the narrow sense, as we see from what follows.

684. 'These', says the Scholiast, 'were prostitutes.' They were also quite ordinary Athenian women's names (cf. 'Lysilla' in *Thesm.* 374), and unless there was a well-known 'firm' or 'team' of prostitutes of whom four bore these names the audience could hardly understand the line as a reference to actual persons.

686. Melesias is not mentioned elsewhere, but Philoxenos in *Wasps* 84 is *καταπύγων*, and it is probable that Ar. has taken the opportunity to name three men whose masculinity could be called in question. The failure, real or alleged, of one Ameinias to fulfil his military duties was current or recent gossip. Cf. 691 n.

687 ὦ πόνηρε: This is not always abusive, but it is certainly brusque. **ἔστ' οὐκ ἄρρενα**: Cf. *Birds* 32 *ὢν οὐκ ἀστός*, 'though he is a non-citizen'.

688 ὑμῖν: The variant *ἡμῖν* is less convincing, since Strepsiades is still far from identifying himself with the Socratics. **ἐπεί**: Almost 'I'll tell you why: . . .'

691 τὴν Ἀμεινίαν: Ameinias is the name of a man (or men) ridiculed by comic poets for a variety of social and political offences.

692 ἥτις: The variant would flatten the joke, and Hesychios' entry *ἥτις· ὅστις* must refer to this passage.

694 οὐδέν: Strepsiades has asked 'What is the point of my being taught . . .' (*τί . . . μανθάνω;*), and the answer seems to be 'There is no point ⟨sc. in going on⟩'—because of Strepsiades' lack of interest. Cf. Eur. *Med.* 64, where the old man, in reply to 'What is it? Don't begrudge telling me!', says *οὐδέν* ('It's nothing')· *μετέγνων καὶ τὰ πρόσθ' εἰρημένα*. In both passages the sense is close to 'Never mind, never mind!' **δευρί**: Socrates gestures towards the bed, and perhaps pulls back the blankets for Strepsiades to get in.

696. Strepsiades has retreated from the bed in horror.

697 αὐτὰ ταῦτ': Strepsiades' point is that he can do everything required without getting into the bed; *αὐτά* is almost 'complete' or 'unimpaired'.

698 οὐκ ἔστι παρὰ ταῦτ' ἄλλα: = *Wasps* 1166; 'there's no alternative to this.' Socrates stands sternly by the bed, and Strepsiades gets into it fearfully.

(ii) **700–6.** *Strophe. The Chorus encourages Strepsiades*

In the MSS. this stanza is sung by Socrates. But: (i) Socrates' *οὗτος τί ποιεῖς;* in 723 shows that he has not been aware that Strepsiades is lamenting the bugs instead of thinking, and therefore Socrates should not be present during 700–22; (ii) the antistrophe (804–10) responding to 700–6 must be sung by the Chorus (*δι' ἡμᾶς . . . μόνας θεῶν*), and everywhere else in Ar. similarly widely spaced strophe and antistrophe are either choral or part-choral; (iii) there is evidence that in Heliodoros' text 708 (*v.* p. xxxi), given to Socrates in our extant MSS., was uttered by the Chorus; (iv) we have already seen that the MSS. attribution of 457–60, 462–4, and 466–75 to Socrates is demonstrably wrong (cf. p. 114).

The extent to which the Chorus identifies itself with Socrates is noteworthy, especially in relation to the advice given by Socrates in 740 ff. and 762 ff.

The metrical analysis of 700–6 ~ 804–9 is:

(1) 700 f. ~ 804 f.
– – ⏑ – | – ⏑ ⏑ – – ⏑ ⏑ – ⏑ – – |
(2) 702–4 ~ 806 f.
⏑ – | ⏑ – – ⏑ – ⏑ ⏑ – ⏑ ⏑ – ⏑ – | ⏑ – ⏑ – – |
(3) 705 f. ~ 808 f.
⏑ – ⏑ | ⏖ ⏑ – ⏑ – – ⏑ ⏑ – ⏑ – ⏑ – |

(1) is an iambo-choriambic tetrameter of the form *ia ch ch ba*, i.e. choriambic dimeter + aristophanean. (3) is an iambo-choriambic tetrameter of the form *ia ia ch ia*. There are several possible analyses of (2); that adopted here begins with *ia* and ends with *ia ba*. Its second element is found in predominantly choriambic contexts, e.g. Eur. *El.* 439 κοῦφον ἅλμα ποδῶν Ἀχιλῆ ~ 449 ἱππόταν τρέφεν Ἑλλάδι φῶς.

706 ends a sentence. 809 ends in mid sentence, and there follow two more verses, to which nothing between 706 and 707 responds. It is also remarkable that Ar. nowhere else ends a stanza with any acatalectic aeolic colon such as -στω γλυκύθυμος ὀμμάτων. If Ar. intended Strepsiades' cries of pain to 'interrupt' the strophe, it can only be said that he does nothing like this anywhere else; and he makes abundant use of cries of pain, joy, or surprise. A more likely explanation is that he cancelled, in the process of revision, what originally followed 706 but never composed a fresh version to fill the gap; cf. 887 f. n. The source of the metrical analysis in the scholion on 804 knew of nothing responding to 810–13.

700 φρόντιζε δὴ καὶ διάθρει: Both these verbs are intransitive; σαυτόν is object of στρόβει, and πάντα τρόπον an adverbial phrase with στρόβει.

702 στρόβει πυκνώσας: στρόβει in *Wasps* 1528 refers to energetic dancing, coupled with παράβαινε κύκλῳ. With πυκνώσας, which in Hdt. ix. 18. 1 is used of an army closing its ranks, there is an element of contradiction; in 'gathering oneself together' one does not 'whirl'. But the highly metaphorical words of the Chorus (πυκνώσας is meant to suggest πυκνός, 'wise', familiar from epic onwards) are accompanied by Strepsiades' contortions as the bugs bite him; he twists and turns (στροβεῖ), shrinks into as small an area of the bed as possible (πυκνοῖ), and at 704 (πήδα) gives a frantic jump.

703 ταχὺς . . . 705 φρενός: Cf. Socrates' advice, 743 f. The nominative adjective ταχύς, agreeing with the subject of πήδα, serves the same function as an adverb, 'quickly'.

705 ὕπνος . . . 706 ὀμμάτων: Cf. 415, 732.

(iii) **707–22.** *Strepsiades in torment*

There may be parody here of a tragic hero expressing his agony in anapaestic verse; cf. Eur. *Hipp.* 1347 ff.

In the MSS. Socrates utters both 708 and 716. But the Scholiast on 707 ff. distinguishes between 707 and 708 as *τὸ μὲν τοῦ πρεσβύτου* and *τὸ δὲ τοῦ χοροῦ*, and *οὗτος τί ποιεῖς;* in 723 can hardly be uttered by the same person as 716. See p. 137 on Socrates' absence from the stage.

708 τί πάσχεις; τί κάμνεις;: For the dramatic effect of bacchiac rhythm, which is far commoner in tragedy than in comedy, cf. *Lys.* 711 *ἀληθῆ ἀληθῆ* and 716 *ἰὼ Ζεῦ*, in an elaborate paratragic setting (706–17).

710 οἱ Κορίνθιοι: It is possible that *κόρεις*, 'bugs', was current slang for 'Corinthians' (cf. the modern 'Jerries' = 'Germans', etc.), and that the point of the joke is its reversal.

711–15 καὶ τὰς πλευράς . . . καί μ' ἀπολοῦσιν: Combination of symmetry and assonance to this degree is unusual, though there are comparable passages in Comedy. Ennius used the same device for tragic effect in a passage called by Cicero (*Tusc.* iii. 44) *praeclarum carmen . . . et rebus et uerbis et modis lugubre: 'haec omnia uidi inflammari, Priami ui uitam euitari, Iouis aram sanguine turpari.'* **δαρδάπτουσιν:** The word is predominantly epic, but not necessarily alien to Attic; cf. 995 n. **καὶ τὴν ψυχὴν ἐκπίνουσιν:** In Homer *ψυχή* is sometimes treated as a kind of vapour which escapes when the body is pierced by a weapon. *ἐκπίνουσιν* suggests that it is here associated with 'life-blood'; cf. the metaphor of Soph. *El.* 785 f. *τοὐμὸν ἐκπίνουσ' ἀεὶ ψυχῆς ἄκρατον αἷμα*—and, of course, it often means simply 'life'.

718 φροῦδα . . . 719 ἐμβάς: For the repetition cf. *Lys.* 962 ff. *ποῖος γὰρ ἂν ἢ νέφρος ἀντίσχοι, ποία ψυχή, ποῖοι δ' ὄρχεις, ποία δ' ὀσφύς, ποῖος δ' ὄρρος κτλ.* Since *Clouds* contains at least one clear parody of *Hecuba* (1165 ff. ~ *Hec.* 171 ff.) it is probable that here too the model is another part of the same lament, *Hec.* 159 ff.: *τίς ἀμύνει μοι; ποία γέννα, ποία δὲ πόλις; φροῦδος πρέσβυς, φροῦδοι παῖδες.* Ar. does not use *φροῦδος* much, but he does not confine it to paratragedy. **χρήματα:** As at the start of the play, not as an immediate consequence of initiation; he has not yet learned anything which will alter the situation. **χροιά:** Cf. 103 n., 510 ff. **ἐμβάς:** Cf. 497, 858.

721 φρουρᾶς ᾄδων: 'Singing ⟨a song⟩ of (= belonging to, characteristic of) guard-duty' is intelligible in itself and was no doubt an expression commonly used of passing the time in tedious or uncomfortable circumstances. Cf. the watcher in Aisch. *Ag.* 16 f. For the syntax, cf. *Wasps* 1225 *ᾄδω . . . Ἁρμοδίου* ('one of the songs in which Harmodios is apostrophized') and—a somewhat different relationship

—Men. *Dysk.* 432 f. *αὔλει . . . Πανός*, 'play one of the tunes which are acceptable to Pan' (or 'which belong to the cult of Pan').

(iv) **723–90.** *Socrates loses patience with Strepsiades*

723 οὗτος τί ποιεῖς: Socrates puts his head out of the door (cf. 726–9, 731 n.). The expression *οὗτος τί ποιεῖς* (*πάσχεις, δρᾷς*) is used when the person addressed has begun to do something which he has not been doing hitherto or when the speaker notices something which, either through absence or through preoccupation, he has not hitherto noticed. Cf. 1502. Since Strepsiades is not doing anything new, but is simply continuing to be bitten by bugs, the words are a strong indication that Socrates did not speak 716 and has not been present during 700–22.

726 ἀπολεῖ κάκιστ': With these angry words, more a threat than an imprecation (cf. *Ach.* 294 f. *σοῦ γ' ἀκούσωμεν; ἀπολεῖ, κατά σε χώσομεν τοῖς λίθοις*) Socrates bobs back into the school.

727 οὐ μαλθακιστέ' . . . 729 κἀπαιόλημ': The MSS. give these words to Socrates. There is no objection to Socrates' passing from threats to encouragement in the course of half a line—such a change of mood, often required for a succession of different kinds of joke, would be characteristic of comedy (cf. 646 f.)—but the shorter we make Socrates' absence or withdrawal from the scene the harder it becomes to understand 731, 'Well, now, first of all let's see . . .' 727–9 must be uttered by the Chorus. **ἀποστερητικός**: -*ικός* was a fashionable suffix at this time; cf. 318 n.

729 τίς . . . 730 ἀποστερητρίδα: 'If only someone would . . .!'; cf. *Lys.* 1086 *τίς ἂν φράσειε κτλ.*, 'I wish someone would tell me . . .' One *ἐπιβάλλει* bedclothes—cf. the words *ἐπίβλημα* and *ἐπιβλήτια*—but one does not *ἐπιβάλλειν* anything *from* bedclothes; nor is *ἐπιβάλλειν γνώμην* meaningful in itself. If, however, we take *ἐξ* in a sense in which 'instead of', 'after', are blended (cf. Dem. xviii. 131 *πλούσιος ἐκ πτωχοῦ γεγονώς*, 'having become rich, though formerly a beggar') the point is: 'Socrates has put bedclothes on me; now, I wish that someone would put an idea into my head.' *ἀποστερητρίδα*, not the only possible way of forming a feminine corresponding to *ἀποστερητής* and by no means the only possible feminine adjective cognate with *ἀποστερεῖν* (cf. 728), reminds us of *αὐλητρίς* and *ὀρχηστρίς*, and there may be a point here foreshadowing 734: Strepsiades thinks of *γνώμην ἀποστερητρίδα* as a personable young woman materializing in his embrace under the bedclothes. It is also possible that *ἀρν-* is meant to suggest *ἔξαρνος* (cf. 1203), in which case Strepsiades would also mean: 'I can deny that I've borrowed the money; all I need now is an idea of how to get away with it.' This, however, is far-fetched, in that denial is not so much a step towards *ἀποστερεῖν* as an aspect of it, and Strepsiades can hardly venture on denial until he thinks he has mastered the technique of *ἀποστερεῖν*.

731 φέρε νυν: Socrates now bustles out of the school and crosses to Strepsiades, who is lying motionless. **πρῶτον**: Cf. p. xxxii. **ὅτι δρᾷ, τουτονί**: *ἀθρήσω τουτονὶ ὅτι δρᾷ* = *ἀθρήσω ὅτι δρᾷ οὑτοσί* would be commonplace Greek; the word-order here is unusual, but cf. *Eccl.* 1125 *φράσατέ μοι . . . τὸν ἄνδρ' ὅπου 'στί, τῆς ἐμῆς κεκτημένης* = 'Tell me where my mistress's husband is.'

732. Strepsiades, whose thoughts have been far away, jumps guiltily.

734 τὸ πέος: This reflects a common assumption of vulgar humour, that an adult male cannot be in bed alone and awake for long without masturbating (cf. 676 n.). The Scholiast suggests that Strepsiades throws back the bedclothes and sits up, imitating masturbation with the comic phallus (cf. 538 f. n.). This is an inference from 735 *ἐγκαλυψάμενος* and 740 *καλύπτου*, and it may be wrong.

735 ἐγκαλυψάμενος: Right over his head (in order not to be distracted from thought by sights and sounds), to judge from *Frogs* 911 f. *ἐγκαλύψας . . . τὸ πρόσωπον οὐχὶ δεικνύς*.

737 αὐτός . . . λέγε: Cf. 636 f. *αὐτός* and *πρῶτος* together constitute an established expression; cf. Thuc. vi. 88. 8 'the Corinthians, having voted *αὐτοὶ πρῶτοι* for help to Syracuse, also sent envoys to Sparta with the Syracusan envoys.' The clause *ὅτι βούλει* serves as object of *ἐξευρών* and of *λέγε*.

738 ἁγὼ . . . 739 τόκων: = *ἃ ἐγὼ φροντίζειν βούλομαι· βούλομαι γὰρ περὶ τῶν τόκων φροντίζειν.*

740 σχάσας . . . 742 σκοπῶν: In other (and less colourful) words: do not commit yourself at once to that approach to the problem which you have already tried in vain, but cast around (lit. 'cut adrift your thought thin'; cf. 229 f.) and see if it may not afford a purchase when approached from a different direction. *κατὰ μικρόν* = 'a step at a time'. *ὀρθῶς διαιρῶν καὶ σκοπῶν* is advice of a different kind, but equally alien to people like Strepsiades. *διαίρεσις* is a philosophical procedure prominent in Plato's late dialogues, but not earlier; and, in a general sense, it is essential to all rational thought.

742 οἴμοι τάλας: Strepsiades has obeyed the command *καλύπτου*, and now the bugs are busy on him again.

743 κἂν ἀπορῇς . . . 744 ἄπελθε: Cf. 703 ff., and for *ἄπελθε* cf. Eur. *Iph. Taur.* 546 *ἄπελθε τοῦ λόγου τούτου.*

745 ζυγώθρισον: This must be cognate with *ζυγόν* in the sense 'beam of a balance', and mean 'weigh up'.

746. We have to get Strepsiades out of bed at some point, to introduce mobility into the ensuing dialogue and put an end to the jokes about bugs. The Scholiast says that he gets up now, and it would be appropriate if Socrates is arrested on his way back into the school by Strepsiades' clambering excitedly out of bed. The bed can be taken into the school by students or slaves at any point from 748 onwards.

748 τὸ τί: Strepsiades has perhaps paused for a moment, to put his idea into words; Socrates is in effect saying 'Go on!' Cf. 694. In 775, however, *τὸ τί* is not an interruption.

749 γυναῖκα . . . 750 σελήνην: 'Suppose . . .' Cf. 769 ff.; no 'apodosis' emerges. Cf. Pl. *Grg.* 513 A, 'What they say of the women who draw down the moon, the Thessalian women.' Menander's *Θεττάλη* portrayed this theme, and the Scholiast says that the women of Thessaly are called witches 'to this day'. **πριάμενος**: *ὠνεῖσθαι* and its aorist *πρίασθαι* are used normally of buying slaves and (not surprisingly) of 'buying' people, i.e. corrupting them by bribery. There is no certain instance of their meaning 'hire', 'engage the services of', and before we give *πριάμενος* that sense here we should reflect that not all slaves were barbarians. Minor wars, of which there was no lack in Thessaly, put an abundance of Greek slaves on the market.

751 λοφεῖον: In *Ach.* 1109 this is a box in which *λόφοι*, 'plumes', 'crests', are kept; whether the word was also used of a box in which a mirror was kept, as Pollux suggests (probably by inference from this passage) is doubtful. Strepsiades thinks of the moon as big enough to need a *λοφεῖον* and also, like a mirror, as needing a receptacle which will protect it against abrasion.

752 κάτροπτον: This is how the word is spelt in all Attic inscriptions down to the late fourth century; etymological pedantry won the day later.

756 μῆνα: Cf. 17 n.

757 εὖ γ': It is not necessary to suppose, either here or in 773, that Socrates' approval is sarcastic or that he is outwardly indulgent to Strepsiades while inwardly despondent about the prospects of such a pupil. In Ar.'s eyes the absurd suggestions of Strepsiades are similar in kind to the Socratic experiment with the flea, and Socrates' approval of them is part of his indiscriminate ridicule of intellectuals. **προβαλῶ**: Cf. 489 n.

758. 'If a lawsuit for five talents were entered against you'.

763 μηλολόνθην: The cockchafer and related species, handsome and conspicuous beetles which spend much of their life on the wing. The reference is to a children's game, tethering a cockchafer by a thin thread and letting it buzz round. The game is still played.

766 ἤδη: 'Before now', almost 'ever'. **παρὰ τοῖσι φαρμακοπώλαις**: It is not obvious at first glance why dealers in *φάρμακα* should sell burning-glasses, but 'remedies' and prophylactics included amulets, bracelets, and rings made from metals and stones which were believed to have magical properties. Medical writers and practising doctors did not believe this, but the gap between the doctor and the layman was surprisingly wide. Cf. *Rep.* 426 B, 'No *φάρμακα*, cautery, or surgery, no spells or amulets or anything else of that kind, will do him any good.'

767 ταύτην: Cf. 83 n.

768 ἅπτουσι: This is our earliest mention of a glass lens; its use for lighting a fire is taken for granted.

769 φέρε τί δῆτ' ἄν: In the MSS. Socrates says these words, whereupon Strepsiades proceeds with *εἰ ταύτην κτλ.* The changes of speaker must be removed; cf. 154 n.

770 γράφοιτο: We might have expected that the *γραμματεύς* would *γράφειν*, the prosecutor *γράφεσθαι*—particularly as the Secretary of the Council is instructed in so many surviving Attic decrees to *ἀναγράψαι* the decree, not *ἀναγράψασθαι*, even though he did not wield the stonecutter's tools himself. But strictly speaking it is the *ὑπογραμματεύς* who holds the tablet and handles the stylus, while the *γραμματεύς* tells him what to write; hence one can say of the *γραμματεύς* either *γράφεται*, 'he sees that it is written down', or *γράφει*, 'he writes it' = 'he causes it to be written'. For the middle cf. 368, and on the causative active 245 n.

771 ὧδε: 'Like this'; Strepsiades demonstrates.

772 ἐκτήξαιμι: The details would be written on a waxed tablet; cf. 19 n.

773 σοφῶς γε: Cf. 94, 757 nn. **νὴ τὰς Χάριτας**: This oath is related by the Scholiast to the story which we find in Pausanias to the effect that Socrates was not only the son of a sculptor but a sculptor himself and that he made the statues of the Graces—in the Propylaia. Socrates in Pl. *Euthyphro* 11 B does indeed refer to Daidalos as 'our ancestor', and it is not unreasonable to interpret this in the light of *Smp.* 186 E, where the doctor Eryximachos uses the expression 'our ancestor' of Asklepios; but we do not know on what evidence the story about the Graces was based. It is by no means necessary as an explanation of the admiring oath *νὴ τὰς Χάριτας*. **οἴμ' ὡς ἥδομαι**: The Scholiast remarks 'In ordinary usage we commonly say *οἴμοι* when someone rejoices', but there is no exact parallel in Ar.

775 ξυνάρπασον: Cf. 490 n. The word is used of sensory perception in Soph. *Aj.* 16.

776 ἀποστρέψαις: = *ἀποστρέψειας*. **ἀντιδικῶν**: We cannot know for certain whether Ar. intended -*δί*- (genitive plural of *ἀντίδικος*) or -*κῶν* (nominative participle of *ἀντιδικεῖν*), 'rebut a lawsuit brought by adversaries' or 'rebut a lawsuit in presenting your (opposing) case'. The second alternative seems the less tautologous; neither word occurs elsewhere in Ar.

777 μέλλων ὀφλήσειν: Lit., 'being about to incur a penalty', i.e. 'when you were obviously going to lose'. **μαρτύρων**: Less was documented in Greek transactions than in ours; 'signatures' were not evidence at all, and although seal-impressions made by a seal-ring were, documentation did not have the finality which we accord it. So much turned upon witnesses; cf. Dem. l. 30, 'I wanted to make the reckoning while the sailors were still there to testify to what had been spent, so that if he afterwards denied anything I could at once refute him.'

779 ἐνεστώσης: 'Still to be heard', 'pending'; a technical term.

780 καλεῖσθ': Another technical term. **τρέχων**: Logic might be thought to demand the aorist *δραμών*, but usage does not; cf. 1213.

781 ἔγωγ': Repudiating *οὐδὲν λέγεις* (cf. 644 n.): 'I *am* saying something', i.e. 'It is *not* nonsense.'

782 εἰσάξει: The word is commonly used of the magistrate who refers the case to the court; but since any verb can bear a causative sense (cf. 245 n.) *εἰσάγειν* is also used (cf. 845) of the litigant who causes his adversary to be brought into court.

783 ἄπερρ': Socrates' patience is at last exhausted, and he wants no more to do with Strepsiades. **διδαξαίμην**: We expect the active; hence the conjectures *διδάξαιμεν* and *διδάξαιμ' ἄν* (for repeated *ἄν* cf. *Birds* 127 *ποιάν τιν' οὖν ἥδιστ' ἂν οἰκοῖτ' ἂν πόλιν;*). But emendation seems unjustified when we consider Pl. *Rep.* 421 E *οὓς ἂν διδάσκῃ, χείρους δημιουργοὺς διδάξεται*. Ar.'s audience *may* have made a difference between *διδαξαίμην* and *διδάξαιμι*, interpreting the former as 'supervise (*or* take charge of) your education'; I would feel no confidence in asserting or denying this. Cf. 368 n.

785 ἅττ' ἂν καὶ μάθῃς: 'Anything that you *have* learned'.

786 ἐπεὶ τί: Virtually = *τί γάρ;* The question is put in justification of the statement made in 785.

787 φέρ' ἴδω . . . 789 τίς ἦν: The luckless Strepsiades has even forgotten (but only temporarily; cf. 1247 ff.) the word *κάρδοπος*. **μέντοι**: Cf. p. xxxii.

790 ἐπιλησμότατον: Morphologically surprising as the superlative of *ἐπιλήσμων* (we expect *ἐπιλησμονέστατον*), but not wholly unparalleled (Sophron has *καταπυγοτέραν*), and emendation is impossible.

(v) **791–803.** *Strepsiades seeks advice from the Chorus*

We naturally expect Socrates to depart into the school at 790; but 803 shows that he is on stage throughout 791–803. It is not impossible to guess at a reason for this. During 791–3 he stamps around in a fury, and makes for the door of the school. At 794 he pauses and listens in curiosity. At the mention of 'son' in 795 he shows a more lively interest, perhaps cupping one ear and raising the index finger of the other hand in the air. At 797 he begins to creep towards Strepsiades from behind, rubbing his hands (or whatever the Greek gesture of pleasurable anticipation may have been); by 803 he is very close to Strepsiades. See 804–13, 813 nn.

792 ἀπὸ γὰρ ὀλοῦμαι: Cf. 1440. This separation of prefix from verb survives in Comedy notably with *ἀπολλύναι* and words of similar meaning; cf. *Frogs* 1047 *κατ' οὖν ἔβαλεν*. **γλωττοστροφεῖν**: Cf. *Frogs* 892, where Euripides prays to *γλώττης στρόφιγξ*: the idea goes back to *Il.* xx. 248 *στρεπτὴ δὲ γλῶσσ' ἐστὶ βροτῶν*.

794 ἡμεῖς . . . 796 μανθάνειν: On the tragic rhythm of these lines cf. 1458 n.

797 ἀλλ' ἔστ' ἔμοιγ' υἱός: We want 'I *have* a son', not '*I* have a son', and may therefore be inclined to emend to *ἀλλ' ἔστί μοι γ'*. This, however, would give the sense 'But I *have* a son, *anyway*!' What we have, I think, is a combination of *ἀλλά* in the sense 'Why, yes!' and the common *ἔγωγε* = 'yes!' (e.g. 769), with which *Lys.* 896 f. *ὀλίγον μέλει σοι . . .;—ἔμοιγε νὴ Δία* has some affinity. **καλός τε κἀγαθός**: Cf. 101 n.

798 ἀλλ' οὐκ ἐθέλει γάρ: 'But, as he doesn't want . . ., what . . .?' Cf. *Wasps* 318 *ἀλλ' οὐ γὰρ οἷός τ' ἔτ' εἴμ' ᾄδειν, τί ποήσω;*

800 καὶ Κοισύρας: Cf. 48 n. The variant *τῶν* will not do. 'The ⟨women⟩ of Koisyra' is not Greek for 'women like Koisyra' or even 'women descended from Koisyra'. *καί* here is akin to Aisch. *Pers.* 749 f. *θεῶν ἁπάντων . . . καὶ Ποσειδῶνος*.

802 ἐξελῶ: Strepsiades repeats the threat which he uttered vainly in 123.

803. Strepsiades rushes into his own house.

(vi) **804–13.** *Antistrophe. The Chorus advises Socrates*

We expect Socrates to go into the school when Strepsiades tells him to (803), but the Chorus now addresses him. It is, of course, quite possible for a chorus to apostrophize an absent character in valediction or when awaiting his appearance (as in *Wasps* 286 ff.). Also Dikaiopolis must be inside the skene while he is addressed by the chorus in *Ach.* 842 ff., for he comes out at 864 in the belief that the Boiotian flautists who strike up at 862 are buzzing insects. There, however, there is no doubt whom the chorus is addressing; but here there is, for the words *ἆρ' αἰσθάνει . . . θεῶν* are equally appropriate whether addressed to Socrates or to Strepsiades, and in the absence of any clue it is not until 808 that we realize that *ὅδ'* must be Strepsiades. (The sense precludes the possibility that *ὅδ'* refers to Pheidippides.) I suggest, therefore, that when Strepsiades departs at 803 Socrates remains on stage for a moment, perhaps rubbing his hands expectantly and jigging with pleasure. He must, of course, go into the school well before 814, for we have to imagine 814–59 as taking place outside Strepsiades' house.

804–9 respond to 700–6. We then have:

(1) 810 f. – ∪ ∪ – –|∪ ∪ – –|∪ ∪ –|
(1) 812 f. ∪ ∪ –|∪ – – –|∪ – – ∪ ∪ –| ∪ – –|

(1) is a pure choriambic trimeter. (2) is an iambo-choriambic tetrameter of the form *ia ia ch ba*, i.e. iambic dimeter + aristophanean, the catalectic form of 705 f. ~ 808 f. For the strong stop within the first metron of (2) cf. 1155. ∪ ∪ – ∪ – is not a common form of iambic metron in Ar.'s lyrics, but cf. *Ach.* 1040 *κατάχει σὺ τῆς χορδῆς τὸ μέλι*: the synizesis *ταχέως* would not be Aristophanic.

806 μόνας θεῶν: Cf. 331, 365, 423 f. nn.

810 γνούς: 'Realizing when a man . . .'; cf. Pl. *Ap.* 27 A *ἆρα γνώσεται . . . ἐμοῦ χαριεντιζομένου.* **ἀπολάψεις**: 'Lap (up)', 'lick (off)'. There is no other example of (*ἀπο*)*λάπτειν* or (*ἀπο*)*λείχειν* in the sense 'extract money', but cf. the metaphorical sense of 'eat', 'drink', 'swallow' (815 n.) There is a variant *ἀπολέψεις*, 'skin', 'peel', 'strip'. This may sound to us an appropriate metaphor, but whether it can mean in Greek 'extract money' turns on a partly corrupt entry in Photios. *λέπειν* means 'wound', 'beat', elsewhere in comedy. The future here is not quite equivalent to an imperative, but rather to 'You will, I hope (I am sure, I have no doubt) . . .'; cf. 633 n. and Lykurg. *Leokr.* 67 *κολαστέον ἐστὶ τοῦτον . . . καὶ οὐ τοῦτο λογιεῖσθε, εἰ κτλ.* **ὅτι πλεῖστον δύνασαι**: Probably not, as the mood and tense might suggest, 'as much are you *are* ⟨as we know⟩ capable of doing', but simply 'as much as you can'; cf. Soph. *Phil.* 849 ff. *ὅτι δύνᾳ μάκιστον κεῖνο . . . ἐξιδοῦ ὅπᾳ πράξεις*, and 348 n., above.

812 ταχέως: For the effect of the placing of the word cf. *Lys.* 829 f. *ἰοὺ ἰοὺ γυναῖκες ἴτε δεῦρ' ὡς ἐμὲ | ταχέως. — τί δ' ἔστιν;* and a common rhetorical phenomenon, the placing of an adverb in -*ως* at the end of a sentence.

813 ἑτέρᾳ τρέπεσθαι: The Chorus's point is: however exasperated you may be with Strepsiades, *don't miss this chance*, which we, your patron deities, have presented to you. Socrates' greed for money is brought into prominence in this part of the play; cf. 876 n. We discover later that the Chorus has been playing a sinister and treacherous part in this train of events; but we have no grounds yet for suspecting this, so that the undertones of *ἑτέρᾳ τρέπεσθαι* can be perceived only by those who have read or seen the play once already. On *τρέπεσθαι* cf. 88 n.

(vii) **814–66.** *Strepsiades puts pressure on Pheidippides*

Strepsiades and Pheidippides come out of their house, the former in a towering rage and the latter bewildered, sullen, and a little frightened.

Whether the father is driving the son before him or dragging him out after him, we cannot tell. Pheidippides, who thinks that Strepsiades has gone mad (816 f., 844 f.), retreats towards the right-hand end of the stage; Strepsiades moves to slightly right of centre (cf. 825, 866 nn.).

Although in the last scene we were given the impression—and it was dramatically necessary, in order that Socrates might be pushed beyond the limit of his patience—that Strepsiades could not retain in his mind anything that he had been taught, for the purposes of the present scene he is represented (814, 828, 847) as tinctured with Socratic manners and doctrines, though not to a significant degree (854 f.).

814 μὰ τὴν Ὁμίχλην: The oath is of Socratic type; cf. 627. **ἐνταυθοῖ**: Cf. 843. The usage of *ἐνταυθοῖ* in Ar. justifies the statement of Herodian that it is synonymous with *ἐνταῦθα*, at least to the extent that it is used of position (as here) as well as of direction.

815 ἔσθι': 'Eat' is used metaphorically of consuming wealth extravagantly, e.g. *Knights* 258 *τὰ κοινά . . . κατεσθίεις*. Hence one point of Strepsiades' words is: 'You've ruined *me*; now Megakles can support you.' The other point is: '*I*'m not going to feed you any more; you can look after yourself.' So in *Peace* 1116, when the oracle-monger Hierokles has referred to Sibylla as an authority (1095) and has also begged shamelessly for a share in the sacrifice, Trygaios says *τὴν Σίβυλλαν ἔσθιε*. **κίονας**: Cf. 46 n., 124. Columns, not uncommon in Hellenistic houses, were in the fifth century a sign of the owner's wealth or pretensions.

816 ὦ δαιμόνιε: Cf. 38 n. **τί χρῆμα**: Cf. 2 n.

817 οὐκ εὖ φρονεῖς: Here plainly equivalent to *παραφρονεῖς* (cf. 844, 1475).

818 ἰδού γ' ἰδού: Cf. 1469. **τῆς μωρίας**: 'What stupidity!'

819 τὸν Δία νομίζειν: Omission of the article *τὸ* in this type of expression is comparatively rare; cf. 268. But *τόν* should not be emended to *τό*; it can be explained as deictic, 'that Zeus' or 'your Zeus'.

820 ἐτεόν: Cf. p. xxxii.

821 ἀρχαϊκά: For the derogatory use of *ἀρχαῖος* cf. 915, 984, 1357, 1469, and for similar ideas, 398 n.

822 γε μήν: Cf. 631. **πρόσελθ'**: So in Eur. *Alc.* 779, Herakles, somewhat drunk and genially offering worldly wisdom to Admetos' slave, says *δεῦρ' ἔλθ' ὅπως ἂν καὶ σοφώτερος γένῃ*. **ἵν' εἰδῇς πλείονα**: We would say 'learn *better*', but *πλέον* (or *πλείω*) *εἰδέναι* suggests special knowledge which is denied to others; cf. Thuc. vii. 49. 4 *ὑπόνοιά μή τι καὶ πλέον εἰδὼς ὁ Νικίας ἰσχυρίζηται*, 'a suspicion that Nikias' insistence was founded on knowledge which they did not possess'.

823 ἀνήρ: 'Grown up', and no longer *παιδάριον*; cf. *Wasps* 1185, 'Are you going to tell stories about mice and weasels *ἐν ἀνδράσιν*?' The common sense 'a real man' does not apply here.

824 ὅπως δέ . . . μηδένα: 'Mind you don't . . .' Strepsiades remembers that what he learnt at the school is a 'mystery', and he adopts the same attitude as the student in 140 and 143.

825 ἰδού: Pheidippides has moved close to his father, in compliance with the command *πρόσελθε*; cf. 82 n.

827 ἀλλὰ τίς: Naturally Pheidippides asks, '*Who*, then, ⟨rules the universe⟩?'; cf. Strepsiades' own question, 368, and p. xix.

828 Δῖνος . . . ἐξεληλακώς: Cf. 381 n.

829 αἰβοῖ: Cf. 102 n. **ἴσθι . . . ἔχον**: We would say 'I assure you', just as we say 'I will tell you . . .' or 'I will explain . . .' where Greek says 'Hear now . . .' or 'Learn . . .'

830 ὁ Μήλιος: There is little doubt that the reference is to Diagoras of Melos, who was regarded, justly or not, as impious, became proverbial for impiety, and in later times is described as an atheist. It appears from *Birds* 1073 f. that when *Birds* was produced (spring 414) Diagoras had been outlawed by the Athenians, possibly during the religious reaction engendered by the mutilation of the herms and the profanation of the mysteries in 415. The Scholiast gives an alternative reference to 'Aristagoras of Melos, a dithyrambic poet', who divulged secrets of the mysteries in words and dance. We have no other information about him; some poetry was attributed to Diagoras, and the name in the scholion may simply be a slip.

831 τὰ ψυλλῶν ἴχνη: Cf. 144–53.

832 τῶν μανιῶν: Cf. *Peace* 65 *τὸ γὰρ παράδειγμα τῶν μανιῶν ἀκούετε*: 'his madness' there, and 'your madness' here. The article is not usual in the expression *εἰς τοσοῦτο*+genitive+'go', 'arrive', etc.

833 χολῶσιν: Cf. *Peace* 66, 'What he said when his madness (*ἡ χολή*, cf. 65 *τῶν μανιῶν*) began'. Side by side with an older belief that madness was a supernatural visitation, the Greeks of Ar.'s time, doctors and laymen alike, tended increasingly to attribute it to injury (cf. 1275 f.) or to biochemical causes, particularly to diffusion of bile. This was, of course, consistent with a belief that the biochemical change was induced in the first place by a god. Excess of bile was most commonly regarded as causing a pathological degree of *anger*; but anger is clearly irrelevant here.

834 φλαῦρον: The word is used especially of ill-treatment, abuse, and slander, cf. 1157. **δεξιούς**: Cf. 148 n.

835 ὑπὸ τῆς φειδωλίας: In expressions with *ὑπό* in the sense 'through', 'because of', the article is sometimes present, more often absent.

836 ἀπεκείρατ': Pheidippides (14 n.) and other young men of high social pretensions wore their hair long, but not artlessly; a Socratic could no doubt keep his own hair short by using a carving-knife.

The Scholiast observes that the meanness imputed to the philosophers by Ar. could in other circumstances be praise of their *ἀρετὴ καὶ καρτερία*. **ἠλείψατο**: Cf. 442 n., 920.

837 λουσόμενος: Washing in warm water, such as was provided at bath-houses, was common enough, especially in cold weather, but could be regarded as a luxury, especially when the weather was tolerably warm, and therefore (*a*) was avoided by ascetics in real life and by philosophers in comedy, out of meanness and indifference to ordinary pleasures, and (*b*) was frowned on by moralists as degenerate and enervating. Note especially 991, 1044 ff., and Hermippos: 'A good man ought not to get drunk or wash in warm water.' The fact that warm water cleanses better than cold does not seem to have been considered.

838 καταλόει μου τὸν βίον: Many forms of *λούειν* imply an alternative imperfective stem *λο-*, e.g. *Wasps* 118 *ἀπέλου* = *ἀπέλουε*. The point is obscure. It was the custom for the members of the family to wash themselves after a funeral; therefore 'you wash yourself as if I were dead' is in itself intelligible. It was also the custom to wash a corpse before the funeral; therefore 'you wash the dirt off me as if I were dead' would also be in itself intelligible. But *λούω* (or *ἀπολούω*) *τί σου* is not Greek for 'I wash something off you', whereas *ἀπολούω τι* and *ἀπολούομαί τι* are Greek respectively for 'I wash something off' and 'I wash something off myself'. It seems that *καταλόει τὸν βίον* must mean 'you are washing away my *βίος* off yourself', i.e. 'you are consuming my livelihood by washing yourself', washing standing for the young man's luxurious life in general; for *κατα-* cf. 857 *καταπεφρόντικα*. The ambiguity of *βίος*, both 'life' (as opposed to death) and 'livelihood' prompts the simile 'as if you were washing yourself after my funeral'.

840 καὶ μάθοι: 'What could one *learn* . . .?' Cf. 1344.

841 ἄληθες: So accented, an exclamatory question, incredulous and indignant.

842 παχύς: It is surprising that this sense (cf. our 'dense', 'thick') does not recur in comedy; similar pre-Hellenistic instances are rare.

843 ἐνταυθοῖ: Cf. 814 n.

844. Strepsiades rushes into the house. Pheidippides soliloquizes.

845 παρανοίας: If a man was incapacitated by insanity or senility his son could obtain through a lawcourt the right to administer the family's property. **εἰσαγαγών**: Cf. 782 n. **ἕλω**: Cf. 591.

847. Strepsiades emerges with a slave who is carrying a cock in one hand and a hen in the other. They are live birds, tied up enough to make their struggles ineffective (I presume it would be cheaper and easier to borrow a couple of birds than to make convincing models). We do not want Strepsiades to carry the birds himself, for we need to be rid of them by 852 or soon after, and there is no dramatic opportunity for Strepsiades to re-enter the house. **τοῦτον τίνα νομίζεις:** Not 'what do you think this is?' *νομίζειν* (~ *νόμος*) means 'accept (*or* treat, practise) as normal'; cf. Lys. x. 17 *τὸ ἀπίλλειν τοῦτο ἀποκλῄειν νομίζεται*, 'This word "*ἀπίλλειν*" means what is now denoted by "*ἀποκλῄειν*".' Hence, lit., 'this <as being> who do you accept as normal?', almost 'You know this creature; what do you call him?'

848 καλῶς γε: 'Good!'—not because Pheidippides is right (he is, in Strepsiades' view, wrong), but because he has given the answer which the argument requires.

850 καλεῖν: Cf. 433 n.

852 ταῦτ' ἔμαθες τὰ δεξιά: Not 'Did you learn these bright ideas?' but 'Are *these* the bright ideas which you learnt?'

853 παρὰ τοὺς γηγενεῖς: *γηγενής* is normally used of the Giants (e.g. *Birds* 824); cf. *Frogs* 825 *γηγενεῖ* ('gigantic') *φυσήματι*. Its point here is probably that the Giants were enemies of the Olympian gods, and so are Socrates 'the Melian' and his students. *γηγενής* seems, however, to be used as a more general pejorative (suggesting 'subhuman') in Alexis, *ἄροτρον, βῶλος, γηγενὴς ἄνθρωπος*, and it may have been a fashionable word with young men like Pheidippides. Cf. the Latin *terrae filii* in the sense 'nobodies'.

855 ἐπελανθανόμην ἂν . . . ἐτῶν: Cf. 129 n. For the phrase *ὑπὸ πλήθους ἐτῶν* cf. Xen. *Hell.* vi. 3. 15 *ὑπὸ πλήθους κακῶν*.

856 θοἰμάτιον: Cf. 497.

857 καταπεφρόντικα: Cf. 838 n.

858 τὰς δ' ἐμβάδας: Cf. 719 n. **ποῖ τέτροφας:** Cf. *Wasps* 665 *καὶ ποῖ τρέπεται δὴ 'πειτα τὰ χρήματα τἄλλα*, 'And where does the rest of the money go then?' (*or* 'And what is done with . . .?').

859 ὥσπερ Περικλέης: Plutarch tells the story. When Perikles' accounts came up for scrutiny after the crushing of the Euboian revolt in 445, it was seen that he had entered ten talents as spent *εἰς τὸ δέον*: the Assembly, knowing that this sum had been given as a bribe to bring about the Spartan king's withdrawal of his army from Attica, wisely asked no questions. *ἀπώλεσα*, between which and *δέον* there is almost a logical contradiction, gives the expression a comic twist. On *-κλέης*, cf. p. xxxi.

860 ἀλλ' ἴθι: They move together, Strepsiades dancing ahead impatiently, Pheidippides reluctantly, towards the school.

860 εἶτα . . . 861 ἐξάμαρτε: 'Furthermore', introducing a fresh argument (cf. 1214 n.), then, lit., 'Do wrong in obedience to your *father*.' The point is: 'Never mind whether it's wrong or not; do it because your father wants you to'; cf. Herodas 1. 61 f., where an old woman is coaxing a younger woman into adultery: *ἀλλ' ὦ τέκνον μοι Μητρίχη*, *μίαν ταύτην ἁμαρτίην δὸς τῇ θεῷ* (sc. Aphrodite). This is better sense than the usual interpretation 'If only you do what I want you to, you can do what you like afterwards, for all I care'; if we say that Strepsiades means *πιθόμενος εἶτ' ἐξάμαρτε* we are missing the point, for we do not want '*in spite of* having obeyed, you can do wrong'. Although '*if* you obey, *then* you can do wrong' would be meaningful, it could not be extracted from *εἶτα*.

861 κἀγώ τοι ποτέ: Cf. Soph. *Phil.* 799 ff., where Philoktetes implores Neoptolemos to end his sufferings: 'O my son . . . burn me! *κἀγώ τοι ποτέ* brought myself to do this to Herakles.'

862 οἶδ': Unless this is parenthetic, in which case *πιθόμενος* is a participle dependent on the verb *ἐπριάμην*, we have asyndeton, in 863. Asyndeton is more natural than parenthetic *οἶδα*, and there are abundant parallels, e.g. 758, 779, 817, 874.

863 ὀβολόν . . . ἠλιαστικόν: The daily fee for jury service was three obols at the time of the play. There are no good grounds for believing that it was ever one obol or that Ar. is being pedantic about Strepsiades' younger days. I print *ἠλιαστικόν* because in fifth-century Attic inscriptions, where the sign H represents the sound [h], it never appears in the word *ἠλιαία*.

864 Διασίοις: Cf. 408 n. **ἁμαξίδα**: There is no reason why this should not mean 'toy cart' (cf. the diminutive *κλινίς*, *κιστίς*, etc.). The alternative explanation, that *ἁμαξίς* was a kind of cake, may be the product of centuries of inflation; at a time when the sculptors who worked on the Erechtheum were paid one drachma a day, one obol (= $\frac{1}{6}$ drachma) was a fair price for a toy cart. Cf. also 880 n.

865 ἦ μὴν σύ: Cf. 1242.

(viii) **866–88.** *Strepsiades presents Pheidippides at the School*

866–8 δεῦρο . . . ἀναπείσας: Socrates comes out in response to this call —not, I think, displaying eagerness, but with nonchalant dignity; cf. the patronizing tone of 868 ff., and 876 n. **νηπύτιος**: A purely epic equivalent of *νήπιος* (cf. 105 n.).

869 κρεμαστῶν: This was the reading adopted explicitly by the Scholiast. *κρεμαστὰ σκεύη* (as opposed to *ξύλινα σκεύη*) are the sails and ropes of a ship, and *κρεμαστά* is treated as a technical term in Xen. *Oec.* 8. 12 *διὰ πολλῶν δε τῶν κρεμαστῶν καλουμένων πλεῖ* (sc. *ναῦς*). The MSS. have *κρεμαθρῶν*; in defence of this it could be pointed out that Socrates first appeared (218) *ἐπὶ κρεμάθρας*: but the rarity of the scansion *θ|ρ* in comic iambic trimeters (cf. 1468 n.) is a considerable objection to it. Socrates thus appears to be using an expression like our 'know the ropes'; but, of course, we are also meant to remember the *κρεμάθρα*.

870 τρίβων: As a noun, *τρίβων* means a workaday cloak which has worn thin. Clothes were hung up and beaten when they were cleaned; since *ἐπιτρίβειν* is used (e.g. 972) of beating people, Pheidippides probably means not 'if you were hanged' but 'if you were hung up ⟨sc. like a slave being beaten⟩'—a common procedure.

872 f. ἰδού . . . διερρυηκόσιν: 'With his lips loosely apart' suggests the lack of mobility and precision in articulation which characterizes infant speech, and this suits *ἠλίθιον, νηπύτιος* (868), and the tone of 878 ff. It may be that slackness of articulation, with inadequate movement of the lips, was characteristic also of the class of young men to which Pheidippides assimilated himself, but we do not have to assume this. In *κρέμαιο* the lips meet on *μ*, part on *α*, stretch a little on *ι*, and are rounded on *ο*. *μ* is an easy sound for infants; difficulty in pronouncing rolled *ρ* (unlike difficulty in pronouncing the very rare sound written 'r' in English) is not apparent in the movement of the lips; thus the only pronunciation which makes sense of Socrates' words is something like [k(r)emæw]. *κρέμαιό γ'* must be wrong, for it would require interpretation as *κρέμα͡ιό γ'*, *κρέμεό γ'*, or *κρέμαυ γ'*, and when Pheidippides uttered the word in 870 its scansion was normal. Emendation to *κρέμαι'* is advisable. An alternative emendation *ἰδού γε κρέμαι'* is not impossible; for *ἰδού γε* cf. 818 and 1469.

874 ἀπόφευξιν: Cf. 167. The repetition of *ἀπόφευξις* in *Wasps* (558, 562, 645) and its occurrence in Antiphon suggest that it was in forensic use in the fifth century.

875 κλῆσιν: An ordinary legal term, as we see from 1189, and not confined to the fifth century. **χαύνωσιν**: This is the language of rhetoric, not of law; cf. *δείνωσις* in a series of rhetorical terms in Pl. *Phdr.* 272 A. In Eur. *Andr.* 931 *τούσδ' ἐχαύνωσαν λόγους* seems to mean 'talked misleadingly (inciting me to vanity)'. This suggests that *χαύνωσις* is 'making something out of nothing', a successful kind of forensic deception. **ἀναπειστηρίαν**: Cf. 96 n. Adjectives in -*(σ)τήριος* are abundant in fifth-century Attic, including Tragedy, and also in prose, e.g. Thuc. vii. 53. 4 *σβεστήρια κωλύματα* and iv. 81 *ἄνδρα . . . δραστήριον*.

876 ταλάντου: Socrates is a clever salesman. Having in effect refused Pheidippides as a hopelessly immature pupil—and having thus created an agonizing anxiety in Strepsiades—he adds musingly, 'All the same, for a *talent* . . .', implying that he might be able to teach Pheidippides, but it cannot fail to be very difficult and very expensive. A talent is a prodigious fee. Euenos of Paros charged 5 mnai ($\frac{1}{12}$ of a talent) for a complete course and Prodikos charged the same sum for an *ἐπίδειξις* which, he claimed, was adequate instruction in the correct use of words. **Ὑπέρβολος**: Cf. 551 n., 1065; the implication is that Hyperbolos' prowess as a persuasive speaker owes nothing to his native wit but everything to an abnormal effort on the part of a teacher.

877 ἀμέλει: Cf. 422 n.

878 εὐθύς γε τοι . . . τυννουτονί: Falling in with Socrates' treatment of Pheidippides as a little boy, Strepsiades recites the trivialities which seem to a doting father evidence of precocity in his son. At *τυννουτονί* he puts his hand a couple of feet from the ground—or, for comic effect, much lower.

879 ἔνδον: i.e. before he was old enough to leave the house and join other boys in the streets or field.

880 ἁμαξίδας τε †σκυτίνας: What 'leather carts' are, is not easy to explain or imagine, unless a cart with leather traces could be so described. Since a passage of Antiphanes is cited by Athenaios once as *σοφιστῶν . . . συκίνων* and again as *σοφιστῶν . . . σκυτίνων*, it has been suggested that Ar. wrote *συκίνας*, 'of fig-wood'. But phrases denoting physical objects often mean something quite different from what they seem to mean literally.

881 πῶς δοκεῖς: In effect, 'you can't imagine!' Cf. 1368, where *πῶς οἴεσθε* is syntactically integrated.

883 ὅστις ἐστί: Cf. 113 n.

884 τἄδικα λέγων: On the rhythm cf. p. xxxvi.

885 πάσῃ τέχνῃ: This expression does not refer to sophistic technique, but makes an imperative or its equivalent into an urgent plea; cf. 1323.

886 αὐτός: 'He will learn by himself'; 887 tells us why.

887 ἐγώ . . . 888 δυνήσεται: In some MSS. the whole passage is spoken by Socrates; the others have *Στ.* at the beginning of 887. But the Scholiast assumes change of speaker at *τοῦτο*, treating the allocation of 887–9 to Socrates as a variant. He is certainly right. *ἐγὼ δ' ἀπέσομαι* must be spoken by Socrates, giving point to 886, and we see from 1105 ff. that Strepsiades is present during the contest between Right and Wrong; on the alleged presence of Socrates at 1105, *v.* n. It is necessary for the actor who plays the part of Socrates to take the part of Right or Wrong, for otherwise we should have five actors on stage (cf. p. xii), and Socrates' previous absences (700–22, 726–30) make his absence now perfectly in character; we can imagine him engaged in scientific experiments. *τοῦτό νυν κτλ.* must be spoken by Strepsiades, for there is no one present to whom Socrates could meaningfully address such a plea. Obviously it is not for Strepsiades to see that Pheidippides learns Wrong, and after the contest he is treated as choosing. There he uses much the same terms (1107 f.) as here and above (882). **νυν:** We expect a choral song at this point, especially as the actor playing Socrates, having gone into the school not earlier than the middle of 887, has to change costume and appear as Right in 889 or as Wrong not later than the beginning of 891. The absence of a song, a sign of the incomplete revision of the play (cf. p. **xxix**), was noted in antiquity, and the text as known to the source of the Scholiast contained the entry *χοροῦ*. Such an entry was normal practice in the fourth century to indicate a song of which the words were irrelevant to the action of the play and (presumably) were not composed by the poet; it is frequent in the MSS. of *Wealth*.

(F) **889–1114**. THE CONTEST OF RIGHT AND WRONG

On the names and characters of the contestants, cf. p. **xxiii**.

In formal structure, and to some extent in content also, this section of the play has something in common with the first part of the dispute between Aischylos and Euripides in *Frogs* (754–1098).

The decision taken in consequence of the dispute, 1105–12, corresponds roughly to the much more elaborate process of decision in *Frogs* 1414–81; nothing corresponds to *Frogs* 1099–1413; but, of course, a second formal dispute is in store for us in 1321–1451 below.

(i) **889–948**. *Anapaestic dialogue*

Cf. *Frogs* 830–74. Right strides out of the school, and gestures angrily to Wrong to follow him. He speaks in a tone of contempt and indignation which he maintains most of the time down to 1085 f. Wrong is nonchalant and very much in control of the situation. The statement of the Scholiast that Right and Wrong are presented in the guise of fighting-cocks is not supported by anything in the text and may originally have referred to the first version of the play (cf. p. xxx).

In this anapaestic sequence there is no paroemiac before the last kolon. Coincidence of metron-end with word-end is almost universal, and elision at metron-end is common. On the rhythm of 916 and 932 *v.* nn.

890 καίπερ θρασὺς ὤν: As *γάρ* and *ἐπεί* sometimes give not the reason why an event just stated occurred but the reason why the statement was made, so *καίπερ* here has the point: '⟨I tell you to⟩ show yourself although you are bold ⟨and do not need to be told⟩.'

891 ἴθ' ὅποι χρῄζεις: Borrowed from Euripides' *Telephos*; cf. 921 f. n.

892 ἐν τοῖς πολλοῖσι: Shameless Wrong is the opposite of the modest Hippolytos (Eur. *Hipp.* 986 f.) and of the *persona* ingratiatingly assumed by many speakers in the courts.

893 ἥττων γ' ὤν: *γε* is 'Yes, but . . .'

898 ἀνοήτους: Right does not spare the audience, though he hopes (918) that they will come to their senses one day. Cf. 208 n.

902 Δίκην: In Attic *δίκη* is not a synonym of *δικαιοσύνη*, except in certain phrases, e.g. *ἐν δίκῃ*, and Wrong refers to 'the virgin daughter of Zeus' (as Hesiod calls her), who, when she is injured by mankind, 'sits beside her father and tells him of men's unrighteousness'. Wrong denies the existence of Dike just as Socrates (367) denies the existence of Zeus.

905 f. τὸν πατέρ' αὑτοῦ δήσας: The chorus in Aisch. *Eum.* 640 ff. makes the same point against Apollo—who, like Right, is provoked to an emotional outburst. Zeus' temporary ill-treatment of Kronos was disquieting, to judge from the way in which Hesiod, who relates the savage behaviour of Kronos himself in detail, slips lightly over it (73). On the position of *αὑτοῦ* cf. 515 f. n.

906 αἰβοῖ . . . 907 λεκάνην: Cf. 102 n. A *λεκάνη* was the usual receptacle for vomit. **καὶ δή**: 'Verbal pointing', and not always at the beginning of a clause; cf. *Lys.* 65 *αἵδε καὶ δή σοι προσέρχονταί τινες.*

908 τυφογέρων: Used abusively of old men in *Lys.* 335.

909 καταπύγων: Cf. 529 n.

910 ῥόδα . . . 912 γιγνώσκεις: Wrong's complacency is imitated later by Pheidippides (1328 ff.). **χρυσῷ πάττων**: 'Sprinkling with gold' suggests the odd and wasteful procedure of throwing gold dust over a person. It seems (despite the numerous instances of *πάττειν* = 'sprinkle') that the words must mean 'adorn all over with gold ornaments'; cf. *Knights* 500 ff. *νικήσας . . . ἔλθοις στεφάνοις κατάπαστος* ('bespangled'), and *χρυσόπαστος* is an epithet of a tiara in Hdt. viii. 120.

913 οὐ δῆτα πρὸ τοῦ γ': Right means: hitherto, what I am saying to you would have been regarded as *μολύβδῳ πάττειν.*

915 πολλοῦ: 'Exceedingly'. **ἀρχαῖος**: Cf. 821 n.

916 διὰ σὲ δέ: ⏑⏑⏑⏑ is an abnormal resolution in anapaests, but common phrases and formulae often justify metrical abnormality (cf. 1066). In *Birds* 1753 we find *διὰ σέ* where –⏑⏑ is expected, possibly a formula from hymns. **φοιτᾶν**: sc. to school, as commonly; more fully expressed in *Knights* 1235 *παῖς ὢν ἐφοίτας εἰς τίνος διδασκάλου;*

920 αὐχμεῖς: Cf. 442 n.

921 ἐπτώχευες: 'You were a beggar', and therefore despised; this leads on to the theme of the next line.

922 Τήλεφος . . . φάσκων: Euripides' *Telephos* represented the Mysian king as appearing disguised as a beggar at Agamemnon's court. The play, produced in 438, seems to have made a great impression, perhaps because the audience liked to see splendid costumes in tragedy and were shocked by a realistic portrayal of beggar's rags; Ar. exploits the play very fully in *Acharnians* and *Thesmophoriazusae.*

923 ἐκ πηριδίου . . . 924 Πανδελετείους: The first two words suggest living off scraps which he saves in a bag (cf. the disguised Odysseus in *Od.* xiii. 437 f.); *γνώμας* both reminds us of the stage Telephos and suggests that Wrong in the old days had nothing except his clever talk. Pandeletos is characterized by the Scholiast as a sycophant and active politician; this may be pure guesswork—he may indeed have been a proverbial character.

925–6. Possibly Ar. intended the two actors to speak simultaneously. For interrupted utterance cf. 1221 f., and for the part-repetition of one speaker's words by the other cf. *Wasps* 1484 *καὶ δὴ γὰρ σχήματος ἀρχή — μᾶλλον δέ γ' ἴσως μανίας ἀρχή.* **τῆς σῆς πόλεως θ'**: 'Yours, and ⟨that⟩ of the city . . .'

928 λυμαινόμενον τοῖς μειρακίοις: We are reminded of the charge against Socrates (Pl. *Ap.* 24 B), *τοὺς νέους διαφθείροντα.*

929 Κρόνος: Cf. 398 n.

930 γ': 'Oh yes, I will . . .!' **σωθῆναι**: The translation 'to be saved' sounds rather evangelical; perhaps 'if he is not to come to any harm'.

932 ἔα: Either ἔᾰ, as implied by *Frogs* 1243 ἔα (i.e. ἔ') *αὐτὸν ὦ τᾶν*, or ἔ͜ᾱ, which would be in keeping with the normal contraction εα > ᾱ, but cannot be proved metrically.

933 κλαύσει . . . ἐπιβάλλῃς: Wrong has moved to take hold of Pheidippides, and Right now threatens violence, which is averted by the Chorus.

938 φοιτᾷ: Cf. 916 n.

940 πρότερος: Cf. *Eccl.* 1082 *ποτέρας προτέρας οὖν κατελάσας ἀπαλλαγῶ;*

941 τούτῳ δώσω: It was sometimes held (rightly or wrongly) that the first speaker has an advantage, but Wrong knows better.

(ii) **949–58.** *Strophe*

Cf. *Frogs* 875–84. Responsion to 1024–33 is normal at the beginning and end, but highly irregular in 953–6 ~ 1028–31 (the Scholiast comments that there are alternative analyses of the strophe).

<table>
<tr><td>(1)</td><td>949 f. ~ 1024 f.</td><td>– – ⏑ –</td><td>– ⏑ ⏑ – |</td><td>– ⏑ ⏑ –</td><td>⏑ – – |</td></tr>
<tr><td>(2)</td><td>951 f. ~ 1026 f.</td><td>⏓ – ⏑ –</td><td>– ⏑ ⏑ –</td><td>– ⏑ ⏑ –</td><td>⏑ – ⏒ |</td></tr>
<tr><td>(3)</td><td>953 f.</td><td>⏑ ⏑ ⏑ ⏑ –</td><td>– | ⏑ –</td><td>– | ⏑ – | ⏑ – ⏑ – |</td><td></td></tr>
<tr><td></td><td>1028 f.</td><td>– – ⏑ ⏑ ⏑</td><td></td><td>– ⏑ | – – – | ⏑ ∩ ||</td><td></td></tr>
<tr><td>(4)</td><td>955 f.</td><td>– ⏑ | ⏑ –</td><td>– ⏑ ⏑ | –</td><td>– ⏑ | ⏑ –</td><td>– | ⏑ ⏑ – |</td></tr>
<tr><td></td><td>1030 f.</td><td>– ⏑ ⏑ –</td><td>– ⏑ ⏑ – |</td><td>– ⏑ ⏑ – |</td><td></td></tr>
<tr><td>(5)</td><td>957 f. ~ 1032 f.</td><td>– ⏑ ⏑ –</td><td>⏑ – ⏑ –</td><td>– ⏑ ⏑ –</td><td>⏑ – – |</td></tr>
</table>

(1) and (2) are iambo-choriambic tetrameters of the form *ia ch ch ba*; cf. 700 f. ~ 804 f. (3) in the strophe is *ia cr lek* (cf. *Birds* 851 f. ~ 895 f.), in the antistrophe *ia lek* (cf. *Wasps* 734 ~ 746). The text of these lines

will be discussed ad loc. (4) in the strophe is a choriambic tetrameter, in the antistrophe a choriambic trimeter. On the problem of responsion posed by (3) and (4) cf. 1310 ~ 1319 and *Wasps* 540 ff. ~ 644 ff. (5) is an iambo-choriambic tetrameter of the form *ch ia ch ba*; cf. 567 f. ~ 599 f.

949 τὼ πισύνω: 'These two who trust in . . .'

952 γνωμοτύποις: The chorus describes Aischylos and Euripides in *Frogs* 877 as *ἀνδρῶν γνωμοτύπων*. **μερίμναις**: Cf. 101 n.

953 ὁπότερος . . . 954 φανήσεται: The order *λέγων ἀμείνων* (MSS.) gives the rhythm ⏑⏑⏑⏑– –⏑– ⏑–– ⏑–⏑–, *ia cr ba ia*. The final sequence *ba ia* is rare enough in tragedy (one example is Eur. *Hec.* 946 f. *διδοῦσ', ἐπεί με γᾶς ἐκ πατρῴας ἀπώλεσεν*) and has no indisputable parallel in comedy; *Thesm.* 1015 *φίλαι παρθένοι φίλαι* is heavy paratragedy. Normal comic rhythm (and, incidentally, possible comic responsion with 1028 f. when the latter has undergone emendations required on linguistic and stylistic grounds) is restored by transposing *λέγων* and *ἀμείνων*.

955 νῦν . . . 956 σοφίας: Cf. *Frogs* 883 f. *νῦν γὰρ ἀγὼν σοφίας ὁ μέγας χωρεῖ πρὸς ἔργον ἤδη*. **ἀνεῖται**: *ἀνιέναι* is used of tossing up dice etc. in games of chance; hence *κίνδυνον ἀνιέναι* = *κίνδυνον ἀναρρίπτειν*.

957 φίλοις: Because the Chorus is well disposed to the school, and both Right and Wrong are inhabitants of the school.

(iii) **959 f.** *κατακελευσμός*. Cf. 476 n. and *Frogs* 905 f.

(iv) **961–1023.** *Speech of Right*

Cf. *Frogs* 907–91.

963 μηδέν': This seems the probable interpretation of *ΜΗΔΕΝ*, rather than *μηδέν*, 'not at all'. Cf. *Wasps* 1047 *μὴ πώποτ' ἀμείνον' ἔπη τούτων . . . μηδέν' ἀκοῦσαι*.

964 εὐτάκτως: Unobtrusive passage through the streets is an aspect of *σωφροσύνη*, and it was part of Spartan legislation for boys. **εἰς κιθαριστοῦ**: Cf. p. xxiii; and on the syntax, 508 n.

965 κωμήτας: The boys from the same 'quarter' of the city. **γυμνούς**: Cf. 498 n.

966 προμαθεῖν: The point of *προ-* is that they will later be expected to know it by heart and sing it; cf. 476 n. **ἐδίδασκεν**: sc. *ὁ κιθαριστής*. **μηρώ**: No doubt it was a schoolboy joke to push the genitals up, or to try to push the foreskin back, by movements of the thighs.

967. The evidence for the sources of these quotations is extremely tangled, but it suggests that the former comes from either Stesichoros or a certain Lamprokles and the latter from Kydias (who is mentioned in Pl. *Charm.* 155 D, and his name is written against a lyre-player leading a komos in an Attic vase-painting).

968 ἐντειναμένους: Singing the song in the mode traditional for that song. *ἐντείνειν* is used (Pl. *Phd.* 60 D) of casting given matter into metrical form (*τόνος*) and (Pl. *Prt.* 326 A) of giving musical form to poetry. Similarly, a man *ἐντείνεται*, 'pitches', his own voice (Aischin. ii. 157).

969 καμπήν: Pherekrates uses *ἐξαρμονίους καμπάς* of the musical innovations of Kinesias; presumably 'modulations'.

'970'. After 969 Brunck (following a suggestion of Valckenaer) inserted a verse in the same metre, about musical styles, cited in the *Suda*. It is absent from the papyri, and must have been absent from the text known to the composer of the scholion on 958, where the total of anapaestic tetrameters 959–1008 is given as *μθ'* (= 49).

971 Φρῦνιν: In Pherekrates Music, personified as a woman, complains (the passage is full of sexual *double entendre*) of her treatment by Phrynis: *κάμπτων με καὶ στρέφων ὅλην διέφθορεν . . . ἐν ἑπτὰ χορδαῖς δώδεχ' ἁρμονίας ἔχων*. Phrynis was a Mytilenean citharode who won the prize at the Panathenaia in 456. Right is thus condemning as a modern innovation something with which Ar. himself had grown up.

972 πολλάς: sc. *πληγάς*.

973 παιδοτρίβου: Cf. p. xxiii and 508 n.

973 μηρόν . . . 976 καταλείπειν: Cf. pp. xxv f. **ἀπηνές**: A surprising word, meaning 'cruel' (cf. Pl. *Lg.* 950 B *ἄγριον καὶ ἀπηνές*, of a repressive law), not 'indecorous'. The point is that the sight of a boy's genitals 'torments' his lovers, just as Eros himself is by tradition a cruel and merciless power (*ἀπηνής* in Theognis 1353); Alexander jokingly described beautiful Persian women as 'a pain in the eyes' (Plu. *Alex.* 21. 10). Right's revelation of the tastes of the generation which he champions can be made plain by change of tone in 973 and 974. **ἀνιστάμενον**: For the use of the singular in a generalization of this form cf. *Eccl.* 300 f. *ὅσοι πρὸ τοῦ μέν, ἡνίκ' ἔδει λαβεῖν ἐλθόντ' ὀβολὸν μόνον, καθῆντο*. The plural *τοῖσιν ἐρασταῖσιν* is no obstacle; many lovers competed for the favours of a handsome boy. **ἥβης**: The genitals, as elsewhere in comedy.

977 ἠλείψατο . . . 978 ἐπήνθει: These lines are crucial for the interpretation of the character of Right and the manner in which Ar. regards this contest. First, it is as if a modern preacher, having thundered 'No girl ever wore trousers in those days!', continued 'And sometimes you glimpsed the satiny flesh on the inside of her thighs.' Right speaks 977 indignantly, 978 dreamily, as his imagination runs away with him, and then pulls himself together in 979. Secondly, we must ask what visual effect, described in 978, is incompatible with anointing with oil below the navel. *χνοῦς* looks easy; it is normally 'down', especially on the face, and it seems that Right likes immature pubic hair to be fluffy, not plastered flat with oil. But in Theokr. 27. 50 a girl's breasts are *μᾶλα . . . χνοάοντα*: there, as here, *μῆλα* are fruit with a firm texture but a matt surface—quinces or apricots rather than glossy apples—and *χνοάοντα* is 'velvety' (obviously not 'hairy'). *δρόσος* denotes any liquid, including dew and drizzle (Aisch. *Ag.* 560 f.), vaginal secretion (*Knights* 1280 ff.), and semen, whence, like *γόνος*, it can mean 'offspring' (Aisch. *Ag.* 141). Following *αἰδοίοισι, δρόσος* would at first suggest 'semen' to Ar.'s audience, but a more realistic picture is obtained if we take it as referring to Cowper's secretion, which in some individuals is emitted when the penis is fully erect. What stimulates the imagination of Right, as a connoisseur of homosexual play, is the contrast between the matt surface of the penis as a whole and the secretion revealed by pushing back the foreskin.

979 οὐδ' ἂν μαλακήν . . . 980 ἐβάδιζεν: Cf. 54 n. **τοῖν ὀφθαλμοῖν**: Ar. always uses the dual when referring to one person's eyes, e.g. 362, 411.

981 ῥαφανῖδος: It seems that *ῥαφανίς* was not simply the very small root we call 'radish', but a generic name covering some much larger species; cf. 1083 n.

982 ἄννηθον: We find *ᾱ̆ννηθον* as a medicine for enteritis in *Thesm.* 486, *ᾰ̆νηθον* and *ᾰ̆νητον* as a condiment, and *ᾱ̆ννησον* as a medicine. Where there is no metrical control the confusion is increased immeasurably, since in most passages there are variant readings; in Plin. *NH* both *anesum* and *anetum* are condiments and medicines! If we stick to Ar., we read *ἄννηθον* here. Alternatively, we could emend to *ἄννησον* in *Thesm.* 486 and keep *ἂν ἄνηθον* here. The former seems to me the wiser course.

983 ὀψοφαγεῖν: They are expected to be content with the staple diet of bread and wine, and not to be choosy over other foods. Pl. *Rep.* 372 E thinks of *ὄψα* primarily as salt, olives, and cheese, but elsewhere the word is applied to meat and fish. Obviously no one believed that boys in the old days survived on a purely farinaceous diet, and if we regard *ὄψα* as that element of diet in which variety is possible, and the part to which the cook's competence and imagination make a difference, we can see how a regard for *ὄψα* could be stigmatized by champions of austerity. **ἐναλλάξ**: Presumably this was considered too relaxed and confident a posture in the presence of one's elders.

984 ἀρχαῖα: Cf. 821 n. **Διπολιώδη**: The festival *Διπολίεια* was held in honour of Zeus Polieus. It was perhaps despised by the younger generation as overladen with archaic ritual and devoid of the athletic contests which made other festivals interesting. **τεττίγων**: The reference is to the custom, mentioned as out of date by Thuc. i. 6. 3 and in *Knights* 1331, of wearing in the hair a golden brooch in the shape of a cicada.

985 Κηκείδου: 'A very early dithyrambic poet', according to the Scholiast. Which of the many forms of his name presented by the MSS. and testimonia is right, we can hardly determine. One Kedeides was *διδάσκαλος* of a tribal chorus on an occasion when Kleisthenes (cf. 355) was its choregos, in the late fifth century; if he was an old-fashioned poet and a contemporary of Ar., the emendation *Κηδείδου* should be adopted and the Scholiast rejected as having made a bad guess. **Βουφονίων**: Part of the Dipolieia.

986 Μαραθωνομάχας: *-μάχης* has somewhat more of the flavour of archaic poetry than *-μαχος*, but both have parallels.

987 εὐθύς: 'Right from the start'.

988 ἀπάγχεσθ': Ostensibly with indignation at their feebleness, but we may be meant to infer also that the lowering of the shield deprives him of his favourite sight.

989 τὴν ἀσπίδα τῆς κωλῆς προέχων: The reference is to the *πυρριχισταί* who danced at the Panathenaia naked, wielding a hoplite shield energetically. *κωλῆ* is the haunch of animal or man (cf. 1019 n.), often mentioned in connection with the partition of meat after a sacrifice. If a man is physically weak, he cannot dance for long holding a heavy shield with his forearm at right angles to his chest or moving it quickly up and down; his arm flops and the shield covers his side from shoulder to knee. The exaggeration 'holding it in front of his haunch' is typical drill-sergeant's language. **ἀμελῇ τις**: With *τῆς* instead of *τις*, *τις* must be understood, and this superimposes an abnormality on what would otherwise be an unobjectionable inconcinnity (cf. 975 n.) of *αὐτούς* with *ἀμελῇ*. **Τριτογενείης**: For the justification of *-ης* cf. 614 n. This is a name of Athena from Hesiod onwards: a name rather than an epithet; the adjective is *τριτογενής*, which accompanies *Παλλάς* in dedications. Cf. *'Ηριγένεια* in *Od.* xxii. 197 f., not to mention *'Ιφιγένεια*.

990 πρὸς ταῦτα: 'Given this', 'in response to what I have said'.

991 μισεῖν ἀγοράν: Cf. Isoc. vii. 49, idealizing the youth of primeval Athens: *οὕτω δ' ἔφευγον τὴν ἀγορὰν κτλ.* **βαλανείων**: Cf. 837 n.

992 φλέγεσθαι: Modest boys were expected to blush readily, but this is a strong word, referring rather to a surge of emotion—anger and shame—when one is the object of ridicule; on *σκώπτειν* cf. 1267.

993 ὑπανίστασθαι: An obvious mark of respect in ancient as in modern times.

994 περὶ τοὺς σαυτοῦ γονέας: *περί c. acc.* is used of the sphere or direction in which an error or offence falls. **σκαιουργεῖν**: Cf. 629 n. The word here refers more to *bêtises* than to the serious offences such as striking one's parents.

995 ὅτι τῆς Αἰδοῦς μέλλεις τἄγαλμ' †ἀναπλήσειν†: 'By doing which' (or 'by experiencing which') 'you are likely to ...'; cf. Thuc. vi. 33. 5 f.

'(Great expeditions come to grief) *ὅπερ καὶ Ἀθηναῖοι . . ., τοῦ Μήδου . . . σφαλέντος, . . . ηὐξήθησαν.*' *Αἰδώς* is personified, as elsewhere in serious poetry. Shameless behaviour is an offence against her, as Justice is 'manhandled' by unjust rulers in Hesiod's description, and the offence is described metaphorically as doing something to her statue; obviously we need some word meaning 'mutilate', 'deface', or 'defile' (*μολύνειν* in the Scholiast's paraphrase). *ἀναπιμπλάναι* means 'infect', and is freely used in metaphor, e.g. 1023, but it is not used without specification of the disease or condition transmitted, and one cannot 'infect a statue' as one can infect a person or a community with immorality. *ἀναπλάττειν*, '(re-)mould', is used of building up, improving, or repairing, never of mutilating. *ἀναπλήττειν* is unexampled (future *ἀναπλήξειν*). I suspect that Ar. wrote *ἀμαλάπτειν* (cf. Soph. fr. 427), *ἀμαλάψειν* or (*ἀ*)*λαπάξειν* (cf. Aisch. *Ag.* 130); for the occasional comic use, apparently without paratragic point, of words associated with archaic poetry or tragedy cf. *Peace* 380 *ἀμαλδυνθήσεται* and *Wasps* 188 *ἰνδάλλεται*. I cannot think that the idea that a good man is himself an *ἄγαλμα* (or *εἰκών*) of Modesty, or even that he 'has a statue of Modesty in his heart', despite the 'sanctuary of Justice in one's own nature' (Eur. *Hel.* 1022) and the 'altars of Justice and Eunomia and Aidos in all men' (Dem. xxv. 35), would occur to the audience. But even if the latter were intended, the primary point that shameless action is a mutilation of the statue of Aidos is still valid.

996 ὀρχηστρίδος: Dancing-girls and flute-girls were normally slaves; it would be unfair to say that they were necessarily prostitutes as well, but they could be prostituted, and they could certainly be importuned in a manner which a free woman would resent.

997 μήλῳ: Throwing fruit at a man was a means by which a girl could suggest to him, without committing herself in words, that she would let him try to seduce her. **εὐκλείας**: The prostitute was despised, as often in those societies which have made most use of her; and chastity in the adolescent was admired as an aspect of *σωφροσύνη*, just as one admires those who can endure hunger, thirst, and cold. The conventional attitude of Right (which, as often happens with conventional attitudes, did not necessarily have any close relation to realities of conduct) is expressed also in Lys. xiv. 25, where the younger Alkibiades is blamed: *ἐκώμαζε μεθ' ἡμέραν, ἄνηβος ἑταίραν ἔχων.*

998 ἀντειπεῖν: Cf. Lys. xix. 55, 'I am thirty years old, and I have never yet contradicted my father', in a parade of the speaker's virtues. **Ἰαπετόν**: Brother of Kronos, so that calling a man 'Iapetos' makes the same point as calling him 'Kronos' (398 n.).

999 ἡλικίαν: Everywhere else *μνησικακεῖν* is used absolutely or that which is recalled with opprobrium is put in the genitive. **ἐξ ἧς**: 'That time of ⟨his⟩ life when you were looked after as a fledgling'. Cf. 562 n.

1001 τοῖς Ἱπποκράτους υἱέσιν: Whether this Hippokrates was the son of Ariphron and thus the strategos killed at Delion in 424 (Thuc. iv. 66. 1, 101. 2) we do not know for certain. He probably was, for (i) one of his three sons was named Perikles, and Ariphron was a brother of the great Perikles, and (ii) from Lys. fr. 43 it appears that the 'sons of Hippokrates' were orphaned. The boys are ridiculed as simpletons in comedy. **βλιτομάμμαν**: *βλίτον* is a vegetable described by Pliny *Nat. Hist.* xx. 252 as *iners . . . et sine sapore . . . unde conuicium feminis apud Menandrum* (832) *faciunt mariti*. Cf. our derogatory use of 'cabbage' and 'turnip'. On -*μαμμαν* cf. 1383 n.; *βλιτομάμμας* means what *βλιτοφάγος* would mean.

1004 ἑλκόμενος: Involved in litigation, as witness or supporter or defendant; cf. 1218. **γλισχραντιλογεξεπιτρίπτου**: -*εξεπιτρίπτου* (cf. *ἐπίτριπτος* as a term of abuse) expresses, I think, the speaker's emotional attitude; 'sticky-argumentative-accursed'.

1005 Ἀκαδήμειαν: This locality, 1 km NW of the city perimeter, did not have in Ar.'s time the associations which it later acquired, as 'The Academy', through Plato. It was a public park and gymnasium, dedicated to a local god Akademos perhaps in the time of the Peisistratidai. **ἀποθρέξει**: 'Run off'; where to, is immaterial.

1007 ἀπραγμοσύνης: Aristophanes of Byzantion decided that this must be the name of a flower that grew in the Academy. Maybe; but more probably this is a characteristic Aristophanic mixture of concrete and abstract, as in *Birds* 1539 ff. *τὴν εὐβουλίαν, τὴν εὐνομίαν, τὴν σωφροσύνην, τὰ νεώρια, τὴν λοιδορίαν, τὸν κωλακρέτην, τὰ τριώβολα.* **φυλλοβολούσης**: Poplars do not 'cast their leaves' in spring, and *φυλλοβόλος* and its cognates are attested (from the fourth century B.C.) only in that meaning. Possibly Ar. intended the word to mean 'shaking its leaves' (in *Birds* 1481 *φυλλορροεῖν* is used of shedding leaves).

1010 καὶ πρὸς τούτοις: Normally *προσέχειν τὸν νοῦν* takes a simple dative, not *πρός*: hence emendations *καὶ τούτοισιν* and *καὶ πρὸς τούτοισιν* (with *ἔχῃς*).

1012 λαμπράν: The variant *λευκήν* will not do, as a white skin, desirable in a woman, is always shameful in a man; cf. especially *Frogs* 1091 f., 'slow, white, fat', of a man out of training.

1014 πυγὴν μεγάλην: Muscular young people are commonly depicted in vase-paintings with buttocks jutting out above massive thighs, and *ἄπυγος* is a derogatory word. It was a standing joke against the Athenians that they wore down their buttocks by rowing, and in *Frogs* 1070 f. we encounter the idea that too much sitting around and talking 'wears down the buttocks'. **πόσθην μικράν**: An abnormally small penis is characteristic of gods, heroes, and youths on vase-paintings, an abnormally large one characteristic of barbarian slaves and of some types of satyr. Possibly the Greeks shared the common popular belief that there is a correlation between size of penis and sexual appetite.

1017 ὠχράν: A strong, sunburnt man is *μέλας*.

1019 κωλῆν μικράν: Apart from a few MSS. which have nothing between *γλῶτταν μεγάλην* and *ψήφισμα μακρόν*, the majority say 'small buttocks, a large *κωλῆ*'. But this will not do; the underdeveloped man has a small haunch; we do not want *μικράν* twice in the same kolon; and we miss either a reference to the penis or a surprise substitute for it. *ψήφισμα μακρόν*—'a long decree', suggesting preoccupation with politics—gives precisely the new twist needed. The idea that *κωλῆ* can = 'penis'—i.e. that a straightforward term for one part of the body can denote a different part, in a context to which the straightforward meaning is highly relevant—is not attractive; the only comparable passage would be Eur. *El.* 1023 *διήμησ' Ἰφιγόνης παρηΐδα*, which, however, I interpret as 'severed ⟨from the body⟩ the face of Iphigeneia'. The common use of words meaning 'tail' for 'penis' is different, because we do not have tails.

1022 Ἀντιμάχου: A man of this name is the object of Ar.'s malice in 1150.

1023 καταπυγοσύνης: Cf. 529 n. **ἀναπλήσει**: Cf. 995 n.

(v) **1024–33.** *Antistrophe*

1028 ἄρ' ἦσαν: The variants *δ' ἦσαν ἄρ'* and *δ' ἄρ' ἦσαν* are both inappropriate. Elsewhere in Ar. *δέ* and *ἄρα* are combined only when a change of subject is emphasized (e.g. 410 *ἡ δ' ἄρ*) or a 'change of direction' (only *Birds* 393 *ἐτεὸν ἦν δ' ἄρ'*). With an emotive expression like (*ὡς*) *εὐδαίμων* we find simple *ἄρα*: e.g. *Frogs* 19 *ὦ τρισκακοδαίμων ἄρ' . . . οὑτοσί*, 1195 *εὐδαίμων ἄρ' ἦν, εἰ κτλ.* *ἄρα* may either precede or follow the imperfect of *εἶναι*: cf. *Peace* 819 *ὡς χαλεπὸν ἐλθεῖν ἦν ἄρ' κτλ.* ~ *Wasps* 821 *ὡς χαλεπὸς ἄρ' ἦσθ' ἰδεῖν*. If we delete δ' and read *ἄρ' ἦσαν*, then *εὐδαίμονες ἄρ' ἦσαν οἱ* responds to *ὁπότερος αὐτοῖν ἀμεί-*.

1029 τότε: *τότ' ἐπὶ τῶν προτέρων* (MSS.) would not be impossible in a different context, but will not do here. 'Those who lived at that time' (i.e. 'in your time') did not exactly live 'in the days of *οἱ πρότεροι*', but were themselves *οἱ πρότεροι*. Moreover the reference of *τότε* is normally understood from the context, as in 1215 and 1456, and not amplified. Delete *ἐπὶ τῶν προτέρων*, and we have *ζῶντες τότε* responding to *-νων λέγων φανήσεται*, on which cf. pp. 153 f.

1030 πρὸς τάδε σ': *πρὸς οὖν τάδ'* (MSS.) conflicts with Ar.'s unvarying practice elsewhere; he never uses a connecting particle with *πρὸς τάδε* or *πρὸς ταῦτα*, whether in choral lyric or in dialogue.* Cf. Aisch.

Eum. 545 ff. πρὸς τάδε τις . . . αἰδόμενός τις ἔστω. This example, in which the postpositive τις is repeated, suggests the solution πρὸς τάδε σ', with repetition of σε. Similar repetition occurs in *Ach.* 383 f. νῦν οὖν με . . . ἐάσατε ἐνσκευάσασθαί μ' κτλ. and Men. *Dysk.* 805 f. διόπερ ἐγώ σε φημὶ δεῖν . . . χρῆσθαί σε γενναίως. With πρὸς τάδε σ' the verse is wholly choriambic, as is the responding verse; cf. pp. 153 f.

1031 κομψοπρεπῆ: Cf. 649 n.; -πρεπῆ perhaps hints at speciousness.

1033 ἀνήρ: Here 'your opponent'; the translation of this word must vary from context to context. Cf. 1035.

(vi) **1034–5.** κατακελευσμός

(vii) **1036–1104.** *Speech and Victory of Wrong*

1036 πάλαι 'γὼ 'πνιγόμην: So in *Frogs* 1006 Aischylos, when invited to reply to Euripides, says θυμοῦμαι μὲν τῇ ξυντυχίᾳ καί μου τὰ σπλάγχν' ἀγανακτεῖ: but he, unlike Wrong, is angry at having to argue with Euripides at all. For πάλαι with the imperfect cf. *Birds* 1670 ἐθαύμαζον πάλαι (implying καὶ ἔτι θαυμάζω).

1037 ἅπαντα ταῦτ': 'All those ⟨arguments⟩'.

1041 πλεῖν ἤ: Cf. 1065 n. **στατήρων**: στατήρ is not used of any Attic coin in documentary inscriptions, but it is often used of foreign gold coins, and in comedy staters are of gold. Athens had no gold coins until at least 407/6.

1042 ἔπειτα: 'Nevertheless', 'in spite of that'.

1043. 'See how I'll refute . . .'

1044 ὅστις: 'For he . . .' **θερμῷ . . . λοῦσθαι**: Right has implied this in 991. Cf. 837 n.

1046 κάκιστον: The frequent associations of κακός and κακία, as applied to persons, with cowardice, the least forgivable delinquency in the Greek adult male, colour κάκιστον here.

1047 εὐθύς . . . ἄφυκτον: Cf. 126 n.

1048 f. ἄριστον ψυχήν: Lit., 'best in respect of soul', i.e. 'most valiant'.

1050 Ἡρακλέους: The leading question hardly permits of any other answer. The comic Herakles is a glutton (e.g. *Birds* 1583–1694); Herakles in serious literature is above all a benefactor of mankind, a slayer of monsters, and the ideal of male courage, strength, and endurance. The metron ⏑ – ⏑ ⏑ – in iambic tetrameters is normally restricted to proper names and formulae (cf. 1066).

1051 Ἡράκλεια λουτρά: Warm springs were the gift of Hephaistos to Herakles. Cf. Hdt. vii. 176. 3 on the altar of Herakles by the warm springs at Thermopylai.

1052 ταῦτ' . . . 1054 παλαίστρας: As in 906 f., Right has no answer. **βαλανεῖον**: Cf. 837 n.

1055 ἐν ἀγορᾷ τὴν διατριβήν: = *τὴν ἐν ἀγορᾷ διατριβήν*: cf. *Ach.* 636 *ἀπὸ τῶν πόλεων οἱ πρέσβεις* = *οἱ ἀπὸ τῶν πόλεων πρέσβεις*.

1057 ἀγορητήν . . . ἅπαντας: Nestor in *Il.* i. 248 and iv. 293, but also Peleus (vii. 126). Wrong is playing on the changes in meaning of *ἀγορά*: in epic, 'assembly', 'meeting-place' and '(sc. public) speech', later 'city centre' as the focus of public life, and 'market'.

1058 ἄνειμι: Wrong develops his points methodically, in a way used by historians and orators. Cf. 1075, 1408.

1063 Πηλεύς . . . μάχαιραν: Peleus (cf. Hippolytos, Bellerophon, and Joseph) resisted the advances of Hippolyte, the wife of his host Akastos, and was accused by her of trying to seduce her. Akastos thereupon contrived that Peleus should be left defenceless in a region full of wild beasts, but Hephaistos brought him a knife. Both Sophokles and Euripides composed a *Peleus*; cf. 1154 f. n. *τήν* presupposes that the hearer knows the story to which the speaker alludes; cf. 179 n.

1064 ἀστεῖόν γε: On *ἀστεῖος* cf. 204 n.

1065 Ὑπέρβολος: Cf. 551 n. **οὐκ τῶν λύχνων:** 'The man from' (*οὐκ* = *ὁ ἐκ*) 'the lamp-market'; cf. *Wasps* 789 *ἐν τοῖς ἰχθύσιν*. Hyperbolos is called *λυχνοποιός* in *Peace* 690 and a retailer of lamps in *Knights* 1315. It does not follow that he made them with his own hands or personally kept shop; cf. 581 n. **πλεῖν ἢ τάλαντα πολλά:** *πλεῖν* (or *πλέον*) *ἤ* is not always 'more than'; cf. Antiphon vi. 44, where 30 and 20 days add up to *πλεῖν ἢ πεντήκοντα*, i.e. 'a full 50 days'. *τάλαντα πολλά* is 'a vast amount of money'; cf. Thuc. vi. 31. 5, where 'if anyone had reckoned up the total expenditure . . .', followed by a list of all the different categories, leads to the climax *πολλὰ ἂν τάλαντα ηὑρέθη . . . ἐξαγόμενα*.

1067 Θέτιν: The marriage was not simply a reward for *σωφροσύνη*. According to the *Kypria* and Hesiod, the reason was Zeus' spite against Thetis. Pindar represents Zeus and Poseidon as rivals for Thetis; but they learned from Themis that it was fated that Thetis' son should be 'mightier than his father', and they prudently married her off to a virtuous mortal. Even so, she was hard to catch, and Hdt. vii. 191. 2 suggests a story in which she was boldly carried off by Peleus, not presented to him.

1068 ἀπολιποῦσα: The correct legal term for a wife's desertion of her husband. In the *Iliad* Thetis is obviously not living with Peleus and had not wished to marry him (xviii. 429 ff.). A citation from Sophokles represents her as leaving him, as a goddess might well, when he spoke harshly to her. **ὑβριστής:** *ὕβρις*, treating a fellow citizen as if he were a slave or foreigner, was a serious offence in Attic law, and in gnomic poetry and tragedy it is behaviour which results from man's forgetting that he is not a god and deciding to do as he wishes. *ὑβρίζειν* has special associations with lack of sexual restraint; hence a faint note of admiration, as for roguish virility, creeps into *ὑβριστής*. Wrong goes further in treating *ὕβρις* as an ideal—naturally, since it is the opposite of *σωφροσύνη*.

1069 τὴν νύκτα παννυχίζειν: 'For all-night sport'. On the repetition of the stem, cf. *Frogs* 150 *ἐπίορκον ὅρκον ὤμοσεν* and 1085 f. *δημοπιθήκων ἐξαπατώντων τον δῆμον*. Greek poets were not sensitive to such repetition.

1070 Κρόνιππος: Cf. 398 n. The element *ἱππο-* seems to denote 'monstrous' in *Frogs* 929 *ῥήμαθ' ἱππόκρημνα*, and can be a derogatory intensification. As an element in proper names it could be regarded as having an aristocratic flavour (63 ff.), and it may possibly have been thought old-fashioned; but it is quite common in late fifth-century casualty-lists. Ar. named one of his own sons Philippos.

1073 παίδων: Cf. pp. xxv f. **ὄψων**: Cf. 983 n. **καχασμῶν**: Cf. *Eccl.* 849 *καχάζων μεθ' ἑτέρου νεανίου*: the variant *κιχλισμῶν* is probably accommodation to 983.

1075 πάρειμ': Cf. 1058 n. **φύσεως ἀνάγκας**: The opposition between *νόμος* and *φύσις* was of great intellectual interest in the fifth century. *φύσεως ἀνάγκη* could mean the physical laws of the universe, including the law of mortality. It could also be used as an excuse for illegal or immoral action; cf. Thuc. v. 105. 2, where the Athenians in the Melian Dialogue ascribe *οὗ ἂν κρατῇ ἄρχειν* to the force of *φύσις ἀναγκαία*. Wrong means simply 'sexual desire'.

1076 ἥμαρτες . . . ἐλήφθης: The closest parallels to the accumulated asyndeton in narrative sequence here are found in Menander (e.g. *ὑπεδεξάμην, ἔτικτον, ἐκτρέφω, φιλῶ*).

1077 ἀπόλωλας: Attic law allowed a husband to kill an adulterer caught in the act, and one Euphiletos, for whom Lys. i was written, did so; but there was a less austere alternative (cf. 1083 n.).

1078 χρῶ τῇ φύσει: Cf. 1075 n. 'Do as you will', whether it is right or wrong. **σκίρτα**: Used also of Philokleon's hybristic behaviour in *Wasps* 1305, and cf. Pl. *Rep.* 571 C, where the bestial element in the soul *σκιρτᾷ* when the control of reason is removed by sleep.

1079 πρὸς αὐτόν: sc. to the husband. Cf. *Ach.* 10 f.: 'I was expecting a play of Aischylos. But he' (*ὁ δέ*, sc. the herald) 'proclaimed . . .'

1080 εἶτ' . . . 1082 δύναιο: Helen so excuses herself in Eur. *Tro.* 948 ff. Plato's hostility to tragedy is largely based on the specious arguments which can be drawn from the weaknesses of the gods in legend (*Rep.* 391 E). **ὡς**: sc. *λέγε*.

1082 καίτοι: Wrong imagines the adulterer as using this connection of thought: '*καίτοι ἐγώ . . .*'

1083 ῥαφανιδωθῇ . . . τιλθῇ: An adulterer caught in the act was commonly subjected to grotesque and painful indignities; a 'radish' (cf. 981 n.) was pushed up his anus and his pubic hair was pulled out with the help of hot ash.

1084 εὐρύπρωκτος: A man subjected to *ῥαφανίδωσις* would literally be *εὐρύπρωκτος*. The word is also used as a general term of abuse (like *καταπύγων*), as we see from the following lines, implying enlargement of the anus by habitual subjection to anal coitus.

1087 ἢν τοῦτο νικηθῇς ἐμοῦ: Wrong is going to 'prove', by appealing to standard comic assumptions, that a majority are *εὐρύπρωκτοι*: from which (he implies) it follows that to be such is not a *κακόν*. The syntax of *νικηθῆναι* is accommodated to that of *ἡττηθῆναι* and *ἥττων εἶναι*.

1089 συνηγοροῦσιν: Although prosecution for an offence against the state was initiated by an individual, the state could appoint *συνήγοροι* to help in (virtually, sometimes, to take over) the presentation of the case. *συνήγοροι* are naturally treated in comedy as unpopular, like tax-collectors today.

1091 τραγῳδοῦσ': Cf. the portrayal of Agathon in *Thesmophoriazusae*; but *εὐρυπρωκτία* does not appear elsewhere as a joke against tragic poets, actors, or dancers.

1093 δημηγοροῦσι: It is a common joke that those who are prominent and fluent speakers in the Assembly are *εὐρύπρωκτοι* for physical reasons.

1095 οὐδὲν λέγεις: Cf. 644 n.

1096 θεατῶν: Cf. 208 n.

1099 τουτονί . . . 1100 τουτονί: Vilification of the audience is a common humorous device in comedy. **κομήτην**: Cf. 14 n.

1102 ὦ κινούμενοι: Right now treats Wrong and the audience together as one side in the battle which he has lost. *κινεῖν* is one of the many slang terms in comedy for heterosexual (cf. 1371) or homosexual intercourse.

1103 πρὸς τῶν θεῶν . . . 1104 πρὸς ὑμᾶς: To outstrip his pursuers, or to fight, a man discards his himation; hence a hoplite's slave would discard it when deserting in the field. Obviously, however, those addressed in *δέξασθε*, before Right starts running, cannot be the same as the people to whom he is deserting. I suggest that Right exclaims *ὦ κινούμενοι* to the audience at large, flings his himation towards Strepsiades and Pheidippides (addressing *δέξασθε* to them), and then bounds out of the orchestra into the audience—whence, when the scene is over (1114), he will depart quietly. **ἐξαυτομολῶ**: The rhythm – – ⏑ ⏑ – ⏑ – – has been foreshadowed in the iambic tetrameters (1066, 1083), and is appropriate in the last verse of the sequence because of its resemblance to the common 'aristophanean' clausula – ⏑ ⏑ – ⏑ – –.

(viii) **1105–12.** *Pheidippides enters the School*

Socrates is off stage, and the part of Right or Wrong has been taken by the actor who played Socrates. There is no time for a change of costume, and no formal grounds for positing a lost choral song between 1104 and 1105. Therefore it is Wrong, not Socrates (to whom the part is given in the MSS.), who now addresses Strepsiades and takes over Pheidippides. The way has been prepared for this by 919, 929 ff., 937*b* f., and 990, where Right and Wrong were presented as rival prospective teachers of Pheidippides. The situation was correctly understood by the composer of Hypothesis III (q.v.) and by the Scholiast on 1102, where Pheidippides is described as *τῷ ἑτέρῳ παραδοθείς*.

1106 διδάσκω: 'Am I to teach him ...?'
1108 στομώσεις: 'Give a sharp edge to'.
1109 γνάθον: Neither 'jaw' nor 'cheek', but one cheek plus that side of the upper and lower jaws; hence the term *ἑτερόγναθος*, used of horses.
1111 κομιεῖ: 'You'll get him back ...'
1112. The only person who can grumble at this point is Pheidippides himself (on *ὠχρόν* cf. 103, 120). Strepsiades is enthusiastic, Right is defeated, Wrong is triumphant, and the Chorus has not yet sounded its first note (1114) of foreboding.

(ix) **1113 f.** *Valediction*

1113. An iambic tetrameter of the form *ia ia ith*, with resolution in the first component of the ithyphallic. **χωρεῖτε**: As all four actors depart, the variant *χώρει* is inappropriate at this point. The utterance is of the same character, and fulfils the same purpose, as the Chorus's *ἴτε δὴ χαίροντες ἐπὶ στρατιάν* in *Ach.* 1143; cf. 510 n. The theatre is left free for the 'second parabasis'.
1114 μεταμελήσειν: Now the role of the Chorus begins to change. *σοι* cannot be Pheidippides (who has not taken the decision himself, and in any case will be far from regretting it); it might conceivably be Wrong, since the school will in the end be demolished; but it is pretty certainly Strepsiades, whose reason for repentance will be emphasized and clarified in 1307 ff. *οἶμαι κτλ.* are uttered behind his back as he capers triumphantly into his house; cf. 804 ff. n. (The attributions in the MSS. are complicated; see app. crit.)

(G) 1115–1130. SECOND PARABASIS

The Chorus now address the judges; they speak as clouds, promising favours in return for award of the first prize and threatening vengeance for an adverse verdict.

The combination of the maintenance of the Chorus's role with rupture of dramatic illusion occurs in the birds' address to the judges at a similar point in the action, *Birds* 1101 ff.

The metre is the trochaic tetrameter catalectic.

1115 f. τοὺς κριτὰς . . . φράσαι: '⟨On the subject of⟩ the judges, we want to tell you what they will gain . . .' **δικαίων:** The poet naturally pretends that the award of the first prize to him will be just and right. **ἡμεῖς:** The variant *ὑμῖν* would in other circumstances be preferable; cf. the oratorical formula *βούλομαι δ' ὑμῖν εἰπεῖν*. But in 1117 f. the Chorus is speaking directly to the judges; hence although (lit.) 'we wish to tell you (sc. the audience), ⟨with reference to⟩ the judges, what they will gain . . .' would be possible—for the chorus-leader could face the middle of the audience in speaking 1115 f. and then turn towards the judges' seats for 1117 f.—it is awkward, and on balance I favour *ἡμεῖς*.

1117 ἐν ὥρᾳ: 'At ⟨the appropriate⟩ time of year'.

1120 ἄγαν: *ἄγαν* and *λίαν* function freely as indeclinable adjectives when preceded by the article (e.g. *Thesm.* 704 *τὴν ἄγαν αὐθαδίαν*), and their adjectival character lingers about them even when there is no article; cf. 1236 n. on *ἔτι*.

1122 πρὸς ἡμῶν: 'At our hands', with what follows.

1123 χωρίου: The normal Attic for 'farm'.

1126 πλινθεύοντ': The reference is to making bricks by drying mud or clay in the sun.

1128 γαμῇ: Rain was especially unwelcome at a Greek wedding, because the procession to the bridegroom's house and the dancing outside his house were in the open and torchlit. **ἢ τῶν ξυγγενῶν ἢ τῶν φίλων:** A partitive genitive playing the part of a nominative or accusative is rare; one example is Xen. *Hell.* iv. 2. 20 *ἔπιπτον ἑκατέρων* (sc. *τινές*). Emendation to *ἢ τῶν ξυγγενῶν τις ἢ φίλων* should be favourably considered; on the article in such cases cf. 622 n.

1130 Αἰγύπτῳ: The point is: he would rather be in Egypt because of the rarity of rain there, despite its unpleasant remoteness (as one might say 'at the North Pole') and the equally unpleasant reputation of its inhabitants.

(H) 1131–1213. THE HOMECOMING OF PHEIDIPPIDES

(i) 1131–53. *Strepsiades comes to fetch his son*

Strepsiades comes out of his house, soliloquizing. He is carrying some object, or leading some animal, which he is going to present to Socrates (cf. 1146 n.); or one of his slaves is carrying or leading it. On the social relationship portrayed cf. 1147 n.

1131 πέμπτη . . . 1134 νέα: Cf. 17 n. After the twentieth day of the month the count was reversed, so that the penultimate day was *δευτέρα* and the last day *ἕνη (τε) καὶ νέα*, lit., 'belonging-to-the-last-unit-of-time and new ⟨day⟩'. Then the first day of the next month was *νουμηνία*, as we see from 1191 and 1195 f.

1135 πᾶς γάρ τις . . . οἷς: 'Every one of those to whom . . .'. **ὀμνύς:** 'With an oath'.

1136 πρυτανεῖ': This is the sum of money paid to the state as a deposit by the prosecutor and forfeited if he lost the case; cf. 1180.

1137. *δεῖσθαι μέτρια καὶ δίκαια* is a stock phrase in the orators.

1138 τὸ μέν τι: Cf. *Wealth* 1179 ff. *ὁ μὲν ἂν ἥκων . . ., ὁ δέ τις ἂν δίκην ἀποφυγών, ὁ δ' ἂν . . . τις κτλ.*

1139 ἀναβαλοῦ: 'Put off' says much the same as 'don't take now' (1138), but this does not matter. Strepsiades is portraying himself not as speaking to one creditor and asking for different favours in respect of different parts of the same debt, but as speaking to each of several creditors and using different approaches.

1145 παῖ: He knocks at the door of the school, and Socrates appears. We might have expected a student to open the door, just as in an ordinary household a slave (if available) would (cf. 132 n.), but that would be dramatically inconvenient and time-wasting at this point. **ἀσπάζομαι:** A normal formula of greeting; in Hellenistic letters the imperative = 'Give my regards to . . .'

1146 τουτονί: In several passages of comedy an object is referred to solely by a demonstrative pronoun in the same gender as its ordinary Attic name, and the text gives us no further help in identifying the object. The Scholiast (recalling 668 f.) suggests that Strepsiades has brought a sack (*θύλακος*) of flour; but I would be surprised if Ar. missed a comic opportunity here. Possibly *τουτονί* refers to an emaciated he-goat or a decrepit dog; or (to remind us simultaneously of 54 f. and the complex 179–497 ff.–856 f.) he brings a tattered *χιτών*: he could appear with it folded under his arm and only reveal its true nature while speaking 1146.

1147 ἐπιθαυμάζειν: No doubt a current euphemism for 'pay money to' or 'give a present to'. Cf. 428 n.

1148 τὸν υἱόν . . . 1149 εἰσήγαγες: Three translations are possible: (1) 'And tell me whether my son has learned that argument, that ⟨son⟩ whom you took into' (cf. 1212) 'your school a little while ago.' (2) '. . . that argument which you took indoors . . .'. (3) '. . . that argument which you brought into the theatre . . .'. Since Socrates has shown that he remembers (1145) who Strepsiades is, (1) is the least natural translation and should be rejected unless there are real objections to the other two. (2) is in fact objectionable because Socrates was not present at 1114 and did not 'take' Wrong indoors. There remains (3). A poet is said to *εἰσάγειν*, 'bring in' (sc. to the theatre) whatever he 'puts on' (cf. 546). If he composes a scene in which a character comes out of the skene, he *ἐξάγει* that character; cf. *Peace* 744, where *ἐξῆγον* = 'caused to come out of the skene', and *Frogs* 946, where *οὑξιών* = 'the character who comes out of the skene'. Now Right and Wrong came out of the skene, so that strictly speaking Socrates *ἐξήγαγε* them; but *εἰσάγειν* seems from 546 to be the more general term, 'stage', and Socrates in fact 'staged' the contest for the benefit of Strepsiades and Pheidippides. I conclude that (3) is the sense in which Ar.'s audience would accept 1148 f.

1150 Ἀπαιόλη: Cf. 729.

1152 μάρτυρες: Cf. 777 n.

(ii) **1154–70.** *Song of triumph and lyric dialogue*

Strepsiades bursts into a song largely composed of tragic phrases; some of these come from extant tragedies, some from tragedies known to the ancient commentators, and one suspects that there may have been specific sources for the rest. The mixture of metrical genres is characteristic of tragic monodies—especially a mixture of anapaests and dochmiacs; cf. Eur. *Hec.* 181 ff. and 1069 ff.

(1)	1154	⏑–⏑–| –⏑|– ⏑–⏑–|
(2)	1155	⏑–|⏑–| –⏑– ⏑–⏑–||
(3)	1156	––⏑|– ––⏑|– ⏑–|⏑–|
(4)	1157	––⏑– ⏑|–⏑|– ⏑–⏑∩||
(5)	1158	–⏑|⏑–|⏑⏑–|
(6)	1159	–⏑⏑–⏑⏑|–|
(7)	1160	–––|– –|––|
(8)	1161	⏑⏑⏑|⏑–| ––|⏑– ––|⏑–|
(9)	1162	–⏑⏑–|⏑– –|⏑⏑–|⏑–|
(10)	1163 f.	–⏑⏑–|⏑–| –⏑⏑|–⏑∩||
(11)	1165	–⏑⏑|––|| ––––|
(12)	1166	×⏑⏑|–|⏑∩| } *or* –⏑⏑|–|⏑⏑| ⏑⏑–⏑|⏑–|
(13)	1167	⏑⏑–⏑|⏑–| }
(14)	1168	–⏑⏑|–⏑∩||
(15)	1169	⏑⏑⏑|⏑–|
(16)	1170	⏑⏑⏑–|⏑∩|

(1) and (2) are iambic trimeters of the form *ia lek*, abundant in tragedy (e.g. Eur. *Andr.* 1031 ~ 1041). (3) and (4) are iambic trimeters. (5) and

(6) are dactylic hemiepe, which are closely combined with dochmiacs in Soph *Aj.* 881 ff. ~ 927 ff. (7) is an anapaestic paroemiac. (8) is an iambic trimeter. (9) and (10) are pairs of dochmiacs. The dochmiac dimeter occurs in 'skolia', drinking songs (e.g. *Wasps* 1245 ff.), but I feel that the audience would not associate the rhythm with skolia in this paratragic pot-pourri. (11) is an anapaestic dimeter. Hiatus after *παῖ* is attested in dialogue (1145) and is acceptable in lyric, for *παῖ* has the character of an exclamation. (12) and (13) either together constitute an anapaestic dimeter containing the rare sequence – ⏑ ⏑ ⏑ ⏑ – (cf. Eur. *Hec.* 145) or (12) is a dochmiac and (13) an anapaestic metron. (14) is a dochmiac. (15) is an iambic metron; for the textual problem, to which the metrical analysis is relevant, *v.* n. ad loc. (16) is a dochmiac; for the textual and dramatic problem there cf. 1171*a* n.

1154 βοάσομαι . . . 1155 βοάν: Variously attributed to Sophokles' *Peleus*, to Euripides' *Peleus*, and to a play of Phrynichos. There is no evidence to support any decision between the alternatives. **ὦ 'βολοστάται**: 'Moneylenders'. We are encouraged to assume that Strepsiades owes to real moneylenders, but the creditors who appear shortly are probably not that; cf. p. xviii.

1156 τἀρχαῖα: 'Capital', a technical term. **τόκοι τόκων**: There is good word-play here on *τόκος* in its ordinary sense 'interest' and its poetic sense 'child'. Coupled with *αὐτοί* it reminds us of formulae used in decrees which honour, curse, or outlaw, e.g. *πρόξενον εἶναι καὶ αὐτὸν καὶ παῖδας*. But *τόκοι τόκων* also appears as a straightforward term for 'interest on interest' in Theophrastos.

1157 φλαῦρον: Cf. 834 n.

1158 οἷος: = *τοιοῦτος γάρ*: cf. 7 n.

1159 τοῖσδ' ἐνὶ δώμασι: The school; the expression is highly tragic.

1160 ἀμφήκει: Cf. 1108 ff.

1161 ἐχθροῖς βλάβη: This is normal Greek morality; so Theognis declares *τοῖς δ' ἐχθροῖς ἀνίη καὶ μέγα πῆμ' ἔσομαι.*

1162 λυσανίας: Another word of tragic type.

1163 τρέχων: Whether Socrates is so obsequious as to run is doubtful; but clearly he goes in to fetch Pheidippides.

1165 ὦ τέκνον . . . 1166 πατρός: A close parody of Eur. *Hec.* 171 ff. *ὦ τέκνον, ὦ παῖ δυστανοτάτας—ἔξελθ' ἔξελθ' οἴκων—ἄιε ματέρος αὐδάν.* Cf. 718 n.

1167. Socrates and Pheidippides come out of the school.

1169 ἄπιθι λαβών: If the variants *ἄπιθι σὺ λαβών* or *ἄπιθι συλλαβών* were right, this would be the only lyric utterance of Socrates in the play. I suspect that *σύ* is a relic of the gloss *τὸν υἱόν σου* and *συλλαβών* either a fluke or an arbitrary emendation. *λαβών* gives as good sense as *συλλαβών*: cf. 1105 *τοῦτον ἀπάγεσθαι λαβών.*

(iii) **1171a–1213.** *Pheidippides shows his mettle and is welcomed home*

1171a ἰοὺ ἰοῦ: The lyrics end at 1170 and 1171*a* is an exclamation *extra metrum*, as in 1 and 1321.

1171b πρῶτα . . . 1172 πρῶτον: Cf. p. xxxii.

1172 f. ἐξαρνητικὸς κἀντιλογικός: Cf. 318 n.

1173 τοὐπιχώριον: Cf. 208 n.

1174 τί λέγεις σύ: 'What do you mean?', uttered aggressively—a usage recognized by the Scholiast as a current (*εἰώθαμεν κτλ.*) method of browbeating (*καταπλῆξαι*) an interlocutor.

1175 καὶ κακουργοῦντ': 'Even in the act'. The point is that whereas *ἀδικεῖν* is a very wide term, *κακοῦργος*, in Attic law, is a man who commits theft or violence in a form which admits of arrest in the act and summary punishment. *δοκεῖν ἀδικεῖσθαι κακουργοῦντα* would be no mean achievement. **οἶδ' ὅτι**: Cf. the tagging on of 'I'm sure' in English.

1176. This line, which weakly summarizes the point of the preceding lines and is yet co-ordinated with them by *τε*, may be an interpolation, expanding a gloss on *ἐπανθεῖ. βλέπος* is cited from Ar. by Pollux but is not necessarily from this play.

1179 τις: Not *τίς*, '*What* day is . . .?' *γε* in Strepsiades' answer is 'Why, yes, the one on which . . .' Pheidippides, for the purpose of the argument, pretends not to know a term in general use, but even within this pretence he can guess that *ἕνη* refers to a unit of time.

1180 εἰς: Cf. 562 n.

1182 ἡμέραι: The plural, which is common enough with *δύο* (e.g. 1189) is better suited than the dual to bring out Pheidippides' point.

1184 γένοιτ' ἄν: Strictly potential, 'unless the same woman can be . . .', and preferable to the variant *γένοιτο*, 'unless the same woman were to be . . .'.

1185 νόμον: One more reminder of the fact, often unavoidably obscured in translation, that *νομίζειν* is the verb corresponding to *νόμος*: cf. 847 n.

1186 νοεῖ: 'Intends'.

1187 Σόλων: Since Solon was the codifier of the Athenian laws in VI in., there was a tendency to speak of all the laws as his, even those obviously of later date; whereas we speak of 'English law', 'French law', etc., the Greeks commonly named the real or imagined lawgiver and spoke of 'the laws of Solon', 'the laws of Lykurgos', etc. It was axiomatic with public speakers in the fifth and fourth centuries that Solon's legislation was democratic.

1191 θέσεις: sc. *τῶν πρυτανείων*. **νουμηνίᾳ**: Pheidippides, equating *νέα* with *νουμηνία*, is arguing that the traditional expression *ἕνη καὶ* *νέα* means 'the last day of the old month and also the first day of the new month'.

1194 ἀπαλλάττοινθ' ἑκόντες: i.e. 'settle out of court'.

1198 προτένθαι: These officials were reponsible for seeing that the food prepared for the festival Apaturia was satisfactory. **παθεῖν**: A less obvious word than the variant *ποεῖν*, it implies, in accordance with ordinary Greek psychology, being compelled to do something—by impulse, appetite, error, or external pressures (e.g. custom). Dikaiarchos even speaks of the holding of a twig while singing skolia as a *πάθος*.

1199 ὑφελοίατο: *-αται* and *-ατο* (= *-νται* and *-ντο*) disappeared from Attic after the fifth century B.C.

1200 ἡμέρᾳ μιᾷ: The dative is due to the prefix *προ-*: cf. *πρότερον* (or *ὕστερον*) *δέκα ἡμέραις*, etc.

1201 κάθησθ': Cf. our 'And you just sit there . . .!'

1202 ἡμέτερα κέρδη τῶν σοφῶν: = *κέρδη ἡμῶν, τῶν σοφῶν.* **ὄντες**: I punctuate before this word, not after it, to give the sense 'for you are' or 'and you are . . .', in view of examples such as Dem. xxiii. 109 *ὑμεῖς δ', ὄντες Ἀθηναῖοι, κτλ.*

1203 ἀριθμός, πρόβατ' ἄλλως: Cf. Eur. *Tro.* 475 f. *ἀριστεύοντ' ἐγεινάμην τέκνα, οὐκ ἀριθμὸν ἄλλως, ἀλλ' ὑπερτάτους Φρυγῶν* and Ar. *Wealth* 921 f. 'Wouldn't you like to have nothing to do all your life?'—*ἀλλὰ προβατίου βίον λέγεις.*

1205 ᾀστέον μοὐγκώμιον: *ἐγκώμιον* and *ἐγκωμιάζειν* are freely used in the fourth century of formal praise in prose or verse, but in fifth-century usage *ἐγκώμιον* is especially a poem celebrating someone's victory. Pindar refers to his *ἐπινίκια* as *ἐγκώμια μέλη* or *ἐγκώμιοι ὕμνοι*.

The metrical analysis of the song is:

(1)	1206	⏑⏑|– –	⏑⏑⌒|
(2)	1207	– –⏑–|	–⏑–|
(3)	1208	– –|⏑–	–|⏑–|
(4)	1209	– –⏑–	–⏑–|– –⏑–|
(5)	1210 f.	– –⏑|–	⏑–|⏑|– –|⏑–| –⏑–|
(6)	1212 f.	– –⏑–	⏑|–⏑–| –⏑|– ⏑– –|

(1) is an ionic dimeter catalectic. (2) and (3) are iambic dimeters, of the form *ia cr*, as in *Peace* 1128–30 ~ 1160–2; if the variant *ἐκτρέφεις* were right (and linguistically there is little to choose) (3) would be *ia ia*, but the ancient metrical analysis in the scholion supports *τρέφεις*. (4) is an iambic trimeter of the form *ia lek.* (5) is an iambic tetrameter of the form iambic dimeter (*ia ia*)+cretic dimeter (*cr cr*). (6) is an iambic tetrameter of the form iambic dimeter (*ia ia*)+ithyphallic (*cr ba*). 1212 f. belong metrically inside the framework of the song, though in sense outside it.

1206 μάκαρ: A conventional opening; cf. Eur. *Ba.* 565 *μάκαρ ὦ Πιερία.* **Στρεψίαδες:** Possibly names in -(ι)*άδης* could have a vocative in -(*ί*)*αδες* as early as V; confusion between 1st– and 3rd-declension masculine names in -*ης* had certainly begun by IV. But there is no other sign of this in the text of Ar. (e.g. *Wasps* 401 *ὦ . . . Τεισιάδη*). Strepsiades is under the impression that abnormal morphology makes his utterance poetic. The composers of epitaphs were under the same impression, as we see from their mixture of dialects, which often runs counter both to locality and to genre. Abundant excuse for this conception of poetic language was, of course, provided by the alternative forms used in epic, e.g. *Il.* i. 337 voc. *Πατρόκλεες* ~ 345 nom. *Πάτροκλος*.

1207 f. ὡς . . . χοῖον: = *ὡς σοφὸς ὤν, καὶ ὅτι τοιοῦτον . . .*

1213. Strepsiades and Pheidippides go into their house.

(I) 1214–1320. STREPSIADES ROUTS HIS CREDITORS

(i) 1214–58. *The First Creditor*

The First Creditor, a fat man (1237 f.), arrives with a summons and with a witness (cf. 777 n.). The witness is a sympathetic listener and has no speaking part (cf. 1246 n. and p. xii).

On the 'identification' of the creditors in ancient commentaries cf. p. xviii.

Although Strepsiades had proved a hopelessly forgetful pupil, and the whole point of giving Pheidippides sophistic training was that Pheidippides should do his arguing for him (cf. 1228 f.), it is actually Strepsiades himself who carries off these scenes—confusedly (1247 ff., 1278 ff.) and with recourse to insolence (1237 f., 1260 ff.) and violence (1296 ff.), but with his memory considerably improved.

1214 εἶτ': This way of opening an indignant speech, conveying the impression that the speaker has been grumbling before we first hear him, is characteristic of later comedy.

1215 εὐθύς . . . τότε: 'At the time', when asked.

1217 ὅτε: Cf. 7 n.

1218 ἕλκω: Cf. 1004. **κλητεύσοντα:** Clearly the technical term in Ar.'s time for acting as witness to the delivery of a summons (*κλῆσις* 1189). The creditor himself says *καλοῦμαι* (1221).

1219 δημότη: Strepsiades.

1220 ἀτάρ . . . 1221 ζῶν: One naturally sympathizes with any creditor who has to deal with Strepsiades, but the First Creditor is slightly absurd; he is working himself up to do an embarrassing and distasteful job (cf. p. xviii). There may, however, be a further a[illegible]ion to Athenian litigiousness; cf. 208 n.

1221 τίς οὑτοσί: Strepsiades puts his head out of th[illegible]door, and no doubt comes right out of the house on saying *μαρτύρο*[illegible]

1222 μαρτύρομαι: Addressed possibly to the creditor's [illegible]itness, but more probably (cf. 1226) to the world at large.

1223 τοῦ χρήματος: Cf. *Birds* 1046 *καλοῦμαι Πεισέταιρον ὕ*[illegible]*ς*.

1225 ψαρόν: Aristotle uses the same word of dark colourin[illegible] birds. There is no reason, so far as we know, why a horse which w[illegible]*ψαρός* should not also be *κοππατίας*: but it is evidently not impo[illegible]t to Ar. that we should identify this creditor as 'Pasias'. Cf. p. xv[illegible]

1226 ὃν πάντες ὑμεῖς ἴστε: 'When you all know that I . . .' Streps[illegible]s looks round at the audience as though at a crowd which had gathe[illegible]

1228. Most of the primary MSS. begin the line with *τὸ χρέος*, a co[illegible]tinuation of the creditor's words. But some MSS. which have *τὸ χρέος* also have, in Strepsiades' reply, words which must have originated in attempts to make an iambic trimeter out of a line which began with *μὰ Δί'*. Sense and dramatic style alike suggest rejection of *τὸ χρέος* (which in Attic should be *τὸ χρέως*, in any case) and the adoption of Triklinios' *μὰ τὸν Δί'*; cf. *Eccl.* 336 *μὰ τὸν Δί', οὐ γὰρ κτλ.* 'Oh no I didn't, because Pheidippides hadn't yet learned . . .' is not a very logical answer to 'You swore you'd pay it back', especially as later in the scene Strepsiades does not so much deny the loan (1256) as cheerfully defy the creditor to recover it. But in the immediate context denial of the loan is uppermost (1225 f., 1230 ff.), and the muddled logic of 1228 is very much in character.

1232 ἀπομόσαι: Throughout the Classical period the swearing of an oath was—or could be treated as—a weighty matter, because of the divine punishment which might fall upon a perjurer (cf. 397 n.).

1233 ἵν' ἂν κελεύσω 'γώ σε: *ἵνα* = 'where'. If a man swore in the sanctuary, or before the altar, of a god he could not so easily feel that maybe the god had not heard him swear; hence he would be more frightened of perjury.

1234 τὸν Δία, τὸν Ἑρμῆν, τὸν Ποσειδῶ: A trio is common (cf. 627), and Zeus, Apollo, and Demeter appear as the *θεοὶ ὅρκιοι* prescribed by the state; but we sometimes find larger companies.

1235 κἂν προσκαταθείην: Strepsiades adopts a mood of cheerful cynicism; he means 'I'd even pay for the fun of it'—and there may be a point in 'three obols', matching the three gods of the oath.

1236 ἕνεκ' ἀναιδείας ἔτι: *ἔτι* possibly functions as an adjective qualifying *ἀναιδείας*, 'this additional shamelessness'; cf. 1120 n. But the interpretation 'May you come to grief *one day*' (or '. . . *in the end*') is more probable, given the threatening tone of Eur. *Alc.* 731 *δίκας δὲ δώσεις σοῖσι κηδεσταῖς ἔτι*.*

1237 ἀλσὶν . . . 1238 χωρήσεται: Strepsiades pats the creditor's belly, pretending that one could make a good wineskin out of it; hides were salted as a preliminary to tanning. **χοᾶς**: One *χοῦς* = 3·2 litres.

1240 καταπροίξει: Good comic diction, but also Ionic in the fifth century; not in fourth-century Attic prose. **θεοῖς**: Virtually = 'your saying "*θεούς*"', the quoted word being accommodated to the syntax of its new context. Cf. 63 n.

1241. Lit., 'and Zeus being sworn by is ridiculous to those who know'.

1243 f. ἀλλ' εἴτ' . . . ἀποκρινάμενος: 'But tell me whether . . . , and then let me go away.'

1245. Strepsiades rushes into his house. As we shall see, he has recovered his memory since 786 ff.

1246 ἀποδώσειν σοι δοκεῖ: The creditor addresses the whole line to the witness, who no doubt replies with a nod or a shrug. One Scholiast attributes the whole line to the witness. Another refers to an interpretation which gave *τί σοι δοκεῖ δράσειν* to the creditor and only *ἀποδώσειν σοι δοκεῖ* to the witness, an interpretation which is not reflected in the sigla of any primary MS.

1247. Strepsiades reappears with a kneading-bowl.

1252 οὐχ ὅσον γ' ἔμ' εἰδέναι: Lit., 'not to-such-an-extent-as me at least to know'. The elementary humour here is like that of *Peace* 824: 'You've come back, master?'—'So someone's told me!'

1254 καὶ τοῦτ' ἴσθ': 'And I can tell you . . .!', threateningly, as in *Birds* 1408 *οὐ παύσομαι, τοῦτ' ἴσθ' ὅτι, πρὶν ἂν κτλ.*

1255 ἢ μηκέτι ζῴην ἐγώ: A more colloquial and less melodramatic utterance than 1220 f.; cf. *Lys.* 531, where *μή νυν ζῴην* = 'I'm damned if I will!' Creditor and witness stalk off, and Strepsiades calls the next line after them defiantly.

1256 προσαποβαλεῖς: Cf. our expression 'throw away' = 'pay' (or 'give') 'to no purpose'. *προσ-* = 'as well'.

1257 καίτοι . . . 1258 κάρδοπον: Presumably uttered in a tone of contemptuous pity, as one might say 'It's a shame to take your money!' **'κάλεσας**: If the meaning were 'You named the kneading-bowl in a foolish way' Strepsiades would himself be lapsing into the normal usage which he has ridiculed, and this would certainly have a humorous point, but it could not be understood without doubt. *καλεῖν* commonly means 'use the word', 'say'.

(ii) 1259a–1302. *The Second Creditor*

Strepsiades has gone, or is just going, into his house. The Second Creditor comes on limping and battered, for a reason which he explains indirectly in 1264 and directly in 1272. Ar. is aiming at the greatest practicable variety and contrast between the two creditor-scenes. The element common to both is Strepsiades' introduction of irrelevant items of sophistic lore (1247 ff. ~ 1279 ff., 1290 ff.), naïvely applied sophistic technique (1225 ff., ~ 1237 ff. ~ 1269, 1274 f., 1286 [cf. Pheidippides in 1179]), and insolent violence (1253 ~ 1296 ff.).

On the 'identification' of the Second Creditor cf. p. xviii.

1261 τῶν Καρκίνου τις δαιμόνων: The natural inference is that Karkinos had composed at least one tragedy in which a god had been portrayed as lamenting. But in *Wasps* 1501 ff. and *Peace* 781 ff. (cf. 864), Ar. refers to the sons of Karkinos, one of whom (*Wasps* 1511) is a tragic poet, identified here by the Scholiast as Xenokles. The joke is complicated; we expect 'one of the *sons* of Karkinos'; we get *δαιμόνων* instead, and the creditor utters (1264 f.) lines which are in fact taken from a tragedy by Xenokles.

1263 κατὰ σεαυτόν νυν τρέπου: The same unsympathetic reply is given by Dikaiopolis in *Ach.* 1019 to the farmer who answers *ἀνὴρ κακοδαίμων* to the question *τίς οὑτοσί;*

1264 ὦ σκληρέ . . . 1265 ἀπώλεσας: The Scholiast says that these words are taken from the *Tlempolemos* (or *Likymnios*) of Xenokles, with substitution of *θραυσάντυγες* for *χρυσάμπυκες*, and that they are spoken in the play by Alkmene when Likymnios had been killed by Tlempolemos. Alkmene was Likymnios' half-sister. That Tlempolemos killed Likymnios is mentioned in *Il.* ii. 661 ff.—an accidental killing, according to a Scholiast on Pindar. Possibly in Xenokles' play Tlempolemos contrived that Likymnios should be killed in an 'accident' while driving a chariot.

1269 ἄλλως τε μέντοι: 'Especially'; cf. p. xxxii.

1272 ἵππους: '⟨Chariot drawn by⟩ horses', as normally in epic. **γ'**: 'Yes . . .'.

1273 ἀπ' ὄνου καταπεσών: Pl. *Lg.* 701 C says, 'One must keep on reining in the argument as one does a horse, not, as if there were no bit in its mouth, be carried away by the argument and *κατὰ τὴν παροιμίαν ἀπό τινος ὄνου πεσεῖν*.' *ὄνου* there is a correction by the second hand of one MS.; the first hand, and the other MSS., have *νοῦ*, which does not make much of a proverb and does not suit the rest of Plato's metaphor. 'Fall' must belong to the proverb as known to Ar. and Plato. *ἀπὸ νοῦ*, which, unlike *μετὰ νοῦ*, *κατὰ νοῦν*, etc., does not occur as an independent adverbial phrase, must be an ancient pun on the proverb.

1275 αὐτός: As distinct from your money. **ὑγιαίνεις**: Cf. 833 n. and *Birds* 1214 *ὑγιαίνεις μέν;* = 'Are you in your right mind?'

1276 ἐγκέφαλον: Although their terminology presupposes that thought and feeling are functions of organs located in the trunk, the Greeks could not fail to observe the effects of injury to the brain. So Hippokrates: 'When the brain has been shaken, the patient necessarily loses the power of speech at once.' **ὥσπερ**: Not 'I think you have, as it were, had your brain shaken' but 'I think you are like a man who has . . .'. Cf. *Peace* 234 f. *ὥσπερ ᾐσθόμην . . . θυείας φθέγμα*, 'I caught a sound like that of a mortar.'

1279 πότερα . . . 1281 πάλιν: This is a scientific problem not explicitly raised earlier in the play, but it was generally assumed in the fifth century that rain water is drawn up by the sun. Cf. 272 n.

1285 ἀλλ' εἰ . . . 1286 ἀπόδοτε†: 'Well, if you're short, pay me ⟨only⟩ the interest on my money' is good sense, but the transition from the singular *σπανίζεις* to the plural *ἀπόδοτε* (the variant *ἀπόδος* does not scan, and Thomas's *γε* has no true parallel) is odd. Pheidippides borrowed the money (1268 ff.), but why should he be brought into the payment of the interest if it is Strepsiades' shortage of money which prevents the repayment of the capital? We want the emphasis to fall on '*interest*' and the right answer may well be *ἀλλ' εἰ σπανίζετ' ἀργυρίου, τὸν ⟨γοῦν⟩ τόκον ἀπόδοτε.*

1286 τοῦτο . . . θηρίον: Lit., 'This ⟨thing⟩, interest, what beast is it?' On *θηρίον* cf. 184 n.; the extension of the word beyond the realm of living creatures is perhaps facilitated by the ambiguity of *τόκος* (cf. 1156 n.). On the order of phrases cf. 379.

1288 πλέον πλέον: Cf. *Frogs* 1001 *μᾶλλον μᾶλλον*: the idiom sounds colloquial, and perhaps usually was, but cf. Eur. *Iph. Taur.* 1406 *μᾶλλον δὲ μᾶλλον πρὸς πέτρας ᾔει σκάφος.*

1289 ὑπορρέοντος: Nowhere else used of time; ctr. Aisch. *Eum.* 853 *οὑπιρρέων . . . χρόνος.*

1292 δίκαιον: The equation of *δίκη*, righteousness and justice among men, with cosmic order and physical laws, is implied by Parmenides, and Alkmaion regarded health as depending on the *ἰσονομία* of the *δυνάμεις* in the body. An ordinary Athenian might not always have put the matter quite as the creditor does, but it is dramatically desirable that the creditor should be trapped into implying that his own demand for interest is *ἄδικον*. Solon said of the sea *ἢν δέ τις αὐτὴν μὴ κινῇ, πάντων ἐστὶ δικαιοτάτη*: we might almost say that the sea 'behaves itself' if not set in motion by some external force.

1292 κᾆτα . . . 1295 σόν: A curiously similar argument from the order of nature is offered by Iokaste in Eur. *Phoen.* 543 ff., when she suggests that Eteokles and Polyneikes should divide their inheritance as day and night divide the year.

1296 ἀπὸ τῆς οἰκίας: Most MSS. have *ἐκ*, not *ἀπό*, but in Ar. *ἐκ τῆς οἰκίας* is used only of movement which must, or can, be through the door from the interior of the building: 123, 802, *Wasps* 266, etc. Contrast *Wasps* 456 *παῖε . . . τοὺς σφῆκας ἀπὸ τῆς οἰκίας*, where the action, as here, takes place outside the house.

1297 φέρε: A slave brings out the goad, as we have to assume on many similar occasions when a character cries *φέρε . . .*, *δότω . . .*, etc. **μαρτύρομαι**: Cf. 495 n.

1298 ἐλᾷς: Cf. 28 n. **σαμφόρα**: Cf. 23 n.

1299 ὕβρις: Cf. 1068 n. **ἄξεις**: Cf. 633 n. 'Pull ⟨the chariot⟩' makes sense; interpretation as *ᾄξεις*, 'go quickly' is perfectly possible but not necessary. **ἐπιαλῶ**: Setting aside the nonsensical and unmetrical *ἐπὶ ἄλλων*, many of the wide range of interpretations offered by the Scholiast all stem from one error, the belief that the last four syllables of the line were *ἐπὶ ἅλω*, 'on to a threshing-floor', which is in fact ruled out by the hiatus. A compound verb is the only possibility, and the epic *ἐπιάλλειν* is suggested by *Od.* ix. 288 *ἑτάροις ἐπὶ χεῖρας ἴαλλεν*, 'he laid hands on my companions'.

1300 πρωκτόν: Cf. 164 n. Strepsiades refers not to a stab in one buttock, which all ages have regarded as irresistibly funny, but to the cruel practice of goading a draught-animal in the anus. **σειραφόρον**: Cf. 122 n.

1301 ἔμελλόν σ' ἆρα: The creditor, naturally, has fled. Strepsiades means 'Aha! I *thought* I'd make you get a move on!' Cf. Dionysos in *Frogs* 268, when he has silenced the frogs: *ἔμελλον ἄρα παύσειν ποθ' ὑμᾶς τοῦ κοάξ. ἆρα* = *ἄρα* in this and many other usages.

1302 ξυνωρίσιν: Cf. 15 n.

(iii) **1303–20.** *Lyric system*

The Chorus now prepares us for the disaster which is about to fall upon Strepsiades, and in its very first words condemns his conduct.

(1) 1303 f. ~ 1311 f.

– – ∪ – ∪ – ∪ – – – | ∪ – (|) { ∪ – | ∪ ∪ – – | / ∪ – ∪ – – – || }

(2) 1305 ~ 1313

⏓ – ∪ – – | – ∪ – |

(3) 1306 ~ 1314

⏓ – ∪ – ∪ – ∪ ⌓ |

(4) 1307–10*b* ~ 1315–20

(*a*) – – ∪ – – – ∪ –

(*b*) – ∪ – ∪ | – ∪ –

(*c*) – ∪ – – | – ∪ –

(*d*) { – | – ∪ – – – ∪ – / – ∪ – ∪ – ∪ – | – – ∪ – | }

(*e*) { – – †∪ | ∪ – | ∪ –† | / – – ∪ – ∪ | – – | }

(1) is an iambic trimeter + reizianum; on balance, I prefer not to regard a verse as ending with *ὁ γάρ* ~ *ὅπερ*. For the abnormal responsion

cf. 1312 n. (2) and (3) are iambic dimeters. (4) is a continuous iambo-trochaic 'pnigos' consisting of (*a*) iambic dimeter; (*b*) and (*c*) lekythia; (*d*) iambic dimeter in the strophe, and in the antistrophe a sequence which can be interpreted either as *cr ia ia* or as *lek ia*; cf. the metrical analysis of 953 f. ~ 1028 f.; (*e*) the strophe is, I believe, corrupt (cf. 1310*b* n.), and the antistrophe is an iambic dimeter of the form *ia ba*.

1303 ἐρᾶν: Cf. 1459.

1310a ὧν: On the genitive cf. 22 n., but note also that the text of the next line is suspect.

1310b τι κακὸν λαβεῖν: In itself the expression is commonplace, but I find it very hard to believe in λήψεταί (sc. ὁ γέρων ὅδε) τι πρᾶγμ' ὃ τοῦτον ποήσει τὸν σοφιστήν (= τὸν γέροντα τόνδε) . . . τι κακὸν λαβεῖν, and the transposition κακὸν λαβεῖν τι solves only the metrical problem of responsion 1310*b* ~ 1320, leaving the stylistic problem untouched. I suspect that τι κακὸν λαβεῖν is a gloss which has ousted a more recherché expression, perhaps (sarcastic) καλόν γ' ὄνασθαι: for ὄνασθαι cf. Eur. *Med.* 1025; for sarcastic καλόν cf. ἀστεῖον in 1204; and for this type of γε in mid sentence cf. *Wealth* 1043 πολιὰ γεγένησαι ταχύ γε νὴ τὸν οὐρανόν.

1312 ἐζήτει: If this variant is right the sequence ∪ – ∪ – – – (found in [e.g.] *Birds* 1314 ~ 1326 and Soph. *El.* 479 ~ 495) must respond to the reizianum (1304) ∪ – ∪ ∪ – –. The responsion which I posit seems to me hard to avoid in 1349 f. ~ 1395 f., where text, sense, and style leave us little freedom of manœuvre. The principle involved is that of 'syllable-counting' without regard for quantity, a principle plainly enough attested in *Wasps* 274 ff. ~ 282 ff., where μῶν ἀπολώλεκε τὰς ἐμβάδας ἢ προσέκοψ' ἐν responds to ἐξαπατῶν καὶ λέγων ὡς φιλαθήναιος ἦν καί and εἶτ' ἐφλέγμηνεν αὐτοῦ to διὰ τοῦτ' ὀδυνηθείς. Related to this is a series of irregularities involving three or more shorts, e.g. *Birds* 333 ff. ~ 349 ff.

1318 ἴσως δ' ἴσως: 'Perhaps—perhaps—he (sc. Strepsiades) will wish (cf. 1129) that he (sc. Pheidippides) were dumb.'

(J) 1321–1511. PUNISHMENT OF STREPSIADES AND SOCRATES

(i) 1321–1344. *Altercation between Strepsiades and Pheidippides*

Strepsiades rushes frantically out of the house, clutching his head and his face and shouting for help. Pheidippides comes out after him. Whereas Strepsiades is agitated, and shows this in his movements and gestures, Pheidippides is nonchalant, self-possessed, and dominant (cf. 799 εὐσωματεῖ γὰρ καὶ σφριγᾷ).

This is the beginning of what will be presented as a contest similar in form to the contest of Right and Wrong. The play is not unique in possessing two contests, but it is unique in possessing two on so elaborate a scale. We may distinguish seven stages:

(i) 1321–44. The violent altercation between Strepsiades and Pheidippides (in iambic trimeters) corresponds to the altercation between Right and Wrong in 889–948. In neither case is there actual violence on stage; the violence has already been committed, while there it is threatened and narrowly averted (933). An interesting difference lies in the fact that Right and Wrong were persuaded by the Chorus to argue (934 ff.). Strepsiades and Pheidippides are not persuaded by any intervention of the Chorus; Pheidippides is all too ready to argue his case (1334), and this is wholly in character with the sophistic education he has received, whereas Strepsiades' readiness to listen (1344), dramatically necessary if the contest is to proceed, is not entirely in character.

(ii) 1345–50. The Chorus sings a strophe, addressed to Strepsiades. The equivalent strophe in the previous contest was addressed to both participants impartially (949–58).

(iii) 1351–2. The Chorus invites Strepsiades to explain how the quarrel started; cf. the invitation to Right (959–60) to state his case.

(iv) 1353–90. Strepsiades tells the story. He is interrupted (1359 f., 1377 f., 1379) by Pheidippides; (iii) and (iv) are in iambic tetrameters. Their equivalent in the contest of Right and Wrong was in anapaestic tetrameters; note, however, that Right was interrupted by Wrong (984 f., 1000 f.), and that he ended with an anapaestic pnigos (1009–23), just as Strepsiades ends with an iambic pnigos (1386–90).

(v) 1391–6. The Chorus sings the antistrophe, commenting on what Strepsiades has told them. The antistrophe which followed the argument of Right commented on his speech and exhorted Wrong to reply (1024–33).

(vi) 1397–8. The Chorus invites Pheidippides to reply; cf. the invitation to Wrong, 1034 f.

(vii) 1399–1451. Pheidippides replies. After introductory remarks, interrupted (1406 f.) by Strepsiades, he proceeds by interrogation; so Wrong, after similar introductory remarks (1036–42), interrogated Right. (vi) and (vii), like the equivalent portions of the earlier contest, are in iambic tetrameters. Right took the initiative in 1083, and the final pnigos was a dialogue; the last words were spoken not by Wrong, but by Right (1102–4), proclaiming his own desertion. Similarly, Strepsiades takes the initiative in 1430, the pnigos (1445–51) is a dialogue, and the last words are spoken by Strepsiades. We proceed immediately to dialogue in iambic trimeters between Strepsiades and the Chorus (1452 ff.), just as the desertion of Right was immediately followed by dialogue in iambic trimeters between Wrong and Strepsiades.

The parallelism of structure between the two contests emphasizes the extent to which Pheidippides has emerged from his education a replica of Wrong; we shall see how he reproduces not only the rhetorical methods but even the actual words of Wrong.

1321 ἰοὺ ἰού: Cf. 1 n.

1322 δημόται: It is natural enough that a man should call on his neighbours for help; it is less natural, to our way of thinking, that his cry for help should presuppose that his relatives and the other members of his deme are within earshot, but this is in fact true to life; cf. 210 n.

1323 πάσῃ τέχνῃ: On this expression (which here goes with *ἀμυνάθετέ μοι*) cf. 885 n.

1324 γνάθου: Cf. 1109 n.

1325 φήμ': 'Yes', as often.

1326 ὁρᾶθ': Addressed to the world at large; cf. 1225 f.

1327 τοιχωρύχε: *τοιχωρύχος*, in the strict sense, is a man who digs or breaks through a wall in order to steal—a species of *κακοῦργος*, liable to summary execution. The word is used, however, as a highly general term of opprobrium.

1328 αὖθίς με . . . 1330 ῥόδοις: Pheidippides adopts, in the face of his father's vituperation, precisely the tone adopted by Wrong in 910–12; note in particular 910 *ῥόδα* and 912 *πάττων*. **ἆρ' οἶσθ':** We would say 'Don't you . . .?' rather than 'Do you . . .?'; cf. *Birds* 797, where the Chorus, after recounting all the advantages of having wings, says *ἆρ' ὑπόπτερον γενέσθαι παντός ἐστιν ἄξιον;* **πόλλ' ἀκούων καὶ κακά:** 'Being called a lot of bad names'. **λακκόπρωκτε:** Since *λάκκος* is 'cistern' or 'reservoir', *λακκόπρωκτος* carries the same implications as the common *εὐρύπρωκτος* (cf. 1084 n.), but at a more advanced stage of grossness and fantasy. Like *καταπύγων* (cf. 529 n.), it could be used as a term of general opprobrium.

1330 τοῖς ῥόδοις: 'Those roses', i.e. those abusive names.

1333 καὶ πῶς: Cf. 717.

1336 ἑλοῦ . . . λέγειν: The joke is against the sophistic exercise of 'blaming and defending the same thing' (cf. p. xx). Dramatically speaking, it is appropriate, for Pheidippides has already committed himself to what is, from the standpoint of *νόμος* (cf. 1038–42), *ἥττων λόγος*, but it serves to bring out his readiness to defend in words even what he does not accept in practice.

1338 μέντοι: The sense is plainly 'I *have* had you taught . . .', spoken bitterly. There is no exact parallel for this sense of *μέντοι*, but cf. 187 and p. xxxii.

1344 καὶ μήν: Strepsiades gives an assurance of his readiness to listen here and now.

(ii) **1345–50.** *Strophe*

(1) 1345 ~ 1391	⏓ – ⏑ | – ⏒ – ⏑ – – – ⏑ – |
(2) 1346 ~ 1392	⏓ – ⏑ ⏑ – – ||
(3) 1347 ~ 1393	– – ⏑ – – – ⏑ – – – ⏑ – |
(4) 1348 ~ 1394	⏒ – | ⏑ ⏑ – ⌓ ||
(5) 1349 ~ 1395	⏒ – ⏑ – ⏑ – ⏑ – | ⏒ – ⏑ ∧ ||
(6) 1350	⏑ – ⏑ – – – | }
~ 1396	– – ⏑ ⏑ – – | }

(1) and (3) are iambic trimeters; (2) and (4) are reiziana. If my text is right, (5) is an iambic trimeter; (6) in the strophe is a verse of the type presented by a variant at 1312 and here, as there, it responds to a reizianum. Cf. 1349 f. n.

1345 σὸν ἔργον: 'It's up to you.'

1349 δῆλον . . . 1350 τἀνθρώπου: As the text stands in the MSS., the elided λῆμ' (followed by ἐστι τἀνθρώπου, which was the text assumed by the author of the metrical analysis in the scholion) 'responds' to ἂν in 1395, which must be the last syllable of a verse, since it is followed by 'pause'; to take 1395 f. as a single verse would give a responsion of unparalleled eccentricity:

1349 f.	– – ⏑ – ⏑ – ⏑ – – – ⏑ – – ⏑ – – –
1395 f.	⏑ – ⏑ – ⏑ – ⏑ – ⏑ – ⏑ ⏑ – – ⏑ ⏑ – –

If we delete *ἐστί* in 1350 and adopt both *γε* and *τοι* in 1349, we achieve responsion in 1349 ~ 1395; on 1350 ~ 1396, see above. *γέ τοι* is peculiarly appropriate; cf. *Wasps* 1415 f. *ἔρχεται καλούμενός σε· τόν γε τοι κλητῆρ' ἔχει.*

(iii) **1351–2.** *The Chorus invites Strepsiades to tell his story*

1352 ἤδη λέγειν χρὴ πρὸς χορόν: The Chorus speaks as if it were a producer telling an actor what to do next. This is unique; the self-references of the Chorus in lyrics (e.g. 564) or in addresses to the audience are generically different, and the rupture of dramatic illusion in *Ach.* 416 *δεῖ γάρ με λέξαι τῷ χορῷ ῥῆσιν μακράν*, though comparable in degree, is a special case because Dikaiopolis is there speaking to Euripides and asking for the loan of tragic stage-properties. It may be that *πρὸς χορόν* was a technical theatrical term; the Scholiast treats it as such. If Ar. had wished to write *πρὸς τὸν χορόν* he could have omitted *χρή*: cf. 433 n. **πάντως δὲ τοῦτο δράσεις:** *πάντως* is a word of many meanings: 'in every way', 'at all costs', but also 'in any case', even 'admittedly'. The future is not indisputably used by Ar. in an imperatival sense; indeed, this use is ill attested in Attic, and in Pl.

Prt. 338 A ὧς οὖν ποιήσετε καὶ πείθεσθέ μοι κτλ. the demonstrative ὧς points to an archaic formula. The Chorus, then, is not saying to Strepsiades 'Please do this' but 'You will do it *anyway*' (sc. 'even without my telling you to do it'). cf. *Eccl.* 704 ποῖ θεῖς οὗτος; πάντως οὐδὲν δράσεις ἐλθών, 'What are *you* running after? You won't achieve anything, anyway' (sc. 'so there is no point your running'). The remarkable first half of the line suggests that the Chorus's point is not '(you will tell us) because you, Strepsiades, are bursting to air your grievances', but 'because it is in the script of the play'; the rupture of dramatic illusion in the whole line constitutes the joke.

(iv) **1353–90.** *Strepsiades' story*

The quarrel began when Strepsiades asked Pheidippides to sing a song (we, deprived of the music, would call it a lyric poem) of Simonides, and Pheidippides objected to singing while drinking after dinner. Strepsiades then asked him to recite something from Aischylos. Pheidippides expressed contempt for Aischylos and extolled Euripides. Strepsiades, still forbearing, then heard him recite from Euripides; horrified at the content, he expressed himself vehemently, and they came to blows.

The quarrel turns on two issues: the traditional practice of singing after dinner, and the rival merits of old and contemporary poets.

For the practice of singing at parties our best evidence is *Wasps* 1219 ff., where Bdelykleon is coaching his father for respectable company and says 'The flute-girl has blown a note . . . mind you take up the skolia' (i.e. as is shown by what follows, 'take up a song which someone else has begun'). That not all songs called 'skolia' in the fifth century were anonymous products of Attica is proved by a citation from *Banqueters*, 'Take it' (sc. the myrtle-branch? Cf. 1364 n.) 'and sing me a skolion of Alkaios or Anakreon.' As we see from 1355 f., since boys of middle- and upper-class families had been taught to play the lyre and sing (cf. pp. xxiii f.), they were expected, when grown up, to be able to accompany their own singing on the lyre. That intellectuals in Ar.'s day were coming to despise this practice is attested by Pl. *Prt.* 347 C ff. There Socrates, wishing to end a lengthy discussion of a passage of Simonides, says that educated men have no need of the 'voices of others'—that is, of instrumental players *and poets* (347 E 3)—but can occupy themselves, while drinking, in question and answer, using their own voices and their own resources. This is a natural enough development in an age of expanding intellectual activity.

Ar. represents men past middle age—e.g. Dikaiopolis in *Ach.*—as uncritically fond of Aischylos while ridiculing Euripides and other contemporary poets. (Sophokles, whose distinguished career in tragedy began fourteen years before the death of Aischylos and continued until the year after the death of Euripides, is only rarely and briefly mentioned by Ar., and nowhere before *Peace*.) This antithesis is the subject of the second half of *Frogs*, where much is made (1043 ff.) of the objection which Strepsiades here brings against Euripides, immorality of subject and characters. It is not wholly intelligible, at first sight, that it should be wrong for Euripides to portray Phaidra, unhappy victim of a goddess's malice and murderess only by proxy, but right for Aischylos to portray Klytaimestra, who embraces both adultery and murder with determination and whose measure of moral responsibility is as disputable as such things are (though the terms are different) in real life. We must, however, remember that by modern standards the Greeks were curiously indifferent to questions of responsibility, and the plea that such-and-such a character in drama is a victim of the gods should not be introduced into this problem at all. Secondly, whereas Aischylos made his audience feel that they were witnessing monstrous events of the distant past, full of grandeur and fear but essentially remote and—in a strict sense of the word—inhuman, Euripides *involved* the audience in these same heroic events (cf. *Frogs* 954 ff.); the point is not directly made in *Frogs* or anywhere else, but there is no doubt that the biggest single contribution to this involvement was the element of generalization, necessarily embracing heroes of the past and contemporary Athenians alike, which Euripides introduced into his characters' speeches (e.g. *Med.* 230 ff., on the status of women). Therefore Euripides was disturbing; Aischylos was not, because he had been dead for more than thirty years when *Clouds* was written, and his work had become classical. There is a third reason for the antithesis between Aischylos and Euripides, which is perhaps the most important reason of all. Few men, unless they are of abnormal artistic sensitivity or are professionally interested, are capable of comparing objectively poetry or music composed after they are forty with the poetry and music which they were taught to admire when they were twenty; and most men do not even try. Those who were in their twenties during the last decade of Aischylos' career were in their sixties during the Archidamian War; this fact was the essential determinant of the antithesis between Aischylos and Euripides as Ar. presents it.

1355 τὴν λύραν: Cf. p. 182.

1356 ᾆσαι . . . ἐπέχθη: Lit., 'to sing Krios, how he was shorn' is normal Greek; the addition of 'a song of Simonides', giving *ᾆσαι* two objects, complicates the syntax but in no way obscures the sense. The poem contained the words *ἐπέξαθ' ὁ Κριὸς οὐκ ἀεικέως*, exploiting the fact that *κριός* = 'ram'.

1357 ἀρχαῖον: Cf. 821 n. **εἶν'**: Cf. p. xxxviii. **κιθαρίζειν**: *λύρα* and *κιθάρα* are named as separate objects by Pl. *Rep.* 399 D, but *κιθαρίζειν* covers both, λυρίζειν being a Hellenistic word. In *Knights* 989 ff. it is the κιθαριστής who teaches boys to play the λύρα.

1358 ὡσπερεί . . . ἀλοῦσαν: Women sang then, as they do now, in performing monotonous manual work, and a couple of their songs have survived in Plutarch.

1359 ἀράττεσθαί: A cogent emendation of ἄρα τύπτεσθαι: – – ⏑ ⏑ – is not unexampled in iambic tetrameters (cf. p. xxxvi), but it is abnormal, and we cannot feel confident that whatever is communicated by ἄρα was so important to Ar. as to make this rather ugly abnormality unavoidable. For ἀράττεσθαι cf. 1373 ἀράττω.

1360 τέττιγας: The cicada is the singer par excellence; cf. Pl. *Phdr.* 258 E–259 D, where Socrates invents an aetiological story, telling how cicadas were once men who 'singing, took no thought for food or drink, and died before they realized what they were doing'.

1361 μέντοι: Cf. p. xxxii.

1363 μόλις μέν, ἀλλ' ὅμως, ἠνεσχόμην: 'I put up with it with difficulty, but still, I did put up with it.'

1364 ἀλλά: The kind of ἀλλά used with imperatives in the sense 'well, then' or 'at any rate' (as in 1369) is here retained in indirect speech; cf. Eur. *Or.* 1562 ὡς ἂν ἀλλὰ παῖδ' ἐμὴν ῥυσώμεθα. **μυρρίνην**: Dikaiarchos said that 'those who sing at drinking-parties do so with a branch of bay or myrtle in the hand, in accordance with an old tradition'. There are no grounds for thinking that in Ar.'s time recitation from tragedy was normal after dinner. Strepsiades is compromising by not demanding a song to the lyre; but he preserves appearances by the myrtle-branch.

1366 πρῶτον: Pheidippides is sarcastic (cf. 8, 647 nn.). For πρῶτος as a term of praise cf. Eur. *El.* 82.

1367 ψόφου . . . κρημνοποιόν: Now Pheidippides drops his sarcastic tone. ἀξύστατος is probably 'incoherent', applied to the poet because it could be applied to his work; cf. Aristotle's dictum, 'the plot of the play must συνεστάναι in such a way . . .' The splendidly expressive word στόμφαξ evidently means 'bombastic ranter'. κρημνοποιός, lit. 'cliff-maker', 'crag-maker', speaks for itself; the same metaphor seems to be used in *Knights* 626 ff. ἐλασίβροντ' ἀναρρηγνὺς ἔπη τερατευόμενος . . . κρημνοὺς †ἐρείδων. The charges that Aischylos is 'full of noise', 'bombastic', and 'makes mountains out of poetry' are precisely the charges brought against him by 'Euripides' in *Frogs*, especially 1056 f. ἢν οὖν σὺ λέγῃς Λυκαβηττοὺς καὶ Παρνασσῶν ἡμῖν μεγέθη: Dionysos says much the same, in complimentary terms, in 1004 πυργώσας ῥήματα σεμνά. It is quickly demonstrable that the average word-length in Euripides is smaller than in Aischylos, but debatable how far popular literary judgements are founded on subliminal perception of statistics rather than on a few memorable passages. The charge of 'incoherence' is not specifically made in *Frogs*, but is implied in Euripides' criticisms of Aischylos as 'cheating a simple-minded audience' (909 f., cf. 989 ff.) by the enigmatic silences of his characters (910 ff.).

1369 τὸν θυμὸν δακών: A man may bite his lip to fortify his spirit; the old men in *Wasps* 1083 boast that they fought at Marathon 'standing man to man, eating the lip in fury'. 'Biting my spirit' must be what we would express as 'biting *back* my anger'. **ἀλλά:** Cf. 1364 n.

1370 ἄττ': Cf. 113 n. **σοφά:** Cf. 94 n.

1371 ἦγ': The MSS. have ᾖσ', ᾖσ', or ᾖσεν. *ῥῆσις* is a speech (cf. *Ach.* 416, referring forward to 496 ff., and cf. the cognate words *ῥῆμα* and *ῥήτωρ*), and nowhere else does anyone 'sing' a speech; note *Wasps* 579 f. *πρὶν ἂν ἡμῖν . . . εἴπῃ ῥῆσιν* and 1095 *ῥῆσιν εὖ λέξειν*. The reference might conceivably be to a monody, of the kind for which Euripides was famous e.g. *Hec.* 154 ff., 197 ff., 1056 ff. One might say that its content justifies *ῥῆσις*, its character *ᾄδειν*. But in Theophr. *Char.* 27. 2 the MSS. have *ῥήσεις μανθάνειν . . . καὶ ταύτας ἄγων παρὰ ποτὸν ἐπιλανθάνεσθαι*, and this seems to me decisive. **ἐκίνει:** Cf. 1102 n.

1372 ἀδελφὸς . . . ἀδελφήν: *ἀδελφός* (*ὁ ἀ-*) is probably the right interpretation; cf. 97 and 558. The play concerned is *Aiolos*, and the brother and sister are Makareus and Kanake, Aiolos' children. The point of *ὁμομητρίαν* is that marriage between children of the same father but different mothers was permitted by law at Athens. **ὦ 'λεξίκακε:** The epithet is associated with Herakles, but it is by no means certain that when an Athenian expressed a horrified reaction by this word he had any particular deity consciously in mind.

1373 κἀγὼ οὐκέτ': *-γὼ* and *οὐ* are scanned as one syllable.

1376 κἀπέτριβεν: The variant *κἀπέθλιβεν* may be right. *θλίβειν* is 'press', 'squeeze'; *ἀποθλίβειν* means 'pinch *off*'; *ἐπιθλίβειν* ('press') does not appear before Hellenistic times. But I suspect that *ἐπιτρίβειν*, one of the commonest words in comedy, was corrupted through the familiarity of *θλίβειν*, *θλῖψις* in Biblical and Patristic Greek in the metaphorical sense 'affliction', 'oppression'.

1378 σοφώτατον: For the phrasing cf. *Frogs* 143 f. *θηρί' ὄψει μυρία δεινότατα*. **σοφώτατόν γ':** *γε* is often used when the second speaker repeats a word from the first speaker and *agrees* with it. There is no true parallel for a usage which would give us here, 'What, *Euripides* a *genius*?' We must, I think, interpret *σοφώτατόν γ'* as expressing heated sarcasm (as in English, 'Oh yes, very clever . . .'); it has affinities with the sarcasm of 647 and 1064 and the common *καλ- γε*. **ὦ:** The variant *ὤ* shows that on one ancient interpretation the words mean 'Ah, what am I to call you?', with a strong stop after *ἐκεῖνον* (on *ὦ* and *ὤ* cf. 219 n.). This would be plausible if *σοφώτατόν γ' ἐκεῖνον* could be a self-contained indignant question, 'What, *he* a genius?'

As we have seen, that is an unlikely interpretation; Strepsiades begins as if he were going to continue 'when he ...' (*ὅστις* ...), interposes a vocative, is about to use something like the epithets of 1327, but realizes that none of them is strong enough to express his feelings. Hence, 'Oh yes, very clever, you—what am I to call you?' Cf. Dem. xviii. 22 *εἶτ', ὦ—τί ἂν εἰπών σε τις ὀρθῶς προσείποι;—*.

1379 ἀλλ': He abandons the attempt to find a suitably opprobrious name, reflecting on the probable consequences. **ἐν δίκῃ γ' ἄν**: Cf. p. xxxii.

1380 ὅστις κτλ.: 'Considering that I ...' On the sentiment and argument cf. 861 ff.

1382 εἰ μέν γε βρῦν ... 1385 προυσχόμην σε: On *ἄν* cf. 54 n. *βρῦν*, *μαμμᾶν*, and *κακκᾶν* do not strike us as plausible baby-words; but *βρῦ*, *μαμμᾶ*, and *κακκᾶ* do, and we must accept the evidence of this passage that when they were used by parents in talking to infants (i) *μαμμᾶ* and *κακκᾶ* were treated as feminine nouns (note 1390 *'πόησα κακκᾶν*: cf. fr. 543. 5 *ὄκῳ* = 'repetitions of the word *ὄκως*'), and (ii) *βρῦ* was treated not like the uninflected *γρῦ* but like *δρῦς* or *μῦς*. This interpretation is supported by Theokr. 15. 13 f., where *ἀπφῦς*, 'daddy' (spoken to a baby) has an accusative *ἀπφῦν*. *κακκᾶ* has a cognate in adult language, *κάκκη* (*Peace* 162); *μαμμᾶ* does not stand in so immediate a relationship to *μάμμη*, for that means not 'food' but 'mum', 'ma'. Cf. also 1001 n. **κακκᾶν ... ἐξέφερον ἄν**: lit., 'and you didn't get ahead ⟨of me⟩ saying "kakka", and I took you ...', i.e. 'Before you could say "kakka", I took you ...' **προυσχόμην**: Sanitation in Greek households was rudimentary, and possibly 'outside' was good enough for children. A house might have an outside *κοπρών*, but not always even that, if the implications of *Eccl.* 320 ff. are to be trusted.

1386 βοῶντα ... 1390 κακκᾶν: This pnigos, concluding one side of the contest, as 1445–51 concludes the other (cf. p. 151), has an effect as if one were to 'stretch' an iambic tetrameter into a 'decameter'; *ἔτλης* is the only point at which verse-end is possible, for the iambic metre depends on treating *ὅτι*, *-αρέ*, and *-μενος* each as two brevia. **οὐκ ἔτλης**: 'You didn't go to the trouble ...'

(v) **1391–6.** *Antistrophe*

1392 πηδᾶν ὅτι λέξει: 'Leap, ⟨wondering⟩ what he's going to say'.

1396 ἀλλ' οὐδ' ἐρεβίνθου: Almost '—why, not even ...'; cf. Men. *Sam.* 143 f. *ἀποδέδρακέ με ἀλλ' οὐδὲ μικρὸν συλλαβών*. *ἐρέβινθος* is 'chick-pea', and 'we wouldn't accept it at the price of a chick-pea' means 'we wouldn't give a fig for it'.

(vi) **1397–8.** *The Chorus invites Pheidippides to state his case*

1397 σὸν ἔργον: Cf. 1345. **ἐπῶν:** Cf. 541 n. **κινητὰ καὶ μοχλευτά:** *μοχλευτής* in 568 referred to Poseidon, who causes earthquakes and is imagined as moving the earth with a lever (*μοχλός*). Unlike *μηχανή* and its derivatives, the derivatives of *μοχλός* are not used metaphorically until the first century A.D., but it is hard not to discern something like the metaphorical sense of 'engineer' in this passage; otherwise we must think of *καινὰ ἔπη* as something massive to be shifted, not as something complicated to be constructed. Many nouns in -*της*, denoting types of craftsmen (often neglected by students of Greek style), are known from Athenian building inscriptions of the fifth and fourth centuries, or from Pollux, and sometimes from those sources alone, and it is reasonable to suspect that a *μοχλευτής* was a specialist in constructional problems. *κινεῖν* has, of course, a wide range of metaphorical senses.

(vii) **1399–1451.** *Pheidippides' argument*

1402 τρί': Three is a proverbially insignificant number; cf. *Ach.* 598 'We were elected—' '—Yes, by three cuckoos.' **ἦν:** Cf. 530 n.

1404 λεπταῖς: The adjective qualifies all three nouns; cf. Thuc. vi. 49. 4 *οὔτε πλοῦν πολὺν οὔτε ὁδόν.* **μερίμναις:** Cf. 101 n.

1406 τοίνυν: Cf. 254.

1407 ἵππων . . . τέθριππον: On the repeated stem cf. 1069 n. **τυπτόμενον ἐπιτριβῆναι:** On the rhythm cf. 1063 f.

1408 ἐκεῖσε δ' . . . μέτειμι: 'Pursue that point in my argument . . .'; cf. the methodical exposition of Wrong, 1058 and 1075.

1409 ἐρήσομαι: Pheidippides, like Wrong, proceeds by asking his opponent questions and exploiting the answers.

1409 παῖδά . . . 1414 τοὐμὸν δὲ μή: Pheidippides now turns to good account the traditional father's argument (1380 ff.): 'Repay me for my care for you in your childhood.' **τοῦτ' ἔστ' εὐνοεῖν, τὸ τύπτειν:** Cf. Antiphon i. 5 *εἰ νομίζει τοῦτο εὐσέβειαν εἶναι, τὸ τὴν μητέρα μὴ προδοῦναι.*

1414 καὶ μὴν . . . γε: Cf. 4. **ἐλεύθερος:** A free man could strike his own children, but he himself could not be struck with impunity.

1415 κλάουσι . . . δοκεῖς: The line is an adaptation of Eur. *Alc.* 691, where Pheres, indignantly refusing to die in place of his son Admetos, says *χαίρεις ὁρῶν φῶς, πατέρα δ' οὐ χαίρειν δοκεῖς;* Since the words *πατέρα δ' οὐ κλάειν δοκεῖς*, so far as the sense goes, could have been uttered by Strepsiades, implying, 'Since a father is capable of feeling pain, he should be spared', and since the quotation is an iambic trimeter surrounded by tetrameters, it is not surprising that the MSS. show various traces of attempts to introduce changes of speaker and to fill out the line; these two things are to some extent, but not completely, interdependent. It need hardly be said that it would make nonsense of the argument to divide the quotation between Pheidippides and Strepsiades; it is the second half which makes Pheidippides' point, and the first half is determined by the second. The only issue is whether three syllables are missing at the end of the line, and, if so, what they were and who spoke them. Of what we find in the MSS., only *τιὴ δή* would scan; but we do not encounter precisely this expression elsewhere in Ar. The decisive argument against *τιὴ δή;* is not, however, its form, but the fact that wherever an expression of this type occurs it asks a genuine question, 'Why?' or 'What do you mean?', and is immediately answered by the other speaker.

1416 φήσεις: For this asyndeton at a step in a reasoned argument cf. *Ach.* 540 *ἐρεῖ τις, οὐ χρῆν· ἀλλὰ κτλ.* **τοὖργον**: Being beaten does not seem to us an *ἔργον* on the child's part, but an *ἔργον* is not always creative; cf. *Birds* 165 f. 'Don't fly around everywhere with your beaks agape, *ὡς τοῦτ' ἄτιμον τοὖργον ἐστίν*', though even there the translation 'behaviour' suggests itself. For the uncertain boundary between doing and suffering in Greek cf. 1198 n.

1417 δὶς παῖδες οἱ γέροντες: This truism is found also in Kratinos (more concisely, *δὶς παῖς γέρων*) and, in elegant tragic dress, in a fragment of Sophokles, *πάλιν γὰρ αὖθις παῖς ὁ γηράσκων ἀνήρ*.

1420 ἀλλ' οὐδαμοῦ νομίζεται: We are not to imagine that Strepsiades is necessarily taking non-Greek peoples into account. The Greeks were aware that no two Greek cities had identical *νόμοι*, and a man could criticize those of his own city by comparison with others. For the purposes of argument it was possible to generalize about 'everywhere' and 'nowhere'; e.g. Xen. *Mem.* iv. 4. 20, 'It is customary everywhere (*πανταχοῦ νομίζεται*) to honour one's parents.'

1421 οὔκουν ἀνήρ . . . 1424 ἀντιτύπτειν: The realization that a given law is the work of people at some time in the past, that these people were not necessarily more intelligent or virtuous than we are, that the circumstances which prompted the law may have differed fundamentally from ours, and that once a law has been made general inertia is apt to protect it from repeal, is a landmark in the history of civilization and must have excited intellectuals in the fifth century. Yet Pheidippides is characteristically Greek in thinking of a *νόμος* not as a 'behaviour pattern' which is eventually codified but as the product of one man's conscious design and one assembly's conscious decision. So Hippias and Socrates in Xen. *Mem.* iv. 4. 19 f. agree that the universal unwritten laws of mankind must have been imposed by the gods because 'the whole of mankind could not meet' (sc. to adopt these laws) 'nor do they all speak the same language'. On the concept of the individual lawgiver cf. 1187 n.

1426 ἀφίεμεν: The word sounds a formal, legal note. Cf. the oath in a document *ap.* And. i. 98: 'All the oaths which have been sworn at Athens or in the fleet or anywhere else contrary to the interests of the people of Athens, *λύω καὶ ἀφίημι*.'

1427 σκέψαι . . . 1429 οὐ γράφουσιν: The idea that birds are free to assault their parents, unrestrained by *νόμος*, is exploited again in *Birds* 755 ff., 1343 ff. A serious sophistic concept of 'the law of nature' existed; cf. 1075 n. Plato was ready to use similar arguments for different purposes, and early evidence for awareness of them is found in Herodotos (e.g. ii. 64, on the behaviour of animals, barbarians, and Greeks in sanctuaries). **ταυτί**: Cf. 83 n.

1430 τί δῆτ' . . . 1431 καθεύδεις: Strepsiades sees without difficulty the fatal flaw in any argument which selects elements common to animals and man but ignores the differences. In most extant Greek discussion of this topic it is the differences which are emphasized; cf. especially Isoc. iv. 28, xv. 254, on the bestial (*θηριώδης*) condition from which civilization and law and the arts first raised mankind.

1432 οὐ ταὐτόν . . . ἐστίν: We have the impression that Pheidippides would find it hard to say why and to defend his own argument against a charge of arbitrariness. For *ὦ τᾶν* cf. 1267. **οὐδ' ἂν Σωκράτει δοκοίη**: Ar. reveals in these four words his awareness that what passes as rational criticism of irrational authority is sometimes no more than transfer of allegiance to another authority.

1433 πρὸς ταῦτα . . . 1435 τὸν υἱόν: 'This being so' (sc. the new 'law' of reprisal) 'do not strike me'; on *πρὸς ταῦτα* cf. 1030 n. The argument of 1434 f. is elliptical: 'Just as I have a right to chastise you ⟨and thus incur a beating myself, now that I am old⟩, so you have a right to chastise your own son ⟨and will thus incur a beating yourself, when you are old⟩.'

1434 καὶ πῶς: Cf. 717.

1435 γένηται: sc. *υἱός*.

1436 κεκλαύσεται: Impersonal (as not uncommonly in 'future perfect' forms), *ἐμοί* being the agent.

1437 ἐμοὶ μέν . . . 1439 δρῶμεν: This address to the old men among the audience is unique in its banality. We cannot say that Ar. was uncertain how to make the transition from 1436 to 1440 and devised 1437–9 as a stopgap, in a moment of fatigue, for no transition is needed; it would have been entirely in character for Pheidippides to proceed straight from his retort to Strepsiades' last point to a fresh argument which excites him intellectually. It seems, therefore, that Ar. is preparing the way—unskilfully, for he is handling a sequence of events of a type alien to comedy—for Strepsiades' repentance in 1462 ff.

1440 σκέψαι . . . γνώμην: Pheidippides persists in treating the occasion as one in which the emotions are not involved (cf. 1336) and the skill and plausibility of the argument are all that matters. **ἀπὸ γὰρ ὀλοῦμαι**: He means, 'No, I don't want any *more* argument—it'll be the death of me!' On the separation of *ἀπό* cf. 792 n.

1442 ἐπωφελήσεις: *ἐπωφελεῖν* (ctr. 753 *τί δῆτα τοῦτ' ἂν ὠφελήσειέν σ';*) does not occur elsewhere in Comedy, and it is possible that there is sarcastic point in *ἐπ-*, 'what *further* benefit . . .?' It must, however, be admitted that it would need an excess of subtlety to discern the sense 'further' in Soph. *El.* 1005 f. *λύει γὰρ ἡμᾶς οὐδὲν οὐδ' ἐπωφελεῖ βάξιν καλὴν λαβόντε δυσκλεῶς θανεῖν.* *ἐπ-* is absent in some MSS., and it is conceivable that Ar. wrote *ἔτ'* ('after this') *ὠφελήσεις*: cf. *Knights* 140 *πόθεν οὖν ἂν ἔτι γένοιτο πώλης εἷς μόνος;* Cf. app. crit. on 654.

1443 τὴν μητέρ' . . . 1444 κακόν: The *μητραλοίας* and the *πατραλοίας* are normally spoken of together, and neither in law nor in rhetoric do we find it explicitly stated that violence against one's mother is more abhorrent than violence against one's father. Yet Strepsiades' horrified reaction receives some support from the importance of matricide as a tragic theme. The point of *καί* is: 'my mother ⟨also⟩, as I did *you*'.

1448 σεαυτόν . . . 1451 ἥττω: For the order *A μετὰ B . . . καὶ Γ*, cf. *Eccl.* 542 f. *αἱ δὲ δὴ Λακωνικαὶ ᾤχοντο μετὰ σοῦ κατὰ τί χὴ βακτηρία;* **βάραθρον**: A gully, near the junction of the northern Long Wall with the city perimeter, into which were thrown the bodies of men executed for offences against the state.

(viii) **1452–63.** *Strepsiades reproaches the Chorus*

1458 ἡμεῖς . . . 1461 δεδοικέναι: Now the Chorus reveals itself, in solemn style, as a member of the supernatural company traditionally worshipped by the Greeks; cf. p. xxviii. They have deceived Strepsiades in order to punish him for his dishonesty, and he accepts (1463) this; it is fully in accord with ordinary Greek theology and ethics. *ἡμεῖς* and *ἀεί* are variants; the latter is tautologous with *ἑκάστοθ'*. Tautology is not in itself a strong argument against a variant (cf. 295, 1279), but *ἡμεῖς* is positively supported by 258 f. *ταῦτα πάντα τοὺς τελουμένους ἡμεῖς ποοῦμεν* and many other passages in which there is no explicit antithesis between *ἡμεῖς* and anyone else. Cf. 1116 n. **ὅντιν' ἄν**: The variant *ἄν τιν' οὖν* is not Attic. The other variant is *ὅταν τινά*, which, though metrically abnormal, is possible (cf. 185 n.) and grammatically sound; the real objection to it is stylistic. The Chorus speaks, and Strepsiades replies, solemnly. If *ὅταν τινά* is right, it is not only an isolated snatch of comic rhythm in a passage (1452–64) otherwise uniform in avoiding resolutions and abnormal diaeresis, but an exaggerated one and—for communication of the sense—wholly unnecessary. The emendation *ὅντιν' ἄν* is surely right; cf. *Peace* 371 f. *ἆρ' οἶσθα θάνατον ὅτι προεῖφ' ὁ Ζεύς, ὃς ἂν (= ἐάν τις) ταύτην κτλ.*

1462 ὤμοι . . . 1464 ἀποστερεῖν: Cf. 1437 ff.

(ix) **1464–75**. *Strepsiades appeals to Pheidippides to help him take vengeance on the sophists*

1465 Χαιρεφῶντα: Cf. p. xxx on the surprising prominence of Chairephon at this point.

1467 ἀλλ' οὐκ ἄν . . . τοὺς διδασκάλους: Why not? Pheidippides, who has cheerfully violated the traditional relationship between father and son, is shocked at the suggestion that he should violate the relationship between teacher and pupil. This is true to life; Pheidippides, like Kallikles in Plato's *Gorgias*, is not abjuring the use of the terms *δίκαιον* and *ἄδικον* (cf. 1332, 1377) but changing their application. It is natural enough that a young man should feel himself bound more closely to his intellectual liberator than to his father; cf. 1432 n. and p. xxiv.

1468 καταιδέσθητι πατρῷον Δία: There are three reasons for supposing these words to be paratragic. One is the prosody of *πατ|ρῷον* (cf. *Knights* 1178 *ἡ δ' Ὀβριμοπάτρα* (– – ⏑ ⏑ – – or – ⏑ ⏑ ⏑ – –); a second, the fact that *καταιδεῖσθαι* occurs elsewhere only in tragedy and Ionic prose. What is most important is that Athenian families and phratries had a cult of Apollo *πατρῷος* but no cult of Zeus *πατρῷος*. But others did; Niobe in Aischylos speaks of an 'altar of Zeus *πατρῷος*', and the title occurs in many inscriptions. As applied to Apollo it was interpreted, by implication, as 'from whom the community is descended'; its earlier implication was 'whose cult has been transmitted within the household'. What exactly it meant in the tragedy from which Strepsiades' words are borrowed is not known, but the borrowing strongly suggests that *πατρῷος* *could* be interpreted as 'whose province is the relationship between fathers and children'; cf. Eur. *Andr.* 921 (Hermione to Orestes) *ἀλλ' ἄντομαί σε Δία καλοῦσ' ὁμόγνιον.* There is no instance of *πατρῷος* used unequivocally in this sense.

The serious tone of the last twenty lines is set aside by the incongruity of tragic quotation; Ar. does not allow us to cease to regard Strepsiades as a comic figure.

1469 ἰδού γε: Cf. 818 n., and 821 n. on *ἀρχαϊκά*: Strepsiades' own words are now being used against him.

1470 οὐκ ἔστ', οὔκ: Cf. *Ach.* 421 *οὐ Φοίνικος, οὔ*: and the idiom is common in fourth-century prose.

1472 ἀλλ' ἐγὼ τοῦτ' ᾠόμην: It is difficult, in the absence of parallels, to extract the sense 'I only *thought* so'; probably 'This was *my* opinion', implying 'You are simply repeating what I told you.'

1473 διὰ τουτονὶ τὸν δῖνον: As the following words show, a dinos is before our eyes in the theatre. Where did it come from? There is no point in the dialogue at which Strepsiades can run indoors and fetch it. And why '*because of* this dinos'? Both questions are answered by the supposition that a dinos, symbolizing the gods of the sophists, stands beside Sokrates' door, just as a conventional herm (1478 ff.) stands beside Strepsiades'. The interpretation of *τουτονί* as 'that which we all know' (cf. 83 n.) is absolutely ruled out by the contrast between the cosmological Dinos and this very different dinos. The point of *διά* is: 'Because of the teaching I received in this school'. Cf. 380 ff.

1475. Exit Pheidippides, probably into Strepsiades' house.

(x) **1476–1511.** *Strepsiades burns the school*

1476 ὡς: 'How . . .!' **ἄρα**: 'After all', 'as I see now'.

1478 Ἑρμῆ . . . 1485 ἀδολεσχῶν: At *Peace* 661 ff. Hermes puts a question to Peace, who is represented on stage as a statue, and pretends to hear her reply; so here Strepsiades addresses the herm standing beside his door and pretends to receive advice. An ancient interpreter tried to give Hermes a speaking part. Cf. 1508 n. *ἀδολεσχία* is idle talk, and sometimes implies that the talk is mischievous or foolish or both. **γραφήν**: Not a lawsuit for damages, but an indictment for an offence against the community—such as the real Socrates eventually had to face. **διωκάθω**: 'Whether I am to prosecute them . . .'. Cf. 1332 n. **οὐκ ἐῶν**: Cf. 1044; 'tell . . . not to . . .', 'say that . . . ought not to . . .'.

1485 δεῦρο . . . 1492 ἀλαζόνες: This is not an unprecedented revenge; Strepsiades is treating the Socratics as if they were accused or condemned for an offence against the state. A fifth-century Lokrian decree provides that when a man incurs exile for proposing the partition of certain land 'his house shall be razed in accordance with the law of homicide', and the Spartans, angry with Agis in 418, fined him and demolished his house (Thuc. v. 63. 2). By 1493 both Strepsiades and his slave are on the roof of the school, the slave hacking off the tiles and Strepsiades, torch in hand, setting fire to the exposed rafters. It is prudent, and normal practice, to begin the demolition of a house from the top, and only what is inflammable can be fired. In any case, a house can be made uninhabitable by destruction of the roof alone. How realistically it would have been possible to do all this in the theatre we do not know, and it is possible that realism would have been taken to the point of setting fire to the wooden set (p. xi).

The slave should come out with the ladder and mattock at 1487 and go up on to the roof while Strepsiades is speaking 1489 f. A second slave brings Strepsiades a torch at 1491, and Strepsiades goes up the ladder at furious speed after declaiming 1491 f.

1489 ἕως . . . οἰκίαν: 'Bring the house down on top of them'; cf. *Ach.* 511 (of an earthquake). 1489 precedes 1488 in some MSS. This is stylistically possible but abnormal; cf. 1458 ff.

1491 τιν' αὐτῶν: Cf. *Lys.* 446 *παύσω τιν' ὑμῶν τῆσδ' ἐγὼ τῆς ἐξόδου*, also determined and threatening.

1493 ἰοὺ ἰού . . . 1507 ἕδραν: We must distinguish between three interlocutors (X, Y, and Z) of Strepsiades. X says (1495) 'What are you doing?', and is answered; Y says (1497) 'Who is setting fire to our house?', and is answered; Z says (1502) 'You there on the roof, what are you doing?', and he too is answered. If the speaker of 1493 comes into view when he cries *ἰοὺ ἰού*, he is no doubt X; if he cries from inside, it does not matter who he is. Either X or Y can say *ἀπολεῖς ἀπολεῖς* (1499). So far as the sense goes, any one of the three can say 1504, and any other one 1505.

It is dramatically appropriate, for three reasons, that Z should be Socrates. His appearance is climactic, and 1503 is a turning of his own words (225) against him. Also, the plural *εἰλήφατε* in 1498 suggests that Strepsiades is treating Y simply as a representative of the school, not as an individual. Now, it would clearly not be appropriate if Socrates were silent while X and Y spoke 1504 and 1505; therefore one of these two lines is spoken by Socrates. In most MSS. he speaks 1504; in some, 1505 is spoken by an unnamed student, and in others by Chairephon. The introduction of Chairephon (about which the scholia are completely silent) is an astute interpretation, giving a symmetrical duet, the last words from the sophists, to the two men whose names are linked in 1465 (cf. p. xix), and variants in 1506 f. may have seemed a decisive argument in its favour. It would be dramatically most effective if Chairephon were the last to appear, chalk-white, thin, and bewildered in the unaccustomed daylight, perhaps winkled out of the burning house by other students. Unfortunately, this would need five actors, and we are not entitled to assume five, however dramatically pleasing the result, so long as the scene can be performed with four. Ar. may well have envisaged X or Y as Chairephon, and the symmetry of 1504 f. suggests that the speaker of 1505 is more important than the third inmate of the school; he may have intended, if the revised version of the play were ever performed, a physical caricature of Chairephon; but he has not left us in the words of the text quite strong enough grounds for adding Chairephon to the dramatis personae.

It is obviously inappropriate that the retort in 1503 should come from the slave Xanthias, or from anyone but Strepsiades, and in any case a speaking part for Xanthias would again mean more than four actors.

1496: διαλεπτολογοῦμαι: Concocted from *λεπτολογεῖν* (320) and *διαλέγεσθαι*.

1498: θοἰμάτιον: Cf. 497 and 856 f.

1503 = 225. So Dionysos in *Frogs* 1471 uses *Hipp.* 612 against Euripides.

1507 ἕδραν: *ἕδρα* is the correct term for the 'station' of a heavenly body; cf. Hdt. vii. 37. 2 *ὁ ἥλιος ἐκλιπὼν* (cf. 584 n.) *τὴν ἐκ τοῦ οὐρανοῦ ἕδρην ἀφανὴς ἦν*. There is a *double entendre*, for *ἕδρα* also means the 'seat' of the body.

1508 δίωκε, παῖε, βάλλε: In some MSS. 1508 f. are attributed to Hermes. They are, of course, uttered by Strepsiades—in a sense, to his slave, but also to himself, for *δίωκε* and other words of the same type are as much war-cries as commands. Cf. especially Xen. *An.* v. 7. 21, 'We suddenly heard a lot of noise, *παῖε παῖε βάλλε βάλλε*, and soon saw a number of men running up with stones in their hands.'

We do not want two actors stranded up a ladder at the end of the play, and the analogy of *Thesm.* 1227 ff., where the last character has rushed off before the Chorus says 'Well, we have had enough sport', suggests that the theatre is clear of all but the Chorus by 1510: Strepsiades and his slave can most easily descend while 1504 f. are being spoken and extravagantly acted. 1506 f. can then be uttered by Strepsiades on the ground, and 1508 f. shouted while he and his slave pursue the inmates of the school out of the theatre.

1510 ἡγεῖσθ' . . . 1511 ἡμῖν: The exodos in *Ach.*, *Peace*, and *Birds* is a song celebrating the hero's triumph; in *Lys.*, *Frogs*, *Eccl.*, and *Wealth* this pattern is variously modified but is still essentially a triumphant celebration. In *Wasps* the dramatic illusion is broken in the very last words (1536 f.): 'No one ever before has taken a comic chorus away dancing.' *Clouds* shares with *Thesm.* a final choral utterance which is little more than the verbal equivalent of dropping the curtain (*μετρίως* occurs in both) but is peculiar in being entirely colourless.

VOCABULARY

Words which are much the same in Greek and English are omitted from this vocabulary (e.g. *γυμνάσιον, κωμῳδία*); so are the commonest words in Attic (e.g. *ἄγειν, ἵππος*) and those of their compounds (e.g. *ἀπάγειν*) and derivatives (e.g. *ἱππικός*) which present no problems. It is assumed that the reader is familiar with the commonest types of verbal set (e.g. *νομιεῖν ~ νομίσαι ~ νομίζειν*).

The English meanings have been chosen with the relevant passages of this play in mind, and many of them would be inappropriate in other contexts.

‡ indicates words which are probably coined for the occasion by Aristophanes.

ἀβέλτερος, stupid
ἄγαλμα, statue
ἄγᾱν, too (much)
ἅγιος, holy
ἀγορεύειν, speak
ἀγορητής, speaker
ἀγρεῖος, boorish
ἄγριος, wild, savage
ἀγροί, country
ἄγροικος, rustic
ἀδελφιδῆ, niece
ᾱ̓δολεσχής, chatterer
ᾱ̓δολεσχίᾱ, chatter
ἀδύνατος, unable
ᾱ̓έναος, eternal
ᾱ̓έριος, aerial
‡*ᾱ̓εροβατεῖν*, tread the air
ᾱ̓εροvηχής, floating in the air
ᾱ̓ήρ, air
ᾱ̓θάνατος, immortal
ἀθρεῖν, observe
ἀθρόοι, all together
ἀθῷος, immune
αἰγίς, aegis
αἰδοῖα, genitals
ᾱ̓ΐειν, hear
αἰθέριος, of the sky
αἰθρίᾱ, fine weather
αἴξ, (she-)goat
αἱρεῖσθαι, choose, elect
αἰσχῡ́νεσθαι, be ashamed
αἰτ-εῖν, -εῖσθαι, ask (for . . .)
αἰτιᾶσθαι, blame
αἴτιος, responsible
ᾱ̓κάματος, tireless
ἀκαρῆ, a moment
ἀκατάβλητος, invincible
ἀκόλαστος, badly behaved
ἀκολουθεῖν, follow
ἀκόρητος, unswept
ἀκρῑβής, precise
ἀκροᾶσθαι, listen
ἄκρον, top, tip
ἀκτίς, ray
ᾱ̓́κων, against one's will
ἀλαζών, braggart
ἀλγεῖν, be pained
ἀλεῖν, grind
ἀλείφεσθαι, anoint oneself
‡*ἀλεκτρύαινα*, hen

ἀλεκτρυών (*m.*, *f.*), fowl, cock
ἀλέκτωρ, cock
ἀλεξίκακος, averter of evil
ἅλες, salt
ἅλλεσθαι, jump
ἁλμυρός, salty
ἄλφιτα, flour, meal
ἀλφιταμοιβός, dealer in flour (meal)
ἁλῶναι, *aor.* ~ ἁλίσκεσθαι, be caught
ἀμαθής, stupid
ἁμαξίς, cart
ἀμελεῖν, neglect
ἀμέτρητος, measureless
ἄμπελος, vine
ἀμῡνάθειν = ἀμύνειν, protect
ἀμύνεσθαι, punish
ἀμφήκης, two-edged
ἀμφορεύς, jar
ἄμφω, both
ἀναβάλλεσθαι, postpone
ἀναβλέπειν, look up
ἀναβοᾶν, cry out
ἀναγεύειν, give a taste
ἀναγιγνώσκειν, read
ἀναγκάζειν, compel
ἀναγρύζειν, utter a sound
ἀναδεικνύναι, display
ἀναίδεια, shamelessness
ἀναιρεῖσθαι, snatch
ἀναίσχυντος, shameless
ἀνακοινοῦσθαι, communicate
ἀναμάττεσθαι, knead up
ἀνάμεστος, full
ἀναμετρεῖν, measure
ἀναπείθειν, persuade
‡ἀναπειστήριος, persuasive
ἀναπλάττειν, remodel
ἀναπλήσειν, *fut.* ~ ἀναπιμπλάναι, infect
ἀνάρμοστος, out of tune
ἀνατέλλειν, rise
ἀνατιθέναι, refer
ἀνατρέπειν, upset
ἀναχωρεῖν, retreat
ἀνδρείᾱ, courage
ἀνδρεῖος, brave
ἄνεμος, wind
ἀνέχεσθαι, endure
ἀνθεῖν, flower
ἄνθος, flower
ἄνθρακες, charcoal
ἀνθρήνη, hornet
ἄνιππος, horseless
ἄννηθον, dill
ἀνόητος, foolish
ἀνοίγειν, open
ἀνταποπαρδεῖν, *aor.* ~ -πέρδεσθαι, fart in response
ἀντερέσθαι, *aor.* ~ -ερωτᾶν, ask in return
ἀντιβολεῖν, entreat
ἀντιγραφή, plea, charge
ἀντιδικεῖν, litigate
ἀντιλογεῖν, argue
ἀντιλογικός, argumentative
ἀνυπόδητος, shoeless
ἀνύσᾱς (*aor. part.*), get a move on
ἄνω, up
ἀξύστατος, incoherent
ἀοιδή = ᾠδή, song
ἀπάγχειν, strangle
ἀπαιόλημα, fraud
ἀπαλλάττεσθαι, go off
ἀπαντᾶν, meet
ἀπαστίᾱ, fasting
ἀπειλεῖν, threaten
ἀπέραντος, endless
‡ἀπεριμερίμνως, thoughtlessly
ἄπερρε, go away!
ἀπερυθριᾶν, brazen out
ἀπέχεσθαι, abstain (from . . .)
ἀπηνής, cruel
ἀποβλέπειν, look
ἀποδεικνύναι, show
ἀποδημεῖν, be away from home
ἀποθραύειν, break off
ἀποκείρεσθαι, have one's hair cut

ἀποκόπτειν, knock off
ἀπολαμβάνειν, get back
ἀπολαύειν, profit (from . . .)
ἀπολιταργίζειν, *slang term for* go away
ἀπομνύναι, deny on oath
ἀποπειρᾶσθαι, test
ἀποπνίγειν, stifle
ἀπορεῖν, be in difficulties
ἄπορος, difficult; helpless
ἀποσείειν, shake off
ἀποστερεῖν, withhold, steal
‡ἀποστερητικός, cheating
‡ἀποστερητρίς (*fem.*), cheater
ἀποσχίζειν, cut off
ἀποφαίν-ειν, -εσθαι, prove
ἀπόφευξις, acquittal
ἀποφθείρειν, get rid of
ἀποχαλᾶν, let go
ἀπρᾱγμοσύνη, minding one's own business
ἅπτειν, light
ἀπωτέρω, at a distance
ἀράττειν, beat
ἀργαλέος, objectionable
ἀργός, idle
ἀργύριον, money
ἄρδειν, water
ἀριθμός, number
ἀριστᾶν, have lunch
ἅρμα, chariot
ἁρμονίᾱ, tuning, mode
ἀρνακίς, lambskin
ἁρπάζειν, seize
ἅρπαξ, robber
ἄρρην, male
ἄρρητος, secret
ἀρτίως, just now
ἄρτος, bread
ἀρύτειν, draw (water)
ἀρχαιϊκός, old-fashioned
ἀσκαλαβώτης, gecko
ἀσκάντης, bed
ἀσκεῖν, practise
ἀσκός, wineskin
ᾆσμα, song, poem
‡ᾀσματοκάμπτης, turner of songs
ἀσπάζεσθαι, greet
ἀστεῖος, smart
ᾀστέον, need to sing
ἀστραπή, lightning
ἀτεχνῶς, utterly
ἀτῑμάζειν, dishonour
ἄτολμος, unventuresome
ἀτραπός, path
ἀτρέμα(ς), ἀτρεμεί, quiet, still
ἀτυχεῖν, fail to get
αὐγή, beam (of light)
αὐλός, (musical) pipe
αὖτε, now
αὐτίκα, at once
αὐχήν, neck
αὐχμεῖν, be dry
αὐχμός, dry
ἀφάλλεσθαι, jump away
ἀφανίζειν, abolish
ἀφάνισις, abolition
ἀφορᾶσθαι, look
ἀφορμᾶσθαι, set off
ἄφυκτος, inescapable
ἄχθεσθαι, be distressed, be annoyed

βαδίζειν, go, walk
βαιός, small
βακτηρίᾱ, stick
βαλανεῖον, bath-house
βάραθρον, pit (of execution)
βαρυᾱχής, βαρύβρομος, deep (in sound)
βάτραχος, frog
βδελυρός, disgusting
βδελύττεσθαι, be disgusted
‡βεκκεσέληνος: *see* 398 n.
βιοθρέμμων, nourishing life
βλάβη, harm
βλαστάνειν, grow
βλέπος, look
‡βλιτομάμμᾱς: *see* 1001 n.

βόᾱμα, cry, shout
βολβός, onion
βόσκειν, feed
βοτόν, animal
βουλεύειν, deliberate
βούλευμα, plan
βρενθύεσθαι, swagger
βροντᾶν, thunder
βροντή, thunder
‡βροντησικέραυνος, making thunder and lightning
βρύειν, teem
βρῦς (*baby-talk*), drink
βυρσοδέψης, tanner
βωμολοχεύεσθαι, play the fool
βωμολόχος, buffoon

γαλεώτης, lizard
γαμψός, hooked
γαστήρ, belly
γαστρίδιον, *dim.* ~ *γαστήρ*
γελᾶν, laugh
γελοῖος, laughable
γέλως, laughter
γεραίτερος, *comp.* ~ *γέρων*
γερόντιον, *dim.* ~ *γέρων*
γηγενής, earth-born (*see* 853 n.)
‡γλισχραντιλογεξεπίτριπτος: *see* 1004 n.
γλοιός, oily dirt
γλυκύθυμος, soothing
γλύφειν, sculpt
‡γλωττοστροφεῖν, ply the tongue
γνάθος, jaw; cheek (*see* 1109 n.)
γνωμίδιον, *dim.* ~ *γνώμη*
‡γνωμοτύπος, creative (*lit.* 'coining judgements')
γονεῖς, parents
γραμματεῖον, notebook
γραμματεύς, clerk
γράφεσθαι, indict; dictate
γραφή, indictment
γρύζειν, murmur
γυμνός, bare

δαιμόνιος, extraordinary
δᾴος, fierce
δάκνειν, bite; worry
δάκτυλος, finger; dactyl
δανείζειν, lend
δανείζεσθαι, borrow
δαρδάπτειν, devour
δᾴς, torch
δασύς, bushy
δείλαιος, miserable
δειλός, unmanly
δειπνεῖν, dine
δεῖπνον, dinner
δενδρόκομος, wooded on top
δεξιός, clever
δέρμα, skin
δέσποινα, mistress
δῆλος, clear
δήμαρχος, annual magistrate at head of deme
δημηγορεῖν, speak in public
δημόσιος, public, state (*adj.*)
δημότης, (fellow) demesman
δημοτικός, democratic
διαβήτης, pair of compasses
διάγειν, spend (time)
διαγράφειν, strike out
διαθρεῖν, look at
διαιρεῖν, classify
διάκεισθαι, be organized
διακῑνεῖν, stir
διακναίειν, wear away
‡διακορκορυγεῖν, rumble
διαλᾱκεῖν, burst
διάλεξις, discourse
‡διαλεπτολογεῖν, pursue a subtle argument
‡διαλφιτοῦν, fill with flour
διαμετρεῖν, measure
διανοεῖσθαι, intend
διάνοια, reasoning
διαρρεῖν, fall loosely apart
διασμήχειν, rub thoroughly
διατήκειν, melt down

διατρίβειν, spend time
διατριβή, time (spent)
διαφανής, transparent
διαφεύγειν, escape
διειδέναι, know well
‡διεντέρευμα: *see* 166 n.
διερός, liquid (*adj.*)
δικάζειν, judge
δικάζεσθαι, litigate
‡δικορραφεῖν, put together (*lit.* 'stitch') lawsuits
δῖνος, (1) rotation, (2) pot
διολισθάνειν, slip through
διορύττειν, bore through
διφθέρᾱ, hide, skin
διφρίσκος, *dim.* ~ δίφρος, chariot-board
διχοίνικον, two choinikes
διψῆν, be thirsty
διωκάθειν = διώκειν
δοκός, beam (of roof)
δρόμος, course
δροσερός, moist
δρόσος, liquid
δρῦς, oak
δυσβουλίᾱ, ill counsel
δῡσκολαίνειν, make a fuss
‡δυσκολόκαμπτος, full of tuneless modulations
‡δυσκολόκοιτος, restless
δύσκολος, unpleasant
δυσμαθής, bad at learning

ἐγείρειν, wake
ἐγκαλύπτεσθαι, cover oneself
‡ἐγκεκοισυρωμένος, like Koisyra
‡ἐγκεκορδῡλημένος, wrapped up
ἐγκέφαλος, brain
ἐγκύπτειν, bend down
ἐγκώμιον, song of praise
ἐγχανεῖν, *aor.* ~ ἐγχάσκειν, laugh (at . . .)
ἐγχειρεῖν, attempt
ἔγχελυς, eel
ἕδρᾱ, seat
εἴδωλον, image
εἶέν, well!
εἰκάδες, twenties (of month)
εἰκάζειν, liken
εἰκῇ, carelessly
εἰκών, image
εἴλλειν, roll up
εἴρων, mock-modest
εἰσᾴττειν, rush in
εἴσοδος, entrance
ἑκατογκεφάλᾱς, hundred-headed
ἐκκόπτειν, knock out
ἐκλείπειν, fade out (from . . .)
ἐκπεπληγμένος, crazy, overcome
ἐκπίνειν, drain
ἐκστρέφειν, turn inside-out
ἐκτήκειν, melt away
ἐκτιθέναι, expose
ἐκτραχηλίζεσθαι, break one's neck
ἐκτρέπειν, turn into a different course
ἐκτρέφειν, bring up
ἐκφροντίζειν, think out
ἐλαίᾱ, olive (tree)
ἔλαιον, (olive-)oil
ἐλαύνειν, drive; ride
ἔλαφος, deer
ἐλέγχειν, test
ἕλκειν, pull
ἐμβάπτειν, dip in
ἐμβάς, slipper
ἐμπιμπλάναι, fill
ἐμπιμπράναι, burn
ἐμπίς, gnat
ἐμφανής, obvious
ἐμφερής, like
ἔναγκος, recently
ἐναλλάξ, crossed
ἐνεστάναι, have begun
ἐνεχυράζεσθαι, (*mid.*) take securities, (*pass.*) be compelled to give securities

ἔνη (τε) καὶ νέα, last day of the month
ἐνημμένος, dressed (in . . .)
ἐνθῡμεῖσθαι, think (about . . .)
ἐνόπλιον: *see* 651 n.
ἐντείνεσθαι, pitch
ἐντετυλίχθαι, be wrapped
ἐντυγχάνειν, meet
ἐξαίφνης, suddenly
ἐξαλῖσαι, *aor.* ~ ἐξαλίνδειν, roll
ἐξαμαρτάνειν = ἁμαρτάνειν
ἐξαμβλοῦν, cause to miscarry
ἐξανέχεσθαι, endure to the end
ἐξαπατᾶν, deceive
‡ἐξαρνητικός, capable of denial
ἔξαρνος, denying
ἐξαυτομολεῖν, desert
ἐξεγείρειν, awaken
ἐξελαύνειν, drive out
ἐξελέγχειν, refute
ἐξέλκειν, drag out
ἐξεπίστασθαι = ἐπίστασθαι
ἐξεργάζεσθαι, perpetrate
ἐξέρπειν, creep out
ἑξέτης, six years old
ἐξευρίσκειν = εὑρίσκειν
ἔξοδος, expedition
ἐξολλύναι = ἀπολλύναι
ἑορτή, feast
ἐπάγειν, step up (pace)
ἐπᾱΐειν, understand
ἐπαινεῖν, praise
ἐπαίρειν, incite
ἐπακούειν, listen
ἐπαναμένειν, wait
ἐπαναπηδᾶν, jump on
ἐπαναφέρειν, refer
ἐπανθεῖν, bloom on
ἐπασκεῖν, cultivate
ἐπεγείρειν, waken
ἐπεμπηδᾶν, jump on
ἐπιάλλειν, lay into
ἐπιδεικνύναι, expound
ἐπίδειξις, display
ἐπιδέσθαι, *aor.* ~ ἐφορᾶσθαι, look upon
ἐπιεικής, reasonable
ἐπιέναι, come on
ἐπιθαυμάζειν, show respect (for . . .)
ἐπιλανθάνεσθαι, ἐπιλήθεσθαι, forget
ἐπιλήσμων, forgetful
ἐπιμαρτῡ́ρεσθαι, call to witness
ἐπιμελής, diligent
ἐπιμένειν, stay
ἐπινοεῖν, have . . . idea
ἐπιορκεῖν, break one's oath
ἐπίορκος, perjurer
ἐπιρρεῖν, flow on
ἐπιστέλλειν, tell, order
ἐπισχεῖν, *aor.* ~ ἐπέχειν, hold on (*intr.*)
ἐπιτηδεύειν, practise
ἐπιτρίβειν, do for, be the death of
ἐπιτυγχάνειν, come upon
ἐπιχώριος, native
ἐπομβρίᾱ, wet weather
ἐπομνύναι, swear in addition
ἐπωφελεῖν, confer further benefit
ἐρασθῆναι, *aor.* ~ ἐρᾶν, be (fall) in love (with . . .)
ἐραστής, lover
ἐρέβινθος, chick-pea
‡ἐρεβοδῑφᾶν, explore the underworld
ἐρέθισμα, provocation
ἐρείδειν, push, slam
ἐρείδεσθαι, struggle
ἐρέσθαι, *aor.* ~ ἐρωτᾶν
ἔρια (*plur.*), wool
ἐρυθρός, red
ἐρωτᾶν, ask (a question)
ἐσθίειν, eat
ἑσπέρᾱ, evening
ἑστιᾶν, feast
ἐτεόν, really
ἕτοιμος, ready
ἔτος, year
εὐάγητος, bright

εὔανδρος, full of good men
εὐανθής, in blooming health
εὔγλωττος, with ready tongue
εὕδειν, sleep
εὐδοκιμεῖν, win applause
εὐηθικός, simple-minded
εὐθύ, straight (for . . .)
εὐκέλαδος, melodious
εὐκλείᾱ, good repute
εὐνοεῖν, be affectionate (towards . . .)
εὔπτερος, with fine feathers
εὕρημα, invention
εὑρησιεπής, never at a loss (*lit.* 'inventive of utterance')
εὐρύπρωκτος, broad-arsed
εὐρωτιᾶν, be covered with mould
εὐστέφανος, adorned with lovely crowns
εὐστομεῖν = εὐφημεῖν
εὔτακτος, orderly
εὐτυχίᾱ, good fortune
εὐφημεῖν, be quiet, say nothing wrong
εὐφραίνεσθαι, rejoice (at . . .)
εὔχεσθαι, pray
εὐχή, prayer
ἐφήμερος, short-lived, mortal
ἐχθές = χθές
ἕωθεν, in the morning

ζάθεος, sacred
ζηλοῦν, envy
ζηλωτός, enviable
ζύγιος, under the yoke
ζυγωθρίζειν, weigh
ζωμίδιον, *dim.* ~ ζωμός
ζωμός, (meat-)soup

ἥβη, youth
ἤθη (*plur.*), character
ἡλιαστικός, for jury-service
ἠλίθιος, silly
ἡλικίᾱ, age
ἡλικιώτης, ἧλιξ, of the same age
ἠμί, I say
ἡμιέκτεων, half-hekteus
ἡμιθνής, half-dead
ἡνίοχος, guider
ἦρος (*gen.*), ἦρι (*dat.*), spring
ἡσυχῇ, quietly
ἥσυχος, quiet
ἠχεῖν, sound

θᾶκος, seat
θαλίᾱ, festivity
θαρρεῖν, be confident
θαυμάσιος, remarkable
θεᾶσθαι, see, watch
θεᾱταί, spectators
θεῖος, (1) divine, (2) uncle
θέμις, permissible
θεόσεπτος, revered as divine
θερμός, hot
θέσις, deposit
θῆλυς, female
θηρᾱτής, hunter, pursuer
θηρίον, animal
θρασΰνεσθαι, be bold
θρασύς, bold
‡θραυσάντυγες, breaking the rails (of a chariot)
θρηνεῖν, lament
θρυαλλίς, wick
θυείᾱ, mortar
θύελλα, gale
‡θυμβρεπίδειπνος, eating only savory at dinner
θῡμός, spirit, anger
θῡμόσοφος, intelligent
θύραζε, out of doors
θύριον, *dim.* ~ θύρᾱ, door
θυσίᾱ, sacrifice

‡ῑ̓ᾱτροτέχνης, medical scientist
ἰδέᾱ, form
ἱερεύς, priest

ἱερομνημονεῖν, serve as delegate to amphictyonic council
ἱκετεύειν, supplicate
ἰκμάς, moisture
ἱμάτιον, outer garment, *equivalent of* overcoat
ἱμείρειν, desire
ἱππάζεσθαι, ride horses
‡ἵππερος, horse-disease; *see* 74 n.
ἱππική, horsemanship
ἱππονώμᾱς, guiding horses
ἴτης, 'tough', brave
ἴχνος, footstep

καθειμένος, hanging down
καθείργειν, lock up
καθεύδειν, sleep
καθίζειν, sit
καθορᾶν, discern
κακοδαίμων, unfortunate
κακουργεῖν, commit crimes
κάλαμος, reed
καλεῖσθαι, summons
καλλίπυργος, towering splendidly
καλύπτεσθαι, cover oneself up
κάμνειν, grow tired
καμπή, modulation
κάμπτειν, bend, inflect
καπνός, smoke, steam
κάρδαμα, cress
κάρδοπος, kneading-bowl
καρπός, crops, fruit
καταβρέχειν, soak
καταγελᾶν, laugh at . . .
καταγέλαστος, contemptible
καταγλώττισμα, tongue-kiss
καταδαρθεῖν (*aor.*), go to sleep
καταιδεῖσθαι, revere
καταισχῡ́νειν, shame
κατακάειν, burn up
κατακλείειν, lock up
κατακλίνεσθαι, lie down
κατακρίμνασθαι, hang down
κατάληψις, seizing; *see* 318 n.
καταλόειν, wash off
καταμιγνύναι, mix
κατανείφειν, snow
καταπάττειν, sprinkle
καταπίνειν, swallow
καταπροίξεσθαι, get away with it
καταπῡγοσύνη, buggery
καταπῡ́γων, bugger
καταρᾶσθαι, vilify
κατασκάπτειν, demolish
κατατοξεύειν, shoot down
καταφροντίζειν, think away
καταφρῡ́γειν, burn up
καταχέζειν, shit on
καταχεῖν, pour . . . over
κατειπεῖν (*aor.*), tell
κατέχειν, possess
κάτροπτον, mirror
καχασμός, guffaw
κάχρυς, parched barley
κεκρᾱγέναι, *pf.* ~ κράζειν, cry out
κελάδημα, sound
κελάδων, resounding
κενός, empty
κεντεῖν, goad
κέντρον, goad
κέντρων, scarred slave
κέραμος, tiles
κεραυνός, thunderbolt
κερδαίνειν, gain, profit
κέρδος, profit
κέστρᾱ, an edible fish
κεφάλαιον, top
κεχηνέναι, *pf.* ~ χάσκειν, have the mouth open (with surprise, stupidity, or laughter)
κήδεσθαι, care (for . . .)
κῆπος, garden
κηρός, wax
κῆτος, sea-monster
κιθαρίζειν, play the lyre
κιθαριστής, lyre-teacher
κίναδος, fox
κίνδῡνος, danger

κῑνεῖν, move; *slang term for* sexual intercourse
κῑνητής, mover
κιχηλᾱ (Doric), thrush (Attic κίχλη)
κιχλίζειν, giggle
κίων, column
κλᾱ́ειν, cry, weep
κλεινός, famous
κλέος, fame
κληρουχικός, for division into allotments
κλῆσις, summons
κλητεύειν, serve a summons
κλῖμαξ, ladder
κλόνος, din
κλοπή, theft
κοῖλος, hollow
κοινοῦν, communicate
κολάζειν, punish
κολετρᾶν, pound, thrash
κολοκύντη, gourd
κομᾶν, wear the hair long
κόμη, (long) hair
κομήτης, long-haired
κομιδῇ, absolutely
κομίζεσθαι, get back
κομψοπρεπής, elegant
κομψός, refined
κοππατίᾱς, branded with letter koppa; *see* 23 n.
κόπρος, dung
κόπτειν, knock
κόραξ, raven
κόρδαξ, a comic dance
κορίζεσθαι, talk fondly
κόρις, bug
κορυφή, summit
κόσκινος, sieve
κόσμος, adornment
κότταβος, a party-game played by slinging dregs of wine
κρέας, meat
κρεμάθρᾱ, (suspended) rope
κρεμαννύναι, hang
κρεμαστά, ropes, rigging
κρημνοποιός, using big words (*lit.* 'crag-maker')
κριμνώδης, like meal
κρῑ́νεσθαι, dispute
κρίνον, lily
κρῑός, ram
κριτής, judge
κρόκος, saffron
κρόταλον, castanet
κροῦσις, striking
κυδοιδοπᾶν, cause an uproar
κύκλιος, (dancing) in a circle
κυλίνδειν, be pushed about
κυνῆ, cap
κυνηδόν, like a dog
κυπτάζειν, peer furtively
κύρβις, an object on which some early laws were inscribed
κύσαι, *aor.* ~ κυνεῖν, kiss
κύστις, bladder
κωλῆ, haunch
κωμαστής, reveller
κωμῆται, those of the same quarter

λαβή, hold, grip
‡λακκόπρωκτος, with capacious arse
λακτίζειν, kick
λαλεῖν, chatter
λαλιά, chatter
λάμπειν, shine
λαμπρός, bright, splendid
λάρος, gull
λάσιος, hairy
λαφυγμός, gormandizing
λεκάνη, bowl
λεπτολογεῖν, argue subtly
λεπτός, thin, subtle
λεπτότης, subtlety
λεύκη, white poplar
λῆμα, spirit
λημᾶν, have discharging eyes

λῃρεῖν, talk nonsense
λῆρος, nonsense
λιβανωτός, incense
λίμνη, lake
λινόδετος, tied by a thread
λιπαρός, bright, glossy
λογίζεσθαι, reckon
λοιδορ-εῖν, -εῖσθαι, abuse, insult
λοῦσθαι (λούεσθαι), wash (oneself)
λουτρόν, bath
λοφεῖον, box
λύκος, wolf
λῡμαίνεσθαι, harm
λύρᾱ, lyre
λῡσανίᾱς, deliverer from sorrow
λύχνος, lamp

μάθημα, study
μαθητής, student
μαθητιᾶν, want to learn
μάκαρ, enviable
μαλακός, soft
μαλθακίζεσθαι, be faint-hearted
μαμμᾶ (*baby-talk*), food
μαρμάρεος, sparkling
μαρτῡ́ρεσθαι, call witnesses
μάσθλης, *slang term for* a resilient man (*lit.* 'leather')
μᾱτιολοιχός, *slang term for* a man who misses nothing; *see* 451 n.
μάχαιρα, knife, sword
μεγαλώνυμος, renowned
μεγασθενής, powerful
μέθυσος, drunk
μειράκιον, young man
μέλε, *vocative used from stand-point of superior insight*
μελιτοῦττα, honey-cake
μέλιττα, bee
μέμφεσθαι, criticize
μέριμνα, thought
‡μεριμνοφροντιστής, 'excogitator'
μεστός, full
μεταμέλειν (*impersonal*), regret
‡μεταφροντίζειν, alter by fresh thought
μετεωρίζειν, be up in the air
μετέωρος, up in the air
μετιέναι, go and fetch
μέτριος, reasonable
μέτρον, measure
μηλολόνθη, cockchafer
μῆλον, fruit
μήν, month
μηρός, thigh
μηχανή, device
μιαρός, foul
μῑμεῖσθαι, imitate
μῑσεῖν, hate
μισθός, pay, fee
μνᾶ, 100 drachmai
μνημονικός, μνήμων, with a good memory
μνησικακεῖν, bring up a grudge
μοιχεύειν, commit adultery
μοιχός, adulterer
μόλυβδος, lead
μορίᾱ, (sacred) olive-tree
μουσοπο(ι)εῖν, put into poetry
μοχλευτής, mover (*lit.* leverer)
μῡκᾶσθαι, bellow
μῡριάκις, innumerable times
μύρον, scent
μυρρίνη, myrtle
μυστοδόκος, receiving participants in the mysteries
μῶν, *particle introducing incredulous questions*
μωρίᾱ, folly
μῶρος, fool(ish)

νᾱός = νεώς
νεᾶν, plough
νεᾱνίσκος, youth
νενησμένος, piled up
νεοττοτροφεῖν, bring up
νέφος, cloud
νεώς, temple

νήπιος, νηπύτιος, silly
νιφόεις, snowy
νοεῖν, mean
νόημα, thought, idea
νόμισμα, coinage
νουμηνίᾱ, new moon, first of the month
νύκτωρ, at night
νύξαι, *aor.* ~ νύττειν, prick

ξηρός, dry
ξυγγενής, kinsman
ξύλον, wood
ξυμβαίνειν, agree
ξύμβουλος, adviser
ξύμμαχος, ally
ξυμφέρ-ειν, -εσθαι, turn out (well)
ξυναρπάζειν = ἁρπάζειν
ξυνέλκειν, pull in
ξυντυγχάνειν, meet
ξυνωρικεύεσθαι, drive racing-chariots
ξυνωρίς, racing-chariot
ξυστίς, charioteer's robe

ὀβελίσκος, (meat-)spit
ὀβολός, obol ($\frac{1}{6}$ drachma)
ὀβολοστάτης, moneylender
ὄζειν, smell
οἰκέτης, slave
οἰκίδιον, *dim.* ~ οἰκίᾱ
οἰμώζειν, cry (with pain)
οἰωνός, bird (of omen)
ὄμβριος, rainy
ὄμβρος, rain
ὀμβροφόροι, bringing rain
ὁμιλεῖν, associate with . . .
ὁμίχλη, mist
ὀμνύναι, swear (by . . .)
ὁμολογεῖν, agree, admit
ὁμομήτριος, born of the same mother
ὀμφαλός, navel
ὄνασθαι, profit
ὀνειροπολεῖν, dream
ὄνος, donkey
ὄντως, really
ὀπτᾶν, roast, fry
ὀρεχθεῖν, beat
ὅρκιον, pledge
ὁρμᾱ́ (= ὁρμή), onrush
ὀρνίθειος, bird's
ὄρος, mountain
ὀροφή, roof
ὀρροπῡ́γιον, backside
ὄρχεις, testicles
ὀρχεῖσθαι, dance
ὀρχηστρίς, dancing-girl
ὁτιή = ὅτι
οὐράνιος, of the sky
οὐρανομήκης, reaching to the sky
οὐρανός, sky
οὐρεῖν, piss
ὀφείλειν, owe, have to pay
ὀφλήσειν, *fut.* ~ ὀφλισκάνειν, incur
ὀφρῦς, eyebrow
ὄψον, relish
ὀψοφαγεῖν, eat delicacies

πάγχρῡσος, all of gold
παιδάριον, *dim.* ~ παῖς
παιδεύειν, educate
παίδευσις, education
παιδίον, *dim.* ~ παῖς
παιδοτρίβης, gymnastics teacher
παίειν, strike
παιπάλη, fine flour
παλαιογενής, aged
παλαίστρᾱ, wrestling-school
παλαμᾶσθαι, devise
παμβασίλεια, mighty queen
παμπόνηρος, thoroughly bad
παννυχίζειν, spend all night
πανουργεῖν, get up to mischief
παντοδαπός, of all kinds
πάντως, in any case
πάππος, grandfather
παραβάλλειν, move sideways

παραδιδόναι, hand over, hand down, provide
παραινεῖν, advise
παρακόπτειν, cheat
παρανοεῖν, be crazy
παράνοια, craziness
παρασκευάζειν, prepare
παρατείνειν, lay out
παραφρονεῖν, be crazy
πάρδαλις, leopard
παρέλκειν, drag on
παταγεῖν, make a noise
πάταγος, noise
πατεῖν, trample
πατρῷος, of one's fathers
πάττειν, sprinkle, coat
παχύς, thick
πέδον, ground
πειθώ, persuasion
πεινῆν, go hungry
πέκειν, shear
πενθεῖν, mourn
πέος, *vulgar word for* penis
πεποτῆσθαι, be on the wing
πεπταμένος, spread out
πέρδεσθαι, fart
περιδέξιος, clever
περικαλύπτεσθαι, cover oneself up
περιλείπειν, leave
περίλεξις, circumlocution
περίοδος, map
περιορᾶν, stand by and see
περιουσίᾱ, abundance
περίτριμμα, *derogatory term for* a well-practised man
περιφλεύειν, singe
περιφορά, course, traverse
περιφρονεῖν, think about . . .
περιφύεσθαι, grow round
περσέπολις, taker of cities
πεύκη, pine
πηδᾶν, jump
πηρίδιον, *dim.* ~ πήρᾱ, bag
πιέζειν, press
πιστεύειν, trust, believe
πιστός, reliable
πίσυνος, relying
πλάγιος, at the side
πλάτανος, plane
πλάττειν, mould, make
πλεῖν = πλέον
πλευρά, side
πλέως, full
πληγή, blow
πλῆθος, number
πλήρης, full
πλινθεύειν, make bricks
πλόκαμος, lock (of hair)
πνεῦμα, breath, blast
πνίγειν, throttle
πνιγεύς, oven
πνοή, breath, blast
ποδαπός, from what country? of what kind?
πολεμίζειν, war
πολεμιστήριον, war-chariot
πολιοῦχος, guardian of the city
πολυήρατος, adored
πολυτίμητος, honoured
πονεῖν, toil
πονηρίᾱ, badness
πονηρός, bad
πόνος, labour
πόντος, sea
πορδή, fart
πορνίδιον, *dim.* ~ πόρνη, whore
πόρρω, far
πόσθη, *vulgar word for* penis
πότης, bibulous
ποτόν, drink
πρᾱγματεύεσθαι, take trouble
πρᾱγμάτιον, *dim.* ~ πρᾶγμα
πράττεσθαι, exact
πρεσβύτερος, older
πρεσβύτης, old man
πρημαίνειν, blow hard
πρίασθαι, *aor.* ~ ὠνεῖσθαι, buy
προαγωγεύειν, procure

προβάλλειν, set (a problem)
προβάλλεσθαι, put forward
πρόβατον, sheep
πρόβολος, bulwark
προδιδόναι, betray
προήκειν, advance
πρόθῡμος, enthusiastic
προῒέναι, let go
προῖκα, for nothing
προμνήστρια, go-between
προνοεῖσθαι, take care
πρόπολος, attendant
προσαποβάλλειν, lose . . . as well
προσέχειν (*τὸν*) *νοῦν*, attend (to . . .)
προσκαλεῖσθαι, summons
προσκατατιθέναι, pay . . . as well
πρόσοδος (processional) approach
προστῑλᾶν, befoul
προσφύειν, graft (on . . .)
πρόσωπον, face
προτένθαι: *see* 1198 n.
προτενθεύειν, get in advance
πρόφασις, reason
πρυτανεῖα, court-fees
πρῴην, the other day
πρωκτός, arse(-hole)
πτελέᾱ, elm
πτύσσεσθαι, wrap round oneself
πῡγή, buttocks
πυκνότης, density
πυκνοῦν, contract
πυρπολεῖν, set fire to . . .

ῥάπτεσθαι, sew on to one's costume
ῥαφανιδοῦν, punish by pushing a radish up the anus
ῥαφανίς, radish
ῥέγκειν, snore
ῥηγνύναι, break
ῥῆμα, word, phrase
ῥημάτιον, *dim.* ~ *ῥῆμα*
ῥῆσις, speech
ῥῑγῶν, be cold
ῥίς, nose
ῥίψασπις, coward who gets rid of his shield
ῥόδον, rose
ῥοῖβδος, whir
ῥύμη, rush

σάλπιγξ, trumpet
σαμφόρᾱς, horse branded with letter 'san'
σέβας, holiness
σέβ-ειν, *-εσθαι*, revere
σείειν, shake
σειρᾱφόρος, trace-horse
σελαγεῖσθαι, shine
σέλῑνον, celery
‡*σεμνοπροσωπεῖν*, wear a solemn face
σημεῖα (*plur.*), evidence
σιδᾱρέον, iron coin
σίδια (*plur.*), pomegranate peel
σιναμωρεῖν, plunder
σισύρᾱ, blanket
σῑτεῖσθαι, feed (on . . .)
σιωπᾶν, be quiet
σκαιός, clumsy
‡*σκαιουργεῖν*, behave badly
‡*σκαλαθυρμάτιον*, trifle
σκίμπους, bed
σκινδάλαμος, sliver
σκιρτᾶν, skip
σκληρός, hard
σκόπελος, peak
σκοπιᾱ́, look-out
σκῡ́τινος, leather (*adj.*)
σκῶμμα, joke (*n.*)
σκώπτειν, joke (*vb.*)
σμῆνος, swarm
σμῖλαξ, bindweed
σμινύη, mattock
σοβαρός, violent, arrogant
σοροπηγός, coffin-maker
σοφίζεσθαι, practise one's art
σόφισμα, invention, idea
σοφιστής, intellectual, professor

σπαθᾶν, use blade (in weaving)
σπανίζειν, be short (of . . .)
σπένδειν, pour libations
σπλάγχνα, guts
σποδεῖν, pound
στέμφυλα, olive-cake
‡στενολεσχεῖν, talk subtleties
στενός, narrow
στερρός, hard, tough
στέφανος, crown, chaplet
στεφανοῦν, crown
στεφανοῦσθαι, crown oneself
στῆθος, breast
στομοῦν, harden, train
στόμφαξ, ranter
στραγγεύεσθαι, hesitate
στρατεύεσθαι, serve as soldier
στρεβλοῦν, torture
στρεπταίγλᾱς, twisting and flashing
‡στρεψοδικεῖν, wriggle out of lawsuits
στροβεῖν, twist, whirl
στρογγύλος, round
στρόφις, 'twister'
στρώματα, bedclothes
στωμύλλειν, chatter
συγγενής = ξυγ-
συγγιγνώσκειν, forgive
συγγνώμη, forgiveness
συγκατακλίνεσθαι, lie down together
συγκολλητής, fabricator (*lit.*, 'gluer-together')
συγκόπτειν, beat up
συγχωρεῖν, agree
συμβουλεύειν, advise
συμβουλεύεσθαι, consult
συμψᾶν, sweep together
συνηγορεῖν, act as advocate
συνουσίᾱ, company
συνταράττειν, turn upside-down
συντρίβειν, smash
σφενδόνη, sling(-stone)
‡σφρᾱγῑδονυχαργοκομήτης: *see* 332 n.
σφριγᾶν, be (physically) fit
σχᾶν, slit; cut loose
σχάσασθαι (*aor.*), cut loose
σχέτλιος, unhappy, unfortunate
σχολή, leisure
σωτήρ, saviour
σωφρονεῖν, behave well, be chaste

ταλαίπωρος, enduring, long-suffering
τάλαντον, talent (6,000 drachmai)
ταμίᾱς, keeper
τᾶν: *a vocative expression*
ταράττειν, disturb
ταρρός: *see* 226 n.
ταῦρος, bull
τέγος, roof
τέθριππος, four-horse team
τειχομαχεῖν, assault (a fortification)
τελεῖν, initiate
τελετή, rite
τελευταῖος, last
τέμαχος, slice
τερατείᾱ, talking of unusual things
τερατώδης, extraordinary
τετράμετρον, tetrameter (*lit.*, 'having four measures')
τετράπους, domestic animal (*lit.*, 'four-footed')
τετράς, fourth day
τετραμαίνειν, tremble (at . . .)
τέττιξ, cicada
τέφρᾱ, ash
τέως, for a while
τηλέπορος, far-reaching
τηλεσκόπος, far-seeing
τηλεφανής, seen from afar
τηλικουτοσί, as old (*or* young) as that
τηλοῦ, far off
τήμερον, today

τηρεῖν, watch over
τῆτες, this year
τίλλειν, pluck
τοιχωρύχος, burglar
τόκος, interest
τολμᾶν, venture
τολμηρός, brazen
τράγος, (he-)goat
τραγῳδεῖν, act in tragedy
τράπεζα, table
τρασιά, figs drying
τραυλίζειν, lisp
τρίαινα, trident
‡**τριβολεκτράπελα**, offensive absurdities
τρίβων, (1) practised, (2) threadbare cloak
τρίμετρον, trimeter (*lit.*, 'having three measures')
τρῖμμα, *derogatory term for* an 'old hand'
τρισμακάριος, thrice-blessed
τριώβολον, three obols
τροχός, wheel
‡**τρυγοδαίμονες**, comedians
τρύμη: *see* 448 n.
τρύξ, half-fermented wine
‡**τρῡσίβιος**, tough, enduring
τρυφᾶν, be fastidious
τρώγειν, chew, nibble
τυννουτοσί, (only) so big
τύπτειν, hit
‡**τῡφογέρων**, silly old man

ὕαλος, glass
ὑβριστής, rogue
ὑγιαίνειν, be in good health
ὑγρός, watery
ὕειν, rain
ὑθλεῖν, talk rubbish
ὑπάγειν, get a move on
ὑπανίστασθαι, get up (from seats)
ὑπένερθεν, beneath
ὑπερβάλλειν, surpass
ὑπέρλαμπρος, most bright
ὑπέρτονος, loud
ὑπερφρονεῖν, look down (on . . .)
ὑπερφυής, extraordinary
ὕπνος, sleep
ὑπολύειν, undo
ὑπορρεῖν, flow on
ὑπόχρεως, in debt
ὑφαιρεῖσθαι, steal
ὑφαρπάζεσθαι, snap up
ὑψερεφής, with high roof
ὑψηλός, high
ὑψικέρᾱτα (*acc.*), high-peaked
ὑψιμέδων, ruling on high

φαγεῖν, *aor.* ~ **ἐσθίειν**, eat
φαλακρός, bald
φανερός, plain (to see)
φαρμακίς, witch
φαρμακοπώλης, druggist
φάσκειν, say (often)
φάτνη, manger
φαῦλος, trivial
φειδωλίᾱ, parsimony
φειδωλός, economical
φθέγγεσθαι, utter
φθέγμα, utterance
φθῆναι, *aor.* ~ **φθάνειν**, get in first
φιλόδημος, democratic
φιλόμουσος, educated
φῑμοῦν, squeeze
φλᾶν, crush
φλαῦρος, derogatory
φλέγεσθαι, blaze up
φληναφᾶν, talk aimlessly
φλόξ, flame
φλυᾱρεῖν, talk nonsense
φοιτᾶν, go (regularly)
φορτικός, vulgar
φρίττειν, shudder
φροντίζειν, think
φροντίς, thought
‡**φρόντισμα**, thought
‡**φροντιστήριον**, school, academy

‡*φροντιστής*, thinker
φροῦδος, gone
φρουρά, guard-duty
φῡρᾶσθαι, blend
φῡσᾶν, inflate
φωνή, voice
φωρᾶν, track down, search (for . . .)

χάλαζαι, hailstones
χαλκεύειν, forge, hammer
χαμαί, on the ground
‡*χαύνωσις*, inflation
χέζειν, shit
χεζητιᾶν, want to shit
χεῖλος, lip
χεσείειν, want to shit
χθές, yesterday
χιονόβλητος, snowed-on
χνοῦς, down, fluff
χολᾶν, be crazy
χορδή, sausage
χορεύειν, dance
χοῦς: *a liquid measure*; *see* 1238 n.
χρέος (*poet.*), *χρέως*, debt
χρῄζειν, want
χρήσιμος, useful
χρήστης, creditor
χροιά, complexion
χρύσεος, golden
χρῡσός, gold
χρῶμα, colour
χρωτίζεσθαι, tinge
χυτρεοῦς, earthenware
χωρεῖν, (1) go on, move on, (2) contain
χωρίον, place, space, farm

ψακάζειν, drizzle
ψᾱρός, dappled grey
ψέγειν, blame
ψήφισμα, decree
ψόφος, noise
ψύλλα, flea
ψῡχειν, cool
ψῡχρός, cold

ᾠζυρέ: *a vocative expression*
ὠνεῖσθαι, buy
ὤφελον, if only . . . had . . .
ὠφληκέναι, *pf.* ~ *ὀφείλειν*
ὠχριᾶν, be pale
ὠχρός, pale

INDEX

CORRIGENDA

P. xviii. 'The non-Attic term δανειστής'. Exceptionally, I trusted LSJ, omitting to consult word-indexes to the orators, and a gross error was the result; δανειστής in fact occurs several times in Demosthenes (e.g. xxxiv 8, lvi 6).

P. 160, 1030 n. The generalization that Aristophanes 'never uses a connecting particle with πρὸς τάδε . . . or πρὸς ταῦτα' is now invalidated by a papyrus fragment of a choral passage almost certainly from Aristophanes' *Heroes*: it begins πρὸς ταῦτ' οὖν ὦνδρες φυλακὴν ἔχετε.

P. 173, 1236 n. The first interpretation offered is hardly worth considering; the second is sustained by several examples in addition to Eur. *Alc.* 731.